KT-545-824

ESSENTIAL BUSINESS STUDIES

2003

WITHDRAWN from College LRC
BOURNEMOUTH & POOLE COLLEGE OF FE
250046560 S

Also in the HarperCollins Essential Series

Essential Accountancy and Finance
Bijon Kar

Essential Business Law
Paul Hilder

Essential GCSE Business Studies
Renée Huggett

Essential Government and Politics
Jim Cordell

Essential Information Technology
Tony Berk

Essential Marketing
Tony Proctor

Essential Mechanics
Owen Elbourn

Essential Psychology second edition
G.C. Davenport

Essential Practical Psychology
Keith Maglennon

Essential Research Skills
Val Bailey et al.

Series Editor: Roger Gomm

ESSENTIAL BUSINESS STUDIES

Second edition

Stephen Barnes
B.Sc. (Econ.)

Collins Educational
An Imprint of HarperCollins*Publishers*

© Stephen Barnes and HarperCollins Publishers Ltd 1997
This book is copyright under the Berne Convention.
No reproduction without permission. All rights reserved.

The author asserts the moral right to be
identified as the author of this work.

Published by
Collins Educational
An imprint of HarperCollins*Publishers*
77-85 Fulham Palace Road
Hammersmith
London W6 8JB

First published in 1993
Second edition published 1997
Reprinted 1997

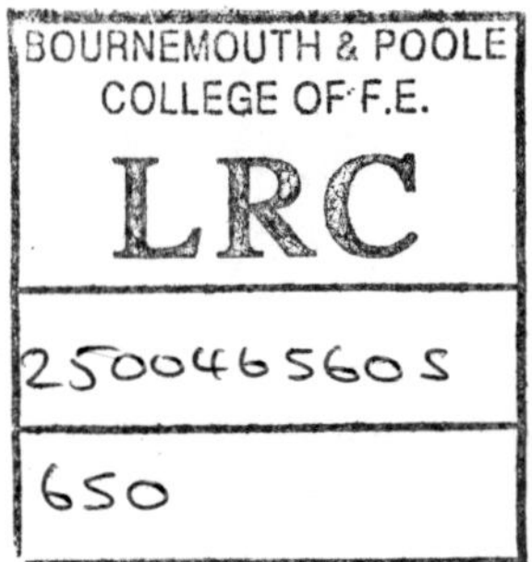
BOURNEMOUTH & POOLE
COLLEGE OF F.E.
LRC
250046560S
650

British Library Cataloguing-in-Publication Data

A catalogue record for this book is available from the British Library

ISBN 0-00-3278581

Project management and editing by Brigitte Lee
Typesetting by Derek Lee
Illustrations by Patricia Briggs
Cover design by Senate
Printed and bound by Scotprint Ltd, Musselburgh, Scotland

Contents

Foreword

Every book in the Essential Series is designed to put you in control of your own learning.

In using this book, you will not only cover the key elements of your course but you will also benefit from the author's use of modern teaching and learning techniques, with the result that you will make the best possible use of your time.

Each chapter in this book has:

- A clear statement of the objectives at the start. This gives you information on the content to follow while setting clear goals to be achieved in terms of your understanding and learning.
- Frequent advice on making your own notes as you work through the material.
- Suggested activities that help you to get involved with the ideas explained and to relate theories to practice. Most activities are case studies or exercises, but some involve personal research.
- Notes in the margin of the text. These may highlight a topic or provide additional material. They are intended to add clarity and interest to your study.
- An evaluation section at the end. This will briefly restate some major themes and provide you with some points for the evaluation and integration of what you have learned – vital to reaching higher grades in your examination.

Successful use of this book will involve some serious work. However, as well as achieving exam success, you may gain a lasting ability to understand and enjoy the business world.

Author's preface

This book - now updated and expanded for its second edition - is subtitled 'a guide to success'. As a good guide, it should keep you company in both your coursework and in your preparation for exams. I have written with direct and recent experience of teaching students on post-16 Business Studies courses, and intend that it should be practical, thorough and friendly from your point of view. As a book, though, it is more than a sequence of examination topics. By this I mean that it has an underlying pattern or paradigm. Business activity is about the human effort to make the best use of scarce resources through adding to their value in consumption. In a market economy the reward for success is profit. However, I hope students will - like this book - ask searching questions about social responsibility, the environment and ethics.

Learning to enjoy a subject is a fast route to examination success. As a teacher, my goal has always been for students to find pleasure and excitement in their studies. Much depends on a lively sense of enquiry. There is a tremendous amount to be discovered about business through everyday life: in the street, at work, in shops and cafés, on television, in newspapers and in magazines. Keep asking questions. Talk to teachers, write letters, make phone calls, argue with friends, challenge yourself.

Essential Business Studies is primarily designed for students on A-level and Advanced GNVQ courses. At A level it is particularly suitable for the AEB, Cambridge Modular and London syllabuses. However, it should also be valuable for students on first-year university courses who need a secure foundation in the subject before tackling more advanced work. In addition, it will provide a thorough overview of the business world for those on courses leading to professional qualifications in banking, accounting, insurance, marketing and personnel. I hope, too, that it will be useful to the general reader who wants a better grasp of the issues in business and economic affairs.

Acknowledgements

The author and publisher would like to thank: Young and Rubicam Ltd for the use of their Cross-Cultural Consumer Characteristics market segmentation model; and Getty Images for permission to reproduce their picture of Adam Smith. The publisher has been unable to contact the copyright holders of Figure 12.1, but will be happy to include an acknowledgement in future reprints.

The author particularly wishes to thank Kidsons Impey (Chartered Accountants) at Brighton; Jane Champ at American Express; Peter Tyson at Body Shop International; Nicholas Bray for advice and word-processing; Victoria Ingham for word-processing; Martin Taylor and Clive Mander for advice and help; Maria Bailey, Keith Brumfitt, David Lines and Nancy Wall for criticism and suggestions; David Myddelton for advice on accounting and finance; John Rowland for ideas and encouragement; Brigitte Lee for editing; Emma Dunlop and Patricia Briggs for editorial and production management at the publishers; and Julie Barnes for all her help and support. Finally, my thanks remain due to many former students at Brighton and Hove Sixth-Form College.

Part 1

Business in Action

Business, market forces and the entrepreneur

Chapter objectives

After working through this chapter, you will:

- understand the meaning of business enterprise
- appreciate business activity as a network of relationships
- be able to classify production sectors and the national work-force
- be aware of the importance of investors
- understand the meaning of the market and market forces
- know how the price mechanism operates
- appreciate the significance of profit
- be able to analyse how and why resources are reallocated between firms
- know the meaning of the following key terms: market, price, consumer surplus, demand, expenditure, utility, revenue, incentive, specialization, money, resources, consumer, producer, production sectors (primary, secondary and tertiary), entrepreneur.

BUSINESS STUDIES

Have you ever wanted to go backstage? Say you had a pass. A pass that meant that you could go backstage – at the theatre – at a pop concert – into television studios.

Now consider a Jaguar car. Think of a pair of Levi's jeans. These products are natural stars. And they too have a backstage. As products they are only possible because of the business behind them. Both a Jaguar and Levi's have classic lines, inspirational design and quality in manufacture. Their 'backstages' are large business organizations. Managers, designers, technicians, craftspeople, accountants, sales staff and advertisers work together in coordinated teams to bring their stars to the stage. And that stage is the marketplace: the shop windows and high streets which we all know.

Business studies is a kind of backstage pass. It may or may not take you into the factories where Levi's and Jaguars are made. But it will take you into the world of many goods and services, so that you can see and experience the excitement of making good products that people want ... and the disappointment of products that people do not want. You will also come across firms and products of which you may disapprove. But the business world is our world. Nobody can stand aside. But not everyone has a backstage pass ...

What does 'business' really mean to you? Some people, as they throw aside the business section of the newspaper, see only negative images: pages of dull figures, boring-looking men in dark suits, ugly factories, drab industrial estates, environmental damage.

All of these exist. But they are only one aspect of a world that is often electric, full of colour and feeling. Business is about being creative. Literally, business means 'busy-ness'. It is about working with people to produce what people want. Thus it is about what we as people decide to do with our resources. These resources are the natural wealth of the earth, the tools and equipment and buildings at our disposal, and our own energy, skills and ingenuity. Business is not an optional extra. It is the condition for our survival. However simply we may try to live, the need for food, shelter and clothing remains.

Specialization

But life is about so much more than survival. Most people wish to live in the company of other people, in households that make up cities, towns or villages. The word 'civilization' ultimately comes from the Greek word meaning a dwelling place. The society and energy of life in modern towns and cities is possible only through the millions of products of business enterprise. We expect foods from all over the world, fashion clothing, comfortable homes. We enjoy luxuries from videos to shampoo, from ice-cream to hi-fi. We demand a vast range of services, too. Leisure services such as hairdressing, holidays, hotels, pubs and clubs seem important. More essential are hospitals, schools and colleges, insurance, banks, police, the fire brigade ... Behind the scenes we have transport, distribution, telecommunications, computing, accountancy, administration, social and legal services, and many more. In any one of these examples, each customer actually consumes business products from thousands of different firms. This is because every firm is interrelated with others. You buy a Mars Bar. One firm imported the cocoa; another refined the sugar. Yet another manufactured the film wrapper. And another designed the lettering ... and made the cardboard boxes in which the Mars Bars were distributed ... and supplied the truck that carried the cardboard boxes to the shops that sold the Mars Bar. There is no beginning and no end to the story. Each firm depends on so many others, in a web of interdependency.

The key principle is **specialization**, which means that each firm concentrates its resources on the product areas in which it has the greatest competitive advantage. For instance, the Mars company has developed unique skills in designing and marketing confectionery that most people enjoy. Very few other producers can equal its skill. In exactly the same way, every individual earns his or her living (or contributes to society) according to his or her specialist skills and aptitudes. Few people still produce a good or service in its entirety. Instead, every production process breaks down into component tasks, each performed by a specialist worker.

▶ **Media Watch**
To get the best out of a business studies course you must keep abreast of the business news. This means a regular reading of the business pages of a quality newspaper or one of the specialist magazines such as *The Economist* or *Business Week*. Radio and TV programmes are also important sources of information. At the time this book was printed the following were regularly broadcast:

- Saturday: Radio 4, 12 noon, *Money Box*
- Sunday: BBC2, 8.50pm, *The Money Programme*
- Monday–Friday: BBC1, 11.05am, *The Really Useful Show* (consumer concerns); BBC2, 12.30pm, *Working Lunch*
- Tuesday: Radio 5, 10.00pm, *News Talk* (money, work and business)
- Thursday: BBC1, 7.30pm, *Watchdog*

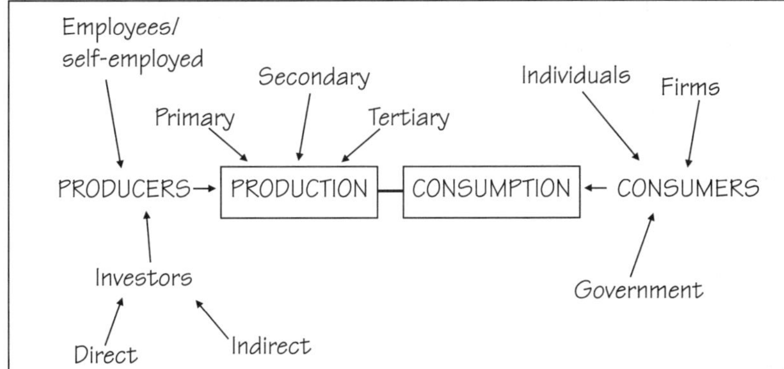

Figure 1.1

▶ A modern economy depends upon the principle of specialization and exchange involving money.

Because modern society is based on such intense specialization, almost no one is capable of meeting all of his or her own needs. Today, people exchange the value of their specialized output for the goods and services that they require. The key medium of exchange is **money**. Modern currencies are worthless in themselves, but they represent **resources**. Money acts as a kind of go-between among consumers and producers. Thus, the specialized work of one person can be exchanged for the equally specialized output of another. For example, a doctor earns money seeing patients in the surgery, while his or her car is repaired at a garage, which will accept money as payment for its services. In a modern economy, people and companies relate to one another in a **business network**.

The Business Network

Any activity that uses resources and whose product is intended for sale or exchange is **business activity**. People are at the centre of business activity, either as **consumers** or as **producers**. Everyone is a consumer, and almost everyone is a producer, at least for some part of their lives. The network of relations between consumers and producers makes up the business world.

Consumers

▶ The government collects statistical data through censuses on households and firms.

Every individual is a consumer because he or she is certain to consume the products of business activity. All firms are consumers because they consume the products of other firms. The government and local councils are also consumers, depending as they do on the products of ordinary firms.

Statistical analysis of the size and changes in consumer groups (see Chapters 5 and 6) provides vital information to firms in attempting to match their output with likely sales.

Producers

Firms are the key producers, but also important are the government (e.g. Department of Social Security), local councils (e.g. education departments) and other public organizations (e.g. the BBC).

Production may be classified by sectors:

- **primary sector** includes all extractive businesses engaged in the production of raw materials, e.g. farming, mining, oil production;

- **secondary sector** includes all manufacturing and construction businesses that transform raw materials into finished products, e.g. the motor industry, electronics, textiles;
- **tertiary sector** includes the production of all services, e.g. transport, banking, health.

Producers have two important identities:

- people who own a business: **investors**
- people who work for a business: **employees**

▶ Investors

Investors
Investors are broadly those who provide finance for a business. This may be by direct investment, in owning a business outright, or in owning shares in a business (see Chapter 3). It may also be indirect through a savings plan, such as a pension fund or a life assurance policy. These funds are then invested in business by specialist managers. In addition, part of people's savings in banks and building societies is lent to firms, but these investments are not equivalent to ownership and are rewarded by interest rather than profit. Finally, it is also possible to 'invest' in the government by buying fixed-interest stocks called **gilt-edged securities**.

▶ Employees

Employees
The country's working population is defined as all those aged between 18 and 60/65 who are available for work. Its size depends on such factors as:

- population trends
- the school-leaving and retirement ages
- women seeking work
- student numbers

Figure 1.2
Adam Smith

Subtraction of the unemployed and those occupied in the armed forces from the total working population gives the total in **civil employment**. A key variable here is the **unemployment rate**, which varies with the overall level of business activity. This in turn depends on the strength of demand from consumers. Governments can influence total demand (see Chapter 33), but only to a limited extent.

MARKET FORCES

The Meaning of the Market

▶ **Adam Smith** (1723–1790). His book, *The Wealth of Nations*, was the first to explain the action of market forces. He argued that the competitive desire for profit was turned by the **invisible hand** of the market into the overall public good. He also warned that firms will try to obstruct competition, which would be contrary to the public interest.

Imagine a large market square, sellers on one side of the stalls and potential buyers on the other. There is continual bargaining over price. Seller and buyer confront each other. Each side has a secret. The seller knows how much the product costs in terms of manufacture, overheads, etc. and will not sell it for less. The buyer knows how much the product is worth to him or her and will not pay more. The game is to strike a **price** on which both sides agree. Provided that the buyer's valuation of a good is higher than the seller's cost, bargaining can occur. The finally agreed price must fall within this bargaining zone and will provide a **surplus** for both sides. The seller makes a **profit**, defined as the difference between the cost price and the selling price. The buyer enjoys **consumer surplus**, which means the difference between the buyer's valuation and the actual price paid. A transaction can then take place. A product moves from seller to buyer, while a sum of money moves from buyer to seller. Both sides are satisfied. The seller can direct finance to the production of further similar products, while the buyer is motivated to earn money to finance further similar purchases. This picture is highly simplified, but it represents the essential dynamic of the market.

▶ Markets enable buyers and sellers to communicate and agree a price. Markets include traditional markets, shops and shopping centres, warehouses, offices, mail and telephone ordering, commodity and finance markets, and the Internet.

▶ Transactions can occur in a market when the buyer enjoys a consumer surplus and the seller makes a profit.

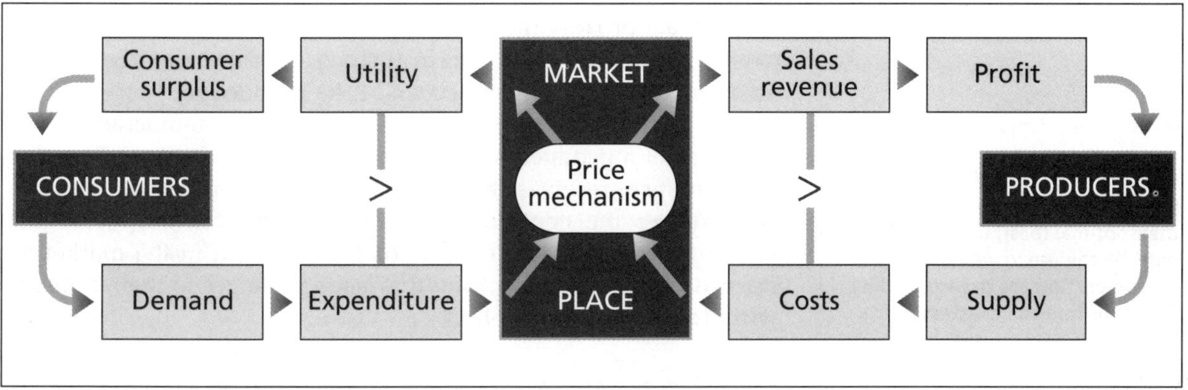

Figure 1.3
Market forces and the price mechanism

This diagram is worth understanding since it explains how the market really works. Start at the 'consumers' box. Consumers have wants, which we call **demand**. If supported by money, this demand becomes **expenditure**, in the purchase of a product, at a price. This product should yield satisfaction – which is called **utility**. The consumer will only make the purchase if the value of the expected utility exceeds the price. Think about this carefully. You are considering the purchase of an ice-cream at 60p. The maximum price you would pay for it is 70p. In other words, you estimate the value of its utility at 70p. The price is less than the utility expected and a purchase can take place. You, the consumer, have made a 'profit' of 10p – this is called consumer's surplus. This surplus will encourage the consumer to make further purchases in future, unless a better product can be found.

Now look at the 'producers' box. The reasoning is an exact parallel. Producers will potentially supply goods or services. This supply incurs business costs. However, the product's sale should yield **revenue**. The producer will only make the sale if the revenue exceeds the cost. The minimum price that he or she would accept for the ice-cream is 50p, since this was its cost to the firm when all outlays are included. The actual price at 60p is greater than the costs, and a sale can take place. The producer has made a profit of 10p. This return will encourage the producer to continue output in future, unless a more profitable product can be found.

The Meaning of Profit

▶ Business enterprise means combining scarce resources so that the added value is greater than the corresponding cost. The surplus is then divided between the consumer (consumer surplus) and the producer (profit).

▶ The reward of profit encourages entrepreneurs to accept the risks of business enterprise.

Profit is an **incentive** to put forward capital (from savings or with a loan) to finance **business enterprise**. The risk of failure - and losses - is counterbalanced by the prospect of success - and profits. Business activity is essential to the creation of wealth. Profit therefore acts as a motor in driving the forces of wealth creation.

Under market forces, the consumer is often said to be king. Every product from every firm must face the test of the marketplace. In their every potential purchase, consumers assess the likely surplus of utility over expenditure. Products that keep failing this test experience falling sales, falling profitability, and the progressive withdrawal of resources from their production. By contrast, products that find consumer approval see rising sales and profitability, attracting new resources to expand their production.

▶ Economic democracy

▶ Profit acts like a directional beacon, channelling resources to their optimal (best) allocation. This must be the use in which consumers find the greatest utility and firms find the greatest profit.

This pattern suggests the idea of **economic democracy**. Every purchase of a product is, in effect, a vote for its continued production. The firm receives the sales revenue and corresponding profit, so ensuring the continued use of resources for output of that product in the future. Products that are rejected in the market are starved of revenue and profit; this leads by stages to their complete withdrawal from production.

PROFIT AND RESOURCE ALLOCATION

Birmingham Biscuits and Coventry Cakes

Birmingham Biscuits Ltd and Coventry Cakes Ltd are two firms of roughly equal size, with products in the same broad market sector. A change in their sales and profitability could be caused by a shift in consumer tastes, or by a change in relative costs. In this case events are triggered by a change in consumer preference, from biscuits to cakes. The consequences unfold as follows:

▶ At Birmingham Biscuits, demand, sales and profits fall, and the firm's hold on resources rapidly weakens. Meanwhile at Coventry Cakes, demand, sales and profits rise and the pull on resources rapidly strengthens. If the trend continues, Birmingham Biscuits will close and the resources released may be re-employed at Coventry Cakes.

	Birmingham Biscuits		**Coventry Cakes**	
	Resources	*Finance*	*Resources*	*Finance*
1	Demand for biscuits falls	Sales fall	Demand for cakes rises	Sales increase
2	Unsold stocks build up	Profits fall	Stocks run down	Profits rise
3	Output is cut back	Investment reduced	Output is increased	Investment increases
4	Machines are sold, staff made redundant	Capital withdrawn	New machines bought, more staff employed	Capital injected

Look carefully at the link between resources and finance. It is very important to realize that finance only represents resources. What happens to the real resources is therefore mirrored in the corresponding financial events.

In reality the pattern will be less neat. A firm like Birmingham Biscuits may react to changed demand and alter its product range. Both decline and expansion are often quite gradual. Rarely are resources so directly exchanged, and in practice there is always a pool of capital and workers seeking more rewarding employment. Often too, neither capital nor labour are particularly mobile, and firms may limp on long after market forces have turned against them. But in the end the market wins. Every day countless millions of consumer-spending choices are made and the invisible messages reach firms in their detailed accounting data. Firms and industries are always expanding and declining with the corresponding changes in their power to attract and retain resources. We are looking at market forces in action.

▶ Competition tends to drive down profits. All firms want to make greater profits than the bare minimum to stay in business. This can only be achieved if they have something special to offer – either a better product or lower costs of production. This 'something special' is called **competitive advantage**.

THE ENTREPRENEUR

The creation of wealth, which people tend to take for granted, depends on the forces of enterprise and the ability to compete in the markets of Britain and the world. Individuals who are willing to accept the risks of business enterprise are called **entrepreneurs** (from the French word *entreprendre* – to undertake). An entrepreneur is a person who commits resources (their own or others') and provides the 'guidance system' within a business enterprise. The entrepreneur's challenge is to engage with market forces and to win: to develop the enterprise that takes the custom, makes the profit, reinvests and expands.

▶ Profit is the reward for efficient use of resources to generate consumer satisfaction. The enterprise that creates the most satisfaction for the fewest resources (lowest costs) is rewarded by the highest profits.

In some ways, enterprise is a state of mind. There is a certain ability to recognize the needs of people that are not being met and then imaginatively to think how they might be met in a practical and cost-effective way. The entrepreneur is self-confident and believes that things can be done better. He or she sees all things as possible and never takes 'no' for an answer. He or she thinks positively about how something might be achieved and pursues the idea with energy and determination.

▶ The government has been anxious to encourage enterprise and has offered incentives to people starting in business or running small firms. The thrust of government policy has been to make even large firms more responsive to market forces. There has also been emphasis on the need to value business and industry more highly.

As a company grows in size and complexity, the role of the entrepreneur often becomes less clearly focused on one person. In a company the capital is divided into shares, which are owned by a number of shareholders. These shareholders elect a board of directors, who make business decisions on their behalf. In a smaller company, the directors are normally also the larger shareholders and form a group of entrepreneurs. In a large national or multinational firm, the directors' proportional shareholding may be quite small and the entrepreneurial functions become very diffuse or scattered. In practice, the careers and often the salaries of directors depend on their firm's success in the market. The transmission of the profit motive through a firm's hierarchy (i.e. levels of seniority amongst employees) is very important in achieving efficiency and customer satisfaction. Some firms will deliberately foster a profit-driven sense of enterprise in the firm through profit-sharing schemes or staff ownership of shares (see Chapter 33).

▶ You will see this sign where I have suggested an activity for you to carry out. Sometimes it will be an investigation, sometimes a case study with questions, sometimes a short piece of written work.

Centurion Cycles and Golden Eagle Ltd

Two cycle manufacturers are located in the East Midlands. Centurion Cycles is a traditional Nottingham-based firm making a conventional range of family and sports models. A reputation for quality does not alter a growing consumer perception of the bicycles as dull and unfashionable. Sales are steadily declining.

Some 25 miles away in Leicester, Golden Eagle Ltd is a new and innovative producer of all-terrain and mountain bikes. As well as catering for specialists, the range has been skilfully adapted to enter the urban cycling and children's markets. Sales are steadily increasing.

Explain carefully how market forces are acting on these firms and their resources.

Evaluation

- In theory, the operation of market forces ensures an optimal distribution of resources. In reality, too, market economies seem to be more dynamic, productive and consumer oriented than any others.
- In small-scale business the entrepreneur is the risk-taking owner or major shareholder whose use of resources to satisfy consumer demand is rewarded by personal profit. In larger firms the entrepreneurial function exists only nominally with shareholders and is transmitted into the firm's management by the elected directors.
- Profit is fundamental in motivating talented people to accept responsibility for managing resources and to inject their creative energy into the generation of wealth.
- Many weaknesses exist in markets. Firms may try to reduce competition through monopoly power or other tactics to fix price and restrict consumer choice (see Chapter 24).
- Economic democracy does not provide equal voting power. Both incomes and wealth are very unevenly distributed and resources are often directed to the production of profitable luxuries for the few, rather than basic necessities for the many.
- Markets tend to consider only the short-run profit. The long run is given a very low value, and thus important investments for the future may not be made where short-term profit is the main goal.
- The market has encouraged ever-increasing consumption without enough regard for the environment, or for the ecosystem on which all life depends (see Chapter 49).

Sole traders, partnerships, cooperatives and franchising

Chapter objectives

After working through this chapter, you will:

- understand the opportunities and problems of being a sole trader
- know how a partnership operates
- understand the principles of a cooperative
- know the meaning of the following key terms: partner, ordinary partnership, limited partnership, producer cooperative, consumer cooperative, business format franchise.

▶ **Media Watch**
For useful background to this chapter you should watch the news and follow the media for examples of the problems faced by small businesses, many of which are sole traders, partnerships and franchises.

SOLE TRADERS

▶ Typical business formats for the sole trader include:
- small-scale retailing, e.g. grocers, newsagents;
- building traders;
- transport services;
- personal services, e.g. child-minding, gardening;
- restaurants, cafés, guest houses;
- arts and entertainment providers;
- smallholdings.

An idea and a small sum of starting capital are all that is necessary to start a business. No permission is needed, no forms need to be filled in. Of course, the enterprise is more likely to succeed with some market research, some business expertise and an adequate sum of starting capital. The one-person business or **sole trader** is the simplest and most common form of business enterprise. Essentially, the individual provides the capital, takes the risk and is rewarded by the whole of the profit (or loss).

Sole trading, as a pattern of business organization, involves few formalities. Financial records must be kept for tax purposes, and VAT registration is required if annual turnover exceeds £50,000. The sole trader will also be subject to all normal business laws, such as those relating to employment or health and safety. Sole traders have great flexibility. They can discover and meet their customers' needs without reference to any head office or set of rules. The product range, marketing and hours of business can all be adjusted to suit local needs, and the response to changing demand can be immediate. Customers can be provided with a high degree of personal service, which may be preferred to the more anonymous service of large firms. Overheads such as office space and administration costs are usually low, so that price can be very competitive. Sometimes the variety of products offered is greater than a larger competitor would be able or willing to stock. Finally, the sole trader is highly motivated since profit is the direct reward for success – and loss is the penalty of failure.

However, very real problems are faced by the one-person enterprise. Starting capital is usually limited to the owner's savings and loan capital will be limited in availability, and often secured on the borrower's home. Liability for debts is unlimited, so that in the event of business failure all debts must be settled, even if this means selling the family home and most of its contents. Expansion is therefore difficult, and ploughed-back profits are often insufficient to take full advantage of any business opportunities. There is little chance of specialization in the management of the business. For example, few sole traders will have the advanced marketing skills that could increase their sales. Similarly, the effective interpretation of accounts needs training and experience. A major drawback faced by all small firms is the higher cost of goods or materials when buying in smaller quantities. Similarly, marketing, transport and borrowing on a small scale all tend to be proportionally more expensive (see Chapter 13). Finally, it can be difficult to keep the enterprise running continuously. The owner may need to make a trip away from the business to market the products, or may simply want a holiday. Equally, there is a risk of the business collapsing if the owner falls ill or dies.

▶ Many sole traders have high materials and bought-in goods costs compared to larger firms.

PARTNERSHIPS

▶ Partnerships are common in retailing, building, farming and consumer services. They are particularly popular in providing professional services such as accountancy, law, architecture and medicine.

Under the Partnership Act (1890), any group of two to twenty people may jointly finance and operate a business enterprise. The rights of the partners, including their share of any profits, are stated in the Deed of Partnership. Unless specified to the contrary, each **partner** carries equal weight in decision making and management. A 'sleeping partner' can choose to contribute capital and share profits but to take no part in running the business. **Ordinary partnerships** carry unlimited liability for debts, but a **limited partnership** is possible (Limited Partnership Act, 1907), where sleeping partners have their liability limited to their capital input. However, at least one partner must always have unlimited liability.

▶ Partnerships depend on trust and cooperation.

By contrast with sole trading, a partnership combines greater financial resources with an enlarged pool of business ideas and expertise. Partners are able to specialize and make different contributions to the business. There are fewer problems with continuity, as an absent partner's duties can always be covered by colleagues if necessary. Nevertheless, many of the limitations affecting the sole trader remain. The ability to raise new finance is still restricted, and all ordinary partners have unlimited liability for all debts. Since the decisions of any one partner are the responsibility of all the partners, a high level of mutual trust is necessary. There is much potential for conflict in decision making, especially if business declines. A partnership can be dissolved voluntarily, or necessarily by bankruptcy or the death of any partner.

COOPERATIVES

▶ There were about 1,500 producer cooperatives in Britain in 1997 employing about 18,000 people.

Producer cooperatives are owned and controlled by the workforce, who elect a team of managers and share the profits among themselves. Most producer cooperatives in Britain are relatively small, with an average of ten employees. As businesses become larger and more complex, it is difficult to run them in a genuinely cooperative way.

Consumer cooperatives are owned by their customers, who join the cooperative society by purchasing at least one £1 share, with a maximum holding of £20,000 in shares. The society functions under the democratic control of the members, who elect a management committee. Dividends are paid to members according to the value of their purchases over a period of time. The only major example of a consumer cooperative in Britain is the high street retail 'Co-op' stores. However, few members participate actively in their management, and trading stamps or price cuts have mostly replaced members' dividends.

▶ Membership of consumer cooperatives has fallen from 13 million in the 1960s to around 8 million today. Mergers have reduced the number of societies to around 50.

Read the following case study and complete the tasks.

Primrose Printers

The impact of computer technology on newspaper printing was sudden and dramatic. Among the many who had found themselves made redundant were ten of the present owner-workers at Primrose Printers. In 1992 they had legally formed a workers' cooperative, each member contributing £10,000 as start-up capital. The premises in Primrose Hill were cramped but the volume of business had expanded rapidly and membership increased to fifteen.

Management meetings were held on a weekly basis with everyone attending – and increasingly long agendas. Problems began to emerge in 1996 when a competitor began trading nearby.

Stuart Leigh, the marketing manager, urged increased spending on advertising and sales. This proposal met with sharp opposition from Martin Cummins, the accountant, who believed that some serious cost cutting was required.

'It's no good being romantic about this business. We need a freeze on wages for everyone. And there's too much waste. I'm afraid that some members believe that what belongs to everyone belongs to no one.'

Wages, too, were a source of conflict. The policy of equal pay for all was popular at first, but now dissatisfaction was surfacing as some members felt that their effort and skills were not being properly rewarded. Lengthy discussions of these issues in meetings led other members to complain that time was being wasted. Moreover, quite small business problems could take an hour or more to resolve. The idea was to avoid voting and reach decisions by general agreement. But as Steve Hursthouse, the computer expert, said:

'Nothing ever gets decided. Our service to customers gets slower. Orders go to commercial rivals. Where will it end?'

1 Summarize the problems being experienced by the business.
2 How far are these the result of being a cooperative?
3 Can you suggest changes which might alleviate these problems?

FRANCHISING

▶ Wimpy, Pizza Express, Tie Rack, Body Shop and the British School of Motoring are all examples of franchising.

A **franchise** literally means a contractual licence granted by one person (the franchisor) to another (the franchisee). The traditional franchise agreement simply meant one firm granting certain rights to another concerning the manufacture or sale of its products. For instance, Heineken lager is brewed under licence in the UK by Whitbread. The modern **business format franchise** was developed in the USA during the 1950s. The concept involves development of a clearly defined business formula by one firm and its expansion by granting licences to other entrepreneurs, who operate the same formula under the terms of a contract.

The business format franchise includes the following key features:

- a contract stating the obligations of franchisor and franchisee;
- the business is owned by the franchisee, who provides a major part of the initial investment;
- the franchisee gains exclusive rights to the use of a business format, including a trade name, and benefits from associated goodwill;
- the franchisor supplies permanent support for all aspects of the operation, e.g. marketing;
- the franchisee pays the franchisor for the rights obtained and for future support.

Taking up a franchise is a means of starting a business with a much reduced risk of failure. The franchisee has a large measure of independence, but also enjoys a great deal of direct and indirect support. The eight major advantages are:

1 **Successful business formula**

The franchisee is launching a business format that is known to be viable. A valuable reputation and well-known name exist from the outset. Access may be gained to various patents, copyrights and trade secrets.

2 **Start-up assistance**

Often the franchisor has options on key high street sites and is sure to provide intensive assistance at the start-up stage.

▶ Franchising can combine the advantages of business operations on a large scale (e.g. purchasing in bulk) *and* on a small scale (e.g. motivated local owners).

3 **Finance**

A franchise often requires a smaller capital investment at the outset than the equivalent independent operation. Bank loans are usually more readily available and less costly for a franchise.

4 **Training and support**

Lack of experience is made good by the franchisor's training and continuous management support. The permanent backing of an expert and sophisticated head office organization is always valuable, but vital when problems arise.

5 **Marketing**

Franchisors will often provide a national advertising and marketing effort that far exceeds anything possible for a small business. They will also carry out in-depth market research.

▶ The **British Franchise Association (BFA)**
The BFA is the central organization for companies engaged in trading through franchise agreements. It has a strict ethical code of practice with which members must conform. It provides for exchange of information and expertise among members. It produces publications giving advice to both franchisors and franchisees. It represents the interests of franchising to the media and the government.

6 **Economies of scale**

A franchising system is able to achieve major **economies of scale** (see Chapter 13) in purchasing, marketing and distribution.

7 **Territory**

The franchisee may be allotted territory within which no rival units of the same franchise will operate. This zoning is designed to ensure that each unit has the potential market base to be fully viable.

8 **Research and development**

The franchisor will have the resources to carry out research and development, so ensuring that the product and allied business format are as advanced and up-to-date as possible.

Despite these substantial advantages, the franchisee will inevitably encounter some problems. Five typical difficulties are:

1 **Controls**
The franchise agreement will specify the rights of the franchisor to exercise some control over the business.

2 **Dependency**
There is a danger of becoming over-dependent on the franchisor and failing to take the necessary initiative and responsibility.

3 **Conflict of interests**
The franchisor's greatest financial concern may be to increase turnover, i.e. the rate at which stock is sold and replenished, in order to maximize growth and fees received. The franchisee will naturally be more concerned with profit.

▶ A franchisee may begin to feel like a branch manager and to resent the influence and control of the franchisor. He or she may come to want greater freedom and more opportunity to be creative.

4 **Franchisor judgement**
Any strategic errors of judgement by the franchisor could seriously affect the franchisee (e.g. excessive speed of expansion or inadequate product development).

5 **Other franchisees**
All franchisees are mutually dependent to some degree. A serious error by one could damage the business of them all.

Make notes illustrating the advantages and disadvantages of sole trading, partnerships and cooperatives. Summarize the benefits and difficulties of becoming a franchisee.

▶ You will see this sign where I have indicated that it would be useful for you to make notes. Always give your notes a heading.

The Soft Shop
As a business format franchise, the Soft Shop offers a wide range of computer software for home and office use. UK sales have been increasing on average at 25 per cent a year over the past six years. There are now twenty-five outlets concentrated in major urban areas, including two owned directly by the franchisor. The start-up capital required is £100,000, of which £12,000 represents a management fee.

You are considering becoming a franchisee of the Soft Shop and running your own branch. List the key questions to which you would need answers before signing an agreement and risking £100,000.

Many real franchise opportunities are advertised each week in *Exchange and Mart*. Send for details of one such opportunity and assess its advantages and disadvantages, under the headings listed above.

Evaluation

- Sole traders and partners are very direct entrepreneurs and represent a pool of energy and ideas essential to an enterprise culture. Such firms may pioneer new products and nurture new business leaders.
- In many markets the advantages of large-scale operation are too great for the very small firm to survive. But gaps in markets may be small and/or local. These are niches that sole traders and partnerships can profitably hope to fill. Such businesses may be effective in opening new markets that are still too small for the commitment of large firms.
- The pattern of such business opportunities changes with time. Food retailing has been squeezed by supermarkets and multiple stores, but inexpensive computer technology is providing new opportunities, for example in desktop publishing.
- Neither consumer nor producer cooperatives are easy to run on cooperative lines if they grow beyond a certain size, and both have found it difficult to attract investment capital from outside without control passing to large investors or creditors.
- Franchising offers an opportunity to start a business with limited capital, based on a product or service which is already commercially proven and with support services provided by the franchisor.

Limited companies

Chapter objectives

After working through this chapter, you will:

- be able to distinguish between private and public limited companies
- understand how a company is formed
- be familiar with the structure of share capital and borrowed funds
- be able to analyse the ownership and control of companies
- understand what is meant by a management buy-out and a management buy-in
- know the meaning of the following key terms: shares (ordinary and preference), debentures, dividend, limited liability, institutional investor, holding company, pyramiding, liquidity, receivership, gearing, venture capital.

WHAT IS A COMPANY?

The term **company** means an organization set up in law to carry on a business with the objective of making a profit. The assets (e.g. land, buildings, machinery) of this organization are owned by a group of people ('company') who each hold a **share** of its capital. These shares are subdivided for convenience into small units, for instance £1 or 50p shares. Shareholders carry rights to vote at meetings and an entitlement to a corresponding proportion of profits.

This form of business is the foundation for the great majority of business activity in Britain and other market economies. There are two essential concepts involved:

1 The company has a legal identity that is separate from that of its owners.
2 The owners' liability for indebtedness is limited to the value of their stake in the company.

▶ The earliest company dates from 1553, when merchants subscribed £6,000 in £25 shares to finance a voyage to discover a new trading route to the Far East. Modern company law emerged through several Acts of Parliament between 1844 and 1862.

▶ **Limited liability** was introduced in the nineteenth century to encourage investment in high-risk capital projects such as railway building.

Private Limited Companies

A **private limited company** is one whose shares may only be sold privately to family, friends and business associates. They are often called family firms. The sale of shares to the general public is prohibited, as is their resale on the Stock Exchange. Often a family or other small group owns most or all of the shares, and this arrangement may be

▶ In 1995–6 there were 1,025,000 private companies in Britain. Most were small to medium-sized companies.

protected by the requirement that an investor wishing to sell his or her shares must offer them first to the other shareholders. The company and its investors enjoy the full privilege of limited liability (indicated by 'Limited' or 'Ltd' in its name). Each year the company must supply the Registrar of Companies with its accounts and other information concerning business activities and organization.

The advantages of forming a private company are clearly those of limited liability and access to greater sources of finance through the sale of shares. As a legal entity the company is also more assured of continuity regardless of circumstances affecting individual shareholders.

However, the actual amount of finance raised depends on the investors available and their readiness to supply risk capital. There is the added complication that many private companies do not wish their shares to be held outside the inner group of directors, in order to avoid any dilution of control.

Public Limited Companies (plcs)

▶ **Companies Acts, 1948–85** These brought about laws designed to protect investors and to ensure that the right of limited liability is not abused. Significant breaches of company laws are a serious offence, while fraud and misconduct by directors can lead to heavy penalties.

The shares in a **public limited company** can be sold direct to the public or to financial institutions (e.g. pension funds). They can be readily resold on the Stock Exchange (see Chapter 22), where their price is publicly quoted. This encourages investors to purchase shares, since they know that they can recover the market value of their holding whenever they wish. With a public limited company there must be at least £50,000 in issued share capital, of which 25 per cent or more must be fully paid up. In practice, the sums involved will be far larger. Limited liability is automatic for all shareholders and the company's name must include the letters 'plc'. Before a company may 'go public' it must submit further details of its affairs to the Registrar of Companies and face a careful check by the Stock Exchange Council in order to protect potential investors. The whole process is quite expensive.

▶ In 1995–6 there were 11,500 public limited companies.

A public company has potential access to unlimited amounts of capital and is likely to be able to obtain loans more cheaply and more easily. It is a common form of organization in industries where the scale of operation must normally be large, for instance oil or banking.

1 Make notes on limited liability and the advantages this has over sole trading or trading through a partnership.
2 Set up a two-column table: one column for private limited companies and one for public limited companies. Make your notes on the two kinds of company in this format.

Forming a Company

A new company – private or public – must register with the Registrar of Companies. This involves providing two key documents:

▶ Memorandum of Association

1 **Memorandum of Association**
This deals with matters of **external** status. It gives the company's name, registered office, trading objectives and capital structure (this is the maximum amount of capital that may be raised plus the nominal value of the shares).

2 **Articles of Association**

▶ Articles of Association

This provides details of the company's **internal** rules. It will specify the arrangements and rules for the sale of shares, shareholders' rights, company meetings, and the election and powers of directors.

There are then various statements and declarations to be made, after which the Certificate of Incorporation is issued.

Share Capital

The Memorandum of Association states the company's authorized capital - the maximum face value of shares that it may issue. The company usually chooses to issue (sell) shares to a lower total value, leaving scope for expansion. When shares are first issued, it may not be necessary for the buyer to pay for them in full. For instance, 50p on £1 shares may be payable with the purchase application, forming 'partly paid' share capital. The outstanding 50p may not be 'called up' until a time many months in the future, when the issue will be 'fully paid up'. This device gives the directors a useful source of promptly available capital which they can request when necessary.

▶ Ordinary shares (equity)

The majority of a company's share capital is usually issued as **ordinary shares** (also called **equity**). In a very real sense, the ordinary shareholders are part-owners of the company and face the risks involved of being in business. They normally have full voting rights on a 'one share, one vote' basis. Any profit, after payment of tax, is divided between **retention** in the business (money ploughed back) and payment of **dividends** to the shareholders. The amount of dividend may fluctuate widely from one payment period to the next. Meanwhile, the market (i.e. resale) value of the shares may rise or fall - often unpredictably.

▶ Preference shares

Some companies issue **preference shares**. These involve less risk than ordinary shares but carry no voting rights. Holders receive a fixed percentage rate of dividend - if sufficient profit has been made - before any payment is made to the ordinary shareholders, as preference shares are given priority over ordinary shares. **Cumulative preference shares** have the advantage that any unpaid preference dividends are carried forward and remain payable as soon as profits permit. **Participating preference shares** allow the holders their fixed-rate dividends, and then to receive an extra dividend if profit is still available after the ordinary dividend has been paid.

▶ **Debentures**: a means of financing a company through fixed-interest loans often secured against company assets.

Debentures are not shares but IOUs or certificates of indebtedness. The holder receives a fixed rate of interest and is a creditor rather than an owner of the company. The interest payment on debentures takes priority over all other types of dividend, and secured debentures have their repayment value attached to specific assets in the company. If the firm is unable to meet its debts, these assets can be sold in order to repay the secured debenture holders. Debentures of public companies are traded on the Stock Exchange and are repayable by a stated date or earlier.

ACT Look at the financial pages of a quality newspaper. Identify examples of companies raising capital through ordinary shares (flotations and rights issues), preference shares and debentures (stocks/bonds).

Ownership and Control of Companies

A sole trader personally owns his or her business. In a private company the few major shareholders are usually directors who make the decisions and manage the firm. A public company is often different. There may be numerous shareholders, large and small, in Britain and abroad. The directors of the company are elected by the ordinary shareholders and have a duty to act on their behalf. All voting shareholders are invited to the company's annual general meeting, where they can propose and vote on resolutions. In practice the directors are in a strong position. Most shareholders do not attend meetings and have no interest in voting. They may have little knowledge of the company's affairs and will usually vote as recommended by the directors. Only in circumstances of extreme mismanagement would they be likely seriously to oppose or, in exceptional cases, to dismiss the directors.

Institutional Investors

▶ The shareholders or owners of most public companies exercise little effective control over the affairs of a business.

Large blocks of shares in public companies may also be owned by financial institutions such as pension funds, insurance companies and various investment and unit trusts, who are known as **institutional investors**. Usually, these professional investors play little part in the control of the company so long as performance is satisfactory. Thus a real gap exists between the ownership and true control of a major plc. Nor do shareholders and directors necessarily have the same interests. The shareholders seek maximum profits and growth in the value of the enterprise. By contrast, so long as return on capital is 'reasonable', the directors may be more concerned to maximize the size or prestige of the firm and the consequences of this for their earnings and career prospects.

Look at the financial pages of a quality newspaper for articles on shareholders' meetings. These are often only reported if there is dissatisfaction with company performance.

What is reported as happening at the meeting and what was the outcome? Remember that if the story describes a 'crowded meeting', this will still mean that only a tiny minority of shareholders turned up. Usually what happens is determined by holders of large blocks of shares – on the whole these will be institutional investors or holding companies (see an explanation of these below).

Holding Companies

Since the shares of plcs are freely traded, it is possible for one company – called a **holding company** – to gain control over other companies through owning 51 per cent or more of their voting shares (less than 50 per cent may still provide effective control). Shares in the holding company may be offered to the shareholders of another larger company, together with some cash incentive. The finance necessary to gain control of the target firm may only be a fairly small percentage of its market value. This device opens the possibility of **pyramiding**. The holding company takes control of 51 per cent of the voting shares in the other company. These enlarged assets are then used to obtain control of the voting rights in a still larger company – and the process can continue. Control of a relatively small company can lead to real control of a far greater business empire.

Management Buy-outs and Management Buy-ins

Management Buy-outs

When the managers act to purchase part or all of a firm, the process is called a **management buy-out**. The negotiation and financing of the deal can be very complex, but the basic idea is straightforward. The managers come to believe that they could run the enterprise more profitably if it were directly within their ownership and control. Often it is a division or subsidiary of a larger firm that managers hope to buy. Since the price will be far beyond the managers' private means, they must obtain support from banks and financial institutions. These outside investors will assess the proposition and, if satisfied, will put up the finance to enable an offer to be made for the business. The banks and institutions involved often hold a proportion of the shares in the new company (an **equity stake**), as well as supplying the loan finance. Later, if the enterprise is successful and it becomes a public company, the investors may sell this stake on the Stock Market.

Why do Buy-outs Occur?

Since the 1960s many very large firms have merged, often carrying into single ownership numerous smaller subsidiaries. Inevitably, some of these subsidiary concerns will perform less well than required by the corporate budgets of their owners. The local managers of the subsidiary may decide that they could achieve greater success if operating independently. Even if subsidiaries are sufficiently profitable, the directors of a large business grouping may wish to concentrate on particular types of products or markets. Thus they will be keen to sell off any activities that do not fit their strategic plan.

Doubt has been growing since the 1980s about the effectiveness of large firms that operate in a range of very different markets. Such firms have also found that expected economies of scale (advantages of operating on a bigger scale – see Chapter 13) may be far less than predicted. Trying to manage tangled strings of factories or shops can prove very difficult. Top managers may feel a lack of effective control. Local managers may feel ignored and become poorly motivated. A fertile situation then exists for a management buy-out.

▶ Management buy-outs are also sometimes made to avert a hostile take-over bid.

The backers of buy-outs are often international financial services and banking firms (e.g. Investors in Industry, CitiCorp) who specialize in providing **venture capital** (risk capital to business). As a bought-out business is revitalized, the value of their stake may grow far faster than the return on a normal business investment. Such investment firms are vigorous in marketing their 'packages' of assistance for achieving management buy-outs.

The advantage of a management buy-out is that more entrepreneurial attitudes will flow through a business. Profitable initiatives may be possible that would not have been allowed before.

Draw up a two-column table headed 'Advantages/ Disadvantages of management buy-outs'. Use the text on page 21 to list the advantages and the text below to list the disadvantages.

Problems for a Buy-out

Most buy-outs are achieved with a high or very high financial **gearing**. This means that they are financed by a small proportion of share capital and a high proportion of debt. It is therefore essential for the buy-out to earn enough profit to meet heavy interest payments. Any rise in interest rates makes this burden even greater.

The institution that has provided the necessary finance will expect to influence management policy making and, if it holds an equity stake, it will require its own business directors to be on the board. Conflicts of interest may arise between the institution and the management: for instance, the institution may want quick financial returns at the expense of longer-term goals.

Given the high level of indebtedness, a buy-out may not be able to raise necessary further funds for investment projects. This problem may contrast with the large-scale investment finance previously available when part of a large group.

Lower-level managers and staff in a buy-out may feel that their career prospects have been reduced by leaving a larger organization. They may also feel less secure. Unless adequate incentives are offered, some key staff may leave.

▶ In 1996 there were 416 buy-outs worth £7.5 billion.

A buy-out can be affected by lack of specialist management services. For example, management accounting or operations research may be well funded in a major public company, but prove more difficult to provide after the buy-out.

The buy-out may also cause some dislocation to markets and customer networks. The newly independent firm will need to prove its reliability and permanence if the customer base is to be retained and expanded.

Northern Lights Ltd

Northern Lights Ltd is a Yorkshire-based chain of fifteen shops selling lighting equipment and accessories. The original owner had sold the business to Sheffield Electrical in 1987, a company itself sold to Hounslow Holdings, a London company with a sprawling empire in fast-moving consumer goods. Sales returns from Northern Lights branches are increasingly disappointing to Hounslow Holdings and high staff turnover is badly affecting the service offered to customers.

Mark Dickinson, the manager of Northern Lights in Leeds, and John Pilgrim, the Harrogate manager, conceive a plan for a management buy-out with subsequent expansion of the business into lighting consultancy and hire services for the entertainment and tourist industries. The likely value of Northern Lights is £1.5 million, but the managers' combined assets total only £125,000.

What arguments could the managers use to persuade a large City bank to provide the financial backing for a buy-out to take place?

Management Buy-ins
A new team of managers is brought in to purchase and lead a business. This is most likely when a potential buy-out situation exists but the existing management team is weak.

Financial institutions may introduce outside managers, with known expertise, to a target firm and arrange the necessary loan and equity finance, with negotiators to assist in clinching the deal.

▶ In 1996 there were 203 buy-ins worth £4.2 billion.

INSOLVENCY AND LIQUIDATION

Solvency means having the ready funds to meet financial obligations. The creditors of a company that is unable to meet such obligations may take legal steps to force the company into **receivership** and **liquidation**. A firm may also announce this step on a voluntary basis. The affairs of an insolvent company are taken over by the **Official Receiver**. His or her task is then to liquidate the firm's assets. This means turning them into cash in order to meet all debts, which are then settled in order of legal obligation. Any funds that remain will be distributed among the shareholders. Often, however, the shareholders will receive nothing, but they will remain protected from actual indebtedness by the privilege of limited liability. Thus some creditors may find that their debts are worthless.

▶ An alternative to receivership is an **Administration Order**. Under the Insolvency Act of 1986, a firm in difficulty may be placed under the control of an external administrator, giving it a period of protection from claims by creditors. The aim will be to re-establish the firm as a going concern.

Read the case study and answer the questions below.

Taylor Tours Ltd
'Too risky,' snapped Malcolm Taylor. 'If we chase off up-market and fail, then we endanger the whole traditional customer base. All that we've achieved will be on the line.'

Duncan Cole, the marketing director, studied his papers. 'I'm sorry, Malcolm. The evidence is there. Our traditional market is crumbling. Look at the market research. Luxury holidays are the future.'

Geoff Taylor looked up. He spoke quietly. 'I think he's right, Malcolm.'

Malcolm Taylor snorted. 'Value for money. That's what our customers expect, and rightly so.' He glowered down the long mahogany boardroom table. There was silence. 'Just who's running this company?' he growled.

Back in 1963 Malcolm Taylor had driven an old battered coach to Paris with his first fare-paying passengers. More trips and better vehicles followed. In those days, he remembered, Brussels and Luxembourg had seemed like exotic destinations. The holidays were all-inclusive, cheaply priced and very popular. As a sole proprietor he made his own decisions, risked his own capital and would find every gap in the market with all the flair of the natural entrepreneur.

Taylor Tours Ltd was formed in 1971 in order to enter the air charter market. Package holidays to Spain and Italy soon pushed coach tours into second place. The shareholders were Malcolm's brother, Geoff, and three other business friends. They became a strong team, although the Taylor brothers retained the controlling interest and Malcolm as managing director always made the final decisions. Expansion was rapid and by the mid-1980s the firm had over a hundred employees. Turnover passed first £5 million and then £10 million.

In 1995, with some misgivings, the decision was taken to 'go public' and launch the company on the Alternative Investment Market, enabling Taylor Tours to issue and sell new shares direct to the public. The price for this injection of capital was a dilution of the directors' control. Additional directors were appointed and soon an insurance company had become a major shareholder.

▶ For smaller, younger firms, the Alternative Investment Market (AIM) was established in 1995. Membership carries less stringent requirements than the main market in terms of past trading performance and accounting disclosure.

It was a slump in turnover and profits that had prompted the present board meeting.

1 Why would Malcolm Taylor be called an entrepreneur?
2 '… the Taylor brothers retained a controlling interest …' What does this mean?
3 Why did 'going public' mean 'a dilution of the original directors' control'?
4 'Just who's running this company?' How would you answer this question?

Evaluation

- The principle of limited liability is the foundation of the modern company. Very few investors would be willing to put forward risk capital if they faced unlimited liability. In effect, the company's identity is detached from its investors. Creditors can only make claims on the assets of the company, not on the private assets of the owners.
- Shares in a company are sold on a permanent basis. In normal circumstances the company will not accept their return or refund the investor. Yet shares are still a **liquid asset** (they can be turned into cash) because of their second-hand market value. The Stock Exchange is a vast market in the second-hand shares of plcs. It is the option of resale that makes investors willing to purchase shares.
- 'Going public' and obtaining a Stock Exchange quotation achieves access to greatly enlarged sources of finance. However, it also means that the ownership of a significant part of the company becomes mobile and unpredictable. Institutional investors may become important shareholders with their own particular interests, while others may build holdings as a platform for hostile take-over bids (see Chapter 24).
- A public company finds that it must satisfy City opinion and maintain sufficient confidence in its prospects to keep the share price at reasonable levels. Given the ways in which companies and their shares move in and out of fashion, this can be a frustrating experience.
- In most private companies, ownership and control are very closely related. For public companies the link may become largely indirect, and in the practical affairs of business management the directors are virtually autonomous (act on their inclination and judgement). From the point of view of the board, the shareholders can seem simply one interest group among others.
- Management buy-outs bring ownership and control more closely into line, since the managers are themselves major owners. Buy-outs of a public company usually involve its being converted into a private company, at least temporarily. However, the heavy loans required for buy-outs put great pressure on managers to succeed and give creditors considerable power over them. Buy-ins involve

bringing a new management team in as owners. Management buy-ins have increased sharply in importance.

4 Public enterprise and privatization

▶ **Media Watch**
Look out for news stories on privatization and former state-run industries.

Chapter objectives

After working through this chapter, you will:

- know the meaning and scope of public enterprise
- understand the case for and against privatization
- be able to describe and assess privatization in practice
- know the meaning of the following key terms: public sector, central government, local government, nationalized industry, quangos, contracting out, deregulation.

THE PUBLIC SECTOR

▶ The public sector includes those organizations owned and controlled by central or local government.

The **private enterprise** of sole traders, partnerships, limited companies and cooperatives together represents the **private sector**. This name is used since each enterprise is owned and controlled ultimately by private individuals. **Public enterprise** means the provision of goods and services by the government or government-controlled organizations. The full range of public enterprise represents the public sector, since it is owned by the government on behalf of the general public. In Britain, the growth of public enterprise has usually reflected the belief that a good or service can be more efficiently or more fairly provided by the public rather than the private sector.

The public sector has four main forms of organization:

1 **Central government**, which is divided into departments or ministries, e.g. the DSS (Department of Social Security), MOD (Ministry of Defence).
2 **Local government**, which includes county and district councils, the new unitary authorities, metropolitan district councils and the London boroughs.
3 **Nationalized industries**, which are state-owned business enterprises.
4 **Quangos** (quasi-autonomous non-governmental organizations) such as boards, committees, commissions etc., which are organized and funded within the public sector yet have considerable independence in their activities, for instance the Universities Funding Council or the Forestry Commission.

▶ Total UK government expenditure in 1995–6 was £300 billion (including £62 billion to support local authorities), representing 42 per cent of national income. There is currently a downward trend in the proportion of national income represented by government expenditure.

The major activities of central government include the provision of defence; health care and social security; support for employment and industry; the maintenance of law and order; spending on education, transport and the arts. These are financed by a wide range of taxes and duties, including:

- income tax (25.4 per cent of total taxation raised);
- value-added tax (VAT) charged at 17.5 per cent on the sale of most goods and services, and excise duty (26.6 per cent of total);
- corporation tax charged on company profits (9.1 per cent of total).

Local government received about 83 per cent of its income from central government, with the remainder raised through council tax, business rates and various charges. County councils provide such services as education, highways, social services and libraries. District and borough councils are responsible for services such as refuse collection, lighting, planning and leisure facilities. For larger urban centres, there are unitary authorities that supply all services. There are also six metropolitan counties (covering conurbations) where the metropolitan district councils provide the great majority of local government functions. In London all services are provided by the boroughs or by government-appointed bodies.

Nationalization

After the Second World War, the new Labour government took over the ownership and management of some key industries, including coal, railways, airlines, electricity, gas and steel. The aim was to protect the interests of the consumer and to ensure sufficient investment. A government minister set broad policy and appointed a controlling board to be responsible for day-to-day management. The boards were required to pursue a mix of business and social objectives, but these were liable to conflict and so caused problems in decision making.

Heavy losses were made by many of the nationalized industries, with few achieving private sector levels of performance. However, some of these loss-making industries were facing inevitable decline as foreign competition intensified (e.g. the decline of British shipbuilding) or underlying markets changed (e.g. the shift from public to private transport). Management difficulties were also caused by the sheer size and unwieldiness of some industries.

▶ The Royal Mail first provided a public postal service in 1635.

▶ The steel industry was nationalized by the Labour government in 1951, privatized by the Conservatives in 1953, re-nationalized by Labour in 1967 and privatized by the Conservatives in 1988.

PRIVATIZATION

Privatization means a transfer in the ownership and use of resources from the public to the private sector. The Conservative government elected in 1979 was determined to carry out a policy of **privatization**, meaning the sale of state-owned industries back to the private sector. This process has run throughout the 1980s and 1990s. Also important have been the **contracting out** of public sector work to private firms (e.g. refuse collection), the **deregulation** of industries subject to state control (e.g. allowing bus companies to compete) and the sale of council houses to tenants.

The arguments for privatizing state-owned industries are:

- Market forces are a greater source of efficiency and value for

▶ Look out for news stories about contracting out.

money than government direction. Increasing competition will lead to better use of resources and more vigorous efforts to satisfy the customer.

- Labour relations should improve when unions and workers recognize that they owe their jobs to the market and not to the government. Management will be motivated to change outdated work practices and to ensure higher productivity.
- Wider share ownership will be achieved through the sale of shares in privatized firms, both to employees and to the general public.
- Government finances will benefit from the proceeds of share sales, reducing the need for state borrowing. There will be less need for subsidies to support unprofitable industries.
- The political objectives of reducing state ownership and handing back more responsibility to private firms and individuals will be met.

Key privatization measures include:

▶ Note that some sales have been in stages: the years quoted signify those in which the government stake fell below 50 per cent, and in many cases to zero.

1979	BP	1987	British Airways
1981	Cable & Wireless		Royal Ordnance
	British Aerospace		Rolls Royce (aero engines)
1982	National Freight		British Airports Authority
1983	Associated British Ports	1988	British Steel
	British Rail Hotels		Rover Group
1984	Sealink Ferries	1989	Water Authorities
	Jaguar	1990	Electricity supply
	British Telecom	1991	Electricity generation
1986	British Gas	1994	British Coal
1986–8	National Bus Company	1994–7	British Rail

The net proceeds from privatization rose from £370 million in 1979–80 to reach a peak at around £8,000 million in 1992–3. By 1995–6 the figure had fallen back to around £2,400 million. Most privatization measures have involved large-scale share offers to the general public as well as to institutional investors. Others have involved management/employee buy-outs (e.g. National Freight) or direct sales to other firms (e.g. the Rover Group sold to British Aerospace and resold to BMW).

Criticism of Privatization

The Conservative Party remains committed to privatization measures and the Labour government, elected to power in 1997, has no plans for re-nationalization. However, there remains a case against privatization:

- Public utilities such as gas, electricity, water and telecommunications are still monopolies with little or no consumer choice available. They may make excessive profits at the expense of their captive market.
- Social objectives are less likely to be served by private enterprise. The social costs and benefits of production (see Chapter 49) may be ignored.
- Public service has been a distinctive ethos of the nationalized industries. Although prone to inefficiency, they have shown integrity and responsibility in attempting to serve all

customers. Market forces respond to buying power, not need. Privatized firms may be unresponsive to individuals and communities with low buying power.
- Wealth and income transfers through privatization are broadly away from society as a whole and towards those who are most powerful and privileged. Shares can only be purchased by those with surplus funds, while privatization issues have often yielded large capital gains. Dividends will tend to be received by those consumers who already enjoy the highest incomes.
- Government finances have been distorted by privatization. The government treats the process of asset sales as income when it really represents liquidation of capital. As the flow dries up, taxes or borrowing will have to increase. Arguably, taxation levels have been cushioned by privatization – again to the advantage of higher-income groups.

Set up a three-column table. Head one column 'In favour of privatization' and one column 'Against privatization'. Make notes for and against privatization in this format. Head the third column 'Privatization in practice' and add to your notes as you read the next section.

Privatization in Practice

It is rather too early to judge conclusively the performance of privatized firms, but observations include the following.

- **Financial performance** has quite strikingly improved following privatization. In most of the companies involved, both return on capital and sales per employee increased substantially.
- **Customer service** is even more difficult to assess. Real improvements in quality have been achieved at Jaguar and British Airways, for example. There is patchy evidence of more customer-oriented service from utilities such as British Gas and British Telecom. Equally, the bodies set up to regulate these industries (e.g. OFGAS and OFTEL) have recorded a rise in consumer complaints and are themselves accused of being ineffective.
- **Labour relations** have generally improved in the privatized firms, but this is also true across the whole economy.
- **Wider share ownership**, both for employees and the general public, has been achieved. In 1983 only 5 per cent of the adult population owned shares, while by the mid-1990s this figure had increased to 22 per cent. However, three-quarters of all investors have only small numbers of shares, while many sell them to realize a capital gain.
- **Privatization offer prices** have been widely criticized for being too low. The government argued that the prices were right given the need for successful flotation and the support of smaller investors. The steep and immediate rise in the value of some privatization stocks does suggest underpricing.

▶ Eight months after British Airways was privatized (1987), only 36 per cent of the original shareholders remained.

▶ In 1984 BT shares increased in value by 88 per cent on the first day's trading.

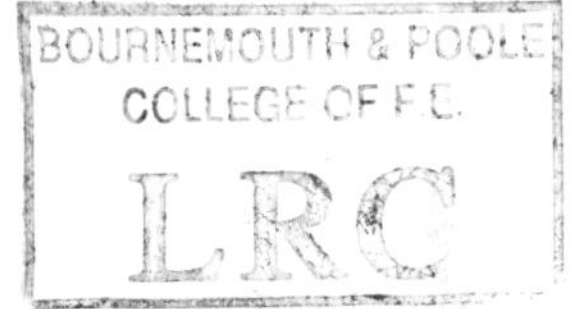
BOURNEMOUTH & POOLE COLLEGE OF F.E. LRC

The debate will probably continue. But the radical shift in balance from public to private sectors is likely to be permanent and may well be extended further.

	Company		
	Amersham International	*British Aerospace*	*British Telecom*
Year privatized	1982	1981	1984
Return on capital			
in year privatized	20.1	8.6	17.7
in 1993–4	30.9	9.4	21.2
Sales per employee (£k)			
in year privatized	30.0	26.7	32.1
in 1993–4	95.4	123.1	87.7

Source: A. Griffiths and S. Wall, Applied Economics, *6th edition (Longman, 1995)*

▶ Try CD-ROM to find old news stories on the privatization of British Rail and other industries.

1 Which company appears to have performed best since privatization?
2 In what ways might this data give an unfair impression of performance by privatized companies?

Evaluation

- Industries run by the state had a broad obligation to operate **in the public interest**. Critics of privatization argue that the drive for profit will push up charges and run down socially useful services.
- Privatization has often left monopolies practically or wholly intact. Though breaking up such monopolies prior to privatization would increase consumer choice and competitive pressure, this has to be set against the risks of losing economies of scale (see Chapter 13) and of reducing the total sale value of the nationalized industry.
- The ultimate business argument for privatization is the effectiveness of market forces in ensuring that producers address the demands of consumers. Profit is the reward for efficiency in the use of resources to match the needs of the market.
- Most public sector organizations have increasingly adopted the methods and style of the private sector. There is now much more emphasis on customer service, quality and competition.
- Social responsibilities can be as effectively met in the private sector as they were under state control. The leading edge of social responsibility in business has been well represented in the private sector (see Chapter 49).
- There is a worldwide trend away from state ownership towards private enterprise. Privatization is occurring in many other countries, including France, Germany, Japan, eastern Europe and Russia.

Part 2

Marketing

5 Market orientation and market segmentation

Chapter objectives

After working through this chapter, you will:

- understand the concept of market orientation
- understand the concept of segmenting markets
- know the typical segmentation criteria
- be able to apply the technique of market segmentation in simple examples
- know the meaning of the following key terms: marketing, product orientation, market orientation, marketing mix, market segmentation, market niche.

WHAT IS MARKETING?

Production is a dynamic process, converting resources into goods and services. **Consumption** is also a dynamic process in demanding, purchasing and using goods and services. **Marketing** means every activity in a firm that aims to join these dynamics together and achieve maximum profitability through the flow of completed sales.

Most larger firms have a marketing department led by a marketing manager or director. This has a range of functions, including those of the traditional sales department. **Market research** is used to identify the potential for new products and the need for the modification or relaunch of existing products (see Chapter 6). Sales are **promoted** through advertising, branding, packaging and point-of-sale display. An optimum range of distribution channels is maintained and filled by a trained and motivated sales force. Finally, price levels are set for strategic profit maximization.These elements of activity combine to form the marketing mix (see Chapters 8–11). Marketing management must coordinate this mix to fulfil corporate objectives. These will be expressed in financial terms through the sales budget (see Chapter 31), which will have been negotiated with the marketing department.

▶ Marketing is **not** another word for sales.

▶ 'Marketing is the management process responsible for identifying, anticipating and satisfying customer requirements profitably.'
Institute of Marketing

'Marketing is the process of determining consumer demand for a product or service, motivating its sale, and distributing it into ultimate consumption, to the continued satisfaction of the consumer, on a realistic profit basis.'
Marketing, Unilever

Make a checklist of the elements of the marketing mix.

Product and Market Orientation

When a firm starts its decision process with the product and works from the product to the market, then it is **product oriented**. If another firm starts its decision process with the market and works from the market to the product, it is said to be **market oriented**.

▶ The concept of market orientation was developed by Theodore Levitt (1960) in *Harvard Business Review.* His famous article, 'Marketing myopia', urged managers to make their first focus the satisfaction of customers rather than crude output of goods and services.

Consider two companies that manufacture garden tools. Firm A aims to maintain its traditional business. It believes that it makes excellent rakes, forks, spades, trowels and so on. Its future therefore depends on the demand for quality garden tools. Firm B does not think that its present products are necessarily its future products. It believes it is a business in the outdoor leisure market, with expertise in garden products. Its future depends on matching its resources to the demands of profitable markets.

Firm A is product oriented; firm B is market oriented.

Test yourself on the concepts of product and market orientation. Use a grid like the one below to enter a product or a market view of what the industry is selling.

Industry	*Product view*	*Market view*
Royal Mail	Selling stamps Collecting parcels and letters Sorting and delivery	Business communication The excitement of receiving a letter Good news Old friends

1 Hi-fi manufacture.
2 Banking.
3 Domestic heating oil.

▶ The division of a market into sectors according to the characteristics of its customers and their usage of the product is called **market segmentation**.

MARKET SEGMENTATION

In any market every consumer is distinct. Your reasons for buying a product will always be different from anyone else's. Every individual has his or her own circumstances, personal motivation and level of income. In this sense each person is a kind of micro-market. Given that the marketing mix is an attempt to achieve an optimum 'fit' between the efforts of producers and the needs of consumers, it follows that ideally a firm would use a separate mix for each single customer. In reality, this is usually only possible in industrial markets (where goods are often made to a given customer specification), or for very expensive products. However, it is possible to identify distinctive groupings of customers within a market.

Segmentation in the Market for Holidays

Harmony Holidays has completed a market research survey which suggests the following customer types:

A families with children
B couples without children
C retired couples
D older single people
E single people aged 18–30
F schools and organized groups

Each of these customer groupings forms a **market segment** and each has its own specific needs. For instance, an all-night disco might appeal to segment E but not to segment C. This approach is segmentation according to **consumer characteristics**.

▶ Segmentation by consumer characteristics

Research also shows that the main attraction for consumers taking a holiday with Harmony varies widely and includes:

- sunbathing and swimming
- social life
- rest
- relief from housework
- sightseeing
- walking and climbing
- pleasure for children

Another whole range of market segments is opened. This approach is segmentation according to **consumer responses**.

▶ Segmentation by consumer responses

Market Coverage Strategy

The use of segmentation depends on the **market coverage strategy**. Firms may choose to:

- aim a standard product at the centre of a mass market, so maximizing sales by satisfying the largest proportion of consumers;
- create a product range designed to target different segments in the market;
- concentrate on the demand of a single segment and market a correspondingly specialized product.

Segmentation is becoming increasingly important as a consequence of the **fragmentation** of the traditional mass markets. Holidays are one example; groceries sold through supermarkets are another. Early supermarkets of the 1960s tended to sell mass-produced foodstuffs and household goods as cheaply as possible and to regard all customers as a single group. Now the targeting of supermarkets includes luxury markets, convenience markets, health markets, vegetarians, one-person households and large families.

▶ Fragmentation has been caused by increasing affluence, enabling many people to look beyond the necessities of life and to demand products that better suit more complex and extended needs.

Types of Market Segmentation

There are many different criteria for identifying market segments. Often consumer characteristics are the basis. These include:

sex	male/female
age groups	0–4, 5–15, 16–24, etc.
household size	1, 2, 3–4, 5–6, etc.
family life cycle	young singles, married with young children, etc.
socio-economic groups	A, B, C1, C2, D, E
education	unqualified, GCSE, A level, etc.
residential neighbourhood	ACORN system
geographical region	London and the south-east, Midlands, etc.
lifestyle	e.g. 'mainstreamers', 'aspirers', 'succeeders', etc.

Segmentation by Socio-economic Grade

GRADE	*Head of household's occupation*
A	higher managerial, administrative or professional
B	intermediate managerial, administrative or professional
C1	supervisory, clerical, junior managerial, administrative or professional
C2	skilled manual
D	semi-skilled and unskilled manual
E	state pensioners, casual and lowest-grade earners

This grading system is the most widely used in Britain. It combines social and economic status, although in reality they do not always coincide. However, grades A, B and C1 are broadly 'middle class', while grades C2, D and E are broadly 'working class'.

▶ Computer technology has made the analysis of point-of-sale and questionnaire-based data much faster and cheaper.

Segmentation by Residential Neighbourhood

A useful development is the ACORN (A Classification Of Residential Neighbourhoods) system of neighbourhood mapping. The population is divided into eleven neighbourhood types and thirty-eight sub-types. Clusters of 150 addresses to cover every household in Britain are classified by their ACORN code. The system can enable marketing activity (e.g. direct mail) to be targeted with pinpoint precision.

Segmentation by Lifestyle

A lifestyle means a way of life. It describes how a person's needs and goals are expressed through his or her work, leisure and social life. Its origins are social and psychological. Its outcomes in business terms are purchasing decisions. The measurement and classification of psychological needs and corresponding lifestyles is called psychographics. A well-known classification system has been developed by Young and Rubicam (a London marketing agency) and is called Cross-Cultural Consumer Characteristics, or '4 Cs' for short.

Cross-Cultural Consumer Characteristics (4 Cs)

The system uses research by US psychologist Abraham Maslow, who developed a well-known 'hierarchy of needs' (see Chapter 35). In each person one of these needs (from the hierarchy) is seen to be dominant and becomes the key factor in determining his or her lifestyle. For example:

▶ About 40 per cent of the population might be classed as 'mainstreamers'.

- **Mainstreamers** have security as their greatest need and are the largest group, forming the foundation of society. They need to be seen as good citizens and do not want to stand out from the crowd. Their homes are neat, tidy and conventional. They buy the products of multiple stores and favour well-known brands (e.g. Ford or Vauxhall cars, Marks & Spencer's clothes, Heinz baked beans).
- **Aspirers** have status as their greatest need. They need to be

noticed and admired by others. Their homes are modern, with plenty of fashionable and technological luxuries. Money is very important: they have a fascination for credit cards and cash. They like exclusive shops and designer products (e.g. Porsche cars, Gucci shoes, Rolex watches, high-tech hi-fi).

- **Succeeders** have a dominant need to control. They are affluent but traditional, ambitious in their careers and autocratic in their need to control organizations and people. Their houses are comfortable, stylish and fairly formal. They buy up-market and reputable products of good quality (e.g. BMW or Jaguar cars, Barbour coats, Wilton carpets).
- **Reformers** seek fulfilment in their lives. They emphasize the quality of life rather than material wealth and find it important to contribute towards the improvement of society. Often highly educated, they are adventurous and ready to pioneer new markets. Their homes are frequently refurbished older properties, with stripped pine and natural materials in the decor. They tend to buy natural and healthy products with a mix of good value, good design and innovation (e.g. Volvo cars, groceries from Sainsbury's or Waitrose and furnishings from Habitat).

Alternatively, segments may relate to the product:

FACTOR	SEGMENTATION CRITERIA
benefit	convenience, indulgence, gift, etc.
attributes	size, colour, features, etc.
loyalty	total, partial, nil
usage rate	daily, weekly, monthly, etc.

Harmony Holidays – Market Segmentation

After careful research, Harmony Holidays decided to relate preferences for sunshine and activity on a holiday.

Three major sectors emerge:

A **Sunbathers** who want an easy undemanding holiday mainly on the beach or in the hotel area.

B **Middle-of-the-roaders** who want a mix of relaxation and moderate activity. Such a segment might be interested in coach tours from their resort.

C **Activists** who place great emphasis on stimulating activity with or without sunshine. They may favour sports, walking and climbing or sightseeing.

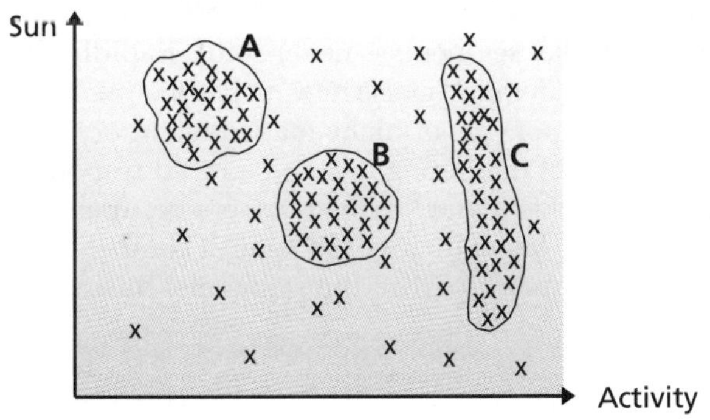

Figure 5.1
Market segmentation: preferences for sun and activity

▶ Most major car manufacturers now offer a range of variants on each model designed to appeal most within different market segments.

Many individuals and families will not fit easily into any one category, but such groupings still form a very useful analysis when setting the marketing mix. Product features and packaging can be adjusted to fit the target customer type. Advertising can appeal to their dominant needs. Distribution can be directed towards optimal outlets.

Nine ways of segmenting markets have been dealt with above. Taking each one in turn, make notes using examples chosen from the holiday business.

Firms have always recognized some limited segmentation in producing, for example, luxury, standard and economy models of a given product. Today, sophisticated segmentation methods open a new and powerful marketing potential. Firms can develop and position products at the centre of their target segments. It follows that the total marketing mix should be highly flexible and capable of fine-tuning according to changes in segment needs.

In many cases new and highly profitable markets are revealed through segmentation. For example, Harmony Holidays may develop specialized sightseeing or walking tours for which customers in these segmented markets may pay a premium price.

Market Niches

▶ The first Habitat shop opened in 1964 selling innovative designs in household goods. The firm developed this niche into a major segment by the 1980s.

A subsection of a segment is called a **market niche**. In terms of its defining characteristics, no segment has a regular shape. Similarly, no product can have equal appeal to all parts of its target segments. The areas of a segment that are partially or wholly untapped by the main producers become niches that offer specialized business opportunities.

Holidays in the Business Market

Figure 5.2 shows a market segment for hotels attracting business clients. The major chains have targeted the segment's central area, offering luxury and a limited degree of character. The niche represents business clients who want only moderate luxury but considerable character. This specialized market is not considered sufficiently large to be worth exploiting by the major chains. However, with a well-targeted marketing mix, the niche will support a profitable smaller business.

▶ The Sock Shop was highly successful during the 1980s but faced growing competition as large stores improved their ranges and merchandising of socks.

The shape of market segments is never static. Rapidly changing patterns of consumer demand cause new niches to appear and others to contract. The components of **niche management** are intensive market research, a tight marketing mix and a rapid response to shifts in demand. No niche is owned by its business occupant. Niche-based firms must always be on their guard against competition from firms positioned in the major part of the segments. Business honey pots attract predators.

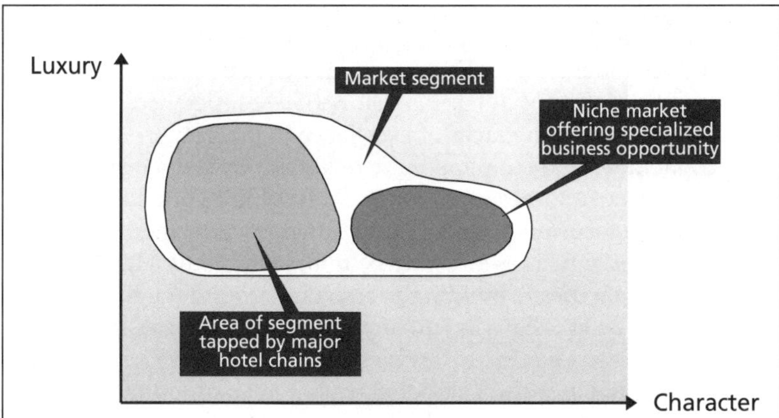

Figure 5.2
The market segment for hotels attracting business clients

Read the following case study and answer the questions below.

Sherwood Shoes Ltd
Sherwood Shoes Ltd designs and manufactures footwear for a mainstream market. Its reputation is for comfortable, practical and reasonably priced shoes. A new market research survey maps consumer priorities when buying shoes.

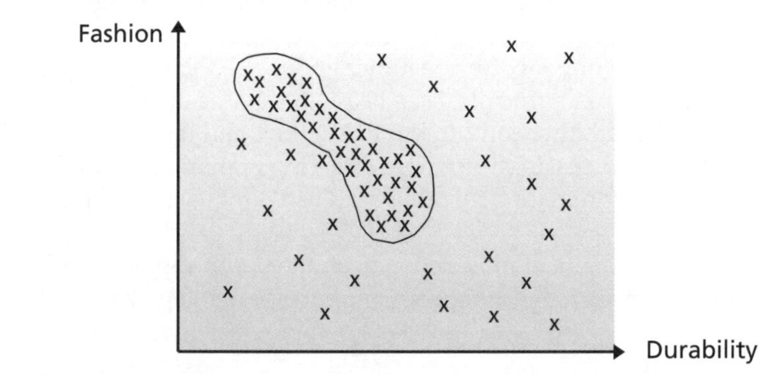

Figure 5.3
Sherwood Shoes: segmentation map

1 What conclusions might the marketing manager draw from the diagram above?
2 Do you foresee any dangers in your answer to Question 1?
3 What other forms of segmentation might the marketing manager attempt?

Evaluation

- Inability to understand and respond to market changes has caused the failure of many firms with good products and reputable brands. Take-over bids are now often based on the claim of superior marketing ability.
- Ultimately, market orientation must relate not just to the customer but to the source of satisfaction in consumption of the product. This means attempting to understand the customer's conscious and subconscious 'world' (see Chapter 9).

- Effective market orientation is carefully guided. Its translation into profitable sales requires management's understanding of the firm's **distinctive competence**. This means identifying areas of excellence in the firm's capabilities and coupling these to known consumer demand.
- Sales is not another word for marketing. Sales orientation means a focus on **pushing** the product towards the customer, who is assumed to be reluctant to buy. Market orientation means building production around the market to such an extent that sales are only the final act in meeting the customer's needs.
- Changing the name 'sales department' to 'marketing department' does not make a firm market oriented. This is only achieved as a complete philosophy, emanating from top management and infusing every operation of the business. The market becomes the touchstone of all decisions.
- Market orientation means that the firm's organizational structure must be capable of tracking its market and adapting rapidly to change. This realization is speeding up the abandonment of rigid hierarchies in favour of more flexible structures, with fewer layers of authority and more emphasis on personal and team initiative (see Chapters 35 and 45).
- The marketing mix for consumer goods used to be on the 'blunderbuss' principle, i.e. a heavy discharge of activity aimed in all directions. In the 1990s, the trend has been towards increasingly accurate targeting of markets and a far more discriminating mix that is adjusted for each market segment.
- Effective segmentation depends on the use of sophisticated market research techniques. Computer technology has made the detailed analysis of markets cheaper, faster and more accurate.
- Segmentation of markets has its counterpart in production, where new technology is making possible a wider range of products and product features at a diminishing cost. It is likely that the product mix will follow the marketing mix in becoming increasingly flexible (see Chapter 14).
- The most extreme form of segmentation involves analysing the special demands of each customer and offering a product to meet precisely their needs. This customization will tend to become more important with advancing production technology, especially in industrial markets.
- Segmentation must be seen as a dynamic analysis. Segment boundaries and patterns are constantly changing, requiring a more adaptable marketing plan.
- By cross-classifying a range of segmentation variables, it is possible to identify very large numbers of possible segments, e.g. 'middle class, male, single, 16–25, central city neighbourhood, aspirer lifestyle'. A danger is excessively fine segmentation, which identifies markets of inadequate size and targets them at excessive cost.

Market research

Chapter objectives

After working through this chapter, you will:

- recognize the scope and importance of market research
- know the main objectives and types of market research
- be able to apply basic research techniques
- understand the use of forecasting
- know the meaning of the following key terms: market research, quantitative information, qualitative information, secondary research (desk research), primary research (field research), samples (random, stratified, quota, cluster), interviews (structured and unstructured), questionnaires, scaled responses, consumer panels, forecasting (quantitative and qualitative), scenario planning.

Market research is the systematic effort to obtain that information which will guide the resources of a business most accurately towards the profitable fulfilment of consumer demand. This implies a strategy of continuous market analysis.

▶ A firm needs information about its customers and non-customers, the perception and use of the firm's products, the response to its marketing effort, and consumer needs that it does not presently fulfil.

Marketing the Grand Hotel

The Grand is a large 150-room hotel situated on the seafront of a major Devon resort. The following type of information would be valuable to the management:

the guests
- numbers?
- business or pleasure?
- singles, families, children, groups?
- occupations?
- income groups?
- home address by region/area?
- type of transport?
- number of nights in hotel?

the facilities
- occupancy rates by room types?
- meals taken? assessment of quality?
- use of bars, games room, discos?
- care of children?

- conference facilities?
- other services?
- special likes/dislikes?

the marketing
- reaction to brochure?
- use of holiday or hotel guides?
- AA/RAC registration?
- perception of price and value for money?
- use of discounts?
- recall of advertising?

the competition
- other local hotels used?
- competing price rates?
- facilities offered?
- food and furnishings – quality?
- rival publicity?

the business environment
national
- national economy: recession or boom?
- growth in incomes?
- inflation?
- interest rates?
- overseas visitors?
- exchange rates?

local
- planned transport improvements?
- shopping developments?
- quality of beaches?
- local events?
- weather statistics?
- local council publicity?

The inset shows just a few of the factors that should be informing the managers of the Grand Hotel. Almost any line of research could split into many more specific enquiries. For example, use of the hotel brochure could be explored in detail. How was it obtained? What other brochures were obtained? Which parts were useful? Was the cover effective? Was there enough information? What image of the hotel did the brochure convey?

▶ Central to market research is the identification of market segments (see Chapter 5).

This type of information enables management to shape its product to fit demand and to target its marketing plan accurately.

The scope of market research embraces every variable that could affect present or future sales. The main areas of enquiry are:

- **consumer research**, which analyses market size and market characteristics, making breakdowns by age, class, income, locality, lifestyle, buying habits, attitudes and values;
- **product research**, which assesses performance in use, variety of uses, use of allied products, after-sales and

maintenance needs, psychological perception of product, rival products;
- **promotion research**, which includes advertising impact, packaging and image perceptions, response to displays and special offers, brand awareness, sales breakdown by territories and sales teams;
- **distribution research**, which explores the breakdown of sales by distribution channels and types of outlet, effects of transit, warehousing performance;
- **pricing research**, which examines sales relative to price, value for money judgements, perceptions of price, effects of income changes, pricing of substitutes;
- **business environment research**, which analyses economic trends, foreign competition, market structure, changes in the law, demographic trends, cultural patterns.

Take each of the six categories of research above and list them with examples of research which might be done for the Grand Hotel.

Information from each of the above areas should feed into the decision process at every level of the organization. Generally, the more strategic the information (e.g. changes in customer average incomes), the more it will be the concern of the board and senior management.

▶ Cadbury spent three and a half years and £10 million on **Project Gift** – a programme to create new chocolate assortments for the 1990s. One result was 'Inspirations'.

MARKET RESEARCH OBJECTIVES

Market research is expensive and must compete for limited resources in the marketing budget. It must therefore work to clear objectives to ensure maximum advantage. The type of enquiry may be:

- **specific**, where an answer is required to a particular problem – for instance, why did sales in East Anglia fall by 25 per cent during April?
- **general**, where the firm wants to monitor broad trends – for instance, the average age of first-time house buyers.

▶ **Specific research** forms a discrete project. The terms of reference are set, the research methods are decided, the results are analysed and the decisions are taken. **General research** is a continuous activity, with reviews at regular intervals that may prompt specific research projects.

▶ The need is for research goals to be well focused. The timings and degree of accuracy required in the presentation of the findings must be decided.

Data gathered must be **relevant**. Information technology has made data collection and processing much quicker and cheaper. However, this can cause **information overload**, where managers disregard data because of its excessive quantity. For a busy manager, one sheet of A4 paper may be far more powerful than a stack of computer printout.

Types of Market Information

- **Quantitative information** answers questions about magnitude. It is usually expressed in numerate form. What percentage of families buy the *TV Times*? How many cans of Orange Fanta are sold on an average day in August?
- **Qualitative information** answers questions of judgement and meaning. What is the image of Woolworths? Why are more women than men vegetarians?

▶ Desk or secondary research

Desk or **secondary research** means the use of information that has already been collected and made available in some form. This may be from **internal sources** such as sales records (by product, area or sales representative), pricing data or customer payment records. More qualitative information will be found in the experience and reports of sales staff, distributors and public relations personnel. Many **external sources** exist, such as trade and employers' associations, specialist journals and government publications. Market research agencies also sell their own specially collected data.

▶ Field or primary research

▶ Firms with limited in-house resources will use a market research agency. Very large firms may have their own research teams and prefer the greater guarantee of confidentiality that this allows. There are about 40 significant market research organizations in Britain with a combined turnover exceeding £380 million.

Field or **primary research** means the collection and collation of original data. This is far more expensive and will usually only be undertaken for a particular purpose (e.g. to test the market regarding a potential new product). In its research the firm will be seeking the answer to specific questions and may use personal or telephone interviews, direct or postal questionnaires, or a panel of potential consumers.

FIELD RESEARCH TECHNIQUES

Sampling

▶ The survey methods selected will depend on the population to be surveyed, the cost and the level of accuracy required.

Few surveys can include the whole of a relevant population as it would be too large. Usually, a **sample** must be selected that is **representative** of a given population. There are various sample types:

- **Random samples**: this means that every member of the population has an equal chance of being selected. Provided that the choice of respondents is genuinely random, then its statistical validity can be precisely calculated. However, respondents may be widely dispersed, making interviews expensive.
- **Quota samples**: to use this method, existing data about, for example, the age and gender structure of the population must be available. The researcher identifies the number of respondents in each category who must be questioned if the sample is to be representative. For example, data may be available to tell the researcher that 30 per cent of biscuit assortment purchasers are women aged 45–60. In 250 interviews the quota for women in this age group will be 30 per cent, or seventy-five. The interviewer finds the right number of respondents to fill each category until the quotas are filled.
- **Cluster samples**: to reduce financial and time costs, a defined cluster of the population may be used as a unit for sampling. Examples could include selected counties, towns, neighbourhoods, firms or colleges. The proportion of the selected population consulted can then be much higher. The distribution of population types within the cluster must be known and allowances made accordingly.

Make a list of the various kinds of sample with a few words of explanation on each. Then add the advantages and disadvantages of each kind.

Data-collecting Techniques

1 Interviews

Personal interviews may be **structured** and based on a printed questionnaire in which respondents are asked a series of questions, perhaps in a shopping centre location. Answers are recorded on paper or portable computer, the interviewer often using a range of given responses from which the consumer is asked to choose. **Unstructured** personal interviews encourage a broader discussion and are often tape-recorded.

Telephone interviews

These are more popular in the USA but are also used in Britain. Short, structured interviews can be conducted quickly, cheaply and with a geographically dispersed population. However, low-income groups without a telephone are out of reach. It can also be difficult to gain the cooperation of respondents.

2 Questionnaires

The design of a questionnaire is vital to its value. Opening questions are normally for **classification** of respondents (by sex, age, occupation etc.). The main questions relate to the subject matter. All questions should be as brief as possible, in number and format. They must be phrased simply and very clearly. Questions should be inoffensive and answers should not rely on calculation. Bias must be avoided in the wording.

Layout should be spacious, clear and organized for easy collation. A range of graduated responses may be offered for a question. For example:

I consider the catering service to be

- ☐ excellent
- ☐ good
- ☐ adequate
- ☐ inadequate
- ☐ very poor

Closed questions are those offering a choice from a fixed range of options only – for instance, 'yes, no, don't know'.

Open questions invite a unique personal response, for instance: 'What made you choose brand X toothpaste?'

▶ When the respondent is likely to be less than honest, disguised questions may be used. For example, the question 'Why do you visit the pub at lunch time?' becomes 'Why do you think people visit the pub at lunch time?'

In a **postal questionnaire** polite letters are sent to the sample population with a questionnaire enclosed, together with a prepaid reply envelope. Instructions must be very clear and some incentive to participate is usually offered, for instance a small gift or entry in a prize draw. Questionnaires may also be attached to periodicals or made part of a guarantee form. The response rate to postal surveys can be quite low.

Questionnaires can also be distributed direct to respondents to be completed on the spot. Where customers are detained, questionnaires may be placed in prominent positions, for instance in a room of a hotel or on seats of a train, in the hope that they will be filled in.

▶ Continuous market research is necessary to ensure a prompt response to changes in consumer preference.

3 Consumer Panels

A small sample of consumers is asked to provide information over a period of time. Vouchers or gifts are often provided as a reward. Panel members may keep records of their purchases, usage of products or choice of radio/TV programmes. Panels may also test new products or discuss their attitudes to products and brands. The method provides valuable in-depth data and helps to reveal trends over time.

List the various ways of collecting information described above. Go back to the example of the Grand Hotel and against each information collection device in your list, write down an example of the kind of marketing information that could be collected using it. For example, for what purposes would it be appropriate to use a questionnaire with closed, graduated questions and for what purposes would it be appropriate to use a consumer panel?

Forecasting

No matter how good the quality of desk or field research, it can only relate to the past. Managers, however, need to anticipate the future.

Quantitative Forecasting

Subjective forecasts are those based on opinion. Sales staff are asked for their estimates of future results; customers may be asked about their buying intentions; panels of 'juries' of experts inside and outside the firm may report on likely projection.

Published forecasts include government macroeconomic data, which may vitally affect the level of demand. Some universities and various other institutions also publish their own economic forecasts.

▶ Qualitative information is vital in setting longer-term strategy (see Chapter 47).

Qualitative Forecasting

This usually attempts to predict how the social, political, economic and technological environment for business will change.

- **Scenario planning** involves exploring the future implications of changes in a key variable, for instance the price of oil. A plastics firm might consider likely, optimistic and pessimistic scenarios based on corresponding projected oil prices.
- **Delphi methods** ask a panel of experts to make individual forecasts without consulting one another. A summary of these views is then provided for each member, who then gives a reconsidered opinion. Repeating the process then creates a converging picture.
- **Value profiles** try to predict changes in social values that affect patterns of consumption. For instance, if marriage becomes more popular, more household goods will be purchased as wedding presents.

List the kinds of forecasting techniques available. Go back to the example of the Grand Hotel. Against each of the techniques listed, note down how it might be used for forecasting in market research for the Grand Hotel.

Read the following case study and answer the questions below it.

The *County Gazette*

A large town and its surrounding villages are served by two local newspapers (excluding free, fixed-circulation titles): the *County Gazette* and the *Weekly Courier*. The average combined circulation of these titles in 1995 was 42,000, rising to 46,000 by 1997. The *Gazette* sold an average of 16,800 copies in 1995 and 17,220 in 1997. Market research conducted by this paper showed that 34 per cent of readers were over sixty, while 22 per cent of the local population were over this age. The editorial board is now considering the introduction of some 'younger' features in order to attract new readers.

1 What evidence points to the need for changes in the style of the *Gazette*? What arguments might be used to oppose 'younger' features?
2 What new market research methods might be used to assess the type of features most likely to increase circulation?

Evaluation

- Marketing expenditure may be too thinly spread across a mass market or too hazily focused for impact. Targeted marketing makes the marketing mix more cost effective.
- Market research should be proactive in identifying business opportunities and anticipating shifts in demand. By contrast, reactive market research would take place only when prompted by difficulties.
- Market research must be up-to-date and the response to its findings must be rapid. Slow decision making using out-of-date research may well carry a firm in the wrong direction.
- Ultimately, market research enables the firm to increase consumer satisfaction by more precisely meeting consumer needs. This increases the value of the product relative to its cost and tends to raise profitability.
- The commissioning of market research should be prioritized according to the ratio of its likely value to its likely cost. Expenditure must be accountable and subject to proper budgeting. Each research project should be reviewed to assess its likely value.
- Market research implicates the whole firm and not just the marketing department. It should be a key ingredient in strategic decision making.
- The use and impact of market research depends on the culture and structure of the organization. The more market oriented the firm, the more responsive it is likely to be towards market research inputs. But there remains the risk of management inertia and resistance to change. Similarly, much depends on the quality of communications. Messages from the market may be compromised or lost through bureaucracy or long chains of command.

7 The product life cycle

Chapter objectives

After working through this chapter, you will:

- recognize the stages in a product's life and be able to apply the concept of a life cycle
- understand the use of extension strategies
- know how to analyse a product portfolio
- appreciate the strengths and limitations of these techniques
- know the meaning of the following key terms: product life cycle, extension strategy, product portfolio, the Boston Matrix.

THE PRODUCT LIFE CYCLE CONCEPT

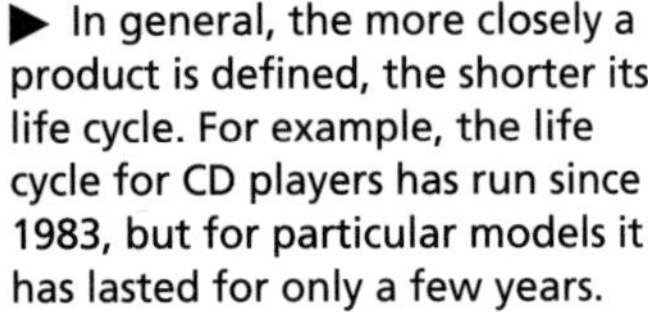

▶ In general, the more closely a product is defined, the shorter its life cycle. For example, the life cycle for CD players has run since 1983, but for particular models it has lasted for only a few years.

Every product has a finite life and can only be marketed with any prospect of adequate profitability for a limited period within the market. Each product has a life of its own, which passes through certain recognizable stages: **introduction, growth, maturity** and **decline**. For some products this cycle is very long (e.g. Lyle's Golden Syrup), while for others it is very short (e.g. most singles in the Top Twenty).

The life of a product may be measured in terms of two critical variables: sales and profit.

▶ This is the 'classic' profile of a product life cycle. Many other typical patterns have been identified.

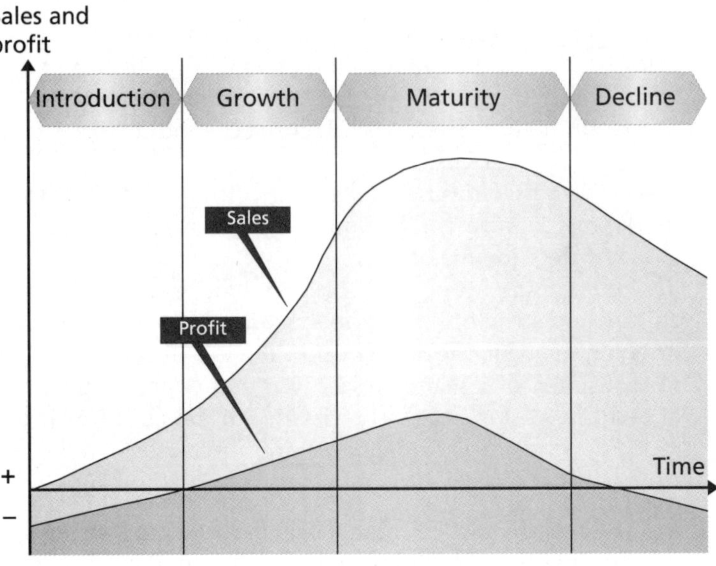

Figure 7.1
The product life cycle

The actual shape of the life cycle will vary widely according to the product and its market. All products have a different length of life cycle and the time spent in each phase may vary from a few days to many years.

The profile of the product life cycle (PLC) provides an important management tool. By identifying the progress of a product through its successive stages, plans and budgets can be arranged for an optimum marketing mix. In addition, the relationship between products can be better coordinated, while management is assisted in making strategic decisions concerning research and development (R&D) and new product launches.

▶ Movements of products along the life cycle may be difficult to detect or predict. The sales curve may follow an unusual or irregular pattern, while external forces such as competition or changes in the economic environment may distort its progress. Constant market research is necessary for the firm to monitor change and to use the PLC effectively.

Stages in the Life Cycle

For a major new consumer product, the following pattern would be typical:

1 Introduction Stage

▶ Introduction stage

This begins with the launch of a new product and its entry into the distribution channels. Competition is usually very limited and promotion will be **informative**, aiming to create **market awareness**. Customers at this stage tend to be innovators who will take risks and feel a need to seek status. Sales will increase only slowly (especially if the product is a major innovation) and overall losses will be sustained, since marketing costs are high and production on a small scale is costly. The pricing strategy may be geared to 'skimming', with a high price in more specialized markets, or to 'penetration', with a low price in potential mass markets. The product may still be modified according to market intelligence, i.e. that which research later reveals about the market.

In practice, many products will fail before reaching the growth stage because of inadequate sales, excessive costs, technical problems or a high risk factor.

2 Growth Stage

▶ Growth stage

Sales increase at an accelerating rate as losses turn into profits and rise steeply. Competitors are attracted to the market with 'me-too' products that have avoided the major development costs. However, the original product is likely to enjoy consumer loyalty and superior distribution. Some smaller firms in the market will be absorbed by larger ones. Promotion will become more persuasive and more strongly brand oriented. A range of product models may be offered by a firm to reach different market segments. Meanwhile, distribution must rapidly widen its coverage and the product may need acceptance by major retail chains.

3 Maturity Stage

▶ Maturity stage

Sales may still be increasing, but the rate of increase declines until a plateau is reached. Weak or small firms may be eliminated as competition intensifies and successful firms attempt to extract profits from a large and established market. Innovators and originators tend to lose their distinctive qualities as branding, advertising and price discounting reach a climax. In consumer markets retailers are crucial to the sales effort, with an emphasis on point-of-sale displays and other sales promotion tactics. In the late maturity stage, falling prices and mounting costs may cause declining profitability, and in a saturated market even the maintenance of market share becomes costly.

▶ Decline stage

4 Decline Stage

Products eventually reach the decline stage through the effects of new technologies or shifts in fashion and taste. The market size begins to contract and, as demand falls, firms may be forced to make deeper price cuts, with profit margins being squeezed. Marketing budgets are cut sharply and over-capacity becomes widespread. Success may be extended by concentrating on best-selling types and models, or by targeting niche markets. At some point, however, managers must decide whether to delete the product or to attempt its relaunch in an **extension strategy**.

▶ Product deletion is often a creative process. The resources that are released can be redeployed to support new product development (see Chapter 8).

Divide a sheet of A4 paper in five horizontally. Head each segment with a stage of the product life cycle; the last column heading will be 'Extension'.

Go back to the activity on Centurion Cycles and Golden Eagle Ltd at the end of Chapter 1. Centurion has a traditional ladies' bicycle called 'Madam', which is in its decline stage. Golden Eagle has a new product called 'Wicked', which has just been launched. With reference to both bikes, make notes on the stages of the product life cycle.

Extension Strategies

As the product moves into late maturity or decline stage, management may try to extend its life through modifications, repackaging or repositioning in the market. The goal is to generate a new phase of profitable sales growth without any major capital costs.

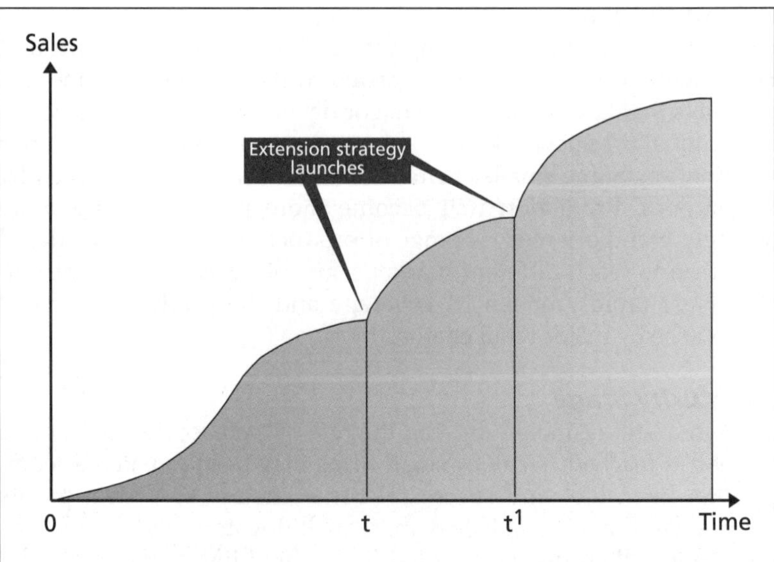

Figure 7.2
Extension strategies

Extension strategies may be based on restyling (e.g. new models of mountain bikes); technical advances (e.g. solar power for calculators); product developments for new markets (e.g. Terry's Chocolate Orange as a moulded bar); wider product range (e.g. new flavours for snack foods); new product uses (e.g. hi-fi for home cinema); more frequent product use (e.g. Cadbury's Creme Eggs throughout the year).

Management will aim to synchronize extension strategies with the PLC pattern and to avoid unsold stocks of the old product.

What advice could you give to Centurion Cycles about extension strategies for 'Madam'?

Evaluation of the Product Life Cycle Method

Strengths

- Provides a clear model for understanding typical changes in product sales and profits.
- By pinpointing product positions of the PLC, the marketing mix can be adjusted to maximum effect.
- Assists planning of a coherent and mutually supportive product portfolio (see below).
- Encourages management to recognize the market as dynamic and to adopt a proactive approach.

Weaknesses

- The PLC is often unreliable and misleading in efforts to forecast events. The movement of products along their PLC may be so erratic that effective analysis is not possible.
- Real sales and profit results are often highly dependent on external factors such as new technologies, tax changes or interest rates.
- Firms may be tempted into self-fulfilling prophecies, for instance withdrawal of marketing support for a product which then collapses when it could have recovered.

THE PRODUCT PORTFOLIO

At any given time, most firms are marketing a range of different products; together these make up the product portfolio (i.e. a 'collection' of products). Each product will have a different life cycle profile and be positioned at a different relative point on its own curve. Generally, firms aim to achieve a balanced pattern of products across the various stages of the PLC. Portfolio management is essential to the firm's stability and long-term growth. It is most important to avoid all major products entering the decline stage at once. Adequate positive cash flow from successful mature products is needed to fund new product research and for promoting launches through the costly introduction stage.

To assist analysis of the business portfolio, a grid is often used.

Figure 7.3
The Boston Matrix

▶ This grid was developed by the Boston Consultancy Group and is often called the 'Boston Matrix'.

Stars are products with a high market share in a fast-growing market. They can earn large cash inflows but require high investment levels to sustain a rising market share. Net positive cash flow may be limited, but potential exists for high cash returns in the longer run.

Cash cows are usually ex-Stars, where market growth has slowed into maturity. Investment in the product is low, yet it can be 'milked' for large positive cash flows.

Question marks hold only a low market share, but in a fast-growing market. If they can be managed towards a higher market share they may become Stars, but high investment is needed. Equally, Question marks with a stagnant or weakening market share may become Dogs.

Dogs have a declining and/or low market share in a static or shrinking market. Usually a firm will dispose of its Dogs, but with low outgoings they can be profitable in specific market segments.

The boxes in the portfolio grid are not secure or self-contained. Markets are dynamic over time and product positions within the portfolio are subject to constant change. The arrows in the diagram represent the general tendency over time for Stars to become Cash cows and for Question marks to become Dogs. Management will aim to achieve a balanced range of Stars, Cash cows and Question marks. Funds generated by Cash cows will finance conversion of Stars into Cash cows and Question marks into Stars.

Read the following case study and answer the questions below.

Country Cakes
The enterprise was launched in 1987 to exploit a widening market niche for cakes with a 'country' image. Based on a small business park near Oxford, the firm's annual turnover has reached about £600,000 and benefits from two major supermarket accounts. The cakes are sold in individual boxes with an average ex-factory price of £1.50. It is estimated that the quality cake market has been growing at around 6 per cent per annum. Sales data for Country Cakes are shown below:

Product	*Numbers sold (000s)*			
	1994	*1995*	*1996*	*1997*
Cotswold Fruit	218	205	193	181
Shire Sponge	129	132	135	127
Cider Apple	16	40	57	66
Natural Carrot	–	8	21	20

1. Using the concept of the product life cycle, analyse the sales prospects for each product.
2. Critically examine the company's product portfolio. What advice would you give about its product mix?

Evaluation

- The concept of product portfolio is very useful in enabling managers to value their product range as an interactive whole. Products can be analysed in terms of their grid positions, and this can then be translated into implications for cash flow and profitability.
- The dangers of this approach lie in oversimplifying reality. Product profitability varies widely, and market share and market growth are only two variables in the decision-making process. It is difficult to classify products on the grid, and there is no guarantee that the cost of higher market share will yield higher net profits.

8 The marketing mix: product

Chapter objectives

After working through this chapter, you will:

- be able to analyse the product from the point of view of the market
- understand the concepts of product value and value analysis
- know how firms develop a product mix and position their products in the market
- understand how new products are developed and why some products are deleted
- know the meaning of the following key terms: product value, value analysis, product mix (width and depth), market position, concept testing, lead time, product deletion.

▶ Ask yourself what the following business enterprises are really selling: (a) a country pub; (b) a maker of fashion shoes; (c) a nightclub.

UNDERSTANDING THE PRODUCT

It is a strange fact that many firms do not know what they are really selling. To list or detail their goods or services is easy. This may define the product in production. But the product in the market, as perceived by the consumer, may be quite different. And since it is the consumer that provides the firm with sales revenue and profit, it is this market perception that must be understood.

▶ Think of some famous cars and the kind of person you would expect to drive them, e.g. VW Golf, Volvo Estate, Morris Minor.

The Mini

One of Rover's most famous cars is the Mini. Launched in 1959, it continues to sell today. Rover is producing a car, but what are customers purchasing? The product itself is like a shell. The essential product may be hidden. Transport ... economy ... convenience ... independence ... fashion ... nostalgia for the 1960s ... surprises ... youth ... fun ... optimism? The Mini is all of these and more. As a classic product it confers good taste on its owner and carries numerous associations from films and advertising. The car has a 'personality' and this is all part of the purchase.

Product Value

Only a product with value can be sold. The total satisfaction that the consumer expects to derive from the product – expressed in money terms – must exceed the price, or no sale will take place. This estimation of value by the consumer is critical and at the heart of any marketing strategy. A product is not purchased for its own sake but for the stream of satisfaction that a consumer expects it to yield.

Objective value refers to the actual qualities of the product that exist independently of the customer. A watch indicates the time to a certain degree of accuracy. It may have other attributes, such as being shockproof and waterproof. All this is real value.

Subjective value refers to those sources of pleasure in a product that depend on the customer's personal feelings. For example, if the watch is a Swatch it may do far more than tell the time. To the buyer it may make an important statement about his or her personality and lifestyle.

Economic value means the consumer's estimate of a product's total value expressed in money terms.

From the point of view of the firm, a product also has a **strategic market value** in its ability to obtain or advance a share in a particular new market. For instance, a maker of professional recording equipment may wish to enter the domestic audio market or a building society may wish to enter the personal loans market. New products act as keys to new markets and build vital reputations.

The economic value of a product may derive from a mainly objective or mainly subjective source, or a mix of the two. A firm may decide to carry out a formal **value analysis** of a given product or product range. This will involve a thorough investigation into a product's source of practical function and consumer esteem and the corresponding cost structure in production. Creative thinking will be directed towards widening the gap between producer cost and consumer value. It does not necessarily mean cost cutting. For example, upgrading a car with real-wood trims and leather seats adds to costs but might add even more to its value in the market.

▶ Tom Peters (1994) stresses the importance of consumer 'delight' in a product. His '1,000 times' principle points to opportunities where a small increase in cost can generate a 'thousand times' greater increase in added value.

Try making a simple analysis of consumer value for the following products under the headings shown below:

1 A home contents insurance policy.
2 A major brand of training shoes.
3 A box of soft-centred milk chocolates.

	Value features	
Product	*Objective*	*Subjective*

Product Types

Consumer goods are those consumed by private individuals or households. There are **single-use consumer goods**, which are for short-term consumption, such as foods, cleaning materials and clothing. By contrast, **consumer durables** provide long-term satisfaction; examples include cars, televisions and furniture.

Consumer services are provided for individuals or households and include repair work, financial services, insurance, holidays, education and health.

Producer goods are those purchased by firms for use in the production process. They include raw materials and components, industrial equipment and machinery.

Producer services are supplied to firms and include maintenance contracts, accounting, legal and secretarial services.

▶ Consumer goods are often divided between:
- **convenience goods**, routine and familiar to the customer;
- **shopping goods**, requiring the customer to shop around;
- **speciality goods**, where customers are loyal to a brand.

PRODUCT MIX

Many firms sell a wide range of products, some closely related and some very different. Each related group of products is called a **product line** and may include a range of models, styles or sizes. The combination of a firm's product lines is called its **product mix**.

▶ Most building societies offer a wide product mix through a range of savings accounts, each with its own brand name, interest rate and conditions.

Product Mix

Silver Blade Ltd manufactures penknives, kitchen knives and scissors.

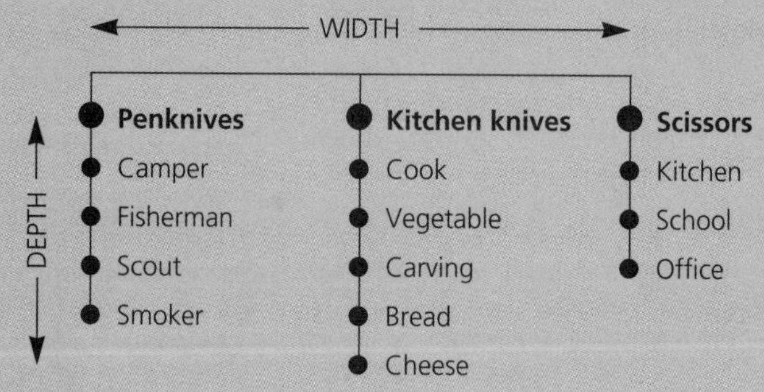

Figure 8.1
Measuring the product mix

The width of Silver Blade's product mix is clearly three.

The average depth in the mix is four $(4 + 5 + 3 = \frac{12}{3})$.

A wide mix provides entry to many different markets, while a deep mix allows access to more segments within a market. This analysis assists managers in recognizing the interrelationships between their products and in building an effective product strategy.

Note the difference between a wide mix and a deep mix and decide what kinds of mix are best suited to what kinds of products.

Market Positioning

Using market research it is possible to identify the **position** that consumers consider a firm or product to occupy in the market. **Market position** can be plotted against criteria such as price, quality, status or image. **Competitive positioning** charts a firm in the context of its rivals. **Company positioning** maps the various brands within one firm's product line. This technique helps to define market segments and to place products within market niches.

▶ Firms may track movements in their market positions through regular surveys of consumers. A relevant marketing mix can then be fine-tuned – or revamped for complete repositioning.

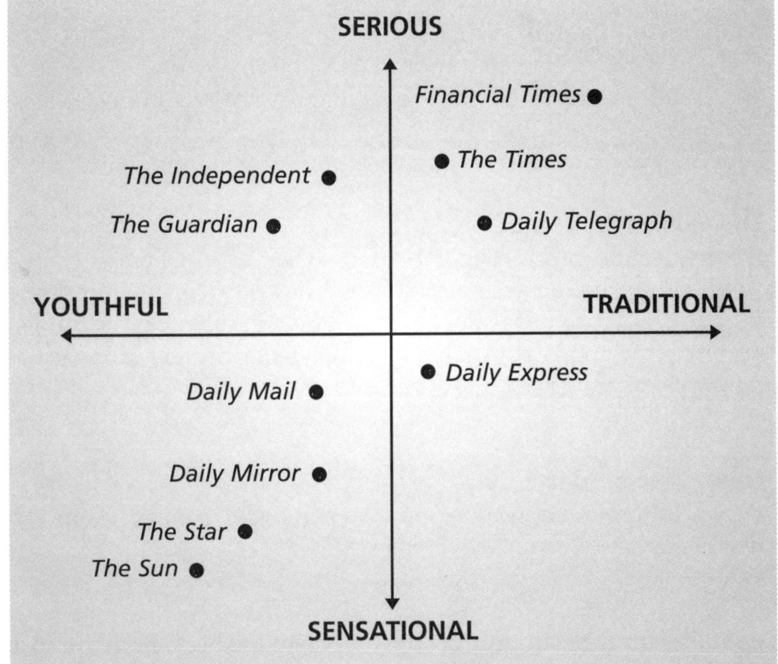

Figure 8.2
Market positioning

The chart makes it possible to distinguish the quality market (e.g. *The Times*), the mid-market (e.g. the *Daily Mail*) and the popular market (e.g. *The Sun*). Management may aim to reposition a product either because the market has moved away from the product or because the product has drifted away from its market.

Define 'market position', then try drawing your own map for car manufacturers or clothes retailers. Use price for your vertical axis and a 'youthful'–'traditional' scale for your horizontal axis.

New Product Development

▶ New products

New products are needed in a firm:

- as a response to changing consumer demand and competition;

- to replace those products reaching the end of their profitable life cycle;
- to provide the basis for expansion.

Although they vary widely in nature (from spearmint Polos to the Boeing 777), there are several categories – shown below – into which most new products fall.

Modified and variant products
Many new products are simply modified versions of old ones. For example, an electronic sewing machine offers an increased range of pre-set stitching patterns. Brand variants are also common, where a firm offers new sizes, colours or flavours.

Imitative or 'me-too' products
These occur when firms produce their own versions of existing successful products to achieve a market share without heavy development costs. Powerful market support is usually necessary.

Diversification products
Diversification products come about when a firm diversifies its product mix and enters an established market. The new product, though similar to its rivals, offers original features. For example, an electrical goods firm already making fan heaters launches a new style of hairdryer.

Innovative products
Significant innovations open new markets – for example compact discs taking over from vinyl records.

The stakes for firms in product development are high. Both the costs and the potential rewards for new products increase with the degree of innovation involved. A modification may be fairly cheap to introduce. The risks of a failure are low since the product is already established. But the likely rewards are often modest. A new product for an existing market is more costly, with a higher risk of failure. However, if a worthwhile market share is taken, then returns may be substantial. A new product for a new market may be very costly, with a longer development period. There is often a dangerously high risk of failure, but the reward for success may be rapid growth in sales and high profitability.

The success rate for new product ideas is remarkably low. Perhaps fifteen to twenty-five viable ideas may be tested to produce one successful idea. Even after launch, the failure rate is high, often with around 50 per cent of new products failing within two years of their launch.

Failure by a firm to introduce new products generally leads to a decline in both market share and profitability. No market stands still. A firm with a stagnant product range will find the gap between the market and its own products gradually widening. Competition intensifies and there is a downward pressure on price. Even a firm whose products are all profitable market leaders must be planning for innovation. In the short term extension strategies may be needed, while in the long run the next generation of products needs developing while time remains.

Senior management should have a clear policy for new product development. The task is the responsibility of the marketing department, but the specific role may be entrusted to a brand manager or new product manager. New product ideas can come from many sources, but they need conscious generation. Large firms have an R&D department, where trained staff search for product improvement and design new product concepts. These can be extremely valuable, but care must be taken to ensure that the work is directed to a proven market need. Thus market research is crucial in pinpointing potential opportunities. The sales department should be channelling important feedback from customers to management. The criticisms of distributors and consumers are a rich source of ideas. Staff suggestions can also be useful, while product planners themselves may use brainstorming techniques to produce the widest possible range of creative ideas.

Processing Ideas

After the elimination of non-starters, the firm must **screen** new product ideas, which involves testing for feasibility. This process requires criteria to be set, against which the ideas may be assessed or formally graded. Likely key factors include market research findings, market expertise, production capacity, skills availability and the existing product mix.

▶ The time lapse – or **lead time** – from a product idea to the actual generation of sales in the market varies widely. A small product modification may take only a few weeks, while a major product innovation in a complex industry (e.g. pharmaceuticals, aerospace) could occupy ten or twenty years. Lead time is important in planning a coordinated marketing mix.

Selected products will move forward to **concept testing**, where consumer responses to the proposed product are collected and evaluated. Products that still remain viable will now face business analysis, where detailed estimates of variable and fixed costs are set against projected sales revenue. Profitability can then be analysed using breakeven analysis (see Chapter 20) and investment appraisal (see Chapter 23). Finally, product development involves translating the ideas into a saleable product. Prototypes will be made and tested; packaging designs will be selected; branding decisions will determine market positioning; market research will continue in the effort to maximize consumer satisfaction.

At the end of all these stages, management must decide whether to launch the product into a test market (i.e. not the mass national market but a moderately large market within a limited geographical area) or to abandon (or mothball) the project. Large sums of money are often at risk and some intuitive decision making is likely. The certainty of success never exists. If a 'go' decision is given, then the product moves into its life cycle and the sales trajectory will deliver the market's verdict.

▶ Product life cycle, see Chapter 7.

Make notes on the process of new product development by drawing a flow chart identifying what should happen at each stage.

Product Deletions

When a product or an extension strategy reaches the decline stage, sales and profit will fall. If the product is **independent** of others in the range, then it certainly should be **deleted** once sales cease to cover variable costs and no contribution is being made to overheads (see Chapter 21). Usually it should be dropped before this point, when it fails to cover **average total costs**, and perhaps earlier still, when its returns fall below a budgeted minimum based on opportunity costs. Of course, managers must be reasonably sure that the decline is not merely caused by temporary circumstances such as a competitor's advertising campaign or a failure in distribution.

If the product is **interdependent** with others in the range, then the deletion decision is more difficult. A product may be unprofitable in itself, but valuable in encouraging other purchases in the range, in retaining a key customer or for the prestige of the brand name.

Use this opportunity to make notes on product deletion, bringing together what you learned about the Boston Matrix and extension strategies in Chapter 7.

Evaluation

- Firms may tend to understand their products in production terms. Management must grasp the meaning of their product in **market terms**, as experienced by the consumer. It is this analysis that enables market-oriented product development to take place.
- Although production and marketing are usually separate departments, their functions are very closely related. The achievement of the best possible product for the market demands detailed knowledge of the technical processes, materials, lead times and costings. The quality of communication between the departments is crucial.
- Market positioning enables management to be more accurate in its market targeting. All elements in the marketing mix can be sharply focused on precise product positions or deployed to shift a product into a more favourable position.
- Models to show product position are plotted according to the perceptions of consumers, **not** management. Targeting a product position is therefore really targeting a picture in the consumer's mind.
- The reality of constant change in markets makes new product planning essential. To be effective, there needs to be a culture of innovation within the firm, where product development is urgent and continuous.
- Assessment of new product ideas is not likely to be objective. Different managers will have different departmental and personal interests that they wish to protect or advance. Caution is needed when a new product idea triggers excessive enthusiasm or opposition.

- Product deletion is a creative activity. Judged correctly, it releases resources within the firm for more profitable uses. Deletions are necessary for products in irreversible decline and for new products that fail to meet sales and profit targets.

The marketing mix: promotion

▶ **Media Watch**
The media are saturated with product promotions. Collect examples of different kinds of promotion and try to work out why companies have chosen particular promotion strategies.

Chapter objectives

After working through this chapter, you will:

- understand how all promotional methods are integrated within the marketing mix
- know how advertising budgets are set and media chosen
- be able to analyse an advertising campaign and its likely impact
- recognize the main types of sales promotion and be able to assess their significance
- know the meaning of the following key terms: promotion, point-of-sale, advertising elasticity of demand, corporate identity.

PROMOTION

▶ Promotion includes:
- **advertising**: all communications designed to increase the priority assigned by the consumer to the purchase of a product;
- **sales promotion**: any tactic in the presentation of a product to the market designed to increase the quantity or frequency of purchase;
- **personal selling**: the efforts of the sales team to maximize the purchases of the product by specific customers over a given time span.

Within the marketing mix promotional activities are intended to increase consumption of the product and so the flow of sales. Consumers arrange the priority of their purchases according to the extent to which their expected benefit (utility) exceeds their expected cost. All promotion aims to increase the consumer's perception of this excess (or consumer surplus).

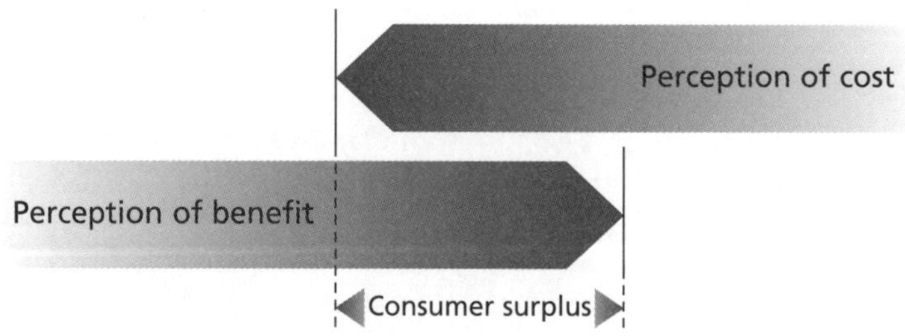

Figure 9.1
Maximizing consumer surplus

The benefit that a product is expected to yield varies with every potential customer. Although the price is usually fixed for consumer products (it may be negotiable in industrial markets), consumers' perception of the price will again vary widely.

Advertising

▶ Marks & Spencer has a very small advertising budget relative to its sales. The firm's reputation is its own advertisement.

Meaning and Function

Some products are said to sell themselves. This means that the consumer demand is so intense and the product is so able to meet that demand that no planned communication between producer and consumer is necessary. For most products this is not the case. The presence of a product needs to be advertised to the population of its target market. Thus advertising is a process of communication designed to stimulate purchase of a given product or brand. This is achieved by influencing consumer behaviour.

For a purchase to occur, the consumer must be aware of the product. The decision to buy then depends on the assessment of expected satisfaction against perceived cost. It follows that advertising will attempt to:

- (A) increase awareness of the product and its availability
- (B) increase expectation of satisfaction
- (C) decrease perception of cost.

▶ Launching a new brand of shampoo:
'The milk of human kindness' (B)
'Four Seasons Shampoo' (A/B)
'Available now' (A)
'ONLY 95p' (C)

Make notes on the functions of advertising (A, B and C) by writing a paragraph for a pamphlet advertising a window-cleaning service.

Much research has taken place to gain an understanding of how advertising acts on the consumer. Two well-known approaches are:

A-I-D-A	D-A-G-M-A-R*
• Attention	• Awareness
• Interest	• Comprehension
• Desire	• Conviction
• Action	• Action

* **DAGMAR** stands for **D**efining **A**dvertising **G**oals for **M**easuring **A**dvertising **R**esults

Both models stress the need to achieve awareness of the product, to generate a belief in its desirability and to trigger the action of purchase.

In pursuit of these aims there are two basic advertising functions:

- **to inform** consumers of the product's existence, availability, purpose, features, specifications and price;
- **to persuade** consumers by intentionally creating a need or desire to purchase and consume the product.

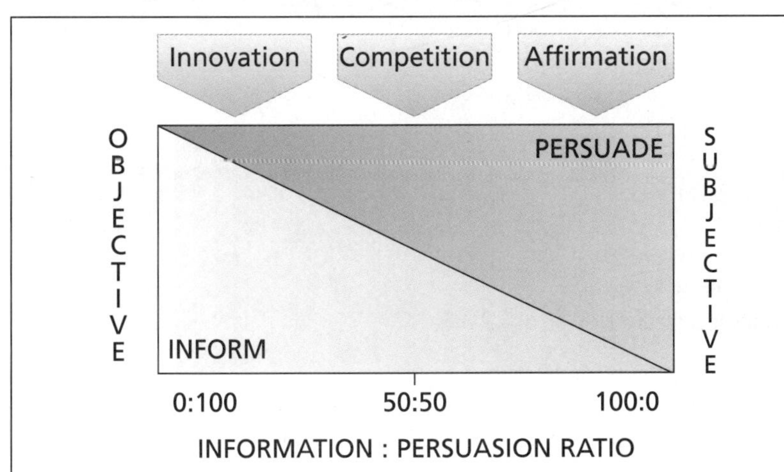

▶ 'Information': dominant when the product is innovative and the consumer is unaware of its qualities and availability. It also has a role in convincing consumers that a product is superior to its competitors.
'Persuasion': dominant when a firm fears competition from similar products, or wishes to protect or extend its market share.

Figure 9.2
The information : persuasion ratio

Advertising Types

Trade advertising is aimed at influencing the managers of distribution channels - those responsible for distribution (e.g. wholesalers and retailers) - to stock and promote a product or brand. It is closely related to personal selling.

Consumer advertising is directed to the end-user of the product, to encourage increased purchasing and usage. This is closely related to sales promotion.

Advertising Media

Each **advertising medium** has its own characteristics:

Television
- high exposure rate
- colour, movement and sound
- can demonstrate the product
- creative: high impact potential

BUT
- expensive
- transient: leaves no record
- difficult to target

Radio
- high exposure rate in target segments
- segmentation of audience possible
- frequent repeat of message
- low cost

BUT
- easily forgotten
- no visual content
- small total audience

Newspapers
- high exposure rate in segment
- strong socio-economic segmentation
- the advert can be retained
- flexible timing
- gain from paper's reputation

BUT
- no movement
- may lack impact
- colour may not be available

Magazines
- specialist readership
- long life span
- links with features
- good colour reproduction

BUT
- timing less flexible
- no movement

Posters
- very high exposure rate
- colour: can be creative
- situational impact

BUT
- conveys limited content
- only suitable for mass markets

▶ Other advertising possibilities include cinema, transport locations, electric and electronic signs and sponsorship.

The subject of either trade or consumer advertising may be:

- the product
- the brand
- the firm or organization (corporate image building)
- the industry
- a point of view (e.g. political campaigns and pressure groups)

Make notes, in a table, on the benefits and shortcomings of different advertising media, contrasting them in terms of expense, exposure and ability to reach closely defined market segments.

Advertising Budgets

There is no simple formula to decide an ideal advertising budget. This is because the exact effect of advertising on sales is not known. In theory a firm should continue to increase advertising expenditure until the profit generated by an extra sale equals the extra cost of achieving that sale. In practice there are some well-known general principles:

- **Percentage of past sales method**, which relates spending to revenue earned on sales already achieved. No allowance can be made for future expansion or contraction of the market.
- **Percentage of expected sales method**, which relates more closely to the market but runs the risk of incorrect sales forecasts.
- **Competitive parity method**, where the firm aims to match approximately the expenditure of its major rivals. This is common in markets with a few dominant firms and tends to act as an upward ratchet in spending levels.
- **Task method**, which rejects the concept of moving from budget to campaign and instead works from campaign needs to budget decisions. Advertising needs are identified and costed with a final strategic decision on the sums that can be afforded. The method implies the setting of clear priorities.

Advertising expenditure varies widely in its effectiveness, according to the product and the market. A useful concept is the **advertising elasticity of demand**:

▶ Advertising elasticity of demand

$$\text{Advertising elasticity of demand} = \frac{\text{percentage change in quantity demanded}}{\text{percentage change in advertising expenditure}}$$

High advertising elasticity clearly suggests a market where advertising is worthwhile. However, an increase in spending does not guarantee an increase in profit, which depends on the cost structure. Advertising elasticity tends to be high in brand-competitive markets and at the early stages of the product life cycle.

Make notes on what advertising elasticity of demand means in terms of making decisions about advertising expenditure.

▶ The advertiser's dilemma: 'Half of all I spend on advertising is wasted. The trouble is, I don't know which half!'

Advertising Campaigns

An advertising campaign or strategy requires careful planning. Management must decide upon its advertising objectives and relate these to the expenditure, timing, targeting and media mix of a campaign. Timing is important. The firm must opt between a 'drip' and a 'burst' approach:

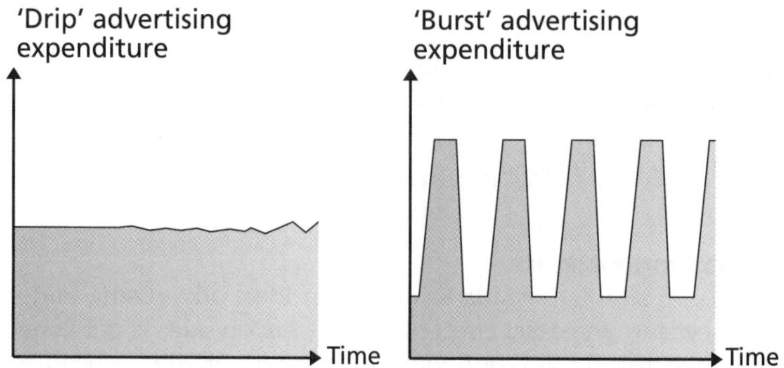

Figure 9.3
Drip and burst advertising

Drip advertising is often related to maintaining brand and product awareness. **Bursts** may depend on competitive pressures and specific events in the product life cycle.

It is also essential to relate the campaign to the elements in the marketing mix. Assuming that target markets for the product are finalized, then the campaign will be assisted by integrated sales promotion. Sales teams will be ready and briefed, with distribution channels well prepared. Pricing policy will have been set, together with sales and profit objectives.

▶ To gain an insight into the world of advertising agencies look at the magazine *Campaign*, which you will find in most large public libraries.

The use of an agency is very common for major campaigns. Agencies can offer a complete range of marketing services, from market research to every part of the marketing mix. Service fees and commission will be charged, but there is the benefit of highly specialized professionalism. Agencies accumulate wide experience and some outstanding talent. The right creative theme for a campaign can be the making of a product (e.g. Levi's 501 jeans advertisements).

SALES PROMOTION

Meaning and Scope

Sales promotion focuses on the **point-of-sale** in the distribution chain. It involves a wide range of techniques designed to increase successful sales outcomes when seller and buyer meet. Included are promotions to the trade, to industrial customers and to domestic consumers. In each case the aim is to accelerate the flow of sales by attracting new customers or by encouraging existing customers to increase their usage rate.

Brands and Identities

The use of names and symbols as a recognizable mark of origin has been common for hundreds of years. Modern brands are powerful and valuable. A firm will try to build favourable associations for its brand. These might be quality or value for money, reinforced through advertising. Once established, the brand itself leads consumers to expect satisfaction and therefore increases sales.

A brand name should usually be short, memorable and have no undesirable connotation, e.g. Flora margarine, Penguin books, Sealink Ferries. Once chosen, a brand must be registered, together with any distinctive trade mark.

Some firms use a single 'umbrella' brand name for their complete product range (e.g. Bic pens, lighters, razors). This ensures a favourable response from consumers to new products under the same brand, while the whole promotional mix can be expressed through a single name. Other firms devise separate brand names for each product (e.g. Distillers' range of Scotch whisky). This tactic increases the sense of product individuality.

There has also been rapid growth in 'own brand' and 'own label' products, sold by national distributors. These are normally manufactured by companies with their own famous brands, which must compete alongside the 'own labels'. A major retailer such as Sainsbury's has a brand identity in its own right and can ensure high-volume sales. The manufacturer selling its product under the 'own label' enjoys large regular orders without any marketing expenses. The original famous brand continues to sell at a higher price in many market segments.

Figure 9.4
The world's top ten brands

Packaging

Over the twentieth century an increasing proportion of products have become pre-packaged. This reflects the importance of packaging in expressing brand identities in a more affluent and sophisticated market. Packaging has the practical task of protecting the product in distribution and in use, but in a real sense it actually **defines** the product. Packaging determines the quantity in which a product is sold (e.g. 400g of chocolates). It may decide the method of usage (e.g. a squirt of washing-up liquid). It certainly expresses image and identity (e.g. Grolsch lager, After Eight mints). Many firms use packaging that is expensive and complex because it increases the customer valuation of the product more than it increases the price (e.g. Biarritz Chocolates). Brands and packaging are very closely linked. Styles of lettering and colour choices for product liveries become vital selling points, e.g. the confident bubbly red lettering on a blue background for Cadbury's Wispa bars. Attractive tins, jars, boxes and even carrier bags are often valued highly by the consumer. The product benefits from a stronger identity and brand loyalty is increased.

▶ Colour is a key element in the appeal of Terry's All Gold chocolates.

Colours have significant psychological and social connotations. Firms use colour in products and packaging to create and communicate brand **image**, i.e. use of psychosocial perception of consumers in the target market.

▶ Important colour associations include:
white – purity, cleanliness
black – power, mystery
purple – indulgence, extravagance
blue – distinction, coolness
green – natural, calm
red – excitement, heat
orange – warmth, comfort
yellow – sunshine, cheerfulness
brown – utility, practicality
silver – refinement, sophistication
gold – riches, luxury

Make notes on the importance of packaging in the promotional mix, taking your own examples from detergents, computer games or compact discs.

Other Promotional Methods

▶ **Point-of-sale promotion**: presentation and promotion of products in the place where they are sold.

Merchandising and Point-of-Sale Display

Merchandising is the art of attracting customers towards a product and stimulating their desire to make a purchase. Despite some functional aspects, shopping today has become less often a practical chore and more often a leisure activity. The environment of shops and stores is carefully planned to be interesting yet reassuring, enjoyable yet convenient. Lighting, decor, fittings and display all help to draw the customer towards a purchase. Physical access to goods is very important, and customers are encouraged to inspect and handle the merchandise. Much of the pressure to buy is invisible. Psychological research has been highly influential. Supermarkets, for example, plan the progress of their customers round the store, 'bouncing' their attention and buying patterns from display to display. The store management can plan the behaviour of customers to a surprisingly high degree.

Make notes on the importance of merchandising and point-of-sale displays with reference to any large high-street store.

Price and Credit

Short-term price cuts are a sales promotion tactic. The chance of a bargain attracts consumer interest, while a lower price will normally raise sales and introduce new customers to the product. Their effectiveness depends on the relative responsiveness of sales to changes in price (see Chapter 11).

▶ Charge-card holders' details provide a valuable database for a company's promotional activities.

The supply of credit has become an important promotional factor. For costly items such as new houses or cars, special credit facilities at reduced interest rates may be offered. Hire-purchase has lost relative popularity but many leading retailers issue their own credit cards, backed by major financial institutions. These not only stimulate sales but also help to solidify consumer loyalty.

Special Offers

The launch of a new product may be assisted by free samples or by special trial packs. More mature products can be promoted with additional 'free' quantities included with the pack (e.g. an extra 10 per cent in volume with soft drinks, or an extra tablet of soap). In highly competitive markets, unrelated gifts may be offered, either directly or through the collection of stamps or coupons (e.g. petrol sales promotions). Product packs may carry opportunities to buy other goods at specially reduced prices, but often require proof of purchase. Promotions may also give away tokens for cash refunds or reductions on future purchases. Competitions and prize draws are another popular device to attract customer interest.

Find examples of companies using price cuts, credit facilities and special offers for promotion. Why do you think these were appropriate for the product?

Exhibitions and Events
These are widely used in industrial markets to sell such goods as vehicles or machinery. A stand at an exhibition can arouse interest and media comment and secure increased orders. Some consumer goods exhibitions, such as the Ideal Home Exhibition, enjoy wide national popularity and act as a showcase for new products. Special local events can also provide a useful focus.

Direct Mail
Sending promotional literature direct to trade and private addresses is increasingly common. It can be targeted efficiently using market research data (see Chapter 6) and is extremely flexible in its timing and format. Mailshots often carry special offers to increase the response rate.

Sponsorship
A firm may agree to fund an organization or project in return for the promotional use of its name in the related publicity. Sporting, artistic, educational and charitable bodies have all used business sponsorship. The sponsoring firm has the added advantage of associating its brand with a respected person or activity. High fees may be paid to sports or pop stars for being publicly associated with a product.

Corporate Identity
Many firms aim to present a unified and easily recognizable image to their market and to society at large. A logo with the organization's colours and consistent graphic design gives the firm a clear identity to which consumers can respond. In the 1960s and 1970s these tended to be efficiency-related with geometric logos, but modern identities are more organic and people-centred.

▶ BP is estimated to have spent £170 million on the new corporate identity it introduced in 1990.

Select an appropriate mix of advertising media for each of these products.

1 'Electrochef' is a new, easy-to-use, inexpensive food processor with a wide range of attachments. 'Fast food that's real food' is the advertising slogan.
2 A travel firm is launching 'Eurostars': coach trips to European cities with cheap hotel accommodation and tickets for major sports events/pop concerts.

Evaluation
- Sales promotion works in the marketplace where sellers and buyers meet. It is a highly flexible part of the marketing mix and can be adjusted or redirected at management discretion.
- All elements in the total mix are intimately related to sales promotion. Its distinction from product development, advertising and distribution is often rightly blurred.
- The largest expenditures are reserved for selling into consumer markets. Sales promotion is also important in industrial markets, but tends to be more discretionary and is often activated through personal selling.

The marketing mix: place

Chapter objectives

After working through this chapter, you will:

- be able to analyse the basic goals of distribution in the mix
- be familiar with the main channels of distribution
- appreciate the role of middlemen
- understand how distribution decisions are made
- know the meaning of the following key terms: distribution channel, distribution chain, middlemen (wholesalers, brokers/ agents), retailers, direct marketing, producer retail outlet, franchising.

DISTRIBUTION

▶ The general rule today is that products must find their consumer rather than the other way round.

The pathways of ownership, transport and storage down which products pass between production and consumption are called **distribution channels**. The successive stages in the process form the **distribution chain**. These chains form a highly complex web of transactions and deliveries which criss-cross physical and financial markets. With large-scale production and increasingly international markets, the distribution chains for one product alone may be lengthy and elaborate.

Since direct producer–consumer contact is usually impractical, firms are needed to act as distributors or **middlemen**. Wholesalers and retailers are middlemen who buy and sell as legal owners of the product. Agents may also deal in the product, but only on behalf of a seller and not as its legal owner (e.g. an estate agent). The most common distribution chains are:

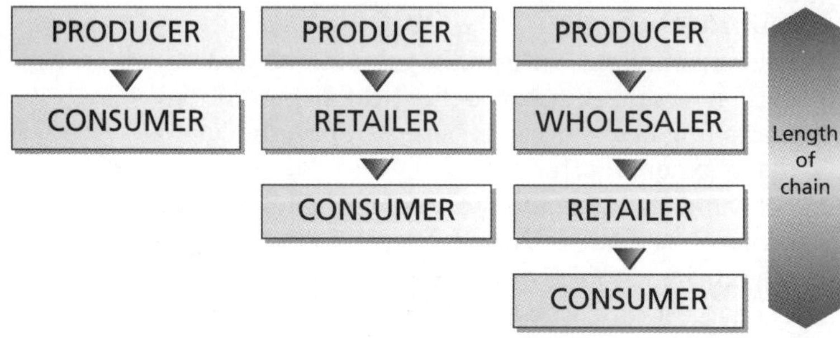

Figure 10.1 Distribution chains

Wholesalers

▶ **Wholesaling**: buying in bulk from manufacturers and selling in smaller quantities to retailers.

The major advantages of wholesaling are:

- **Bulk purchasing**: the manufacturer is able to sell goods in large quantities to the wholesaler, who therefore pays a lower unit price. Stocks of finished goods can be far lower, releasing finance for the manufacturer and cutting handling and warehousing costs. Delivery costs are also reduced and the necessary size of the sales force is smaller.
- **Breaking bulk**: the wholesaler breaks down large purchases of each product into smaller consignments for each retailer. This greatly reduces transport and delivery costs:

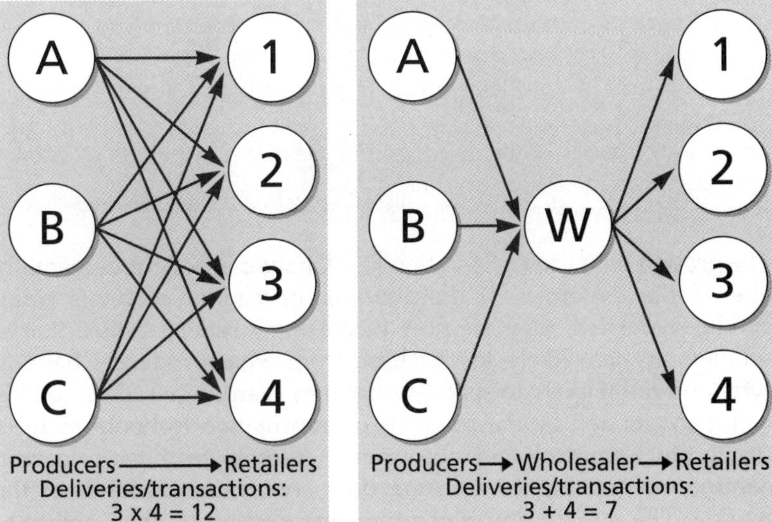

Figure 10.2
The wholesaler: breaking bulk

In Figure 10.2, without a wholesaler, twelve deliveries/transactions are required between the producers and retailers. By using a wholesaler (W), this figure is reduced to seven.

- **Spreading risks**: by moving output into the wholesale trade, the producer avoids the risk that stock may fall in value through deterioration or shifts in market demand.
- **Retailer support**: the wholesaler assists retailers in enabling them to make small orders of the product, which they would otherwise be unable to do. Often help is also given with technical training and sales promotion. In addition, the retailer may obtain vital working capital through the extension of credit.

These benefits carry a cost. First, the wholesaler requires a profit margin, so adding to the final price of the product. Second, control over the precise delivery of the marketing mix moves away from the producer. The product may not be handled, merchandised or promoted in the way the manufacturer intends.

Retailers

The retailer provides:

- variety and convenience for the customer
- merchandising and promotion

- product information and advice
- final pricing expertise
- credit and delivery services
- after-sales service

Some 82 per cent of all shops (283,000 in number) are still small businesses, but large multiple stores have now captured 60 per cent of total retail turnover and the figure is rising.

Key Trends in UK Retailing

- The decline of the small independent retailer and the growth of large multiples.
- The use of cars for shopping, with the corresponding advantages of large 'one-stop' out-of-town stores.
- The shift in market power from producers towards large retailers.
- An increase in franchising, which ties large numbers of small retailers to a single supplier.

The growth of market orientation (see Chapter 5) has fundamentally altered the dynamics of distribution. Instead of channels being producer-pushed, they are now increasingly retailer-pulled. Large retailers are less likely to purchase from what producers have to offer and more likely to specify what they want to sell. This trend is being accelerated by the progress of information technology. Electronic stock control and accounting systems feed back instant, continuous and highly accurate data concerning demand in the market. The market shares of producers depend on their ability to respond with sufficient sensitivity and speed.

These changes in the relationship between producers, wholesalers and retailers are transmitted through the distribution chains, with the effects of change flowing in both directions.

▶ Small local and specialist retailers are, however, likely to flourish in niche markets. For them, the role of the wholesaler is vital in breaking bulk and in supplying goods from a great variety of producers.

The changing structure of distribution is causing a decline in the traditional wholesaler. Very large outlets such as superstores and hypermarkets are taking many wholesale functions to retail level. Meanwhile, consumers in their cars are in effect carrying out the last stage of distribution themselves. Significantly, less than 25 per cent of the grocery trade now passes through wholesalers. Large multiple stores enter into direct contracts with manufacturers and bypass the formal wholesale stage, providing their own central warehouses and distribution system. Shorter distribution chains speed market intelligence and allow final retail prices to be cut to the minimum. Profitability is still possible, but is likely to require the lower margin, high turnover formula (see Chapter 30) of large stores.

▶ **Direct selling**: producer sells direct to consumer.

Direct Selling

Direct selling is widespread in industrial markets where the producer's sales force will negotiate orders with the end-user. It is often essential when trading large items of equipment, where technical specifications are paramount.

In consumer markets, direct selling has two main patterns:

1 **Direct marketing**

A mail order catalogue may be sent to the consumer, who makes his or her selections and then orders by telephone, fax or post. The method is widely used by firms selling clothing, cosmetics, toys, books and household goods (e.g. Next, Grattans, Littlewoods). **Direct mail**, usually targeted by market segment, yields orders for a specific product or product range. It is particularly popular for the sale of financial services, magazines and home improvements. Direct response advertising urges the customer to order goods directly from the producer or retailer. This method uses television, radio and the press and is popular for arts and entertainments, music recordings, novelties and gifts.

2 **Producer retail outlets**

Some producers sell some or all of their output through their own chain of shops. Boots pharmaceutical products, the filling stations of major oil companies and the tied houses of brewery groups are all examples. Franchising has a similar effect (see Chapter 2).

Direct marketing brings a producer closer to the market and reduces distribution costs. Postal shopping, however, loses much of the impact provided by good merchandising and is impractical for lower-value goods.

Agents and Brokers

▶ Brokers (agents) bring together buyer and seller without themselves owning what is bought and sold.

Firms may employ their own agents or pay an external (independent) agent to act on their behalf. Agents are normally rewarded for sales on a percentage commission basis. Single company agents will push only that firm's products, but external agents often have access to a wider network of customers. Raw materials, insurances and housing are all often sold through agents or brokers.

Agents are also widely used in export markets, where their detailed knowledge of local markets, major customers and trading conditions is particularly valuable. However, the use of an agent network abroad can make control of the full marketing process problematic. Even so, it is likely to be far cheaper and less risky than establishing an overseas subsidiary, unless export sales have reached a very substantial value.

Distribution Decisions

The most basic objectives of distribution are likely to be maximization of sales and profitability. Increasing sales can raise market share, strengthen competitive position, reduce average costs and enable the business to grow. The profit margin is critical in determining the level of reward earned by the achievement of sales and is reflected in the return on net assets.

Before setting the distribution mix, the marketing manager should consider:

- **Market coverage**: this must be sufficient to reach sales and market share objectives. It may be intensive, where a product is to be available from many outlets (e.g. a soft drink such as 7-Up) or selective, where outlets are targeted more specifically by market segment (e.g. a luxury hi-fi brand such as Bang & Olufsen).

▶ Luxury products tend to have longer distribution chains. For household necessities chains have generally become much shorter.

- **Cost of distribution chain**: distribution chains are essential in achieving sales, but their cost must be carefully related to their net benefit. In a long chain the total distribution cost may exceed the cost of production.

Figure 10.3
Mark-ups through the distribution chain

- **Distributor services**: the importance of services offered by the wholesaler and retailer varies widely according to the product and the market. If coverage objectives require product availability in a very large number of outlets, then wholesaling is probably essential. If the market is concentrated in the hands of a few major retail multiples, then it is their merchandising and promotional skills that are important. In specialist or highly technical markets, middlemen are vital in providing customer information, advice and after-sales service. Equally, a service whose market is highly dispersed (e.g. insurance) can be sold effectively through direct marketing.
- **Distributor motivation**: wholesalers and retailers are normally selling the products of many firms, including direct competitors. Means must be found to ensure that sufficiently high priority is given to sales of the product concerned.
- **Warehousing and transport**: opting for shorter distribution chains is likely to increase producer stock-holding, warehousing, handling and transport costs. The severity of these increases is a significant factor in constructing the distribution network.
- **Producer control**: lengthening distribution chains are liable to blur the focus of the producer's intended marketing mix. Control diminishes over the producer's presentation and promotion, while final prices may become unpredictable. Increasing control over the active mix will generally raise distribution costs.

▶ Marketing managers must also integrate distribution decisions with other elements of the marketing mix.

Distribution decisions take account of all the above factors, but it is essential to recognize that the variables are **interactive**. An effort to increase coverage may mean a longer or more complex distribution chain. This will add to costs and put upward pressure on final price. Similarly, shortening or simplifying distribution chains might reduce costs and increase sales per outlet. However, reduced coverage could lead to a net fall in total sales and market share. In addition, the producer's average cost will also be influenced by length of production runs and total output levels. The aim of management is to find an optimum balance between these conflicting pressures.

1 Suggest the most appropriate distribution channel(s) for the following products and make notes explaining why you have made these choices:
- specialist books from a small publisher
- a popular brand of biscuits
- a complete business computer system
- up-market delicatessen products

2 Make notes to show how distribution might interact with:
- pricing decisions (see Chapter 11)
- promotion decisions (see Chapter 9)

Read the following case study and answer the questions below it.

Borders Ltd

Borders Ltd is marketing a new board game based on international diplomacy. This is being manufactured in a small factory unit near Jedburgh in the Anglo-Scottish border country.

Alison McCrandles, the marketing director, is now seeking an effective national distribution channel for the game. She has already reached agreement in principle with major wholesalers who would ensure wide retail distribution.

At projected output levels the unit cost will be £4, with a factory-gate price of £5.45. The wholesalers require a 10 per cent mark-up, while retailers will need to mark the product up by a further 40 per cent. Comparable games retail at around £8 and the market is highly competitive.

This morning Ms McCrandles has received a letter from a major UK chain store with branches in all major towns and cities (populations over 50,000) offering to act as sole distributor and working on a mark-up of £2.50 above the factory-gate price.

1 Compare selling prices and profit margins for the two distribution channels.
2 What are the possible advantages and disadvantages of accepting the chain store's offer?

Evaluation

- In consumer goods markets, the balance of power is shifting away from the large-scale producer towards the large multiple retailer. Combined with developments in information technology, this means that the marketing mix is increasingly being shaped at retail level.
- The extent to which producers can directly influence the retail stage depends on their market power and the length of the distribution chain.
- It is probably inevitable that distribution chains will become shorter. Rapid changes in demand require producers to move closer to consumer markets. Consumers

are increasingly discerning in selecting the producer of their choice and are using cars for large-scale, one-stop shopping.

- Within firms the production function is extending backwards through closer cooperation with suppliers, while the marketing function is being driven forwards through the closer relationship with retailers.
- More accurate segmentation of markets is leading to a more complex fine-tuning of distribution channel structures. One firm may adopt a variety of distribution strategies depending on its target markets.
- The growth of very large retailers is exposing smaller producers to the risks of excessive dependence on one buyer. The loss of a particular contract can cause the complete failure of a smaller business.
- The quality of relationships between producers and the relevant wholesaler or retailer is vital to marketing success. Effective transmission of the marketing mix depends on communications and cooperation between the links in the distribution chain.
- Distribution is the least readily flexible element in the marketing mix. However, the changing patterns of market segments and the rapid evolution of distribution channels mean that managers must keep their distribution strategy under constant review.

The marketing mix: price

Chapter objectives

After working through this chapter, you will:

- appreciate the special importance of price in business as a whole and within the marketing mix
- understand the market forces of demand and supply and how they are resolved in price
- be familiar with the major pricing strategies and their associated pricing methods
- be able to analyse commonly used pricing tactics
- know the meaning of the following key terms: price, supply, demand, supply curve, demand curve, price elasticity, cost-based pricing, demand-based pricing, competition-based pricing.

THE MEANING OF PRICE

A **price** is an exchange rate. It states the quantity of one resource that can be exchanged for another. In a modern economy exchange is made more convenient by the use of money, which represents resources. Business is about combining resources to increase their value, and selling them at a price high enough to replenish those resources and leave a surplus of reward.

▶ In a market economy, resources are allocated through the price mechanism.

Within the market, producers measure costs against price. Consumers weigh price against satisfaction. Provided that the value of customer satisfaction exceeds the value of producers' costs, then a price can exist at which sales take place. Price is at the heart of the market. For the firm, the volume of sales multiplied by price yields sales revenue, a proportion of which is profit. But this profit is earned in a competitive market where the consumer has a choice. If another firm can offer more satisfaction relative to price, its sales – and share of the market – will increase. Thus price is also at the heart of competition.

▶ For the firm the volume of sales multiplied by price yields sales revenue.

Demand and Supply

Demand for a product is the quantity that buyers are prepared to purchase in the market over a given period and at a given price.

Say the farms of a particular area produce a distinctive local cheese. At a price of £2 per lb, total sales for the farmers amount to

600lbs per week. A series of values for quantity demanded relative to price – called a **demand schedule** – shows:

price per lb (£)	3.50	3.00	2.50	2.00	1.50
quantity demanded per week (lbs)	250	400	600	850	1,200

When plotted on a graph, the schedule forms a **demand curve** (DD):

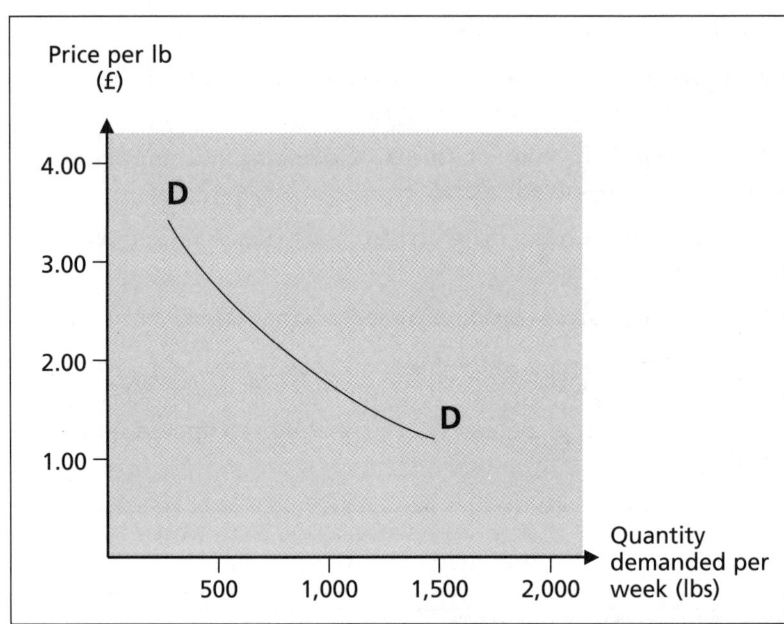

Figure 11.1
The demand curve

▶ Surpluses of unsold goods put a downward pressure on price, while a tendency to sell out exerts an upward pressure.

The demand curve typically slopes downwards from left to right, meaning that at lower prices a greater quantity is demanded. Why does this relationship hold good? Because as the price of one product falls, consumers are able to obtain greater value (utility) in return for their expenditure. Consumer surplus is now higher. Consumption of the product becomes more attractive relative to other products and demand is greater.

Now consider **supply**, which means the quantity of a product that firms are prepared to offer in the market over a given period at a given price. The **supply schedule** for the cheese is:

price per lb (£)	3.50	3.00	2.50	2.00	1.50
quantity supplied per week (lbs)	900	750	600	475	250

When plotted on a graph, the schedule forms a **supply curve** (SS):

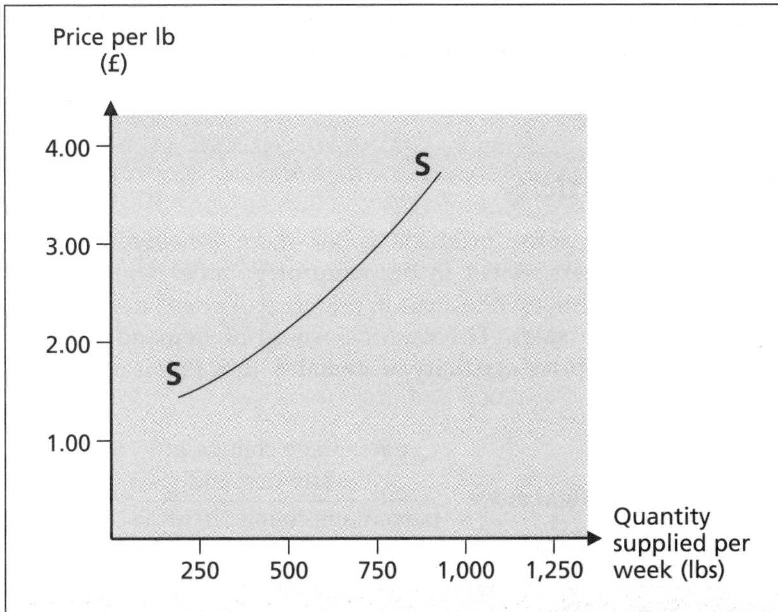

Figure 11.2
The supply curve

The curve typically slopes upwards from left to right, meaning that at higher prices a greater quantity is supplied. Why does this relationship generally hold good? Because, as the price of one product rises, firms are able to obtain greater revenue in return for their costs. Profit is now higher. Production of the product becomes more attractive relative to other products and supply expands.

► A highly profitable product becomes a 'honey pot', prompting increased output from existing firms and attracting new firms into the market.

We can now superimpose typical demand (DD) and supply (SS) curves in a single diagram:

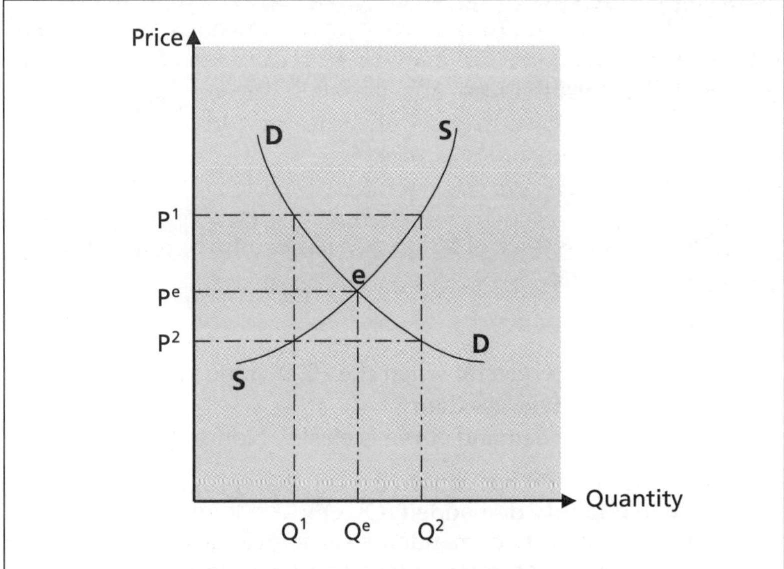

Figure 11.3
Interaction of demand and supply

Only at the **equilibrium price** (e) does the quantity demanded exactly equal the quantity supplied. At this price only the output of firms will correspond with the purchasing intentions of consumers. At a higher price (P^1), a surplus of output will remain unsold (Q^1, Q^2). But at a lower price (P^2), a shortage of output will exist (Q^1, Q^2). Thus the equilibrium price is also called the **market clearing price**.

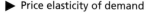

NM Draw your own single demand and supply diagram using the data for local cheese given on pp. 77–8. Mark the equilibrium price and explain briefly its significance.

Demand Elasticity

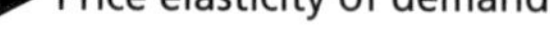
▶ Price elasticity of demand

The demand for some products is far more sensitive to price changes than others. A cut in the price of potatoes will increase demand only slightly, while a cut in the price of crisps may cause a sharp increase in sales. The responsiveness of demand to price changes is called **price elasticity of demand**. Its value is calculated by the formula:

$$\text{Price elasticity of demand} = \frac{\text{percentage change in quantity demand}}{\text{percentage change in price}}$$

Price Elasticity

Lyme Lamps Ltd

This is a recently established business making adjustable reading lights. The firm sells the lights for £20 each and is currently receiving orders for 200 units per week. The marketing director decides to stimulate sales with a price cut to £18 per light. The result is a rise in weekly demand to 260 lights. What is the price elasticity of demand (PED)?

$$\text{percentage change in quantity demanded} = \frac{60}{200} \times 100\% = 30\%$$

$$\text{percentage change in price} = \frac{2}{20} \times 100\% = 10\%$$

$$\text{PED} = \frac{30\%}{10\%} = 3$$

A reduction in the price of lamps has led to a three times greater increase in demand.

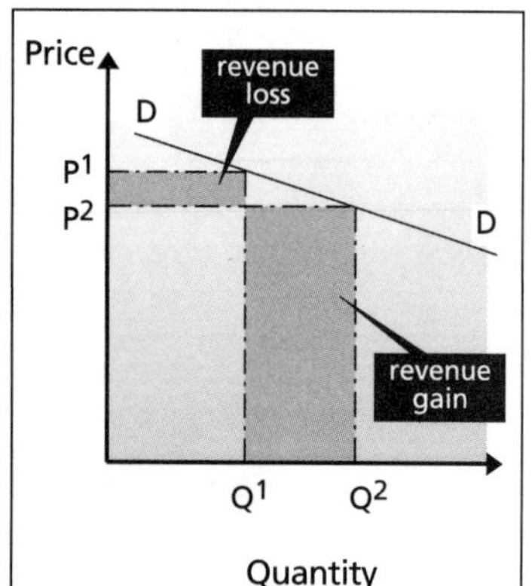

Figure 11.4
Elastic demand

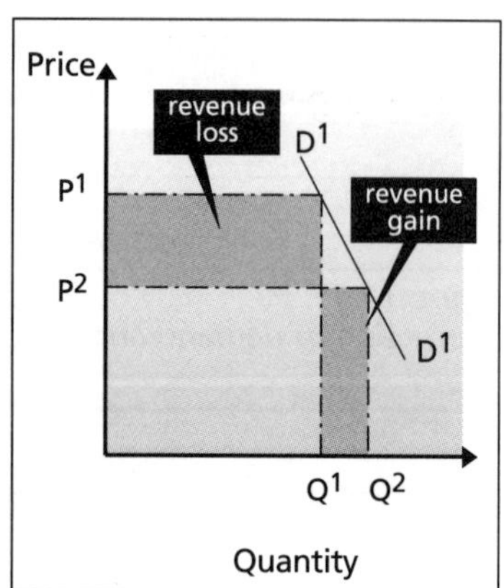

Figure 11.5
Inelastic demand

Demand is said to be **elastic** when the PED value is greater than 1 and **inelastic** when it is less than 1.

In Figure 11.4 the demand curve is elastic. Notice that:

- a cut in price (P^1, P^2) has caused a more than proportional increase in quantity demanded (Q^1, Q^2);
- since price × quantity demanded = sales revenue, we can identify rectangles of **revenue loss** and **revenue gain** (check the coordinates P^1, Q^1 and P^2, Q^2);
- since revenue loss is smaller than revenue gain, net revenue has increased.

In Figure 11.5, demand is inelastic and the price cut has caused a less than proportional increase in quantity demanded. Revenue loss is greater than revenue gain, so net revenue has decreased.

Look again at Lyme Lamps. The revenue change is simply calculated:

original revenue = 200 lamps @ £20 = £4,000
new revenue = 260 lamps @ £18 = £4,680 (up 17 per cent)

Note that this does not necessarily mean an increase in profit.

If the lamps cost the producer £15 each, then:

original profit = 200 × £5 = £1,000
After the price cut, profit = 260 × £3 = £780!

Elasticity and Net Revenue

demand curve	*price change*	*net revenue effect*
elastic	increase	decrease
elastic	decrease	increase
inelastic	increase	increase
inelastic	decrease	decrease

▶ The more exact the definition of a product, the higher is its likely price elasticity. For example, overall demand for lager might be relatively inelastic, while demand for Heineken Export might be relatively elastic.

Demand curves are not static. Changes in tastes, fashions or incomes may cause the demand curve to shift position or change its gradient and hence elasticity.

For example, at the development stage of the product life cycle, the relevant demand curve might correspond to Dd, Dd (Figure 11.6 below):

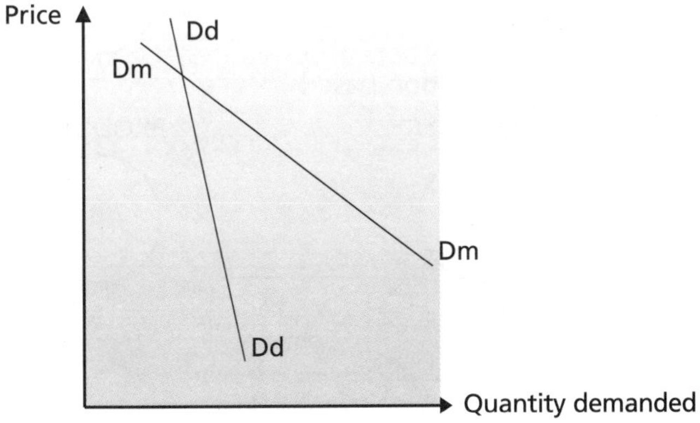

Figure 11.6
Elasticity and the product life cycle

By the maturity stage, the demand has become much greater at most prices, but also much more elastic (Dm, Dm). This may be due to increased choice and competition in the market.

Pricing Objectives and Pricing Policy

Pricing bears directly on a firm's sales revenue and profits. It is therefore the concern not only of the marketing director but also of the managing director and the whole board. With pricing decisions the success or failure of product ranges and even the survival of the firm may be at stake. Pricing objectives flow from overall business objectives (see Chapter 46). Pricing may be concerned primarily with:

- **profitability,** where the emphasis is on return on capital or profit goals for a given period;
- **sales growth**, where the intention is expansion of the firm and its market share;
- **stability or survival**, where the need is either to maintain a position of strength or to ride out a period of difficulty.

These objectives will be translated by marketing management into pricing policies. They will address such issues as price relationships between products or the use of price reduction and discounts. The policy must be fully integrated with the firm's overall marketing intentions and the other elements in the marketing mix.

Pricing Strategies

▶ A pricing strategy may be:
- **cost based**: price works forward from cost towards consumer demand;
- **demand based**: price works backwards from consumer demand towards costs;
- **competition based**: price is determined in the marketplace.

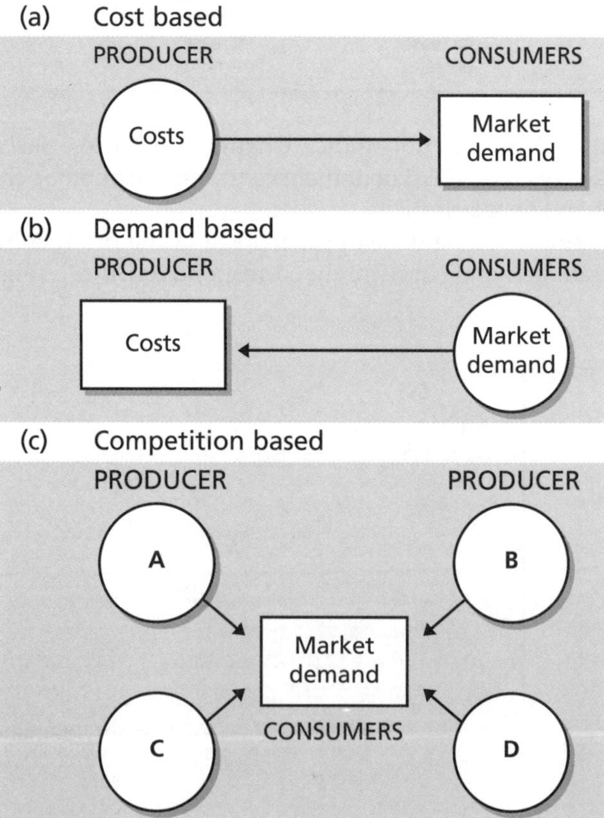

Figure 11.7
Pricing strategies

As you read through the text on various price strategies make notes which (a) briefly define each strategy and (b) say when its use is appropriate.

Cost-based Strategies

This approach begins with the producer. Prices are derived from analysis of costs combined with allowance for profit. Consumer demand is not directly considered. The following are types of cost-based strategies:

- **Cost-plus pricing** involves setting a projected output, calculating total cost per unit and adding a percentage mark-up for profit:

$$\frac{\text{total cost}}{\text{projected output (units)}} + \text{percentage profit} = \text{price}$$

- **Mark-up pricing** is the trade equivalent of cost-plus. The formula is:

  cost price + mark-up percentage = selling price

  The mark-up percentage is only partly profit, since it must also cover overhead costs. The method is very simple and widely used in the retail and wholesale trades. A trader can achieve some relationship with demand by using different mark-up rates for different products.
- **Target return pricing** aims to ensure, through sales, a target rate of return on the related investment. The formula is:

$$\text{unit cost} + \frac{\text{target percentage return} \times \text{investment}}{\text{projected sales volume}} = \text{price}$$

  This method is used in capital intensive firms, when return on investment is a vital factor.

▶ Be careful to distinguish mark-up from margin. For example, a chocolate bar costs 16p from the supplier and sells for 20p.

The mark-up is $\frac{4p}{16p}$ = 25 per cent.

The margin is $\frac{4p}{20p}$ = 20 per cent.

Demand-based Strategies

These emphasize the consumer and take as their starting point the strength of demand. Each method, in effect, attempts to evaluate consumer preferences and requires a basis in market research. The following are types of demand-based strategies:

- **Perceived value pricing** involves research in asking members of the target audience to estimate the price that they would be willing to pay for the product (or product concept). The results then form the basis of the pricing decision. The concept is extended by using perceived value to drive production and costing decisions. If a product concept has a certain perceived value, then the challenge to the firm is to design and manufacture that product to sell at or below perceived value and still meet the profit target.
- **Penetration and skimming strategies** aim for different **market depths** in the life of a product. **Penetration** means the attempt to gain rapid competitive advantage through low price, leading to high sales and a high market share. The approach is valuable if major economies of scale exist, or when the hope is to discourage competitors in a new market. **Skimming** the market means the attempt to gain a high margin by charging a comparatively high price in order to cream off the profit from a smaller market in which demand is relatively inelastic. This can be effective in targeting luxury market segments, or when launching a risky innovation where the need is early payback on investment (see Chapter 23).
- **Variable pricing** involves charging different prices for products that are the same or similar, according to the customer, place or time. For instance, customers above or below certain ages are eligible for reduced fares on trains and buses, while others must pay a higher rate. Theatres charge different rates for different blocks of seats. Phone

calls are cheaper in the evening. This **price discrimination** is possible when a market can be divided. Each section of the market has its own demand curve with its own shape, which can then be exploited.

For example, in Figure 11.8 the demand curve for train travel to London in the rush hour is inelastic (D^{RH}), but becomes elastic during the off-peak period (D^{OP}):

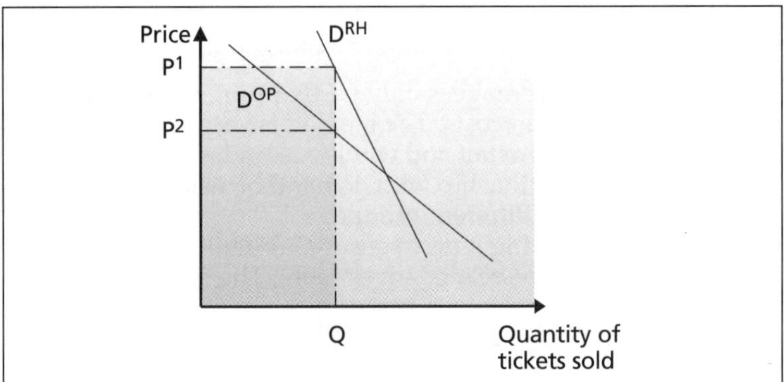

Figure 11.8
Demand for rail travel to London

▶ Demand-based strategies are often closely linked to a product's progress through its life cycle (see Chapter 7).

To fill the trains by selling quantity Q tickets, the train operating company can charge a high price (P^1) in the rush hour but only a much lower price (P^2) at off-peak times. Variable pricing also helps to spread demand across busy and slack periods and to achieve more even use of facilities.

- **Marginal cost pricing** uses the same principle in filling unused production capacity. If a sufficient number of customers is paying the full price and covering the overhead costs, then it may be most profitable to attract additional customers at any price greater than variable cost. For example, a hotel may generate its main revenue and profit during the summer season. It could then offer bargain winter breaks at much reduced prices. So long as these cover variable costs (e.g. meals and staffing), then a **contribution** is made towards overhead and profit (see Chapter 20).

Competition-based Strategies

Except in cases of perfect monopoly, the products of every firm are under pressure from competition. In competitive markets, price is almost always a key factor affecting sales.

- **Going-rate pricing** means setting a price in line with similar products on the market. When there is little difference between products, the individual demand curves become very elastic. The going rate is held down by competition to the lowest realistic price. Any attempt to price above this level will be very difficult. Pricing at the going rate also avoids retaliation by competitors.
- **Price leadership** occurs in competitive markets dominated by a few large firms (a situation called **oligopoly**). One firm may emerge as a price leader whose decisions to change prices are normally followed rapidly by other firms in the industry. In the tea industry, Brooke Bond has sometimes appeared to act in this role. Following the price leader is often the most comfortable option for firms. Changes in costs tend to affect every company at the same time. Besides, to break ranks and increase price alone risks losing market

share, while undercutting competitors may provoke a **price war** in which all firms lose.
- **Bid pricing** is used in markets where firms compete to win contracts. **Bids** or **tenders** are made to the customer, who considers the rival offers and then announces a choice of contractor.

Pricing Tactics

Having established the best pricing strategy for their products, marketing managers use a variety of tactics to fine-tune pricing in the mix.

▶ Pricing tactics must be carefully integrated with the main pricing strategy.

- **Product-line pricing** means pricing a product in the context of other members of the same product line. For example, a producer of kitchen utensils might price a colander with a high profit margin and a cheese grater with a much lower margin. This responds to market pressures but ensures viability of the product line as a whole.
- **Complementary goods pricing** occurs when the sale of the main product leads to sales of complementary products (e.g. pens and ink cartridges). A firm may choose to price a major product at a low margin and rely on a more highly priced complementary product to assist in reaching profit targets.
- **Product life pricing** involves coordinating relative price with a product's progress through the product life cycle. Penetration pricing might be used at the growth stage, but profit might be obtained from the decline stage by skimming the market.
- **Loss leadership** means offering one or a few products at or below cost price in order to attract customers, who will then make other purchases which carry normal margins.
- **Psychological pricing** is the firm's tactical response to consumer perception of price. Products are frequently priced at just below critical price thresholds. A price of 99p, £19.95 or £9,995 invites customers to place the product in the price bracket below the relevant threshold. An interesting alternative tactic arises from the price–quality association. Say a firm introduces a new up-market brand of coffee. The consumer may need psychologically to pay extra in order to believe in the quality or exclusivity of the product. For the producer the cost may be no more than a mainstream brand, but a slightly higher price may increase sales!
- **Experimental pricing** involves testing prices (i.e. trying different prices with customers to determine equilibrium price) in the market and assessing consumer response. This occurs when firms are uncertain about market value. It is common in markets for second-hand goods and unusual luxuries.

ACT Read the following paragraph and answer the questions below:

Fruits of the Earth Ltd buys pineapples from the wholesaler for 85p each. The normal selling price is £1.20, with average sales of 200 per week. After the manager decides on a price cut to 99p, sales rise to 270 fruits per week.

1 Calculate price elasticity of demand.
2 Calculate change in revenue.
3 Was the price cut a wise decision? Give reasons for your answer.

Evaluation

- Pricing has implications that go to the heart of any business enterprise. It is a key determinant of revenue and profit. Decisions about price will tend to involve the most senior management, although tactical measures may originate from more junior managers, e.g. at branch manager level.
- It is essential that price is tightly coordinated with other elements in the mix. The aim is to maximize the positive gap between the consumer's perception of price and value.
- Distribution channels often account for a large proportion of final price. The selection of distribution channel may vitally influence final price in large sectors of the market.
- A price reduction can cause an increase in revenue and a decrease in profits. This applies when the reduction of profit margin outweighs the benefit of extra sales. Equally, a price increase can cause a decrease in revenue and an increase in profit. This occurs when the increase in margin outweighs the negative effect of reduced sales.
- Price elasticity of demand (PED) is broadly higher for luxuries and lower for necessities. However, PED values for individual brands tend to increase with the degree of competition in the market.
- For every product, many customers would be willing to pay a higher price. This fact is the basis of variable pricing, which can only be successful when market segments are easily and securely divided.
- Marginal cost pricing carries the risk that all customers will come to expect the reduced price, so causing a reduction in sales at the normal full price. Managers must also remember that no profit is made until fixed overheads are covered.
- In export markets price will be translated into a foreign currency (see Chapter 43). Since rates of exchange fluctuate, the price payable by overseas customers is liable to move up or down without any change in the UK price quotation.
- Pricing decisions must be closely integrated with budgets for sales and profit. Changes in price may require flexing of budgets (see Chapter 31).
- Price can be so central to corporate objectives that it influences the whole culture of the firm. For instance, a business may be based on the principle of price discounting (e.g. Kwik-Save).

Part 3

Operations

12 Business location

Chapter objectives

After working through this chapter, you will:

- be able to analyse the major factors influencing location decisions
- understand the key location trends of the 1990s
- know the meaning of the following key terms: industrial concentration, industrial inertia, development areas, intermediate areas, inward investment.

▶ **Media Watch**
For this chapter look out for articles about declining and expanding regions of the UK, and stories about towns or regions that are trying to attract industrial investment.

THE LOCATION DECISION

The location decision is fundamental to costs and sales, whether for a new firm finding business premises or for an established firm deciding to expand or consolidate. There are usually a variety of possible locations for every firm, and a range of criteria for assessing their relative advantages and disadvantages. It is most unlikely that there will be any one perfect location, but rather a choice that is judged to be optimal. This means balancing one factor against another and may mean some tough choices for senior management, e.g. should a very low-cost site be accepted if it isolates the firm from its market?

▶ Location decisions are strategic and have a long-term impact. They are not based solely on the current balance of factors but on projections of these factors into the future.

Draw up a table with four columns (one for side headings). As you read about the factors affecting location decisions make notes relating to the following three companies:
1 Manufacturer of products from coconut fibre, imported by sea in bulk.
2 Supplier of in-company training in human-relations skills.
3 High-precision engineering company exporting worldwide.

Factors Affecting a Location Decision

1 **Raw materials and energy**

Raw material supplies explain the location of extractive industries (e.g. coal mining) by definition. Nearness to supplies of raw materials is also essential for manufacturing firms or industries whose processes involve converting large quantities of raw materials into much smaller (bulk-reduced) quantities of finished products. For example, the steel industry requires iron ore and coal, from British or imported sources. The use of electricity and gas from national grids/pipelines has largely freed firms from the location constraints of **energy supplies**.

2 **Markets**

In manufacturing, shorter distances between a firm and its market reduce transport costs and enable the business better to understand and service the needs of its customers. Increasing market orientation highlights the sharpened need for market intelligence and research – and the efficient transmission of the marketing mix. Closeness to **markets** allows exploitation of informed communication channels with customers, increases personal contact and assists after-sales service. Many service industries must obviously locate very close to their target markets. However, in some cases computer networks are able to reduce this need, e.g. 'armchair banking' allows the functions of a traditional branch to be provided over the telephone.

▶ In 1996 the Cooperative Bank announced the closure of all its branches, with services being provided by telephone from an HQ in Skelmersdale, Lancashire.

3 **Transport**

Transport involves customers and staff as well as supplies and distribution. Firms will aim to minimize the cost of transport in terms of money and time. The transport infrastructure is therefore of great importance. For many firms this means connections to the motorway network. Airports, seaports and rail services may also be highly relevant. Despite strong government incentives, it has proved very difficult to attract firms to remote regions such as Cornwall, west Wales or north-west Scotland. Links into Europe are growing in importance, with corresponding advantages for eastern and south-east England. The Channel Tunnel may intensify this factor.

▶ 'Corridors' of business development have grown alongside specific motorway links, e.g. the M4 corridor between London and Bristol.

4 **Rents and rates**

Rents and land prices are a major cost factor for many firms. Demand and supply mean that the most preferred locations carry the highest costs. For example, in 1997 office rents per square foot were up to £45 in central London, around £20 in Manchester and yet only £8 in Plymouth. The **business rate**, introduced in 1993, has meant that local authority rates are now standardized across the country. This change caused some sharp increases, especially in the south of England.

5 **Labour**

All firms employ **labour**: in many firms this is the most important resource and the largest source of costs. An adequate supply of labour with the necessary skills is essential. For example, the motor industry still needs a large engineering-based manual labour force. Local education and training facilities may be important. Salary and wage rates vary widely on a regional basis, tending to be highest in London and lowest in areas of high unemployment. Employers will also be attracted by a harmonious industrial relations record, while a background of union militancy could be discouraging.

▶ In some industries office space is beginning to shrink as 'telecommuting' allows staff to work from home and communicate using phone, fax, computer disks and e-mail. Firms may also use 'hot desking', where work stations are adaptable and shared according to staff needs on periodic visits to the office.

6 **Infrastructures**

Firms need electricity, gas and water services, road connections, drainage, waste disposal systems, legal and financial services, and so on. These elements in the business **infrastructure** vary in availability and cost. City centres, with their concentration of professional, financial and office services, are attractive to many service industries. For manufacturing and distribution, out-of-town sites are often preferred. Here there is better motorway or trunk road access with industrial estates or business parks, where many key services are already provided.

7 **Concentration and inertia**

Many industries become localized, i.e. concentrated in one locality. For example, the ceramics industry is concentrated around Stoke-on-Trent. This concentration provides a wide range of external economies of scale (see Chapter 13) as allied industries develop in the same area. These might include specialist transport and trading facilities, training services, suppliers of equipment and users of by-products. Industrial **inertia** occurs when firms remain in an area after the original location factors have ceased to be relevant. This may make good business sense if the costs of relocation exceed the likely benefits.

8 **Government policy**

From 1945 to 1979 the UK government took a major role in influencing industrial location. It aimed to reduce regional unemployment problems and to prevent excessive urban congestion. Public sector location decisions were directly affected and private sector industrial developments were prohibited in some areas and strongly encouraged in others. Since 1980 the government has placed greater emphasis on market forces. However, there are still many governmental influences on business location. Currently, government provides special help to firms locating in Scotland, Wales and the West Country, plus the industrial West Midlands.

▶ There is some evidence that the 'Assisted Areas' policy has not been a cost-effective means of creating new employment. The emphasis now is on selective rather than automatic aid and the creation of new jobs that would not otherwise have existed.

Figure 12.1

Firms in all assisted areas qualify for '**regional selective assistance**'. This provides project grants made according to costs or jobs created, and training grants related to new investment. This aid is now selective and is supplied at the minimum level necessary for a particular business project to go ahead.

The Department of Trade and Industry also develops industrial estates in assisted areas, which are then let to incoming firms on subsidized terms. Both the UK government and the European Union's 'Regional Fund' direct resources into assisted areas for improvements to the infrastructure, e.g. road or bridge building. Finally, many local councils have active business development policies with their own advertising and advisory services to attract firms.

Since 1945 new and expanded towns (e.g. Crawley or Peterborough) have been established by the government, either to accommodate population movements out of the largest cities or to revitalize assisted areas. Substantial amounts of land and infrastructure for business have been provided as part of each development. The new city of Milton Keynes was the largest project, but the programme is now effectively complete.

9 **Management factors**

Rarely do firms make a location decision without some prior commitments. A new project may be constrained in location by the firm's existing facilities, e.g. warehouses or depots. The degree of decentralization will affect the willingness of managements to see departments or divisions at a greater distance from headquarters. There are significant indirect costs in relocation which arise from general upheaval, interruption to production, inconvenience to customers, etc. Time is also important. A firm may select a site simply because it is available sooner.

▶ Many firms are undergoing managerial change as centralized 'organizational cities' break down into 'organizational villages'. They are becoming more federal in organization, with less emphasis on single location decisions and greater emphasis on a more plural, diverse picture as different functions are split across a wide range of optimal locations.

10 **The environment**

A favourable **environment** for the firm and its staff is now a major locational factor. Cultural, leisure and educational facilities, the countryside, the housing situation and the quality of shopping have all grown in perceived importance. It is usually vital for firms to be able to retain their key staff in any move. The result has often been to favour the southern half of England and cities with a 'good image', such as Bristol. The university, cathedral and market towns are generally enjoying new popularity (e.g. Cambridge or Exeter). Some cities may also be considered to carry higher prestige (e.g. central London, Edinburgh).

The south-east of England as a region remains a key location choice for the tertiary sector. Elsewhere, location decisions tend to favour centres or 'corridors' with good transport links (e.g. Manchester or the M1 through the East Midlands), or with relatively inexpensive skilled labour (e.g. South Wales or 'Silicon Glen' in Scotland).

▶ The Microsoft UK headquarters is at Reading on the M4 corridor.

Local councils and public agencies have continued to play an important part in attracting firms to particular areas. Some individual towns have marketed themselves energetically towards UK and foreign firms, sometimes with considerable success (e.g. Warrington). Meanwhile, investment by foreign firms in Britain – called **inward**

investment – increased sharply from the late 1980s. American, Japanese and Korean firms among others have chosen to site major production facilities in Britain (e.g. the Toyota car plant near Derby). Factors influencing their decision have been comparatively low labour costs, government grants and access to the markets of the European Union.

Decision making regarding location carries real costs. The factors are complex and management may accept an existing or sub-optimal location to avoid excessive expense. And managers do not in practice seek to optimize every factor within their control. Often they will be content to maintain a 'reasonable' solution ('satisficing'). Thus, in many firms, location is not under constant review and must be shown to be **unsatisfactory** before any change is likely.

Primary Products Ltd

Primary Products Ltd uses plastic injection moulding to make a wide range of accessories for young children. These include toys, educational games and playroom furnishings. At present the firm is based in a converted warehouse on a cramped site in south London. The combination of inadequate floor space, rising rents and local traffic congestion has prompted management to consider a major relocation to a new business unit with an office and manufacturing space at Llantarnam Park in South Wales (see p. 91).

What further information about this proposed location would be required by:

(a) the marketing manager;
(b) the production manager;
(c) the personnel manager?

Evaluation

- The decline of the traditional heavy industries (e.g. coal, steel, shipbuilding, textiles, railways) located on coalfields or close to ports has been very significant since the 1950s. The areas affected are beginning to develop a more diversified industrial base and a larger service economy, but major problems remain.
- London continues to act as a hub for the national economy; its reputation as a leading world financial centre is a powerful factor. Although many firms have left London to avoid its congestion and high cost structures, its importance as a market and as a capital city will remain. In addition, the development of the 'Docklands' as a business centre has been one of the largest projects of its kind in Europe.
- Locational forces have become more volatile. The decline of heavy manufacturing, the growth of low-bulk and weight industries and the expansion of the tertiary sector have all made business more 'footloose', or unattached to any one area or locational factor.

- The growth of electronic communications may reduce the importance of central facilities as firms become more scattered by function and less dependent on any specific location. An increasing number of staff are becoming able to work from home, using electronic media including on-line computer and facsimile machines – a phenomenon called 'telecommuting' or 'teleworking'.
- Transport is a vital influence. The motorway corridors reflect this priority and European links are a growing factor.
- The availability of technical expertise and the closeness of universities and research institutions is important to the main 'sunrise' hi-tech industries.
- The issue of quality in the local environment has risen strongly as a priority. This is always stressed in the marketing of a business location.
- The 'Business Park' and 'Science Campus' are offering attractive, carefully managed locations for firms in the light manufacturing, hi-tech and service sectors. Emphasis is placed on a high-quality environment with a wide range of on-site facilities, such as hotels, conference suites, landscaping and security.
- Local councils and public agencies (e.g. the Welsh Development Agency) have played an important part in attracting firms to their areas.
- Foreign investment in the UK increased sharply from the 1980s, especially by Japanese, American and German firms. Low land and labour costs and good transport links have been key locational factors.

13 Scale of production

Chapter objectives

After working through this chapter, you will:

- know how and why firms attempt to grow in size
- appreciate the problems that may be caused by growth
- be able to analyse changes in cost structures caused by changes in scale
- recognize recent trends in scale economies/diseconomies
- understand the practical business context of scale economies
- know the meaning of the following key terms: economies and diseconomies of scale, long-run average cost (LRAC), minimum efficient scale (MES).

ECONOMIES OF SCALE AND LONG-RUN AVERAGE COSTS

▶ Large-scale production often reduces unit cost.

Reductions in cost caused by increasing the scale of production are called **economies of scale**. It is important to realize from the outset that reductions in average cost caused by increases in scale are quite distinct from any downward slope in the short-run average cost curve. While capacity is fixed, we are in the short run. Once capacity is expanded with a larger production line or a new and bigger factory, then we have entered the long run.

▶ The Bic Crystal ballpoint pen, first launched in 1958, is a classic example of scale economies in action.

The size of a firm affects the efficiency of each business function and the organization as a whole. In addition to these **internal changes**, a number of large firms together will also generate an **external** impact on efficiency. Although scale economies are most obvious in manufacturing, exactly the same principles apply to service industries. The eight major economies of scale are summarized below:

1 Production

Plant costs increase with scale more slowly than output. This phenomenon affects factory buildings, machines and most equipment. **Plant utilization** is likely to be higher as scale increases. Costly specialized equipment becomes economic beyond a certain usage rate.

Raw materials and **components** can be purchased in bulk at lower unit prices. Special cost and delivery deals may be negotiated with suppliers.

Maintenance becomes more efficient with specialist maintenance teams and more accurate data concerning breakdown patterns and their causes.

▶ Economies of scale help to explain why two major firms – Unilever and Procter & Gamble – dominate the UK soaps and detergents market.

2 **Marketing**

Finished goods (i.e. goods that have completed all stages of production) may be bulk-purchased at significant discounts. Expert buyers in larger firms obtain the best contracts.

Product development is costly and time-consuming. 'Research and development' and 'new product' departments become viable with increasing scale.

Promotion economies include cheaper advertising rates, national brands to support a full product range, higher productivity for sales teams and falling unit costs for packaging.

Distribution becomes more efficient as fleet and bulk transport systems become justified and fully utilized.

▶ As a world-class oil company, Britain's largest firm – BP – depends on the recruitment of outstanding staff. Its rates of pay and other rewards are always at the top end of the market scale.

3 **Personnel**

Recruitment of higher-calibre staff is easier for the large firm with its wider career structure. Selection is more scientific.

Training and development for staff can be more extensive and sophisticated.

Pay and benefits can often be more generous, enabling larger firms to attract and retain good staff.

4 **Administration**

Administration overheads increase less than proportionally as output and sales increase. Staff and information technology can be more specialized and better used.

5 **Finance**

Raising finance is faster and easier for the large firm. Banks more readily grant long-term loans, given the greater security. Access is gained to the London and international money markets. A public company can issue and expect to sell large blocks of additional shares. Interest rates on larger loans for major firms are lower and close to the banks' base rate.

6 **Management**

Specialist managers can be employed in the larger firm to tackle key business functions and to offer specialized services such as management accounting and operations research (i.e. the analysis of practical problems to achieve optimum utilization of resources available).

Organizational structures can be built for optimum performance. A multi-divisional structure (for different product ranges, for instance) becomes practical, with its own business managers.

7 **Entrepreneurial**

Reduced risk is experienced through increasing scale. Bad decisions, downturns in the market or simple misfortune can be better absorbed by a larger firm.

Diversification into a range of products and markets also provides greater security and stability.

▶ Most of Britain's potteries industry is concentrated in the area around Stoke-on-Trent. Firms there enjoy a network of external scale economies.

8 **External**

Concentration of industry means a clustering of firms in the same industry within a given geographical area. This often leads to the development of a range of specialized local services, e.g. education and training, banking, transport and warehousing. Skilled staff may move more easily between firms.

Suppliers and subcontractors are attracted to the area to provide accessible and compatible services. This is vital for modern integrated production systems and just-in-time stock control (see pp. 125–6).

By-products are more readily marketed.

DISECONOMIES OF SCALE

Increasing scale does not only bring greater efficiency. It can also cause certain costs to increase disproportionately and breeds special types of inefficiency. Generally these diseconomies are far outweighed by scale economies, but beyond a certain size they may dominate and begin to drive up average cost.

The essential nature of scale diseconomies is managerial. The sources of inefficiency affect different organizations to different extents and in different ways:

- **Loss of coordination** can occur as the scale of operations increases. The close-knit structure of a small firm is lost and departments can take on an independent life disconnected from corporate objectives.
- **Bureaucracy** means rules, procedures and paperwork to an exact and specified pattern. This ensures that all parts of the organization operate according to formal plans, but it can also cause unnecessary delays and excessive administration.
- **Inflexibility** arises as management becomes increasingly rigid in its effort to maintain control. This is damaging to market orientation and may prevent exploitation of smaller market segments and niches.
- **Motivation and morale** can decline with increasing scale as the individual feels less directly involved in tasks and less valued personally by the firm. Alienation may develop as staff feel distanced from their work, with a reduced sense of urgency or conviction.
- **Reduction in initiative and creativity** may occur as employees feel that following rules and instructions is more important than ideas or innovation. 'No one listens' may be the staff perception of management, so that creative thinking withers. Senior managers may become highly conservative, believing that their security depends on maintaining the **status quo**.
- **Poor communications** easily develop as a firm grows. Managers become remote from subordinates and misunderstandings occur as messages become distorted through complex communication networks. Excessive delays are likely at bottlenecks in the communication system, while informal communication may degenerate into gossip or an overactive 'grapevine'.
- **Slow responses** to change are typical of large, ponderous organizations. Shifting markets, new technologies or increased competition may prompt a response, but only after elaborate procedures have been followed and the initiative has been lost.
- **Overstaffing** develops as more supervisory layers of management are installed and resistance to change prevents staffing levels from being altered to meet changed conditions. Highly graded jobs that have outlived their usefulness may remain.

▶ In today's fast-changing marketplace, flexibility and speed of response are vital qualities.

▶ 'The specific danger inherent in large-scale organization is that its natural bias and tendency favour order at the expense of creative freedom.'
Fritz Schumacher, *Small is Beautiful* (London, Blonde and Briggs, 1973)

▶ Many firms have been **delayering** during the 1990s. This involves cutting out layers of costly middle management (see Chapter 48) and giving more responsibility to staff 'on the ground'.

- **Weak asset turnover ratio** (see Chapter 30) is often the result of investment in plant and equipment that has not been properly appraised. A large firm is liable to carry an excessive value in under-used assets, while a smaller, leaner business achieves a higher turnover relative to its capital employed.
- **Waste** increases when staff feel diminished responsibility and accountability for their actions. Errors may cause major losses of materials or incur heavy charges, while any corrective action is slow and indecisive. Extravagance may increase as employees feel that 'the company can afford it'.

The Long-run Average Cost Curve

Economies and diseconomies of scale can be represented in the **long-run average cost curve (LRAC curve)** for the firm:

▶ While economies are greater than diseconomies, the curve is downward-sloping and vice versa.

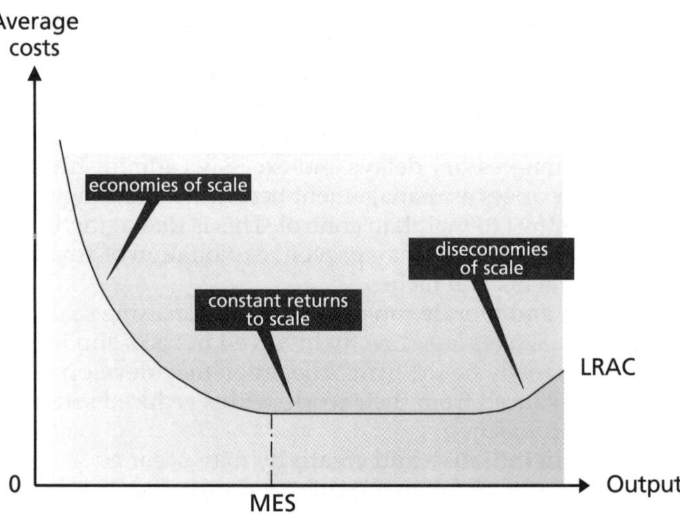

Figure 13.1
The long-run average cost curve

▶ **Minimum efficient scale (MES)**
MES is the smallest scale of production at which most or all economies of scale have been achieved; beyond MES no significant cost economies are gained and diseconomies may set in.
Any point on the cost curve has its own corresponding short-run cost structure covering the output range below that capacity.

The shape of the LRAC curve for a firm is dynamic and subject to important changes. These may affect new investment decisions and the competitive structure of the industry (see Chapter 24). For example, new technologies in production and information systems have pushed some LRAC curves downward with a steeper initial gradient.

Until the 1970s there was a tendency to increase progressively the scale of production in pursuit of ever greater scale economies. This led some enterprises to face unexpected diseconomies, and since then the approach to scale economies has been more sophisticated. Different cost centres within the firm may face widely differing LRAC curves. Management must try to structure the organization so that each cost centre achieves maximum efficiency in terms of its scale.

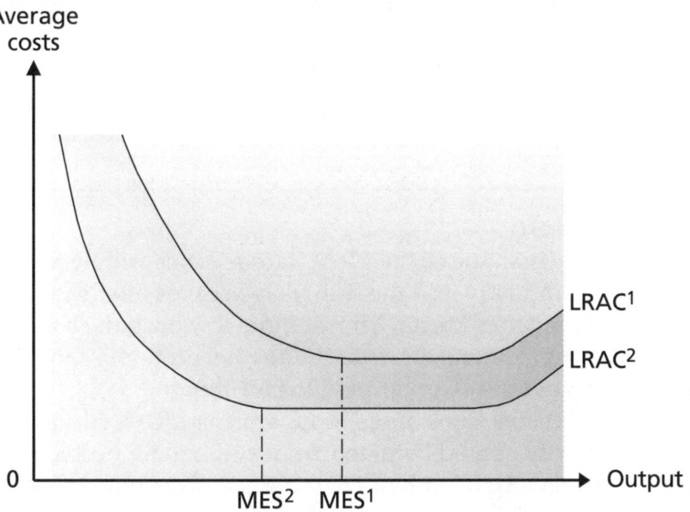

Figure 13.2
LRAC curve and new technology

▶ New technology has made average cost lower at all capacity levels. On LRAC², MES is reached before the output required on LRAC¹; MES² implies that some smaller firms may now be successful in the market.

The general fragmentation of markets in recent years has an interesting relationship with economies of scale. The demand for greater choice and individuality among products has combined with a partial shift up-market, with increased sales of luxuries and specialities. These trends have opened many new opportunities for economic smaller-scale production. Simultaneously, new technology is making large-scale production more flexible and better able to process batches of differing specification within a flow production system (see Chapter 14).

Pennine Pencils

Pennine Pencils began trading on a rural industrial estate in North Yorkshire at the start of 1988. The initial capital employed was £120,000. In the first year, output was only 200,000 good quality pencils, designed for specialist markets. Variable costs were 6p per unit, while fixed costs amounted to £16,000. A profit of 6p per pencil was achieved.

1 What was the average cost and selling price of each pencil?

By 1990 capital employed had risen to £150,000 and output was up to 400,000 units, with fixed costs reaching £28,000. Variable costs were constant but the firm cut its price to 18p per unit.

2 How has average cost and profit changed?

The firm then expanded rapidly and entered the mass market with major chain store contracts.

Key data 1992–6

Year	*Sales (million units)*	*Unit price (pence)*	*Variable cost per unit (pence)*	*Total fixed costs (£k)*	*Capital employed (£k)*
1992	1	15	5	60	220
1994	3	12	5	120	400
1996	8	8	4	200	600

3 Sketch a graph to show average cost for the whole period 1992–6.
4 Suggest an explanation for the downward trend in (a) average variable cost and (b) average fixed cost.
5 Calculate the return on capital over the period.

Evaluation

- The basic shape of the LRAC curve varies widely according to the industry and the firm. Some curves offer early economies and reach MES at quite low outputs (e.g. catering). Others offer continuing net economies up to very high volumes (e.g. car manufacturing).
- Net diseconomies of scale and a rising LRAC curve are primarily caused by managerial and human problems in the large organization. Their onset and severity often reflect more on the organization and its management than on scale alone.
- Small-scale business can achieve valuable scale economies through franchising or joint purchasing and marketing agreements (e.g. an independent hotel within the 'Best Western' group).

14 Production systems

Chapter objectives

After working through this chapter, you will:

- know the basic types of production
- understand process and product layout
- be able to evaluate the forces acting on production management
- know the meaning of the following key terms: job, batch and flow production.

PRODUCTION TYPES

A firm must decide on the type of production process most suited to its needs. This will affect the types of staff to be employed, the kinds of machinery and equipment required and the physical layout of the production process in the space available. These decisions do not only affect manufacturing firms. Service industries (e.g. banking, tourism) also have a production process, which may involve paperwork, person-to-person conversation and the use of information technology.

▶ Within the scope of operations management, the production process is often the most central and costly function.

There are three basic production types:

1 **Job production**: work is to individual customer order; each product is a one-off.
2 **Batch production**: output is in batches, where products pass through each production stage as a group.
3 **Flow production**: continuous standardized output is achieved using a specialized production line.

▶ The choice of production type depends on the nature of both the market and the product.

The differences are best illustrated using a simple example:

Cake Making by Job, Batch and Flow Production

Three firms – A, B and C – make cakes in the same city.

Firm A (job production) takes individual orders for wedding cakes and cakes for special occasions. It works from small premises in the town centre, with one kitchen and a small office. All the staff are highly skilled, but some are only part-time. Each order is produced separately, with about a dozen orders in progress at one time. The kitchen is crowded with equipment and utensils; these are used as and when required.

Firm B (batch production) is a local bakery which operates from a small modern industrial estate at the edge of the town. It receives regular orders for batches of the different kinds of cakes that it offers. Some staff are skilled while others are only semi-skilled. Orders are processed in batches of up to 200 cakes at a time. The equipment is arranged by process: food mixers, ovens, icing machines, etc.

Firm C (flow production) is a large factory owned by a public limited company. Its new plant is on a major industrial estate. Cakes are produced to an exact specification on a continuous basis and output is distributed nationwide by a fleet of trucks. The workforce is semi-skilled or unskilled and works on a shift system. Each stage of production has been broken down into simple operations and there is a separate production line for each type of cake. The costly machinery for each production stage is in constant use.

Set up a three-column table with the columns headed 'Job', 'Batch' and 'Flow' production. Give a brief description of each. As you read on, note down why each of the three cake-making firms noted above might have chosen its mode of production.

▶ Job production usually relates to highly specific or individual markets.

Job Production

Job production is found in small-scale services and manufacturing as well as in major projects such as road and bridge building. Each piece of work is different and to the customer's specification. The firm may be working on a variety of jobs at once, but each one is likely to be at a different stage. Tools and equipment are used irregularly and for a variety of purposes. The layout in the production area is usually fairly informal. Staff need to be skilled and adaptable, often working on their own initiative. Higher pay rates and the use of quality materials may push up costs, but overhead costs such as machinery tend to be lower.

▶ Batch production is often used where a wide product range is necessary or when demand is very variable.

Batch Production

This is typically applied to the manufacture of books and clothes, while production of package holidays has a similar pattern in a service industry. Sufficient demand must exist for output to be in batches or groups. The units in each batch pass through each production stage together. Batches are often to varying specifications and work on a number of batches may be in progress at any one time. Plant and equipment will be more expensive and more specialized but fairly adaptable. IT will be more fully and more productively used through careful management planning. Machinery is likely to be grouped by process, for instance with all cutting machines placed together. The workforce will be moderately skilled, the jobs being fairly specialized but still flexible. Overall costs tend to be reduced through more efficient use of resources.

Flow Production

▶ Flow production is normally best suited to mass markets with constant high levels of demand.

This is essential in the modern production of chemicals, oil, paper, cars, electrical goods, processed foods and many other key industrial and consumer products. Flow production developed in the USA during the 1920s and has spread all over the world as the basis of cheap mass-produced standard goods.

A very large, stable and long-term market for the product is essential. Output is a continuous flow and includes a narrow range of standardized products. Wherever possible, processes are mechanized or automated using costly machines designed for a specific use. These will be arranged according to the planned sequence of processes, forming a production line. The workforce is also highly specialized, using maximum **division of labour**. Tasks are likely to be repetitive and many workers are semi-skilled or unskilled. Efficiency in flow production demands synchronization and coordination between processes to avoid 'bottlenecks', where queues of semi-finished goods build up. The numbers of machines relative to their speed must be matched and **work study** is used to predict accurately the time taken by workers for each task. It is vital that all stocks are reliable in their availability and that breakdowns are minimized by preventative maintenance. Unit costs can be dramatically reduced by bulk materials purchasing and the spreading of overhead costs (e.g. machinery) across very large outputs.

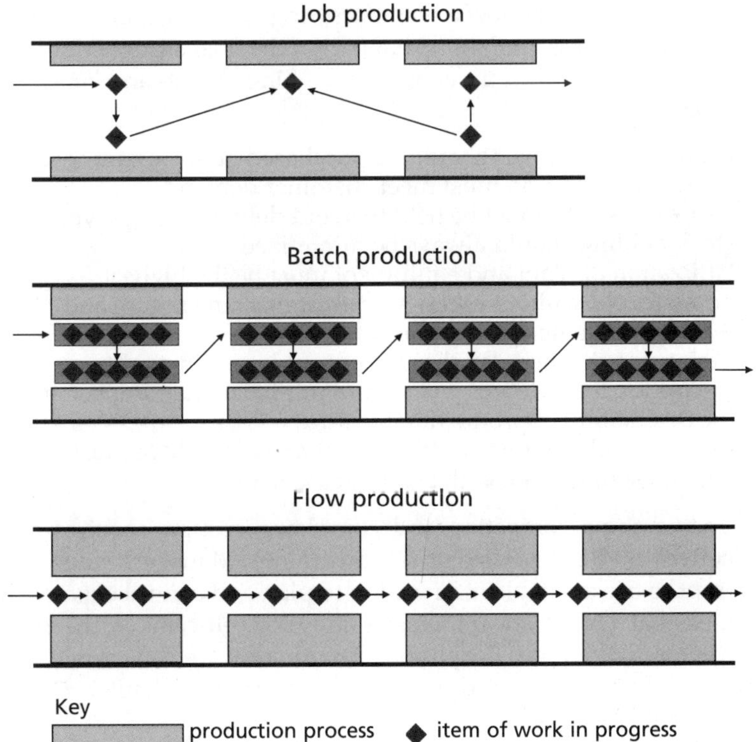

Figure 14.1
Production layouts for job, batch and flow production

Production Layout

The physical layout of production facilities must reflect the type of production. The best configuration of machines and equipment in a limited space will achieve the smoothest and fastest movement of work-in-progress between the stages of production.

Process layout means grouping together the equipment for each process. This pattern is usually applied to job and batch production. Products or product batches can move between processes in a variety of sequences and the workload can be planned for maximum plant utilization.

Product layout means arranging equipment to form a continuous 'line' specially designed for each product type. For flow production this allows the application of division-of-labour principles and specialized machinery. Work-in-progress forms a continuously moving flow down each product line, giving a very high plant utilization.

PRODUCTION MANAGEMENT

Flexible Systems

▶ Closer matching of segmental demand with a specialized product often allows a higher profit margin to be achieved.

Some important changes in the nature of markets are bringing changes to production systems. First, mass markets are breaking up into different segments (see Chapter 5), each needing versions of a basic or generic product. Second, consumer demand is changing increasingly fast and a quick response is essential for competitive advantage.

The production manager is responsible for organizing that precise transformation of resources that represents the firm's product and hence its sales. The bulk of a manufacturing firm's costs arise from its production process, as does a vital part of the final customer satisfaction. This is reflected in the constant weighing of costs and benefits in production decisions:

- Production materials should be purchased at the lowest cost, yet the specification must meet customer demands.
- Sufficient stocks must be held to avoid delivery delays, yet stock holding should always be minimized.
- Utilization of plant and equipment must be the highest possible, but without excessive risk of machine failure and leaving adequate spare capacity.
- Maintenance schedules should prevent lapses in quality or disruptive breakdowns, yet should minimize their impact on the availability of production facilities.
- Labour productivity should be maximized but there must be enough staff to cope with any increase in output.

▶ Close communication between the production and marketing departments within a firm is essential in matching supply and demand.

Balancing these competing and complex pressures requires clear objectives and a knowledge of constraints. Managers must then attempt to use available information to plan and control events. The task has been made cheaper, faster and more efficient by the use of computer technology. Purpose-designed software can provide full on-line information, rapid alert to variances (see Chapter 31) and flexible troubleshooting.

Production planning should be market-led. The quantities of

resources required for each product must be related to capacity and the implications of relevant delivery dates. Flows of output can then be routed through their necessary stages to meet the demands of the market with the greatest possible efficiency. As the starting date for each work schedule approaches, instructions regarding materials, manpower and machine usage are issued (this is called dispatching). The progress of each order must be monitored as it passes through successive production stages. Staff called **progress chasers** may be responsible for ensuring that actual events correspond with the schedule. In large firms this task is now computerized.

Make notes on production planning, using the production and delivery of a training course as an example. Remember that producing leaflets and handouts is also a production process.

Enter ticks in the boxes below to indicate the most appropriate type of production for the business activities listed:

Business activity	*Job*	*Batch*	*Flow*
production of a gourmet blue cheese on Dorset farm	☐	☐	☐
light bulb production for domestic market	☐	☐	☐
printing books on gardening	☐	☐	☐
estate agency	☐	☐	☐
package holiday operation	☐	☐	☐
shipbuilding	☐	☐	☐

What are the most critical factors that determine the optimum type of production?

Evaluation

- In practice firms may combine production types, for instance job/batch or batch/flow. This can occur in various ways. Two separate processes may operate under one roof. Alternatively, a 'basic' product may be manufactured using flow production and then finished in batches to satisfy particular markets. Or batches may be matched to use spare capacity on a flow system.
- One result is that the boundaries between job, batch and flow are tending to become more blurred. New technology is making machinery far more flexible in its application. The traditional production line can become less rigid with its capacity tending to 'soften'. CAD/CAM (computer-aided design and manufacturing) systems and automatic multi-purpose tools combined with faster machine settings are all assisting this trend. One result is that 'limited editions' and 'customization' are becoming simpler and less costly.

- The **mass markets** of the twentieth century are now becoming more discerning, less predictable and less homogeneous (see Chapter 5). They are tending to fragment into many different market segments, so that flow production systems must attempt to meet the different needs of segments and niches in the structure of demand.
- In some firms there can be a danger of separate 'production' and 'marketing' cultures developing, with the respective managers seeming to be on opposite sides. Production managers can lose sight of the customer and the market, while marketing managers lack contact with the realities of production. Much depends on effective communications, senior management teamwork and the quality of strategic leadership.

15 Quality

Chapter objectives

After working through this chapter, you will:

- be able to analyse the meaning of quality in business
- know how quality standards are specified and achieved
- be aware of quality control techniques
- understand the human dimension to quality, the use of quality circles and the concept of quality as a culture
- know the meaning of the following key term: Total Quality Management (TQM).

WHAT IS QUALITY?

Think of quality. What might you picture? The Flying Lady poised on the bonnet of a Rolls Royce? Or the distinctive radiator grille of a BMW?

Think of a Volkswagen. Whether in your mind's eye you see a Beetle or a Golf GTi, you see and feel quality.

Each of these three car manufacturers is held in high regard for quality. The British firm has remained exclusively in a low-volume, top-of-the-market niche, while both German firms have successfully applied the concept of quality to higher-volume mainstream products.

Quality is a feeling. A product that is well made or a service well delivered creates in the consumer a spontaneous sense of satisfaction. A repeat purchase immediately moves from possible to probable. Quality does not necessarily mean a high price or the use of expensive materials. The most ordinary mass-produced product can carry quality. This can be as simple as a plastic pen or a china mug. The product has an honesty in performance and a natural style. Quality is a great seller.

▶ 'There is a central quality which is the root criterion of life and spirit in a man, a town, a building or a wilderness. This quality is objective and precise, but it cannot be named.'

Christopher Alexander, *The Timeless Way of Building* (quoted by Tom Peters and Nancy Austin in *A Passion for Excellence*)

Since the 1980s, quality has been a rising priority for almost all firms. In most markets abundance and low prices were no longer enough. Everywhere consumers have become increasingly discerning and quality conscious.

The quality profile of the market has been fundamentally changed:

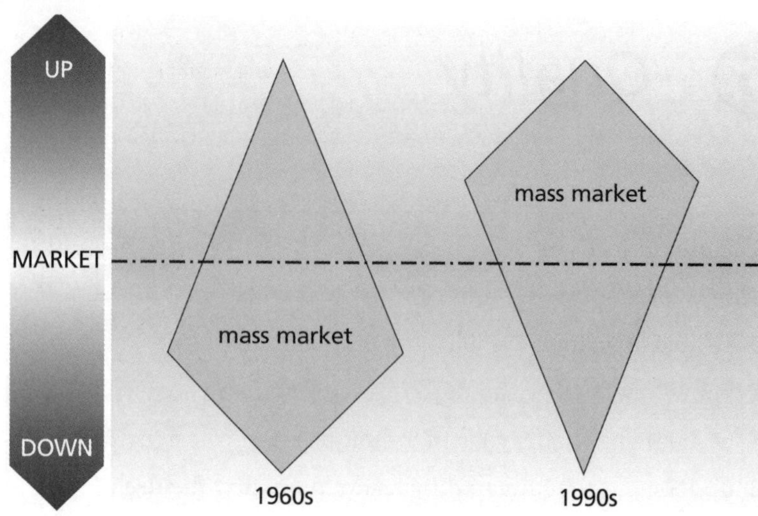

Figure 15.1
The quality profile of the market

▶ Changes in the law regarding consumer protection have also acted as a stimulus to product quality. For example, new food-labelling regulations have made consumers more critical in their response to food additives.

Markets are now fiercely competitive in attempting to deliver the quality that consumers desire. Demand feeds back down the production chain. The specification for industrial products has been steadily rising, while toleration of production defects has fallen sharply.

The rapid growth of international competition has made a major impact on standards of quality. UK producers have either had to match the quality of the best European, American or Far Eastern products or face long-term decline. Market orientation and quality together make a powerful partnership. Major retailers, for example, do not buy what their suppliers offer but use detailed market research to specify to suppliers the quality and price **that their customers demand**.

It is important to distinguish the different meanings of the word 'quality'. **Specification quality** means the level of quality that the product is intended to represent. A Rolls Royce is intended to be of higher quality than a Ford Mondeo. Flying business class is intended to be a higher quality experience than flying economy class. **Production quality** simply means conformity to specification. This is quality defined in a negative sense: the product is not substandard.

Finally, quality also has a more abstract meaning that relates to a product's honesty in performance and excellence in its class. This is difficult to measure but increasingly important. It is closely related to the concept of **total quality**, where, for every part of the entire organization, the highest standard is a permanent goal.

Specification Quality

Not all markets require a high-specification product. Often a lower price is more important. Through careful market research, firms must identify the level of quality that a market requires and the optimum specification in terms of materials, 'finish' and customer service.

Quality, like quantity, is constrained by cost. Consumers would always like a greater quantity of a product for their money; similarly with the wish for higher quality. The producer, as always, aims to maximize the gap between the cost of a product and the price it will command in the market. This price depends on the satisfaction it yields in consumption. Quality increases that satisfaction, but it also increases cost. The relationship is very important.

▶ Notice that an **increase** in cost – and price – can lead to an increase in sales and an enhancement of competitive advantage.

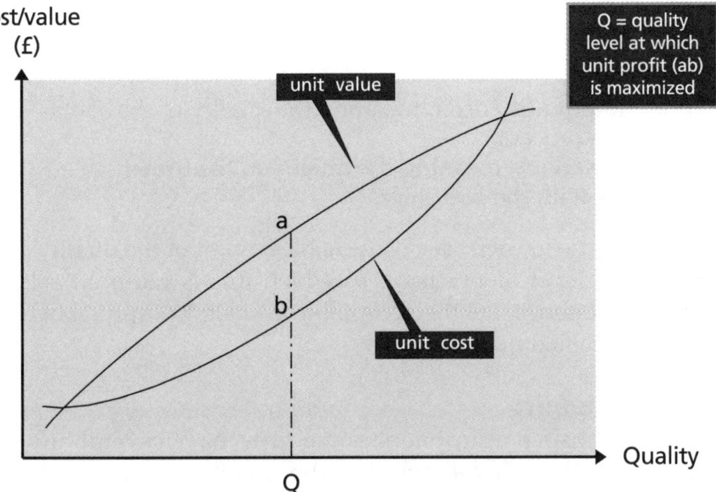

Figure 15.2
The relationship between quality and cost

Notice that:

- the greatest profit (ab) is achieved at quality level Q;
- at extreme levels of low and high quality, production cost is greater than market value.

The diagram does not imply that a middling quality is always the most profitable. For each product and market, the shape of the curves will be different. For instance, men's suits of high quality are very costly to produce but are profitable because their sale value is also much higher. Low-quality T-shirts have a low sale value but are profitable because their production costs are also much lower.

The market is the key. In business terms a low-quality product is not necessarily 'inferior' to its high-quality counterpart. Both may be equally profitable yet be selling in different segments of the market.

The firm must make a clear decision concerning the markets in which it intends to compete. The product can then be specified with the optimum degree of quality relative to cost. This decision making should be ongoing. Changes in consumer taste and incomes will shift the market value curve, while progress in design and technology will impact on the production cost curve.

Production Quality

Once the product has been defined in terms of specification, a production system can be designed to meet this standard within a given cost structure. Quality in production means adherence to the target design and specification. Again, the market will determine the margins of tolerance that can be accepted. Products outside these specification margins can be classed as rejects. In some markets, to deliver consignments in which a limited percentage of the

▶ The key concepts of modern quality control were developed in Japan by two Americans, W. Edwards Deming and Joseph M. Juran, after the Second World War. Their work was celebrated by the Japanese but, ironically, not properly discovered in America until around 1980.

items are rejects will be acceptable, and the cost of ensuring a 0 per cent defect rate would be unacceptable (e.g. nuts and screws). In other markets, total compliance with very high quality specifications is essential (e.g. medicines).

We can sub-divide the concept of production quality as follows:

- **Supplier quality**, meaning the quality of the raw materials, components, sub-assemblies and finished goods purchased by the firm.
- **Production quality** itself, meaning the quality of the actual production process.
- **Customer service**, meaning the quality of the firm's interaction with the customer.

The critical issue in each case is the achievement of the quality specification. The level of precision to which this is required sets the margins of tolerance, i.e. the acceptable limits for output above and below the specified quality.

1 Supplier Quality

Almost all firms have suppliers; some firms have several hundred different suppliers. It follows that the quality of any product at least partly depends on the quality of these supplies. Often when the purchaser and supplier move towards a contract, they are both seeking a long-term relationship. It is in their mutual interest to be certain that the product quality will meet the specification. A detailed agreement to this effect is called Supplier Quality Assurance (SQA). Exhaustive examination and testing of the product are usually necessary and quality parameters must be set for tolerance and rejection. Sometimes the buyer will take technical advice from the supplier, while large buyers may not only state their exact requirements but also expect to look closely at the supplier's premises and financial position. An effective SQA system will greatly reduce the need for **goods inward inspection**. Suppliers may also be graded by the buyer according to their ability to meet reliably the product specification. Grade I status makes the firm an **approved supplier**.

In recent years there has been a strong trend towards reducing the size of the supplier base (i.e. goods are bought from a smaller number of firms). This allows stronger relationships to be developed with suppliers and builds greater confidence in the quality of goods purchased. Correspondingly, many firms no longer accept the lowest tender for a given order but instead make quality and stability the key factors when choosing a supplier.

2 Production Quality

▶ In many markets quality remains discretionary but comes to form a vital part of the marketing mix. It is possible to sell cars where the window winder comes off in your hand. However, reputations are built on cars where it does not.

The aim is to meet the firm's own quality specification at the lowest cost. For many firms in recent years the targets have become tougher. Specifications have risen to meet international competition. Tolerances have been tightened as markets become more sensitive to faults and failures. The traditional approach is one of **quality control**. This often means a system of inspection for each process. Where inspection of every product is impractical (i.e. where the costs would exceed the benefits), mathematical sampling methods are used.

The requirements for any level of confidence for any sample size can readily be calculated using the properties of a **normal distribution**. This would be a single sampling scheme. **Multiple sampling** means taking a number of smaller samples and combining their defect rates to pass or reject the consignment or flow of production. **Sequential sampling** tests a series of items one by one until a critical pass rate is reached.

Defect rates and rejected batches of goods are recorded and this must lead to investigative action. The cause of the failure can then be remedied. This may mean investment in new plant, improved training or a switch of suppliers.

These methods are all corrective, in the sense that they aim for quality **after** the production process has taken place. Increasingly, firms are adopting **preventative** quality systems, which avoid unacceptable work from ever taking place. Approaches include:

- **Automatic quality control**, where electronic sensors detect any drift outside tolerance limits and either alert the operator or trigger a self-correcting mechanism.
- **Quality by design**, where rigorous quality standards are built into the product and its production process.
- **Total quality commitment**, where the whole organization commits itself to quality targets and all staff accept personal responsibility for quality in their work.

▶ See also Chapter 18.

3 Customer Service

The quality of a firm's behaviour towards its customers is of the utmost importance. One serious lapse in conduct by one employee can lose a customer for ever. The standards of the departments and staff that deal with the customer represent the firm's public face and will vitally affect both its immediate sales and its long-term reputation. Clear procedures both to maintain quality and to deal with complaints are essential. There should be flexibility and a swift response in putting right any failure. Training should be combined with a genuine sense of motivation among all staff to satisfy their customer.

▶ Not only must the product be of appropriate quality but its promotion and distribution must also reflect that standard.

Quality Circles

A group of employees meeting regularly on a voluntary basis in company time to discuss questions of quality, costs, output and safety is called a **quality circle**. The idea originated in Japan and has spread to America and Europe. There are usually around five to ten members, including shop floor staff, a supervisor or foreman, plus perhaps a specialist in quality control. The circle selects its own leader and training for members is usually available. The agenda is set by the group, who tackle workplace problems. Ideas are generated and plans are made for testing solutions, with specific targets to be achieved. Quality circles recognize and attempt to harness the practical expertise and experience of ordinary staff. They help to increase the sense of employee involvement and to create a feeling of common cause among managers, specialist staff and shop floor workers.

▶ Quality circles are an important part of kaizen, or continuous improvement; see Chapter 18.

QUALITY AS A CULTURE

▶ Charles Handy says: 'Quality is truth'.

Quality is finally about more than design, specification and defect rates. As the manager at a Lucas automotive parts factory put it: 'Quality is a state of mind'. By this comment he meant that quality is an approach to work, perhaps even an approach to life. It is making personal best performance an active commitment, regardless of circumstance or occasion. Obviously a total quality philosophy means production quality and customer service. But it also means quality in paperwork, in answering the phone, in cleaning a work surface, in welcoming a visitor. The old dependency on inspections, penalties, slogans and targets is replaced by an environment of trust, self-responsibility and continuous learning.

This vision of quality pervading the entire organization is known as **Total Quality Management** (TQM). It means that every individual and team connected with the firm strives for continuous improvement in everything that they do. This in turn is directed towards the goal of customer satisfaction. And 'satisfaction' means more than 'being satisfied'. The ultimate intention of TQM is that customers' reasonable expectations should be exceeded by their actual experience – making satisfaction turn into 'delight'. Moreover, for most firms, business is not based on a single sale but on a stream of repeated sales. It must therefore provide the customer with a stream of repeated satisfaction – or delight.

Quality Assurance

▶ BS 5750 does not specify quality but certifies that the conditions for achieving the company's own quality specification are tested and assured.

Many firms – both in manufacturing and service industries – are gaining external certification for their quality commitment. The British Standard for overall quality assurance is BS 5750 (the equivalent international standard is termed ISO 9000) and means that an organization has in place all the necessary structures and procedures to ensure that quality will be as specified. BS 5750 certification is a source of competitive advantage and may be a required condition for doing business with other companies.

People and Quality

▶ When Rover cars faced a crisis of confidence in the 1980s, the new chairman used his first product launch to generate a recovery of faith among staff in the quality of the model.

Technical sophistication is not enough to achieve quality. Real quality depends on real people, who understand and are committed to the quality specification that they have agreed to deliver. This is most obviously true of customer service, but it is also true of the production process. The importance of motivation (see Chapter 35) can hardly be overstated. Staff need to feel valued, to identify emotionally with their place of work and its product, and to feel personally responsible for quality. The relationship with the product matters. If staff do not believe in their product, then quality is almost impossible. Such a belief can be cultivated by involving staff in new product launches and by keeping everyone informed of performance in the market.

Some firms hold regular morning briefings. These involve managers or team leaders explaining achievements to date and setting plans for the day ahead. It may also be an opportunity for managers to explain the purpose of the work in progress and its significance for the final customer.

Training is very important but can only go so far; pride and self-respect then take over. Quality-driven firms place the greatest emphasis on the morale and welfare of their employees. Marks & Spencer even set conditions for the welfare of employees in **supplier firms**, believing that their morale will affect the eventual quality of the St Michael products.

Recruitment and selection also matter. New employees need to understand the challenge of their job and the standards expected. The firm must kindle in them the motivation to succeed. Much depends on a firm's reputation in attracting the best staff.

Evaluation

- For most firms, market orientation means quality orientation. Customers seek satisfaction from a product, and ensuring that satisfaction - plus a competitive edge - is the role of quality. Failure in quality ultimately means failure in sales.
- Quality in specification should be determined by the market. For this purpose, management requires accurate and up-to-date market research. Quality in production is determined by the firm. To hit targets requires adequate standards and motivation among staff.
- There are two basic approaches to quality. It may be **controlled** as a targeted variable, placing the emphasis on physical inspection. Alternatively, it may be **nurtured** as a culture, placing the emphasis on human motivation.
- The concept of **total quality** means a thorough-going commitment to quality in every aspect of the firm's operations. In creating such a climate, much will depend on the ethos of the firm and the effectiveness of leadership and communications.
- Ensuring the quality of supplies is of increasing importance. Relationships between supplying and purchasing firms are becoming closer as complete production cycles become 'seamless', even between one enterprise and another.
- The nature of national markets often determines the character and extent of quality. It is in the domestic market that firms tend to have their largest sales and where products are first developed. If the market demands quality, national firms will deliver. This then makes a powerful base for exports.

16 Critical path analysis

Chapter objectives

After working through this chapter, you will:

- appreciate the principles of project and network analysis
- be able to draw a simple network diagram using the correct format and notation
- know how to identify the critical path
- understand the calculation and purpose of float time
- know the meaning of the following key terms: network diagram, activity, node, dummy activity, critical path, total float, free float, operations research.

PROJECT ANALYSIS

Most people can think of occasions when they have spent too long doing something trivial while there was something essential that needed doing first. The problem is often spoken of in terms of 'getting your priorities right'. Suppose that a sports club is organizing a party in four weeks' time. The Secretary knows that to arrange food and drink for the correct numbers will take a week, while to send out invitations and to receive replies will take three weeks. And before the event takes place, the club's hall must be redecorated, which will take two weeks. What is the best plan?

▶ Which is the critical activity?

Send out the invitations immediately. During that three weeks the hall can be redecorated. Then when the numbers are confirmed after three weeks, the catering can be arranged in the last week and everything should be ready on the day. Notice that sending out invitations at once is critical to the plan. By contrast, there is up to a week of slack time available before redecoration must begin. In such a simple example this seems fairly obvious, but when a project involves many different interdependent activities, then the same logic becomes vital to efficient operations.

Croyde Construction Ltd

▶ Resources engaged on a project carry an opportunity cost.

This building firm has won the contract to build a new pavilion for a sports club in Bristol. The project manager describes the tasks involved as follows. The foundations must be laid before the walls can be constructed. Glazing can begin while roofing takes place, but wiring and installation of fittings cannot start until the roofing has finished, which in turn allows drainage work to begin. Once this is finished, painting can follow. Meanwhile, decorating can begin when wiring and fitting is complete. Finally, the site must be cleared before the pavilion is handed over to the client.

The club wants its pavilion finished as soon as possible. The firm wants to release its resources for other work as soon as it can, while satisfying the customer and gaining the benefit of cash on completion. So how could the activities in this project be prioritized? Or, put another way, how could the various activities be sequenced for the earliest completion and the avoidance of delay?

Initially it is necessary to identify the activities involved and to estimate how long each activity is expected to take.

Notation	*Activity*	*Duration (days)*
A	Lay foundations	2
B	Build walls	6
C	Glazing	3
D	Roofing	5
E	Wiring and fitting	3
F	Drainage	2
G	Decorating	4
H	Painting	3
J	Clear site	2

A simple flow diagram provides a picture of the work involved:

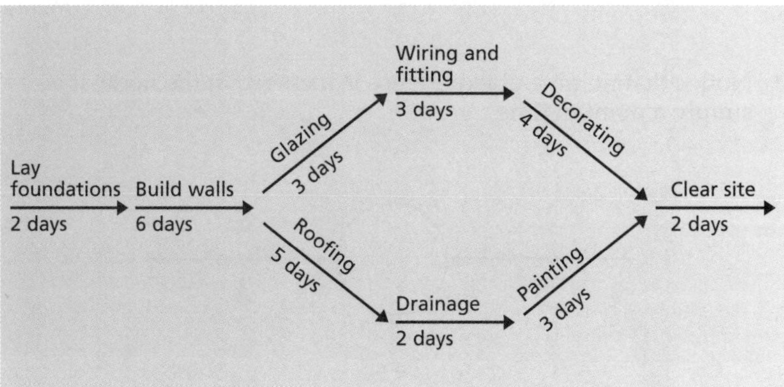

Figure 16.1
Building the sports pavilion: flow diagram

This is useful but rather limited as a tool to assist decision making. But it can be developed into a **network diagram** that is more revealing. First, there are some simple conventions that make networks easier to follow and interpret.

Notice that

- Each distinct stage in the project is called an activity.
- The sequence of activities works from left to right.

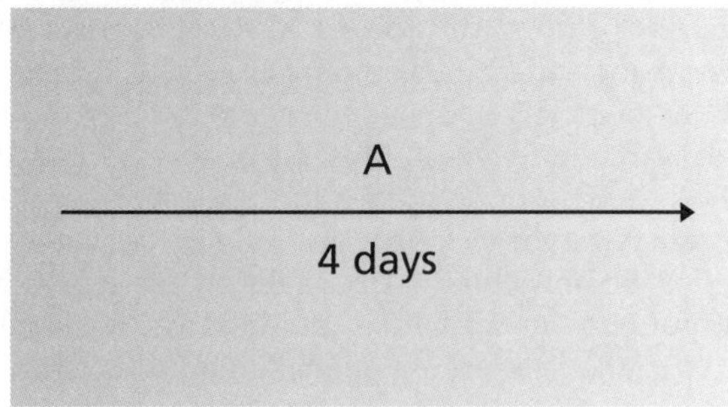

Figure 16.2 (a)
Arrow

Activities may be labelled A, B, C etc. with their estimated duration shown (e.g. four days).

- An activity is indicated by an arrow; arrows are drawn for convenience only and their length does not signify the length of an activity.
- The point at which activities end and others begin is called a **node** and is represented by a circle.

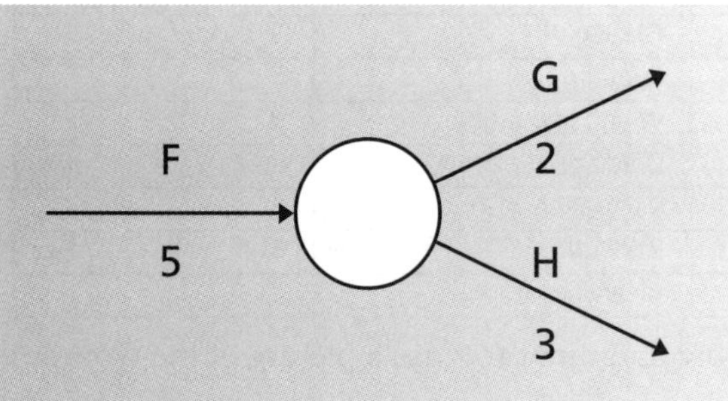

Figure 16.2 (b)
Node

- Notice that no time or experience is incurred at the node; it is simply a point in time.

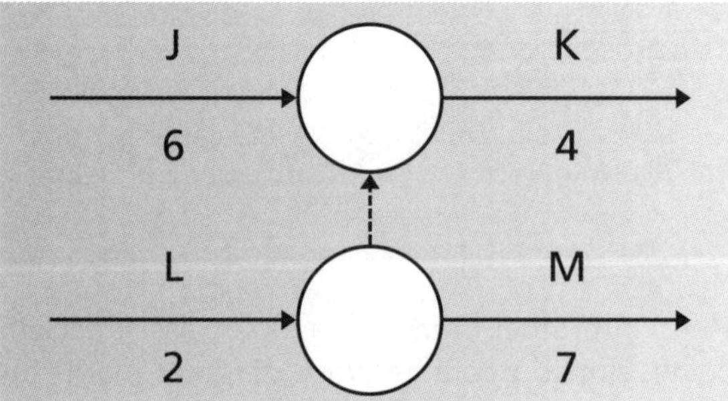

Figure 16.2 (c)
Dummy

- When the start of one activity is dependent on the completion of another that is not in the same sequence of tasks, then a dummy activity must be inserted to show the logical dependency. A dummy is drawn as a dashed arrow. In Figure 16.2 (c), Activity K follows Activity J but cannot be started until Activity L is complete. The dummy indicates this connection.

We can now draw a network diagram to represent the building project facing Croyde Construction.

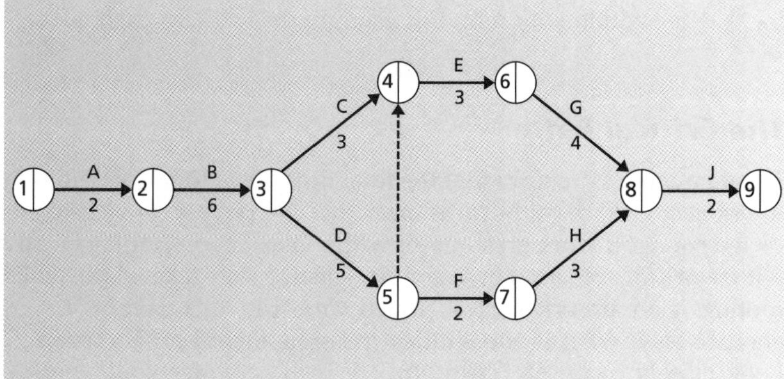

▶ In Figure 16.3 the activity sequence glazing–wiring–decorating can take place while roofing and painting are in progress (subject to the dummy). Thus there are two pathways at this stage in the network.

Figure 16.3
Building the sports pavilion: network diagram

Check carefully the logic of the network:

- Activities A and B must be completed in sequence before any others.
- The network splits after Activity B because there are activity sequences that can run concurrently, i.e. in parallel.
- There is only one pathway after Activities G and H since Activity J can only take place once all others are complete.
- A dummy is needed between Nodes 4 and 5 since work on wiring and fitting cannot begin until roofing work is finished.

▶ Remember that the arrows represent activities and occupy periods of time. The nodes are not activities and are only 'switching points' between activities.

Earliest Start Time (EST)

An activity cannot start until the other activities on which it depends are finished. Using this principle, we work from left to right across the network. Times in the network are measured in terms of completed days, so Activity A begins - or has an EST - at Day 0. It is therefore clear that for Activity B the EST is Day 2. Similarly, Activities C and D have an EST at Day 8. What is the EST for Activity E? Activity C can be finished by Day 11 (2 + 6 + 3). But the dummy indicates that Activity D must also be complete. So the EST for Activity E is Day 13 (2 + 6 + 5).

▶ The nodes are used to indicate ESTs and LFTs:

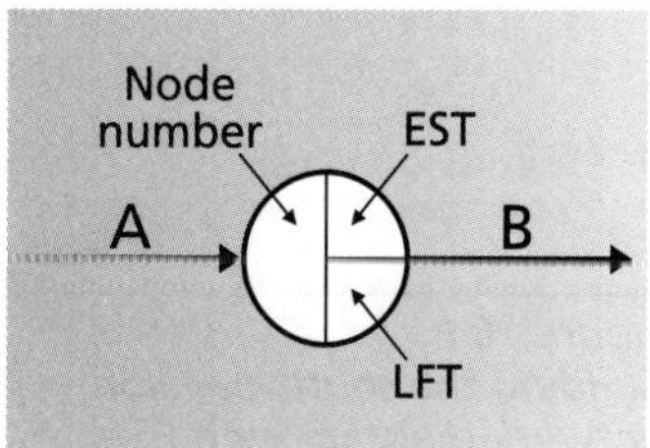

Figure 16.4
Node diagram

The ESTs refer to the next activity (Activity B above), while the LFTs refer to the previous activity (Activity A above).

Draw the diagram in Figure 16.3 and enter the ESTs for each node.

Latest Finish Time (LFT)

Unlike ESTs, the logic for calculating LFTs works from the end of the project towards the beginning. We have established that the total length of the project is 22 days. It must therefore follow that the LFT of the last activity - Activity J - is Day 22. Look carefully at Node 8. If Activity J is to finish by Day 22, it follows that Activities G and H must both be finished by Day 20 at the latest. Now consider Node 6. If Activity G is to be complete by Day 20, then the LFT for Activity E must be Day 16. The same logic leads to a LFT at Node 7 of Day 17.

Now add to your network diagram the LFTs for each node.

▶ The **critical path** through a project is the sequence of activities where any delay must extend the length of the project.

The Critical Path

The data on p. 115 shows that the total time taken for all activities in the project is 30 days. But it is clear that the project could be completed sooner if work on some activities takes place simultaneously with work on others. For example, glazing can take place while roofing is in progress. How much time can this save? Or, put another way, what is the shortest possible length for the project? Look closely again at Figure 16.3. Which activities could not be delayed for quickest possible completion?

▶ The critical path is indicated by a tag:

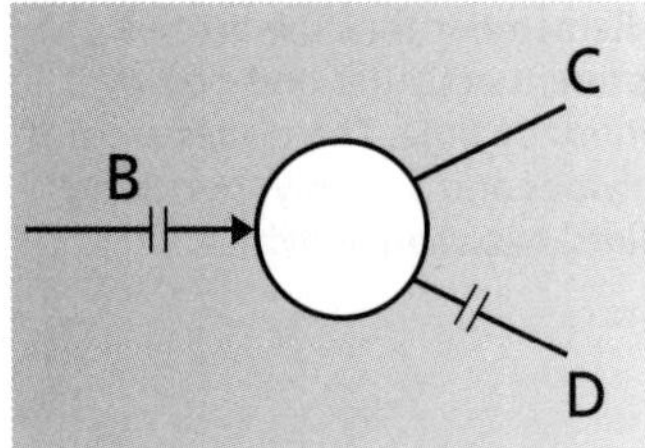

Figure 16.5
Critical path tags

The EST and LFT entries at the nodes provide the answer. If there is no difference between the LFT of the preceding activity and the EST of the following activity then it follows that no delay is possible if the project as a whole is not to be delayed. So the pathway indicated by joining all nodes where LFT = EST is 'critical' to ensuring that the project has a minimum duration. This **critical path** is illustrated in Figure 16.5.

Activities A and B are clearly critical. Any delay here immediately delays the whole project. But Activity C could be delayed while the longer Activity D is in progress. Similarly, if Activity F were delayed it need not extend the project provided that the central Activities E and G are on schedule. Because the dummy is a logical link in the network, it can be a critical path connection – even though it is not a real activity and has no duration.

The critical path can also be found by identifying the longest possible route through the network. At first thought this seems contradictory. But any activities that are not on the critical path could be delayed without delaying the whole project. Any delay to critical activities must by definition cause delay to the total project duration.

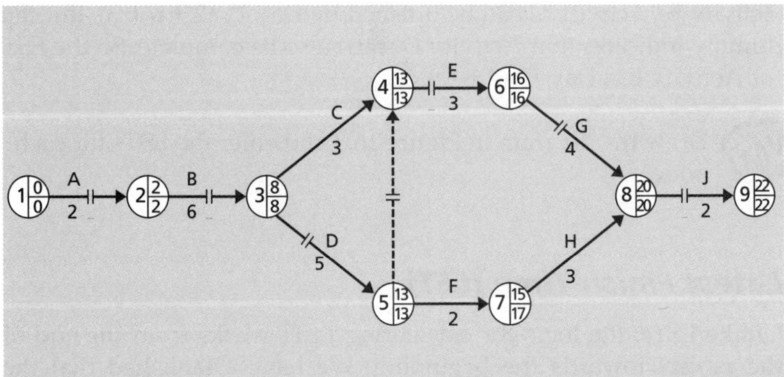

Figure 16.6
Building the sports pavilion: network diagram with ESTs, LFTs and critical path tags

Finding the Float

Once a critical path has been identified, it is possible to analyse the leeway or total float time that exists for each activity.

This is the difference between their earliest and latest start times. We have already calculated the ESTs. The latest start times are simply the LFT of the activity less its duration. So:

total float = LFT *less* activity duration *less* EST.

▶ Total float is always zero along the critical path.

▶ Remember that float time is always available on non-critical activities.

Since there can be no delay to activities on the critical path, it follows that there must be no float time either. Correspondingly, non-critical activities must carry some float or they would be critical. This principle can now be tested:

Total float for

Activity D = 14 (LFT) – 5 (duration) – 9 (EST) = 0 days

Activity C = 14 (LFT) – 3 (duration) – 9 (EST) = 2 days

But what exactly is meant by total float? Total float on Activity H is 2 days (21 – 3 – 16). The same test for Activity F also gives 2 days (18 – 2 – 14). Suppose that Activity F ran 2 days late. The actual start time for Activity H would now be Day 18 and it could not be finished until Day 21, where critical Activity J begins. There is now zero float on Activity H. So the float is not available to each activity but to a pathway of non-critical activities – in this case F and G, extending from Node 5 to Node 8. That is why it is called total float. Once it is used then it is not available again. However, it is possible to measure the float available without delaying the start of the next activity. This is called the **free float**. It is measured in the same way as total float except that we subtract from the EST of the *next* activity instead of the LFT of the activity concerned:

Free float = EST (next activity) *less* duration *less* EST (this activity)

▶ **Calculating float**

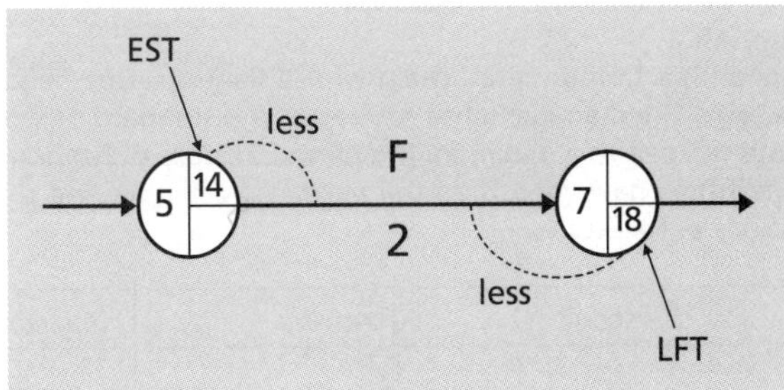

Figure 16.7 (a)
Total float

18 – 2 – 14 = 2 days

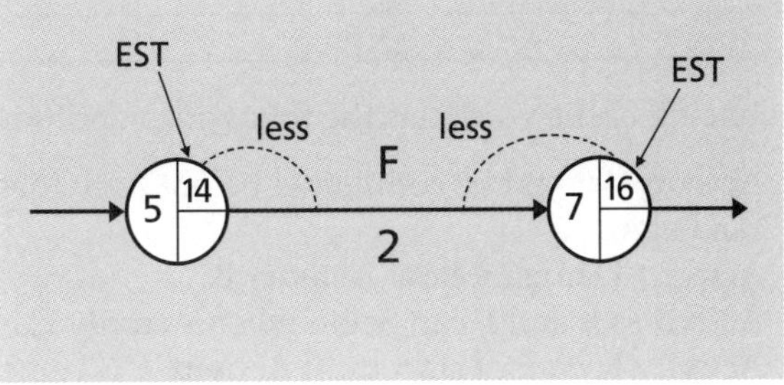

Figure 16.7 (b)
Free float

16 – 2 – 14 = 0 days

We can now draw up a simple table to show the float available with the data for its calculation:

Activity	*LFT*	*Duration*	*EST*	*Total float*	*Free float*
A	2	2	0	0	0
B	8	6	2	0	0
C	13	3	8	2	2
D	13	5	8	0	0
E	16	3	13	0	0
F	17	2	13	2	0
G	20	4	16	0	0
H	20	3	15	2	2
J	22	2	20	0	0

Verify the entries for free float using the information in Figure 16.6. Make a simple table to show the process.

VALUE OF CRITICAL PATH ANALYSIS (CPA)

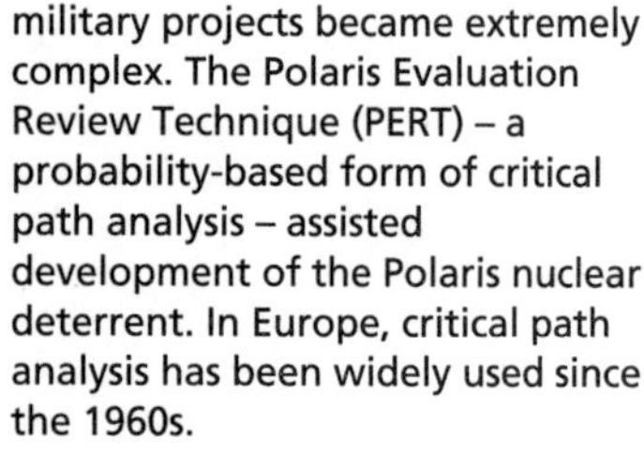

▶ After the Second World War, US military projects became extremely complex. The Polaris Evaluation Review Technique (PERT) – a probability-based form of critical path analysis – assisted development of the Polaris nuclear deterrent. In Europe, critical path analysis has been widely used since the 1960s.

▶ The emergence of low-cost desktop computers has made the application of critical path analysis much easier, faster and cheaper.

CPA is one method from a range of operations research (OR) techniques. They are all designed to make operations management more cost effective. This implies enabling managers to use relatively fewer inputs to achieve outputs of relatively greater market value.

CPA has particularly powerful applications in any kind of project management. A project in this sense can have many meanings. It might involve physical construction or a logistical problem, such as moving a firm's headquarters, or the production of a one-off service such as staging a large conference. It is valuable not only in solving specific problems (e.g. what is the latest date for construction to begin?), but also as a process for thinking analytically and critically about a complex series of planned events.

Savannah

Savannah is a fashion retail chain whose flagship store needs a complete refit. The management requires a high standard of work but is anxious to keep to a minimum the period of store disruption.

The fitters have identified the necessary activities and their likely durations as follows:

Activity	*Duration (hrs)*	*Activity*	*Duration (hrs)*
A	4	E	11
B	8	F	9
C	2	G	10
D	7	H	6

Sequencing of the work has the following conditions:

- Activity A must be completed before Activities B or C can begin.
- Activity D must follow Activity B.
- Activities E and F can begin when Activity C is finished.
- Activity H cannot start until Activity F is complete.

- Activity G requires Activities D and E to be over.
- The project is complete when Activities G and H have ended.

1. Draw a network diagram to represent the project.
2. Calculate ESTs and LFTs throughout and identify the critical path.
3. Which activities could be delayed without preventing earliest completion of the whole project?
4. Activity C is installing some shop lighting. Suppose that what was expected to be a simple task runs into circuit problems and is extended by 3 hours. How is the network affected?

Evaluation

Use of CPA can:

- Break down a project into its component tasks and clarify interrelationships. Practical problems and opportunities can be pinpointed.
- Support efficient planning of human resources, materials and other inputs.
- Assist control of project activities by assigning tight deadlines and a 'time-budget' for events.
- Ensure management and logistical focus on activities critical to prompt project completion.
- Reveal opportunities for savings by making possible just-in-time approach to using resources.
- Improve cash flow by enabling managers to delay expenditures until the latest possible time.
- Allow effective use of 'what if ... ?' questions to explore the implications of delays or unexpected events.

BUT it can also:

- Run the risk of oversimplifying reality with a mechanical type of model that may lack flexibility.
- Lead managers to expect orderly and predictable events when actual outcomes are uncertain and ambiguous.
- Make too little allowance for human behaviour and the motivation of individuals.

17 Stock control

Chapter objectives

After working through this chapter, you will:

- understand the meaning of stock and stock control
- recognize the balance to be set between stockholding and its cost
- be able to use a simple stock control model
- know the main stock management methods, including just-in-time systems
- know the meaning of the following key terms: product stock, service stock, procurement time, re-order level, buffer stock, stock value.

STOCK CONTROL

All goods held by any firm that are not part of the permanent fixed assets (i.e. buildings, plant and equipment, fittings) are **stock**. The purpose of stock is to provide an immediate supply of all goods required in the chain of production and distribution. It provides a form of insurance:

- a demand for any item at any stage can be met without undue delay;
- a failure in any source of supply will not interrupt the production process.

▶ Most firms also hold **service stocks**, which assist the production process: spare parts, lubricants, cleaning materials and office supplies. Their total value is only a small percentage of the value in product stocks.

As part of the **working capital** (i.e. resources that circulate within the business), stock moves through the firm in a continuous cycle. Most stock is held only because it will form part of an eventual sale. As sales are achieved, so stock circulates.

There are three main types of **product stock** held by firms:

- **Raw materials and components** are the goods waiting to enter the firm's productive process.
- **Work-in-progress** means the semi-finished goods within the productive process at any given time.
- **Finished goods** are the completed goods awaiting sale and delivery to the customer.

▶ Stock is the necessary slack in a production system that creates supply to meet demand.

▶ Avoiding over-stocking and under-stocking

Stocks are resources with a money value. Although they circulate around the firm, their average value is a permanent use of resources. The use of any resource has a cost, which must be set against the corresponding benefit received. The purpose of stock control is to achieve an optimum balance between these costs and benefits.

To make notes on the benefits and costs of stockholding draw up a two-column table, one column for benefits, the other for costs.

Benefits of Stockholding

- **Secure supplies** of raw materials and components are assured. Suppliers may be unreliable, while political or industrial troubles could disrupt deliveries.
- **Bulk-purchase discounts** may be obtained by ordering in large quantities.
- **Production planning** is simplified if work-in-progress stocks are sufficient to overcome any imbalances between the throughputs of different processes.
- **Fluctuations in demand** can be absorbed without delays to the customer.
- **Customer choice** includes the full product range.
- **Immediate delivery** can follow all sales.

Costs of Stockholding

1 **Opportunity costs**

Stocks represent idle resources within the firm. These resources could be used for other purposes and the next best such purpose is the opportunity cost. The minimum opportunity cost must be the current rate of interest, since the firm could always invest any surplus funds. In practice, reinvestment of resources in the business itself will probably earn more than the rate of interest. The true opportunity cost of funds tied up in the stock is often around 20 per cent per annum.

▶ If real interest rates are high, efficient stock control could become even more essential.

2 **Physical costs**

- **Warehousing and storage**, including rent, rates and maintenance of premises.
- **Documentation and administration**, which requires office staff and computer time.
- **Checking and handling**, needing specialist workers and costly equipment.
- **Insurance and security**.
- **Falling market value** due to changes in demand, for instance fashion-based or seasonal goods.

Stockholding Policy

Striking the right balance between the costs and benefits of stockholding is rather like walking a tightrope.

The aim is to hold the net cost of stockholding at its minimum. This is made more difficult by continuous change in the key variables. Marketing factors are particularly volatile.

▶ A: the cost of holding stock
B: the cost of not holding stock

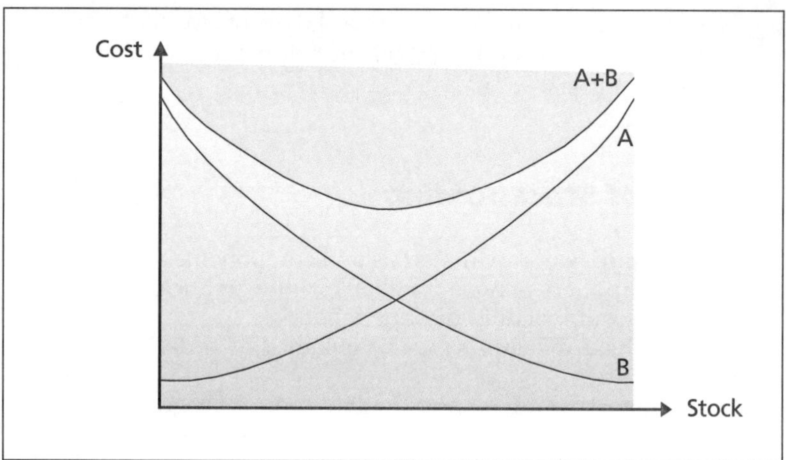

Figure 17.1
The costs and benefits of stockholding

Stock Management

Once a policy is set, production management must attempt to implement it. For each type of stock a range of values must be decided, within which actual stock levels will be allowed to fluctuate. The classic model oversimplifies reality but it is a useful guide:

▶
- **Procurement time**: average period from placing an order to the arrival of supplies.
- **Re-order level**: set according to the procurement time and aims to avoid any entry into buffer stocks.
- **Buffer stock**: the reserve stock which is regarded as a minimum insurance against stockout.

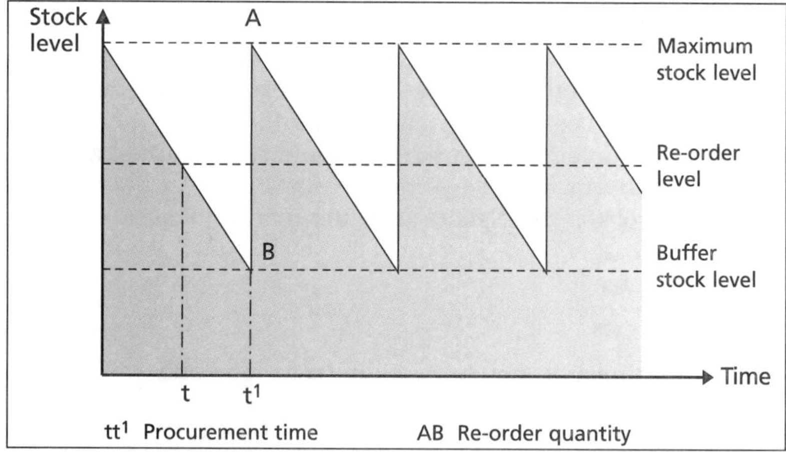

Figure 17.2
A model of stock control management

Notice that:

- The sawtooth pattern of stock usage will in reality be far less regular.
- Actual stockholding will occasionally break through the maximum and buffer stock levels.
- Major changes in the usage rate will show as changes in the down gradients on the graph. Early recognition can prompt corrective action.

In Figure 17.3 below, the usage rate abruptly accelerates:

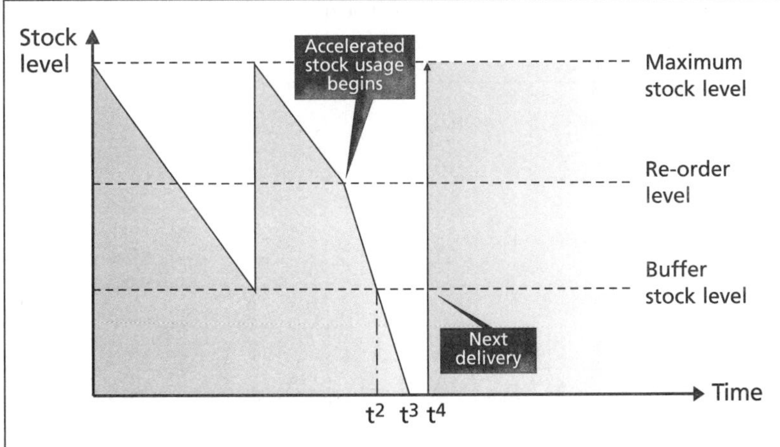

▶ The increased usage rate suggests breaking into buffer stocks by t^2 and complete stockout by t^3 – but no delivery is scheduled until t^4.

Figure 17.3
Increased production and falling stock levels

Effective operation of such a stock control model depends on a flow of accurate and up-to-date information. Many firms now have computerized on-line stock control, which not only provides the required data but also automatically triggers the necessary orders as stock is depleted.

The model must take account of seasonal variation and underlying sales trends detected in market research. Even then, breakdowns or failures in the production process may occur; demand in the market may change unexpectedly; a competitor may launch a hostile initiative; the wider economy may enter recession or boom. The keynote is flexibility.

A firm may assess its relative stock levels using ratios (see Chapter 30).

Stock value is related to sales in two ways:

$$\text{Stock turnover ratio} = \frac{\text{sales}}{\text{stock}}$$

$$\text{Stockholding period in days} = \frac{\text{stocks}}{\text{cost of goods sold}} \times 365$$

The savings from an improvement in stock utilization can be very substantial. Suppose a firm's stock turnover is 2.0 with sales at £100 million, stock at £50 million and profits at £10 million. Assume that the interest rate on the value of stock held is 10 per cent. If stock levels can be halved to £25 million - and the stock turnover ratio increased to 4 - the saving would be about £2.5 million. This boosts pre-tax profit to £12.5 million - a rise of 25 per cent.

Make notes on stockholding ratios using the example of a firm with sales at £150 million, stock valued at £50 million and profits of £8 million.

Just-in-Time Systems

▶ This was pioneered in Japan under the kanban system of delivery. Stock control is fully computerized and orders are made automatically to suppliers, who deliver on a daily or even hourly basis.

In essence, the idea of this system is for stocks to be delivered at - or very close to - the time when they are actually needed. The result is to tighten dramatically the slack links in the production and distribution chain represented by stock. Just-in-time stock control drastically modifies the stock control model.

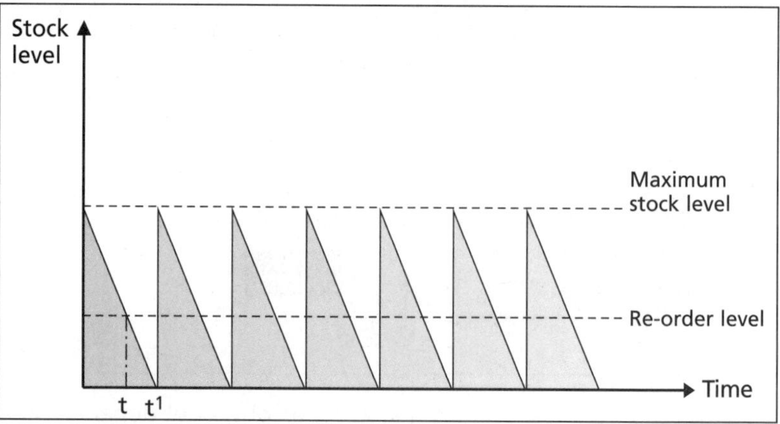

Figure 17.4
Just-in-time stock control

Typically, with this system of stock control:

- the re-order level may be very early in the usage cycle;
- the procurement time (tt[1]) is very short;
- buffer stock is non-existent or minimal.

The system depends on a much closer relationship with suppliers and firms will make reliability a key criterion in awarding supply contracts. Often suppliers will locate physically very close to a major manufacturer (see Chapter 12). The purchasing firm may even provide advisory and training services to its suppliers in order to improve their performance.

The just-in-time principle extends through the whole production chain. Computers are applied in calculating optimal logistics for manufacturing processes. This means that production bottlenecks are avoided and just the right quantities of components are matched to work-in-progress at the start of each operation. Computerization of sales records can connect market demand directly with the production interface. Delivery to the firm's own customers can also adopt a just-in-time approach.

▶ The need for adequate liquidity and working capital may affect a firm's stockholding policy. See Chapter 29.

The net effect of these new approaches is to concertina the whole production and distribution sequence. Stock – and therefore working capital – is reduced and a major competitive advantage is gained in overall costs. A recent study found that firms adopting a just-in-time system could reduce stock by 50 to 90 per cent. This is reflected in the falling stock turnover ratios for manufacturing across the industrial world.

Note the advantages and risks of just-in-time stock control. Use Figures 17.3 and 17.4 in your notes.

Forrest Fashions Ltd

Forrest Fashions Ltd is a major specialist in printed fashion clothing, founded by a young model, Jane Forrest. The factory holds stocks of undyed fabric in 50-metre rolls. With a usage rate of twenty rolls per week, the production manager Sean Fraser aims to ensure that stock levels never fall below forty rolls but do not exceed 160 rolls. Current practice is to place orders in batches of 120 rolls, which take an average of three weeks to arrive.

1 Sketch a stock control chart using this data.
2 The stock level is eighty rolls. A large rush order now arrives which will push the usage rate up to forty rolls per week for the next two months. What action might the production manager take and why?

Evaluation

- Stock control is about striking a balance between the risk of stockout on the one hand, and the cost of stock on the other. Thresholds of acceptable risk vary widely. The chosen solution will depend partly on the culture and traditions of the firm.
- There is no simple formula for calculating optimum stock levels. Each firm, product and market is different.
- Just-in-time increases the stakes in stock control. Without the cushioning of buffer stock, errors translate faster into lost production and late deliveries. The whole decision cycle must increase its speed and be informed by very accurate and up-to-date data.
- Computerized stock control systems are only as good as the model with which they are programmed. In dynamic markets the ground rules of stock control must be under constant review.

▶ Many firms have found themselves over-stocked during times of recession. Trading with lower stock levels reduces this risk.

18 Lean production

Chapter objectives

After working through this chapter, you will:

- grasp the full meaning of lean production
- know how just-in-time production works
- appreciate the advantages of cell production and continuous improvement
- recognize how flexible capacity and shorter development times increase competitiveness
- understand how flexible specialization enables firms to target smaller segments within markets
- know the meaning of the following key terms: Japanization, kanban, autonomous work groups, kaizen, seven-S model.

THE IDEA OF LEAN PRODUCTION

The word 'lean' normally means 'no fat' or, in business terms, 'no waste'.

The idea of lean production has gained widespread currency over the past decade. Essentially, the term means a high and rising level of efficiency in the use of resources to produce goods (and services).

A goal of any firm is to maximize the gap between the value of its inputs and outputs: this is the process of adding value. The techniques of lean production aim to drive down the cost of inputs while maintaining or increasing the market value of outputs. In a sense, this has always been the intention of every business. But there is a world of difference between a generalized intention largely confined to management and an energized determination among staff at all levels. It was the results of this difference that powered the products of Japan into the markets of Europe and America during the 1970s and 1980s.

Low costs and relatively low prices do not in themselves generate competitive advantage. But Japanese firms were so successful in their conquest of world export markets that in many industries no firm could remain competitive without adopting the philosophy of lean production.

It is not surprising that lean production has been associated closely with the 'Japanese Way' and the **Japanization** of so many firms in the western world.

▶ **Japanization** was a response to the success of Japanese exports in the domestic markets of America and Europe.

It is worth thinking carefully about the inner logic of production. Firms only produce because there is a market for their products. In other words, the willingness of customers to pay for a product 'pulls' resources through the production process. In ideal circumstances this consumer 'pull' on resources would be so sensitive that a perfectly undelayed production process for every product would only begin exactly when required. The interfaces of marketing and production would be perfectly connected, enabling the events that link resource ingredients to finished product to become a seamless continuum. Suppose, too, that all the resources necessary for production were totally flexible and could be expanded or contracted in exact accordance with demand. There would now be a situation in which all costs were variable and no resources were ever idle. All the opportunity costs of waste would have been eliminated.

This sounds like a production manager's dream! Although it could never be literally achieved, this has been the aim and strategic thrust of many Japanese firms since the end of the Second World War. And the effort to eliminate waste is not confined to production and the reduction of cost. Marketing is about sales through the perception of high consumer surplus (see Chapter 1). Offering a product for sale that does not quite suit the customer is a waste of potential market value. But if market research is finely tuned and the production process is flexible, then the customer may be suited precisely. Again, a form of waste is eliminated and more added value is achieved.

Just-in-Time Production

This includes and extends the principle of just-in-time stock control. The system is based on market-pull rather than production-push. The Japanese term '**kanban**' refers to the way in which component supplies are 'pulled' through a production process. In its literal form, each stage of production is attended by two bins of components. When one bin is empty, it is wheeled over to the relevant part of the factory with its kanban order card attached. This signals further production of the necessary component, which must be complete before the remaining bin-load is exhausted. The system may be computerized but the principle is the same. Work-in-progress is minimized and the opportunity cost of stock is reduced.

▶ The **kanban** system was developed at Toyota's factories in Japan just after the Second World War.

Just-in-time stock ordering from suppliers works in the same way. Stock is delivered at short notice in relatively small batches. Buffer stocks are minimal and orders are frequent, with the assumption of a prompt and reliable response from the supplier company. The just-in-time principle also holds good at the other end of the production process. Finished goods are not produced for stock but for a specific order or customer.

▶ Every coil of sheet steel produced in a British Steel strip mill has a customer before it is even rolled.

Just-in-time production takes almost all slack out of the system. But it is dependent on excellent communications and relationships, both inside the firm and between the firm and its suppliers.

Cell Production

The traditional mass production factory is arranged for conveyor-belt-style working with a very high degree of specialization in roles and tasks. Division of labour is taken to an extreme, where each worker repeats one relatively simple task many times in a day. Often the individual worker is barely aware of how his or her work contributes to output of the final product. **Cell production** regroups the workforce into a series of mini-production units within the factory. Each unit or 'cell' becomes responsible for a complete stage of production, encouraging a much higher degree of motivation and commitment to the work. In many cases cells also operate as **autonomous work groups** (see Chapter 35), involving the team deciding for itself how the work should be carried out and distributed among members. They are also likely to be responsible for checking the quality of their own work. This all adds to the likelihood of personal and group identification with the specific and total production processes. It also provides a vital sense of **empowerment**, which allows staff to feel control and responsibility in their work and counteracts alienation.

▶ The team becomes an important social group, with its own informal dynamics.

Kaizen

▶ 'Do not waste the gold in the worker's head.'
Toyota

This Japanese word means 'continuous improvement' and is a vital element in lean production. The essence of the idea is that well-qualified, well-trained staff are engaged in a continuous process of proposing small but significant ways of improving efficiency, reducing costs and adding value. Suggestions may relate to the product or the process; they may aim to increase quality or reduce waste.

▶ 'Don't ask me, I only work here' is sometimes said in fun but carries ominous implications for the culture of the firm.

With staff ideas regularly contributed through kaizen groups and quality circles, this is an inexpensive route to improved productivity. By contrast, the tendency of European and American firms has been to neglect the potential ideas and expertise of staff and to rely instead on costly but infrequent injections of capital investment. This brings 'occasional improvement' to productivity, with long periods in which no progress takes place with the wholehearted involvement of staff remaining absent.

▶ Charles Handy (1989) argues that successful firms need a 'learning culture', where education continues through working life and employees develop the habit of asking questions.

Within a firm with the kaizen ethos, all employees become like partners in the enterprise. Often there is an expectation that people are thinking critically and creatively about their work and are not afraid to make any suggestion. Such a firm has a 'learning culture', in which a job is perceived not merely as a way to earn money but as a personal commitment within which the 'whole person' feels able to grow in experience and awareness.

Flexible Capacity

▶ Albright and Wilson is a large chemicals producer in Birmingham. When a machine is said to be at capacity a group of researchers is sent to work with the operator on boosting output. Increases of 20–70 per cent have been achieved without installing new capacity.

Even capacity – the limit to output for a given quantity of fixed assets – can become flexible. When working at 'capacity', adjustments can often be made to machines so that their output is increased.

Firms with subsidiaries abroad may be able to shift work at short notice from factories in one country to another, avoiding bottlenecks in their national capacity. Alternatively, they may have known subcontractors who will accept orders in excess of capacity.

▶ 'Capacity is not what you own but what you have access to.'
Chairman at Bodycote Specialist Coatings, Manchester

New technology is also helping to soften the boundary of fixed capacity. The design of machinery is becoming more flexible in allowing firms to upgrade or expand output at shorter notice and at less relative cost. The increased use of computers and micro-electronics is tending to make capacity changes cheaper to configure and install.

Shorter Development Times

Consumer tastes and preferences are changing increasingly quickly, with market opportunities liable to emerge and disappear before firms have had time to respond. This places a premium on fast-track product development, where the lead times on all stages of conceiving, designing, testing and making available a new product are severely telescoped. Lean production is concerned not only with the sensitivity of market-pull on existing products. It also means the ability to accept and even anticipate changes in the nature and structure of demand and to translate these into modified or new products without delay.

This is particularly important in cases of a significant change to the generic product or in the target market. Very often the firm whose product is launched first gains a large share of the market that subsequently develops. Again, new technology is accelerating product development. Many stages in the process have become computerized, while design and testing is increasingly possible using virtual reality techniques.

Flexible Specialization

This term means the ability of a production system to cope with the need for a flexible range of specialized products. The traditional 'Fordist' mass production lines of the twentieth century were designed for the output of standardized goods. This reflected the mass markets of consumers who appeared to express very similar values and tastes. But growing affluence towards the end of the century has caused rapid market fragmentation. The wide segments of the past are cracking into numerous niches or sub-segments, each of which has its own pattern of preferences for product specification and price.

The challenge of targeting these subdividing markets demands the closest possible communication between the marketing and production functions. One way forward is to offer a fairly limited range of generic products that can be customized in the production process to meet the needs of different market segments. For example, the same confectionery can be offered in different pack styles and sizes, a book or magazine can be produced in different editions, a car can be made with all kinds of different accessories and types of finish. Machines are increasingly programmable and can be reset far more quickly than in the past. Flexible specialization means that the advantages of flow production are applied to batches of the product, each of which is designed to penetrate its own market segment.

▶ Some car dealers can now invite the customer to decide the specifications of their new car on screen. The instructions are passed electronically to the factory where that particular car will be manufactured and prepared for delivery.

MANAGEMENT AND LEAN PRODUCTION

Lean production is more than a collection of techniques or the application of new technologies. It is a kind of philosophy or integrated way of thinking about business management. It takes market orientation to its logical conclusion while waging war on waste of all kinds.

▶ Pascale thought that many American managers saw the soft-S factors as 'froth'. He wrote: 'That froth has the power of the Pacific.'

A key thinker and theorist who has helped to popularize the 'Japanese Way' in America and Europe is Richard Pascale. His book, *The Art of Japanese Management* (1981), has been an international bestseller. Its essential purpose was to analyse and expose the critical differences between American and Japanese management methods that might explain Japan's superior performance. Working with Peters and Waterman, he developed and explained the **Seven-S model** for evaluating management. The hard S factors - strategy, structure and systems - were the traditional strengths of western firms. But the soft-S factors - style, skills, staff and shared values - were taken far more seriously by Japanese companies. Linking fluently these human dimensions with the hard-S factors appeared to be at the heart of Japanese success. Pascale gave particular attention to 'shared values' as providing the 'glue' that held the other S-factors together. He pioneered much current thinking on corporate culture (see Chapter 45) in stressing the importance of the firm as a total human entity and not just a collection of machines and people that happen to be working together.

Blue Line Buses Ltd runs local bus services in six seaside towns along the south coast of England. There is a major depot in each town for maintenance and crewing operations. The whole operation was purchased at the time of bus privatization in the 1980s.

PowerGlide Ltd designs and produces rollerblades and rollerskates. Manufacturing uses up-to-date technology and employs 100 production staff. The process is based on a production line where each worker repeats a single task.

Suggest at least three ways in which each company might use the principles of lean production to improve efficiency.

Evaluation

- Lean production may not in itself supply a firm with a long-term source of competitive advantage. But it is a base on which competitive advantage may be built much more easily.
- The sustained commitment of all managers is necessary for lean production systems to work. A shift to lean production systems cannot be treated as a fashion or a one-off effort to improve efficiency. It requires entry into a genuinely different way of thinking and working.
- Lean production methods make intensive use of new technology but really depend on the quality of

relationships between people and the culture of the firm as a whole.

- It is not only manufacturing industries that can adopt lean production. The distribution chain that ends in retailing has been revolutionized in many cases by the same approach. Other service industries such as tourism or banking are equally able to benefit.
- As the status of staff rises from that of 'worker' or 'employee' to that of 'colleague' or 'partner', the firm is more able to become thoughtful, self-critical and creative at every level.

Part 4

Finance

19 Analysing costs

Chapter objectives

After working through this chapter, you will:

- know the sources of business cost
- understand the differences between variable, fixed, total and average costs
- appreciate the concept of opportunity cost and recognize its business relevance
- know the meaning of the following key terms: direct and indirect costs, overheads, fixed, variable and semi-variable costs, total cost, average cost, opportunity cost.

WHAT ARE BUSINESS COSTS?

▶ Remember: sales revenue minus costs equals profit.

A **cost** arises from the consumption of any resource that has a price. The use of a resource that was in unlimited supply with no transport requirement would have no cost. In practice, virtually every ingredient of a business enterprise carries a cost. The task of management is to combine resources in such a way that their cost is exceeded by their market value. The measure of success is profit.

Timber Traditions Ltd operates from a country town industrial estate. Its business is the manufacture of specialist timber window frames and doors for local builders and private customers. The company accounts list the main costs incurred throughout a year's operations.

A	B	C
materials wages (for production staff)	energy maintenance marketing administration	salaries (for managers and office staff) rent rates insurance depreciation

There are two important observations to be made about these costs:

- Only materials and wages (box A) are actually related to physical manufacturing. The other costs (boxes B and C) are all necessary to the business but are only indirectly related to the actual product.

- The costs in box A will vary in proportion to output. The costs in box B will vary to some extent with output, but not on a proportional basis. The costs in box C are fixed and will not vary in any way with output.

Direct and Indirect Costs

▶ The total direct cost is often called the **prime cost.**

Accounting in a firm shows the resources in use at a given time and the flow of resources leaving (costs) and entering (revenue) the business (see Chapter 25). The recording and analysis of costs is a crucial part of an accountant's work.

All costs that can be related to a particular product are called **direct** costs. These include:

- **Direct materials**: those raw materials and components used in making the product itself.
- **Direct labour**: all work involved in making the specific product.
- **Direct expenses**: any other services required exclusively for output of the product, e.g. design fees or equipment hire charges.

▶ Indirect costs are often called **overheads**.

All other costs within the firm are called **indirect** costs because they do not relate directly to the particular physical product. These are the background business costs – or **overheads** – that are not always obvious.

Indirect costs are also split between:

- **Indirect materials**: all goods consumed in the firm apart from materials for production, e.g. machine parts, cleaning materials, office stationery.
- **Indirect labour**: wages and salaries of supervisors, maintenance and security staff, office personnel, sales teams and management.
- **Indirect expenses**: all other overhead costs including rent, rates, heating, lighting, insurance and depreciation.

▶ **Total cost**: the sum of direct and indirect costs.

The sum of direct and indirect (or prime and overhead) costs is the **total cost**.

This cost breakdown is valuable for accounting purposes in helping to calculate the cost of a particular product and in reaching pricing decisions. It also corresponds with the logic of the 'profit and loss account' (see Chapter 27).

Direct and Indirect Costs

Coffee and a Cake

A customer sits down in a café with a cup of coffee and a small cake. The bill is £1.80. How can coffee and a cake possibly cost so much? The customer may remark that the same items could be served at home for less than 30p. But the bill is not literally for coffee and a cake. The cost of direct materials is certainly small. Even the cost of direct labour and direct expenses may be modest. But the customer is surrounded by indirect costs: the wear and tear on the furniture and fittings; lighting and heating; maintenance and repairs; insurances; office expenses;

cleaning expenses; rents and rates; publicity. It is these costs, plus a profit margin, that make the bill £1.80. The customer may even be getting good value.

Variable and Fixed Costs

So far we have analysed costs in their relationship to the product itself. We will now look at the behaviour of costs relative to the level of output. To illustrate this we will use the following data based on the production of goods vehicles:

▶ These values are graphed in Figures 19.1 and 19.2.

Output (units)	*Total fixed cost (£k)*	*Total variable cost (£k)*	*Total cost (£k)*	*Average cost (£k)*
0	200	0	200	∞
1	200	80	280	280
2	200	160	360	180
3	200	240	440	147
4	200	320	520	130
5	200	400	600	120
6	200	480	680	113
7	200	560	760	109
8	200	640	840	105
9	200	720	920	102
10	200	800	1,000	100

Variable costs (VC) are those that vary in an approximately direct relationship to output. Direct materials and labour are the major examples. For instance, a 25 per cent increase in output by a firm making garden seats will cause a 25 per cent increase in timber usage and a 25 per cent increase in direct labour costs. As shown in the data above, every time output is doubled, variable costs are doubled. These costs are represented on a graph as a straight line in relation to output (line VC in Figure 19.1). In the short run, capacity (maximum output) is fixed.

Fixed costs (FC) are those that do not vary with output. They include such items as rent, rates, insurance and depreciation. On a graph they form a line parallel to the output axis – the line FC in Figure 19.1.

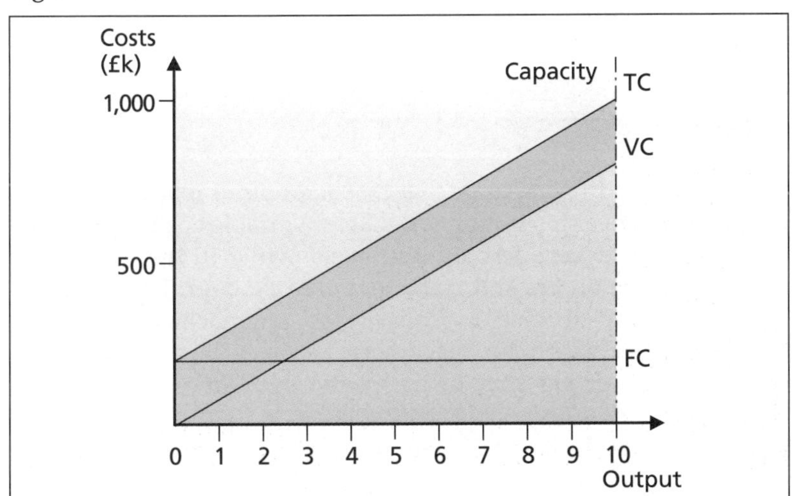

Figure 19.1
Fixed, variable and total costs

Notice that the total cost line (TC) always starts from the platform of fixed costs and not from the origin; at all points TC = FC + VC.

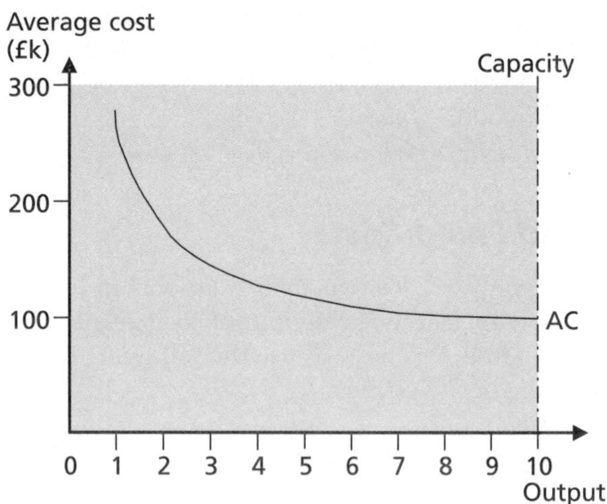

Figure 19.2
Average cost: total cost divided by output

Notice that the curve does not touch the cost axis since it is meaningless to calculate average costs for zero output – the value would be infinity. The average cost curve (AC) is downward-sloping because the fixed costs are being spread over a progressively greater output.

Semi-variable costs are those that vary with output on a non-proportional basis. These are likely to embrace maintenance, heating, lighting and administrative costs and marketing expenses. Within a narrow range of output there may well be little change in semi-variable costs. However, as certain output levels are reached, increases in these costs will occur. For example, an extra maintenance crew will be needed, extra office staff will become necessary, or additional sales representatives must be recruited. In graphical terms, the result will be a roughly stepped pattern.

In practice, most semi-variable costs are composite, including both a fixed and a variable element. For instance, electricity carries a standing charge plus a variable rate for usage. In Figure 19.1 the variable parts of semi-variable costs have been included with variable costs and the fixed parts of semi-variable costs with fixed costs.

Total cost (TC) is the sum of all these cost elements (see TC in Figure 19.1).

Average cost (AC) (see Figure 19.2) is simply total cost divided by the level of output. This relationship forms a downward-sloping curve of declining gradient.

Make notes to define and illustrate variable, fixed, total and average costs in relation to output. Invent your own data for drawing these in graph form.

BUSINESS COSTS IN PRACTICE

Figures 19.1 and 19.2 assume that cost and output relationships are linear. In practice this is highly unlikely. Variable costs will probably be higher at very low output levels owing to the expense of small materials orders and inefficient use of labour. Equally, variable costs tend to rise as capacity is approached, when the matching of labour with machinery becomes less efficient and overtime rates of pay may be necessary. In addition, the variable element in the semi-variable costs is likely to follow the same pattern. For example, the maintenance costs in a factory may rise

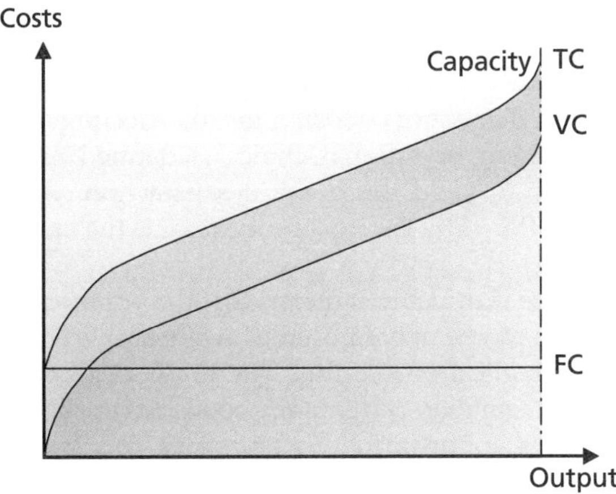

Figure 19.3
A more realistic picture of variable and total costs

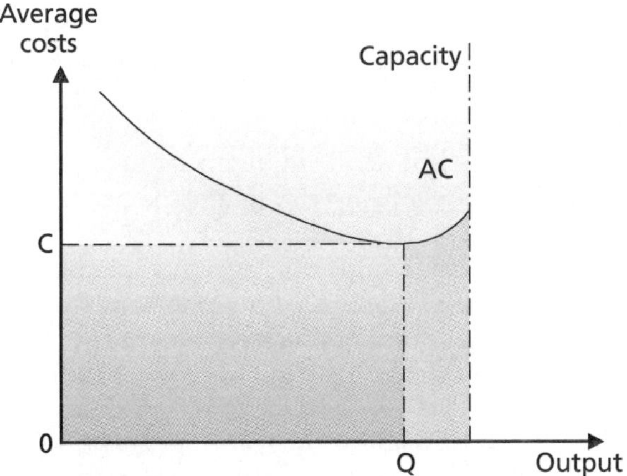

Figure 19.4
Average cost curve

Notice that the initial fall in AC is steeper due to higher variable cost rates at a low output; the trend is still downwards until around 80 per cent capacity is reached because the fixed costs are spread over a greater output. The gentle rise in average cost towards capacity is caused by the high variable costs across this output range; the lowest average cost (OC) is achieved short of 100 per cent capacity at OQ.

sharply when equipment is being used at peak output. Figure 19.3 above shows a more realistic picture of a firm's cost structure.

This pattern means that average cost is likely to be rising over the last 10 per cent or so of the firm's capacity (see Figure 19.4). Partly for this reason, many firms choose to operate at around 80 to 90 per cent of capacity. In addition, it is often advantageous to hold spare capacity to meet fluctuations in demand or a sudden but valuable order.

It is important to remember that the situation described relates to the **short run**, i.e. the period over which capacity is approximately fixed. In the **long run**, capacity can be expanded and a new AC curve may offer a lower minimum average cost. This is caused by economies of scale (see Chapter 13).

Make a copy of Figure 19.3 to add to the graphs you have already drawn. Annotate it to show that in practice the earlier calculations are unlikely to fit reality. Explain why firms often choose to run below maximum capacity.

▶ **Strawberry or vanilla?**
You are offered an ice-cream: strawberry or vanilla? You choose strawberry. Since vanilla was your second preference, the satisfaction expected from the vanilla ice-cream is the opportunity cost of choosing strawberry.

OPPORTUNITY COST

Life – and business – is about choice. Choice means having more than one option. The act of choosing means selecting one option and rejecting the others. A rational choice is defined as selecting the option expected to yield the greatest satisfaction. The satisfaction that would be offered by the next best choice is the **opportunity cost** in any decision.

When a choice is difficult, it means that the opportunity cost is relatively high. We can be uncomfortably aware of this when we make a choice by the smallest of margins. The presence of the second-best choice in our imagination can actually spoil our first choice!

The concept of opportunity cost translates into financial terms.

Opportunity Cost of a Car

Two sisters each receive a gift of £10,000 from an elderly relative. The first sister buys a car with the money. The second sister decides to save hers. What is the difference in their assets after one year?

The first sister has lost £2,000 in depreciation as her car is now valued at £8,000. Disregarding running costs, has her choice of a car carried any other cost? The second sister no longer has £10,000; with the interest rate at 5 per cent she now has £10,500. So the first sister has suffered an opportunity cost of £500 through rejecting the choice of investing the money. Opportunity cost is very real. In calculating the true cost of running a car, it must be included.

It is the same for business. A firm may be deciding how to invest £50,000. For this sum it can either replace its old and outdated machinery or build a new office. If it selects the office, then the opportunity cost will be experienced in more machine breakdowns, higher labour costs or lower product quality. It follows that management must monitor opportunity costs carefully and be ready to make a new decision when opportunity cost exceeds the benefits of an existing choice.

Use the following three headings to classify the costs of running a three-year-old Ford Escort for one year:

1 Variable costs.
2 Semi-variable costs.
3 Fixed costs.

Costs to consider:

- repairs, tyres, oil
- depreciation
- AA/RAC membership
- insurance
- MOT
- servicing
- road tax
- petrol
- parking
- opportunity costs of capital tied up

Now calculate the total cost of running the car over an average 12,000 miles in one year. The result may be surprising…

Evaluation

- The distinction between fixed, semi-variable and variable costs is only meaningful in the short term, i.e. the period in which capacity is fixed. In the long run, fixed costs can be increased (e.g. extend the factory), reduced (e.g. shut down a production line), or reduced to zero (close down and sell assets).
- Although labour is classified as a variable cost, the firm may find that its direct wages bill is fairly constant relative to small variations in output. Harmonious labour relations do not allow for frequent changes in staff levels and recruitment and training costs are better spent if a long-term permanent labour force is retained. In addition, staff morale and loyalty need to be safeguarded.
- Costs are measured for a specific business purpose. Their classification depends on the nature of this purpose. The distinction between direct and indirect costs is the approach of an accountant who is concerned with budgets for costs and profit. The analysis of variable and fixed costs is the approach of a manager or economist who aims to show how costs behave over ranges of output. The different approaches reflect different uses for costing information.
- Simple linear cost models exist to illustrate a principle that is valid. Across limited output ranges they are often close to reality and very useful. Over wider ranges of output they can be highly unrealistic.
- A cost structure is not static. Every cost exists in a dynamic market for resources, the price of which can change without warning. Budgets and cost assumptions must be capable of prompt adjustment as circumstances alter.
- Collecting cost data can be expensive and the impression of accuracy can be deceptive. Managers must judge the level of accuracy that is realistic and cost effective. There is also the risk that managers at any level will under- or overestimate costs to suit their own purposes, for instance setting an 'easy' budget.
- Management accountants use a great variety of technical terms to describe costs. The definition of these terms can vary widely and must always be checked precisely.

20 Breakeven and contribution

Chapter objectives

After working through this chapter, you will:

- know how to draw a breakeven chart
- be able to manipulate a breakeven chart and solve simple problems
- understand the arithmetic method of determining breakeven output
- be able to evaluate the limitations and strengths of breakeven analysis
- understand the concept of marginal cost
- know how to draw up a contribution statement
- be able to apply the concept to business problems and recognize its limitations
- know the meaning of the following key terms: breakeven analysis, breakeven point, margin of safety, profit-volume analysis, marginal cost, contribution costing.

BREAKEVEN ANALYSIS

If any business is to achieve a profit, its revenue must more than cover costs. For this analysis we will make the assumption that all output is sold. As sales increase, so will total revenue. Equally, as output increases, so will total costs. But while zero sales means zero revenue, zero output does not mean zero costs. The minimum cost level for any firm must be the level of its fixed costs. Total costs increase with output from this fixed-cost base. Thus no profit can be made by the firm until total revenue 'catches up' with total costs. For any profitable firm there must be an exact level of output where total costs equal total revenue and the enterprise breaks even.

Constructing a Breakeven Chart

Total revenue = price × volume of sales
Total cost = average cost per unit × volume of output

Thus price/volume and cost/volume are the two key relationships that will determine final profitability. Neither alone is decisive: it is their interaction that managers must analyse.

A simple diagram illustrates the position. Total revenue = TR, total cost = TC, variable costs = VC and fixed costs = FC.

▶ The total revenue line (TR) starts from the origin and, given a constant price at all levels of output, it must be linear and upward-sloping. Until output OA is reached, the firm would be making a loss (TC > TR). At output OA, TC exactly equals TR and the firm is therefore **breaking even**.

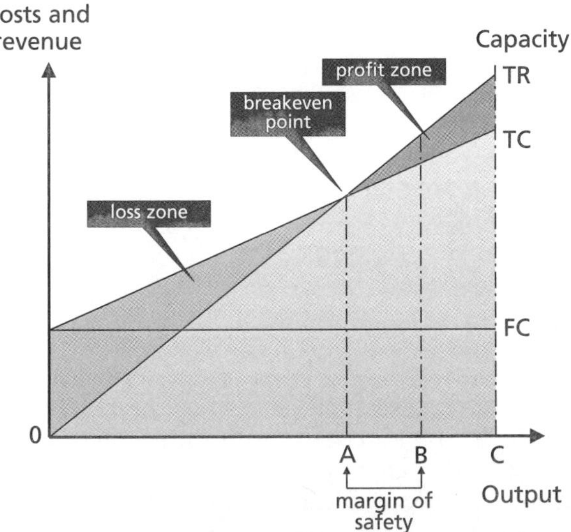

Figure 20.1
Basic breakeven model

The graphical intersection point on the graph is called the **breakeven point** and the whole diagram is known as a **breakeven chart**. At output levels beyond OA a profit is being made and this increases towards maximum capacity OC, as shown by the profit zone.

Suppose the firm is actually operating at about 85 per cent capacity (at OB above). Clearly a profit is being made, but if output were to fall to any level below OA this would lead to losses. The output range of AB is therefore the firm's **margin of safety**.

Breakeven Analysis

Tubular Chairs Ltd

This recently established business produces very modern seating made from moulded plastic and tubular steel. The standardized product sells for £12.50 per unit to wholesalers. The firm's present sales are running at around 9,600 chairs per month (80 per cent capacity).

Costs per chair are as follows:

variable costs:	materials	£3.50
	labour	£2.50

fixed costs amount to £52,000 per month.

We can now draw a breakeven chart to see the firm's profitability relative to output and sales. For clarity, the variable cost line is dropped.

Check carefully how the diagram is constructed: the x-axis

Figure 20.2
Breakeven chart for Tubular Chairs Ltd: 1

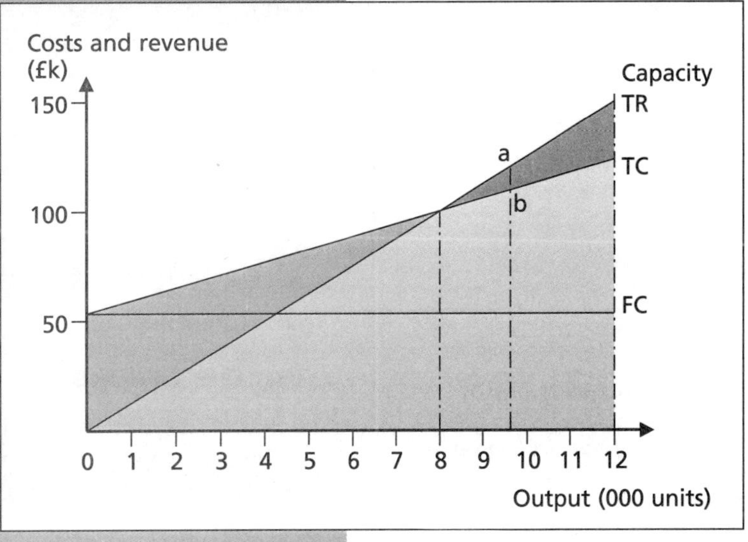

represents output, the y-axis costs and revenue (i.e. money flows).

Since sales are 9,600 units and this represents 80 per cent capacity, maximum output must be 12,000 units.

Fixed costs are given as £52,000 and marked as horizontal to the x-axis.

Total costs:
at zero output = FC which = £52,000
at capacity output = FC + VC = £52,000 (FC) + £72,000 (VC)
= £124,000 (TC)

Total revenue:
at zero output and sales = zero
at 12,000 units capacity output and sales =
12,000 × £12.50 (price) = £150,000

The breakeven point is identified at the intersection of the TC and TR lines, and breakeven output is found to be 8,000 units.

The profit zone begins at the breakeven point and at the firm's present 9,600 units output and sales, profit is £10,400 (vertical distance ab). This can be simply checked:

TR = £120,000
TC = £52,000 + (9,600 × £6) = £109,600
Therefore profit = £120,000 – £109,600 = £10,400
The margin of safety = present output – breakeven output
= 9,600 – 8,000 units
= 1,600 units

Carden Coats Ltd

Carden Coats Ltd manufactures waxed jackets in a small factory on the outskirts of Manchester. Its sole customer is a major UK chain store, which purchases 1,000 jackets each month. The factory's capacity is 1,250 jackets per month. The company charges the chain store £40 per jacket.

Fixed costs per month (£)		*The manufacture of each jacket costs*	
rent	2,400	materials	£12.00
rates	800	labour	£13.00
salaries	5,000		
other	800		

1 Construct a breakeven chart from the data given.
2 (a) What is the present level of profit per month?
(b) What is the breakeven output?
(c) What is the margin of safety at the present level of sales?

Using the Breakeven Chart

▶ Computers greatly assist in manipulating a breakeven chart. A simple spreadsheet package allows investigations of 'what if…?' questions.

The chart does not merely illustrate the firm's existing position. It can be used to explore changes in any of the three key variables: (1) sales volume; (2) costs; (3) price.

1 **Sales volume**

The impact of changes in sales volume is clear from the chart for Tubular Chairs. Any fall in sales below 8,000 units will cause losses. A rise in sales to capacity output would increase profits to £26,000. Notice that a 10 per cent fall in volume to 8,640 units causes a 60 per cent fall in profits to £4,160.

2 **Costs**

Suppose that variable costs increased from £6 to £7.50 per unit.

▶ Output and sales at 9,600 units is now below the new breakeven point (10,400) units. The firm makes a loss of £4,000 (TR = £120,000, TC = £124,000).

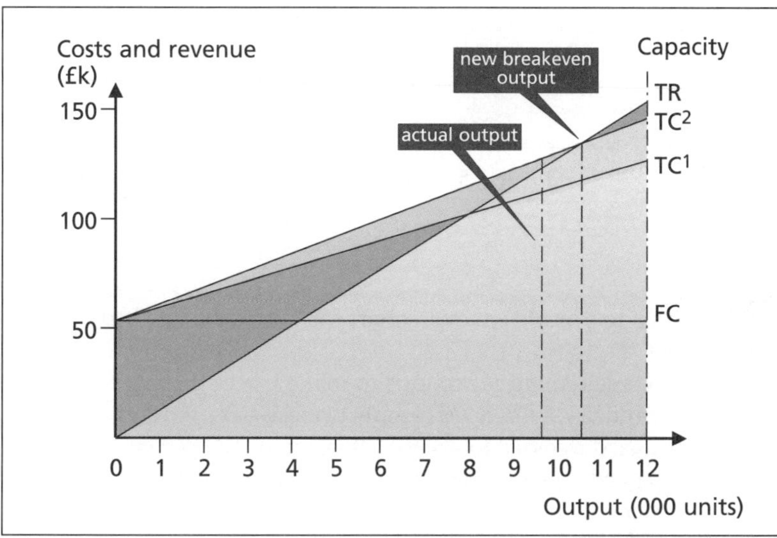

Figure 20.3
Breakeven chart for Tubular Chairs Ltd: 2

Alternatively, with the original variable cost and price, suppose there was a fall in fixed costs to £39,000 per month.

▶ Output and sales at 9,600 units now yields a profit of £23,400 (up 125 per cent), while the breakeven point has fallen to 6,000 units.

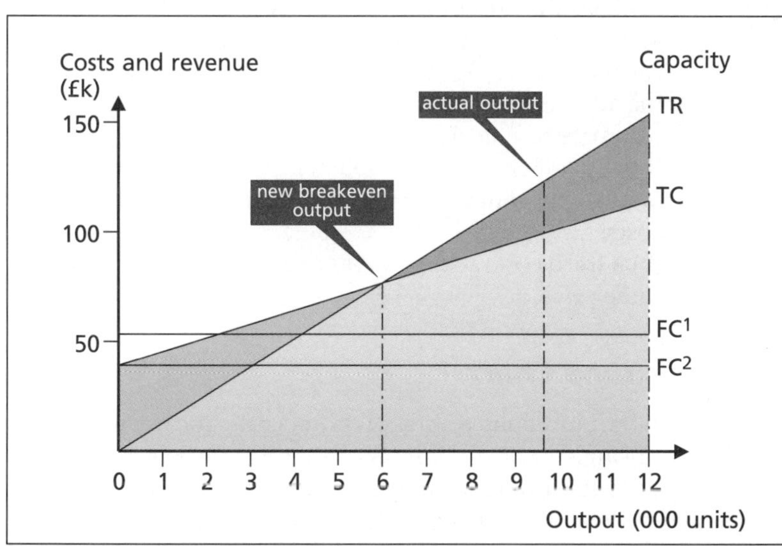

Figure 20.4
Breakeven chart for Tubular Chairs Ltd: 3

3 **Price**

Finally, with original cost and price data, say there was a fall in price obtainable from £12.50 to £11.

Sales of 9,600 units now yield only £105,600, while TC = £109,600. The loss of £4,000 is the same outcome as that caused by the rise in variable costs (above).

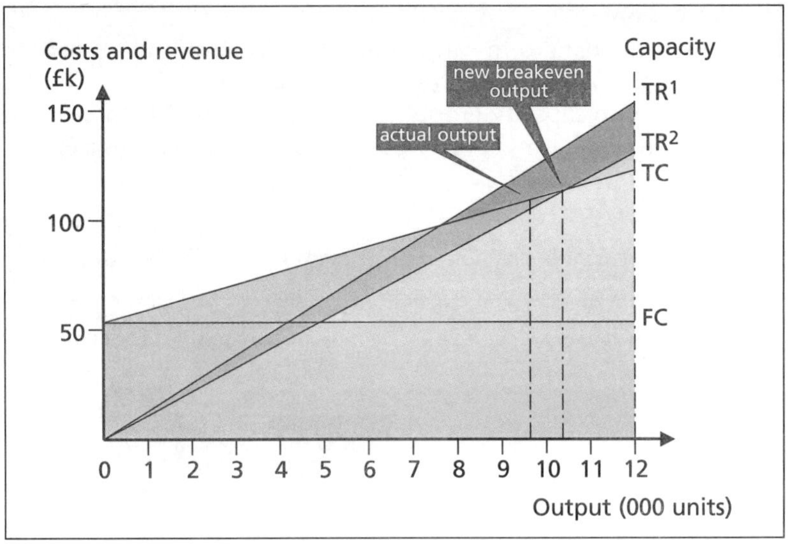

Figure 20.5
Breakeven chart for Tubular Chairs Ltd: 4

Return to your breakeven chart for Carden Coats Ltd.

1 Management is anxious to make use of the excess capacity, which represents unnecessary fixed costs. The board decides to accept the offer of a 20 per cent increase in order size in return for a reduction in selling price from £40 to £38 per jacket. Evaluate this decision with reference to your breakeven chart.
2 Another major retailer will purchase 600 jackets per month on a regular basis at this new price of £38. The firm has the opportunity to rent additional factory space and, for an increase in fixed costs to £18,000 per month, capacity can be doubled to 2,500 jackets a month. Assess the advantages and disadvantages of this plan and recommend a decision.
3 If the plan were to be adopted, investigate the effects of:
(a) a 10 per cent rise in variable material and labour costs;
(b) a third contract to supply a further 600 jackets at the same price.

Profit-Volume Chart

Tubular Chairs Ltd could also express its costs and revenue relationship on a single profit-volume chart (see Figure 20.6).

Against output is plotted loss and profit as an outcome. This is an alternative presentation of the loss and profit zones shown in the breakeven chart. At zero output the loss is the entire fixed overhead expense (£52,000).

The loss diminishes with output because the sales revenue (SR) yielded by each unit exceeds its variable cost, progressively 'paying off' the fixed costs (SR £12.50 – VC £6 = £6.50 surplus).

Zero profit or loss (i.e. breakeven) is reached at 8,000 units and thereafter profit increases with output to reach maximum level (£26,000) at capacity.

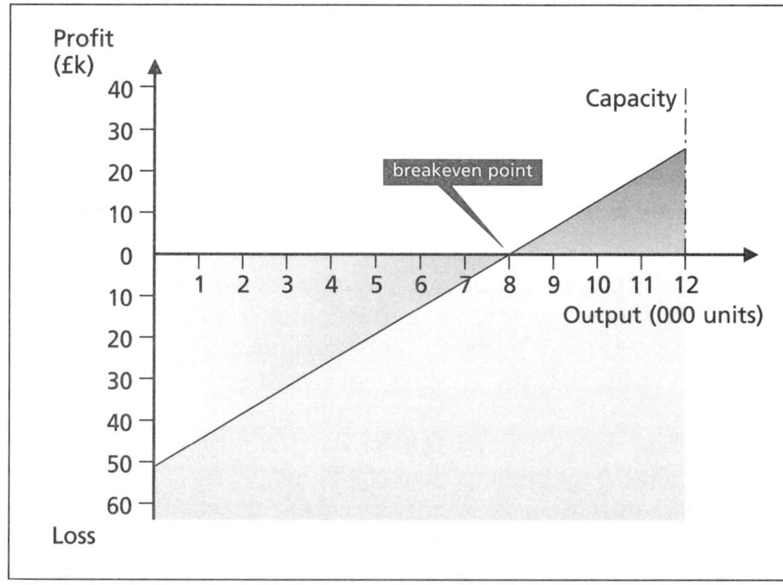

Figure 20.6
Profit-volume chart for Tubular Chairs Ltd

CONTRIBUTION COSTING

Marginal Costs

The cost of producing an item depends on how many are produced. Reducing output means that fixed overheads become a proportionately larger burden and average cost per unit rises. In the most extreme case, if a firm making shoes made only one pair per month, then the cost of that pair of shoes would include the cost of the entire rent, rates and other overheads.

Marginal costs mean the extra cost of producing an extra item.

▶ **Marginal cost**: the extra cost of producing one extra item.

Marginal Costs

Sprint Footwear Ltd

Sprint Footwear Ltd manufactures a single product - running shoes - in one factory. The maximum output (capacity) is 1,000 pairs a month. Costs are as follows:

variable costs per pair of shoes	(£)
materials	8.50
labour	11.50
	20.00

fixed overheads: £9,000 per month
selling price: £35 per pair

How much does each pair cost the firm to manufacture? In this form the question is unanswerable. Suppose the firm produces at capacity 1,000 pairs per month:

variable costs £20 × 1,000	20,000
fixed overheads	9,000
total cost	29,000

Therefore each pair costs 29,000/1,000 = £29

But suppose the firm is working at 50 per cent of capacity. Then:

variable costs £20 × 500	10,000
fixed overheads	9,000
total cost	19,000

Therefore each pair costs 19,000/500 = £38

Clearly the 'cost' of each pair depends entirely on the level of output. A reduction in output means that fixed overheads become a proportionately larger burden and the average cost per unit rises accordingly. Indeed, in the most extreme case, if the firm made only one pair of shoes during the month the cost would be £9,020!

▶ On a factory visit, students may be given free samples that might be quite expensive in the shops. The cost to the firm is not the shop price, nor the average cost, but the marginal cost.

To tackle this problem, we must bring in the concept of marginal cost (MC). As already mentioned, marginal cost refers to the extra cost incurred by producing one additional unit. So if the shoe factory was producing 800 pairs per month, its marginal cost would be the extra cost of producing an 801st pair. Since it makes no difference to fixed overheads whether the firm produces 800 or 801 pairs, it must follow that MC = £20.

Often MC will be constant over a wide range of output, but it may ultimately take the form of a roughly U-shaped curve. In this example, MC is always £20. But if the firm were to sell its entire output at £20 per pair, a heavy loss would occur since the fixed overheads would not be covered. However, if it sold one extra pair by special arrangement at £20, then no loss is incurred as all the other pairs sold at a higher price are covering the fixed overheads.

Make notes on marginal cost by using the data for Sprint Footwear.

Contributions to Fixed Overheads

Given that the firm must pay its fixed overheads regardless of production or sales, it may be very useful for costing purposes to split fixed overheads from the variable costs (i.e. materials and wages for those involved in making the product) of production. Take first the sales revenue per unit sold for Sprint Footwear. Then subtract the marginal cost (equivalent to a constant variable cost). What remains is called a **contribution** towards fixed overheads (FO).

	(£)
sales revenue	35
marginal cost	20
contribution to FO	15

So, if the firm works at 80 per cent of capacity (800 pairs per month), then its contribution costing statement will be:

sales revenue	28,000
marginal costs	16,000
contribution to FO	12,000
less fixed overheads	9,000
profit	3,000

Calculating Contribution and Profit

Contribution costing takes the simple **revenue – cost = profit** formula and, by separating variable costs and fixed overheads, distinguishes two steps between sales revenue and profit:

step 1: sales revenue – variable costs = contribution
step 2: contribution – fixed overheads = profit (or loss)

Provided that sales revenue exceeds variable costs, then a positive contribution is achieved (which may or may not yield a final profit). But if variable costs exceed corresponding sales revenue, then a loss is inevitable and every unit produced can only add to losses.

Make notes on contribution costing using the data for Sprint Footwear, but assume the firm is working at 75 per cent capacity.

Contribution Costing and Business Decisions

Single Product Problems

Teign Textiles Ltd

Teign Textiles Ltd, a small firm in Devon, makes 500 bedspreads each week at an average cost of £10 and with a selling price of £12.50. The factory's maximum output is 600 units per week. One morning the sales manager receives a special request from a new hotel for 100 bedspreads; unfortunately, it can offer only £850 for the consignment. Should Teign Textiles accept the order?

At first glance the answer is clearly no. It would mean a price of £8.50 per bedspread and the loss (selling price – unit cost) would be £1.50 on each one.

Consider now the following costing statement:

	(£)	(£)
variable costs (VC)		
wages	2,500	
materials	1,000	3,500
add: fixed overheads		1,500
total		5,000

▶ NB Assume that all semi-variable costs can readily be related to output and therefore treated as variable.

With output at 500 bedspreads per week, the unit cost is confirmed at £10.

This can be shown in a unit cost statement:

	(£)	(£)
VCs per bedspread:		
wages	5	
materials	2	7
add: fixed overheads		3
total		10

It is now clear that a selling price of £8.50 will cover the marginal cost and still leave a contribution of £1.50 towards fixed overheads. In the absence of any better proposition, the firm should accept the order. This is clear from the following brief contribution statement:

	Without hotel order (£)	With hotel order (£)
sales revenue	6,250	7,100
variable costs	3,500	4,200
contribution	2,750	2,900
fixed overheads	1,500	1,500
profit	1,250	1,400

This principle of selling spare capacity at any price that yields a positive contribution is very valuable, provided that the mainstream market continues to pay the full price.

Make notes on selling spare capacity. To make sure you understand the principle, recalculate the data for Teign Textiles as if the offer were for 80 bedspreads at £640 for the consignment.

▶ Small firms may charge all overheads according to a single yardstick, such as output level or direct labour cost. Larger firms distinguish production overheads from administrative and selling overheads. These must be charged to separate **cost centres**.

Multiple Product Problems

Most firms produce a range of products that can be related to one set of fixed overheads. This range may refer to different sizes, colours, styles etc., or to a portfolio of distinct products. In order to find the marginal cost of one product, it is necessary to extract its component cost elements from each cost centre. A **cost centre** is any identifiable place or process where costs are incurred. So a machine, an office, a loading bay or a whole department could all be regarded as cost centres. Estimates may be necessary when deciding what proportion of costs at a given cost centre are attached to a particular product (e.g. labour costs). Once costs have been assigned to each product, then the various contributions can be calculated.

Contribution Costing with Multiple Products

Peak Plastics Ltd makes plastic kitchen products and its range includes washing-up bowls, plate racks and laundry baskets. Monthly output/sales and prices:

	output/sales (units)	*price (£)*
washing-up bowls	12,000	3
plate racks	8,000	5
laundry baskets	11,000	4

fixed overheads are £30,000 per month

The latest month's results on a contribution basis are shown in the table:

	Washing-up bowls		*Plate racks*		*Laundry baskets*	
	(£)	*(£)*	*(£)*	*(£)*	*(£)*	*(£)*
Sales revenue		36,000		40,000		44,000
Variable costs						
materials	6,000		11,000		7,000	
labour	4,000		9,000		5,000	
Semi-variable cost	7,000	17,000	13,000	33,000	9,000	21,000
Contribution		19,000		7,000		23,000

	(£)
total contribution	49,000
fixed overheads	30,000
profit/loss	19,000

Notice the weak contribution of the plate racks. Indeed, if each product were to share the fixed overheads on a roughly equal basis, then the plate racks become unprofitable:

contribution = £7,000
FO allocation = £10,000
loss = £3,000

However, any positive contribution is valuable in the absence of a better alternative; the plate racks are contributing to the burden of fixed overheads.

▶ Even a negative contribution does not necessarily mean that a product should be discontinued. The reasons for its losses must first be analysed. The product could be in the development stage of its product life cycle with high costs and, as yet, low sales. Alternatively, it might be moving beyond maturity and need an extension strategy (see Chapter 7). It could also be subject to a sudden but temporary cost rise or sales slump.

Make notes on contribution costing for multiple products using the data for Peak Plastics. Complete the picture for yourself by working out the effect of deleting plate racks from the product range and relying on the contribution to overheads by other products.

Calculating the Breakeven Point

It is now useful to return to the breakeven model. Provided that price exceeds variable cost, then a contribution to fixed overheads is made with each successive unit sold. With increasing output, these contributions accumulate until fixed overheads are covered. This is the breakeven point: all costs are exactly covered by total revenue. Thereafter contributions are towards profit.

It follows that the breakeven point is easily calculated:

$$\text{breakeven point} = \frac{\text{fixed costs}}{(\text{price} - \text{variable cost per unit})}$$

$$= \frac{\text{fixed costs}}{(\text{contribution per unit})}$$

▶ Turn back to the example of Tubular Chairs on p. 145. It is now easy to calculate the breakeven point:

$$\frac{£52{,}000}{(£12.50 - £6)} = 8{,}000 \text{ units}$$

Clare's Café

Clare's Café finds that over 75 per cent of its turnover arises from meals and snacks sold over an extended lunchtime period. At present the café is open from 10.00am until 10.00pm. However, takings in the evening have been disappointing and the manager, Clare Haddon, is considering an earlier closing time of 6.00pm. As evidence to support this proposal she shows her partner the following information:

Customers served after 6.00pm, average daily results

		£	£
Sales			68.00
Less costs	materials	28.50	
	labour × £5/hr	20.00	
	power	2.50	
	overheads	25.00	
	(apportioned by time)		76.00
Profit/(loss)			(8.00)

Give your opinion, supported by the information above.

Evaluation

Limitations of Breakeven Analysis

- The distinction between variable and fixed costs is in practice neither precise nor clear.
- Cost assumptions are unrealistic: variable costs will not increase exactly in proportion to output, while fixed costs may change over the range of output represented.
- Sale of all output at a constant price is not certain. Higher sales may mean a lower price and therefore the TR line would probably be curved.
- The multi-product firm may not be able to isolate an accurate cost/revenue structure for one product.
- The key variables – price, cost and volume – are unlikely to be independent and static, but more likely to be **interdependent and dynamic** (changing).
- Data for the chart may be based on doubtful estimates or become outdated.

Advantages of Breakeven Analysis

- It clarifies the key relationship between costs and sales.

- It focuses management attention on devising strategies for profitability.
- It enables managers to explore a wide variety of 'what if' questions by manipulating elements of the chart.
- The smaller the output range, the more realistic the chart becomes. Usually the firm is concerned only with small changes in the variables.

Advantages of Contribution Costing

- Splits direct costs and fixed overheads, so identifying the product's contribution towards overheads.
- Enables sales and pricing decisions to maximize final profit through reference to levels of contribution.
- Avoids any need to use estimates or opinions in allocation of fixed overheads between products. The method keeps to exact data.

Dangers of Contribution Costing

- The temptation is to generate increased sales by making deep price cuts. Positive contributions may still be made, but total contributions may be inadequate when set against fixed overheads.
- Competitive acceptance of cut-price business to fill unused capacity may undermine markets charging 'the standard price' and lead to reduced profitability in the firm or industry.
- The distinction between direct and fixed costs is often blurred (semi-variable costs are a problem), making some assumptions unreliable.
- Marginal cost data can be subject to frequent change. Fixed overheads may also increase abruptly. Thus contribution-based decisions can easily become unrealistic.

21 Overhead costing

Chapter objectives

After working through this chapter, you will:

- grasp the problem of relating overhead costs to individual units of production
- know the overhead allocation methods used in smaller firms
- understand apportionment and absorption systems and their application to different types of overhead cost
- be able to evaluate the significance of overhead costing to management

THE PROBLEM OF OVERHEAD COSTS

▶ How much does a bar of Cadbury's Dairy Milk chocolate cost? It depends on which costs you include.

How much does a product cost? Take the example of a bar of chocolate priced at 30p. How much did it cost? This might appear to be a simple question. Subtract the profit from the price and you have the answer – say 20p or 15p? We assume that the chocolate company knows the answer. Strangely, the chocolate company does not know the answer. In fact, no one knows the answer. There *is* no answer.

At least, there is no absolute and precise answer. It would be easy enough to find the cost of the chocolate *itself* by adding together the labour and materials used in its manufacture. But what about the cost of the machinery? And the heating and lighting? And the office costs? And the marketing expenses? These and all the other overhead costs must be included. If the firm made only one product, we could divide the overhead costs by the number of chocolate bars produced. But the firm makes many different products, which can make many different demands on the many different overhead cost centres. Think again about that one bar of chocolate. How much electricity would you include in its cost? How much machine maintenance? How much computer time? How much advertising?

▶ There is no single correct method of relating overhead costs to a particular product.

These are the kinds of question to which overhead costing attempts to provide an answer. But there can be no perfect or 'correct' solution. Any answer must be an accountant's answer, providing figures that are as true and fair as possible. The issue is clearly of great importance, since profit can only be projected with a cost structure for each product.

Overhead Types

We know that the identification of **direct costs** is straightforward.

By definition, direct materials, labour and expenses relate to the specific product. The problem areas are:

- indirect materials
- indirect labour
- indirect expenses

} these by definition do not relate to any specific product

In accounting terms (see Chapter 25) these costs can be divided between:

- **Production overheads** that are indirect costs arising through the physical production process. They would include factory rent and rates, supervisory labour, maintenance expenses and depreciation.
- **Administrative overheads** that include office rents and rates, labour and supplies and computer costs.
- **Selling overheads** that include all marketing expenses, such as advertising, sales promotion, personal selling and distribution.

▶ **Direct costs** arise directly from output of the product.
Indirect costs include all other expenses in the business.

Simple Overhead Allotment

In small firms the overhead costs are usually lumped together and allotted to each product. A true single-product business is rare, but it allows allotment on the simple basis:

$$\frac{\text{total overhead costs}}{\text{output}}$$

▶ Small firms may charge all overheads according to a single yardstick, such as output level or direct labour cost.

However, a firm whose output is a variety of products or services must find a yardstick for allotment. Most of the major overhead costs increase with time, for instance rent or depreciation. Direct labour costs are also usually time-related and these can be used to provide a simple allocation ratio.

Storm Gear Ltd

Storm Gear Ltd produces waterproof jackets and trousers that sell for £15 and £10 respectively. It is estimated that for the coming year direct labour costs will amount to £400,000 and total overhead costs to £600,000. Overheads will therefore represent £600,000/£400,000 × 100 per cent = 150 per cent of direct labour costs. So for every £1.00 in direct labour costs required by one of its products, £1.50 will be allocated in overheads.

We can now complete a statement for costing and profit:

	Jackets		Trousers	
	£	£	£	£
Sales revenue		15.00		10.00
Direct materials	5.00		2.50	
Direct labour	3.00	8.00	2.00	4.50
Gross profit		7.00		5.50
Overhead costs	4.50		3.00	
Operating profit		2.50		2.50

Notice that this overhead charging rate is based on estimates for direct labour and overhead costs. Actual costs that differ from estimates may make adjustment necessary to avoid distortion in the price and profit structure.

▶ Larger firms distinguish their production overheads from administrative and selling overheads. The production overheads must first be charged to separate cost centres.
• **Allocation** means that the whole of a particular overhead cost is applied to one cost centre.
• **Apportionment** means that an overhead is applied to more than one cost centre according to a selected criterion.
• **Absorption** is the process of charging overheads from a cost centre to the flow of production units through that cost centre.

Overhead Absorption

The system of allotting all overhead costs on the basis of a single criterion becomes too inaccurate for a larger business with many processes and products. Say one production department in a firm generates particularly heavy overhead costs. If four products pass through this department and one does not, it is clearly unsatisfactory for this last product to be burdened with the same proportion of overheads as the others. A more refined system is needed.

Production Overheads

The essential principle is to split up the overheads and distribute them as accurately and fairly as possible. First, overheads are allotted to **cost centres**, for instance machines, processes, departments. Then the total overheads carried by each cost centre are **absorbed** by the various products.

Overhead **allocation** occurs when an overhead is related exclusively to one cost centre (e.g. a computer system in a particular department), which then carries the full burden of the cost concerned.

Overhead **apportionment** means that an overhead provides benefit to more than one cost centre and its burden must therefore be apportioned according to the most suitable criterion.

Eastern Engineering Ltd

Eastern Engineering Ltd has two workshops through which all products must pass. The annual production overhead cost includes the following items:

Item	*Total cost (£)*	*Apportionment basis*	*Details*
Rent	100,000	floor area	Workshop 1 covers 1,500 sq metres Workshop 2 covers 500 sq metres
Supervisor's wages	45,000	direct labour costs	Direct labour: Workshop 1 = £50,000 Workshop 2 = £25,000
Electricity	30,000	metered	Each workshop has consumption meters
Insurance	10,000	net book value (NBV)	NBV: Workshop 1 = £1,200,000 Workshop 2 = £800,000

Apportionment between the workshops will now be on a *pro rata* basis:

Item	Total cost (£)	Apportionment ratio (%)		Apportionment (£)	
		Workshop 1	*Workshop 2*	*Workshop 1*	*Workshop 2*
Rent	100,000	75	25	75,000	25,000
Supervisor's wages	45,000	67	33	30,150	14,850
Electricity	30,000	as metered	as metered	20,000	10,000
Insurance	10,000	60	40	6,000	4,000

Different firms will use a wide range of different criteria for optimal apportionment. Where there is no satisfactory objective basis, a technical estimate is used.

Overhead absorption means the process of charging overheads from cost centres to the flow of output. Each cost centre may receive an apportionment of overheads from a range of sources. The resulting aggregate must then be absorbed by the units passing through the cost centre.

The first step is to select a charging criterion. If the products concerned are identical, then this may simply be the number of product units. For non-standard output, a time-based factor such as machine hours or direct labour hours is likely to be more appropriate.

A rate of absorption per unit is then calculated. For example:

$$\text{Unit absorption rate} = \frac{\text{Total cost centre overhead}}{\text{total output (units)}}$$

The paint shop at Premier Products plc sprays 60,000 products each year and has to absorb an annual overhead cost of £15,000.

▶ The **unit absorption rate** is the overhead charging rate of a particular cost centre to its throughput of production units.

$$\text{Unit absorption rate} = \frac{£15{,}000}{60{,}000}$$

$$= £0.25$$

This rate can then be applied to any required production period or order size. For instance, an order batch of 500 products must be allotted 500 × £0.25 = £125 in paintshop overhead charges. Other firms may choose to use such bases as machine hours or direct labour hours in calculating their unit absorption rate.

▶ As a basis for the unit absorption rate, total output is only appropriate for flow production of standard products. Otherwise machine hours might be adopted where plant and equipment are very costly, while direct labour cost might be applied where paid labour is the dominant cost.

Administrative and Selling Overheads

These costs usually have a slight or complex relationship with the quantity of production or sales. For example, a call by a sales representative may bring a large order or no order at all. Processing an invoice for a £10,000 sale costs no more than an invoice for £10. The normal approach is to charge these overheads directly to unit costs using an absorption rate derived from product costs.

Telford Toys

The company produces sailboats, trucks and shape sorters using two workshops, A and B. Unit direct costs are as follows:

	Sailboats (£)	**Trucks** (£)	**Shape sorters** (£)
Direct materials	4.00	3.50	3.00
Direct labour	8.00	7.50	7.00

There are two major production overheads: rent and power. The relevant apportionment is:

Item	*Total cost* (£)	*Apportionment basis*	*Details*
Rent	40,000	floor area	Workshop A = 200 sq metres Workshop B = 300 sq metres
Power	10,000	metered	Workshop A 25% Workshop B 75%

Sailboats and trucks pass through both workshops but shape sorters are produced solely by Workshop B. Output in the coming year is estimated at 5,000 sailboats, 7,000 trucks and 8,000 shape sorters.

1. What is the total production cost of each toy? Give your reasoning.
2. Administrative and selling costs are budgeted at £20,000 per year to be absorbed in proportion to direct labour costs. Selling price will be based on total cost plus a 25 per cent mark-up. Calculate the price of each product.
3. How far are your costing calculations truly accurate? What possible sources of inaccuracy might they contain?

Evaluation

- Indirect cost – or overhead cost – cannot by definition be directly related to any particular physical product. Whichever allocation technique is used, it is important to realize that the final answer is synthetic. No perfect answer is possible. Management must construct an answer using the best judgement available.
- Any alteration in the overhead allotment system can move a product from apparent profit to loss, or from apparent loss to profit, **without any change to price or sales**. This fact emphasizes the artificial nature of any overhead costing system. It also highlights the need for discretion and consistency in selecting the basis for such a system.
- Inaccuracies in cost estimates that form the basis of absorption rates may cause under- or overabsorption, which will then distort the apparent profitability of different products.
- Although all methods of allocation are arbitrary, for the

purposes of management control over cost and pricing structures, it is the **consistency** of the method that matters. Valid comparisons can then be made over time periods and the monitoring of costs is meaningful.

- Efforts at cost saving often focus on variable rather than fixed costs. Overhead costing, by setting detailed targets, encourages the careful control of fixed costs. On the other hand, overhead estimates may encourage managers to spend 'up to the limit'.

22 Raising finance

Chapter objectives

After working through this chapter, you will:

- appreciate the meaning of finance
- recognize the different types of finance needed by a firm
- know the main sources of finance for fixed assets and working capital
- be able to explain the significance of the Stock Exchange
- understand how firms select their sources of finance
- be clear about the principles of financial gearing
- know the meaning of the following key terms: equity, debt (long-term, medium-term, short-term), working capital, retained profits, share issues, prospectus, underwriting share issues, offers for sale, tendering, placement of shares, rights issue, debentures, Eurobonds, sale and leaseback, venture capital, gearing, trade credits, overdrafts, bill financing, debt factoring.

TYPES AND USES OF FINANCE

Types of Finance

▶ You will find it useful to look at the format of a simple T-form balance sheet as shown in Chapter 26.

There are two basic types of finance available to any business:

1 **Equity**, which is share capital put up at risk by the shareholders. The money is not repayable but, if profits permit, the shareholders receive a dividend. Equity also includes profits that have been retained within the business.
2 **Debt**, which includes all forms of borrowing from sources external to the firm. These funds are repayable and usually carry an interest charge.

The Uses of Finance

There are two essential types of use for all business finance:

▶ Funding of fixed assets and expansion

▶ Provision of working capital

1 **Funding of fixed assets and expansion**, including the purchase of property, plant and equipment and the take-over of other firms.
2 **Provision of working capital**, covering stocks, debtors and cash.

These will now be analysed more fully.

Fixed Assets and Expansion

Every business has assets that represent its physical and trading existence over the longer term. For most firms these include land, buildings, plant, equipment, holdings in other companies and general investments, plus any valuation of goodwill and brand names.

Methods of funding include:

- retained profits
- share issues
- debentures
- Eurobonds
- medium- and long-term loans
- short-term loans
- mortgage loans
- sale and leaseback
- hire purchase
- venture capital

▶Increasingly, some of a firm's most valuable assets are intangible. Human assets do not appear on the balance sheet but are still very real and may be costly to accumulate, e.g. upgraded skills through training.

1 **Retained profits**

Part of after-tax profits - often about one-third - are used to pay dividends to the shareholders. The remaining two-thirds are retained within the company, providing the major source of funding (often over 60 per cent of the total) for asset purchases and investment. Being an internal source of finance, this **ploughed-back profit** can be used at the directors' discretion, with no lenders to satisfy. However, retained profits are not a 'free' source of finance. The opportunity cost of each investment project is the value of the next best option available. The minimum opportunity cost is the interest rate obtainable at the bank. New funds in a business add to the net assets on which management must make an adequate return. For public companies this point is underlined by the market price of their shares and the need to maintain confidence among investors.

2 **Share issues**

▶ Share issues

A company might decide to invite investors to purchase a new issue of shares. A private company will have to arrange this with existing shareholders and business associates. For a public company there is a wider range of options:

▶ **Media Watch**
Look at the financial pages of a quality newspaper for news about share issues. Collect news cuttings to illustrate the topic.

- A **public issue** means that the shares are sold by the company direct to business investors and the general public. The procedure will normally be carried out for the firm by an issuing house - a City institution with the necessary expertise. A **prospectus** will be supplied (and published in the national press), giving full details of the company's business activities and financial performance to date, together with plans and prospects for the future. Investors are invited to apply for an allocation of shares, which may be scaled down if the issue is oversubscribed. An issue is usually **underwritten** (insured) so that any shares unsold through the issue are automatically purchased by the underwriters. The whole process is expensive for the issuing company and often costs around 10 per cent of the issue value.
- An **offer for sale** is also a public issue, with the difference that all the shares are first sold to an issuing house, which then resells them at a higher price. This method may be suitable for a private company that is going public.

- **Issues by tender** set a minimum price for the shares and investors are then invited to make bids for their required allocation. The final price set is the highest consistent with sale of the complete issue.
- A **placing** occurs when most or all of the new shares are sold ('placed') direct to institutional investors such as insurance companies or pension funds. This method can be useful for small and less well-known companies, but a discounted share price will be needed to attract support.
- A **rights issue** involves offering existing shareholders the right to buy additional shares in proportion to their current holding at a reduced price. This does not give the shareholder a profit, since the share price falls to cancel out the gain. However, if the shareholder does not want to increase his or her stake, the rights can be sold at a price that will prevent any loss. Rights issues are a cheap method of raising share capital for well-established public companies.

All shareholders require a return on their investment. A new share issue, again, adds not only to the resources available to management but also to the capital on which a competitive return must be made.

It is important to appreciate that, although the proportion of the adult population who own shares has greatly increased (up to 22 per cent by 1994), these privately owned holdings represent only about 20 per cent of the total value of issued shares, a proportion which has fallen from around 50 per cent in the 1960s. The reason for this reduction is that much business expansion has been financed through **indirect investment** by households, i.e.:

▶ Large financial institutions are the dominant investors in British industry. Their fund managers make many of the key decisions in purchasing new issues and holding or selling existing stocks.

- placing funds with investment and unit trusts
- making contributions to pension funds
- paying premiums to insurance companies

▶ Debentures (loan stocks/bonds)

3 Debentures

A firm with sufficient financial standing may issue and sell promises to pay a given sum at a future date (called the **maturity date**), plus a fixed annual interest payment. These debentures are usually secured on assets of the company (repayment of the loan can be enforced in the last resort by selling those assets). If debentures are quoted on the Stock Exchange, they can be bought and sold with eventual repayment to the holder at the maturity date. Debentures are **not** shares and carry no voting rights. There is a legal obligation on the issuing company to make interest and final payments to debenture holders before any dividends are distributed. Some loan stocks are convertible, which means that at a future date the holder is entitled to convert the loan into ordinary shares at an agreed rate.

▶ Eurobonds

4 Eurobonds

Deposits of a foreign currency in a European bank (e.g. pounds sterling in a German bank or US dollars in a French bank) are called **Eurocurrencies**. These deposits arise from investors seeking higher rates of interest than are available in their home country. They also provide a major source of funds for large companies, which can negotiate long-term loans in Eurocurrencies called Eurobonds.

5 Medium- and long-term loans

▶ Loans

Many firms obtain loans for an agreed period (term) from the banking system. Bank finance used to be primarily short term, but loans are now available for periods of up to twenty-five years. Long-term loans are for a period exceeding ten years and are used to purchase a major asset such as land or buildings. Medium-term loans extend for a period of one to ten years and are used to fund assets with a shorter life span, such as machinery or vehicles. The conditions of the loan are often specially designed to meet the business need. Repayment patterns can be related to the projected earnings of the investment project concerned. This may mean an initial period without repayment or even the delay of repayment until the end of the term. Interest rates can be fixed or variable, or negotiated at agreed intervals. The longer the term and the higher the business risk, the greater the bank's requirement for security. This involves committing a specific fixed asset (e.g. property) to cover repayment in the event of default. Small business owners may be obliged to pledge their private property as security.

▶ Finance managers must ensure that a firm has sufficient liquid assets to make debt repayments as they fall due.

6 Short-term loans

These are bank loans for up to one year granted for a stated purpose, such as the purchase of office equipment. The loan is repaid with interest, usually on a monthly basis.

7 Mortgage loans

If a firm wishes to purchase a major marketable asset such as land or buildings, then a mortgage loan may be obtained using the asset as security. This is exactly the same principle as applies to house purchase. Banks, insurance companies and pension funds all offer business mortgages that may have terms of up to thirty-five years.

8 Sale and leaseback

▶ Sale and leaseback

This means that a major asset is purchased and then sold to a financial institution (often an insurance company), which **leases** it back to the business. Therefore, the firm is renting the asset over an agreed period. The rental charge will relate to interest rates and the asset acts as security.

9 Hire purchase

▶ Hire purchase

A firm purchasing an asset makes one initial payment, while the bulk of the cost is met by a **finance house** (e.g. Mercantile Credit). The remaining balance plus interest and service charges is then settled in a series of instalments over an agreed period.

10 Venture capital

▶ Venture capital

The term means the provision of equity finance (share capital) to support smaller businesses, often in their start-up stages. Many merchant banks have a venture capital subsidiary, while 3i (Investors in Industry) Ventures is Britain's largest source of venture capital. A wide range of business ventures may be supported, including innovative technologies, medical products and professional services. Often the sums provided are relatively small, in the £50,000 to £30 million range. However, the venture capitalist will expect a real influence in the firm's management.

The Stock Exchange

The **Stock Exchange** is a market where buyers and sellers can meet to establish a price and trade in:

- shares in public companies
- stocks or bonds (fixed-interest-bearing certificates of indebtedness)

▶ The London Stock Exchange is the largest stock market in the world after Tokyo and New York. Nearly 10,000 different securities are traded.

At the time of their issue, the sale of these **securities** is called the primary market and does **not** take place on the Stock Exchange. The subsequent sale of second-hand securities – called the secondary market – is the function of the Stock Exchange. This is a vital service as the willingness of investors to buy shares and stocks in the first place is dependent on their ability to achieve a fast, inexpensive resale in this secondary market.

The market operates through 'member firms' whose representatives trade in particular types of security. Their activities are closely regulated by the Stock Exchange Council, which sets the rules of the market and ensures high standards of professional conduct. Member firms are broker/dealers. This means that they buy and sell stocks and shares both on the instructions of clients and on their own behalf. Some members also become 'Market Makers', which means that they will always buy and sell specified securities and unfailingly stand by the prices that they quote.

The organization of the Stock Exchange underwent a basic change (called the 'Big Bang') in October 1986. Much wider membership was introduced, while commission rates were opened to market forces. The old arrangement of face-to-face dealing on the Stock Exchange floor was replaced by a computerized system called SEAQ (Stock Exchange Automatic Quotations).

The prices for securities quoted in the City pages of the newspapers are actually a mid-point between current prices for buying and selling. Transactions can be made instantly via a broker/dealer on the telephone and, after allowance for commission, the buyer or seller will be sent a bill or a cheque. Securities are held for the benefit of dividend or interest payments and for the possibility of capital gain.

▶ A **bull** market is one where share prices are on a rising trend. Among investors, bulls are optimists who buy securities in the hope of reselling at a higher price. By contrast, a **bear** market is one where prices are on a falling trend and bears are pessimists who sell securities in the hope of buying them back at a lower price.

The price of any security depends on the forces of demand and supply. Some market forces act on the individual firm and others on the business environment as a whole. Important factors influencing prices include:

- announcement of trading results (often anticipated in advance);
- significant growth or decline in the market for a firm's products;
- discoveries or breakthroughs, e.g. oil strikes, new drug developments;
- economic events – especially concerning taxation or interest rates;
- City opinion regarding business prospects;
- political issues such as election results.

Quite apart from any personal interests, the directors of public companies cannot ignore the price of their company's shares. They are often under some pressure from 'City opinion', which, if negative, can make new issues difficult to sell and rights issues unattractive. In addition, the fund managers (for pension funds and insurance companies), who often hold a large proportion of a company's equity, understandably expect a reasonable performance from their investments.

Working Capital

Within every business there are resources - called working capital - that continuously circulate, entering and leaving the business in a cycle. **Cash** is needed to buy materials and pay labour. Materials, semi-finished and finished goods are held as **stock**. Sales take place but payments may remain outstanding as **debtors**. The value of resources tied up in these ways fluctuates, but its average value is considerable in most firms (see Chapter 29).

1 **Trade credit**

Firms do not normally pay for their supplies at the time of receipt but benefit from thirty to ninety days (or even longer) as a period of credit. This becomes a long-term source of working capital, although it may involve the loss of discounts for prompt payment. It is especially important for small firms, but large retailers also sell goods at a profit before they have paid the supplier.

▶ Many small firms are starved of working capital through the slow settlement of invoices by the large firms who are their customers.

2 **Overdrafts**

The firm is allowed by its bank to have negative balances ('in the red') up to a maximum sum outstanding for a limited period. Both the period and the overdraft limit can be renegotiated. As a method of borrowing it is very flexible and convenient. Interest (at about 3 per cent above base rate) is payable only on the amount overdrawn and formalities are kept to a minimum. However, an overdraft is intended only to meet short-term needs (e.g. a seasonal lull in sales) and is repayable on demand. In practice, though, many firms continue to renew overdrafts on a semi-permanent basis.

3 **Bill finance**

A **bill of exchange** is a legal document that amounts to a special cheque, usually payable three months after it is signed. A firm supplying goods to another company in the UK or overseas draws up a bill which is signed by the customer. This may then be 'accepted' (guaranteed for payment) by a merchant bank, which will charge a commission. However, the bill can then be 'discounted' (sold at a discount) on the London discount market. The net effect of this is to bring forward the date at which cash is received by the supplier firm.

4 **Debt factoring**

Debt factoring means receiving money in advance on the sums owed to a business. A typical business may have the equivalent of two months' sales owing at any given time (i.e. up to around 20 per cent of the value of annual sales). A **factor** will advance around 80 to 85 per cent on debts outstanding and pay the remaining balance (less charges) as payment is received. In addition, the factor will take over the administration of invoicing and credit control as well as providing protection against bad debts. Such a service strengthens cash

▶ The largest UK debt factor is International Factors owned by Lloyds Bank.

▶ Even if the firm does not use a factor, attention to credit control can release valuable cash by ensuring prompt payment by customers.

flow by releasing large amounts of working capital. This in turn allows the firm to settle its own bills faster, gaining early-payment discounts and a good credit rating.

5 **Reducing stock**

A major item on most balance sheets is stock (see Chapter 17). This again represents resources tied up, which **might** be released to work more profitably in the business. Stock levels may be run down by temporarily reducing output, reducing prices or intensifying the marketing effort. However, the firm must be careful that the value of lost sales or a dented reputation through the greater likelihood of running out of stock does not outweigh the savings.

▶ A firm can reallocate resources inside the business. For example, surplus land might be sold to finance some new vehicles.

6 **Asset sales**

Any asset held by the company carries an opportunity cost, i.e. the loss of benefits arising from the next best use of those resources. A firm can therefore examine its asset stock to find items whose value could be turned into cash and more valuably used elsewhere in the business. This might involve sale of a car park or a surplus warehouse, a piece of underutilized machinery or even the boardroom! There may also be the possibility of rental income from letting underused assets.

▶ Gearing

Gearing

The **financial gearing** of a firm means the proportion of capital employed held as debt, or the ratio between debt and equity (share capital). Taken together, debt and equity act as the driving force of the firm. Their combined action provides the dynamic for production. Their relative sizes represent a gearing relationship (see Chapter 30).

Gearing

A firm is financed by £400,000 in ordinary share capital and £100,000 in long-term loans.

$$\text{gearing ratio} = \frac{\text{debt}}{\text{equity + debt}} = \frac{£100{,}000}{£500{,}000} = 20 \text{ per cent}$$

The gearing ratio has critical implications. Equity yields no fixed rate of return: dividend levels can be determined by the directors. Debt carries an interest rate and interest is an obligatory payment beyond the directors' control. Thus the level of dividends can be related to the firm's performance, but interest must be paid regardless of performance.

▶ As profitability falls, a high-geared firm risks reaching the point at which total profits fail to cover interest payable. If no other sources of ready cash exist, the business may be forced into liquidation.

For a fuller understanding of gearing, consider this analogy: on a bicycle in a high gear you go very fast downhill. Stay in high gear going uphill and you will go slower and slower. Follow the same route in a low gear and you will break no speed records on the downhill section, but equally you will continue to make reasonable progress uphill. Business enterprises have 'uphill' and 'downhill' stretches and their gearing has parallel implications.

Work carefully through the following example to make notes on gearing.

Effects of Different Gearing Ratios

Blue Ltd and Red Ltd are identical companies, except in one respect: they differ in gearing.

	Blue (£k)	**Red** (£k)
total equity	800	400
total debt (interest 10%)	200	600
capital employed	1,000	1,000
gearing	20%	60%

The rate of interest on debt is 10%.

Consider the following results (all amounts in £k):

Year 1: return on capital of 24%

	Blue (£k)	**Red** (£k)
operating profit	240	240
interest payment	20	60
profit before tax	220	180
tax @ 25%	55	45
profit after tax	165	135
return on equity	20.62%	33.75%
interest cover	12	4

It is essential to understand each of the steps above:

- a 24% return on £1 million capital employed means an operating profit of £240,000
- the interest and tax payments involve simple arithmetic
- the return on equity = $\dfrac{\text{profit after tax}}{\text{total equity}} \times 100$
- the interest cover is the number of times that operating profit will 'cover' the interest payable

Now examine the results for years 2 and 3 below.

Year 2: return on capital of 12%

	Blue (£k)	**Red** (£k)
operating profit	120	120
interest payment	20	60
profit before tax	100	60
tax @ 25%	25	15
profit after tax	75	45
return on equity	9.37%	11.25%
interest cover	6	2

▶ High gearing can be a particular temptation to firms when rapid expansion seems possible.

Year 3: return on capital of 6%

	Blue (£k)	**Red** (£k)
operating profit	60	60
interest payment	20	60
profit before tax	40	0
tax @ 25%	10	0
profit after tax	30	0
return on equity	3.75%	0%
interest cover	3	1

When return on capital is **above** the interest rate, shareholders will do best from high-geared Red. Its return on equity will be better than low-geared Blue, which means:

(a) there is more available per share for dividends;
(b) the market price of the shares will rise.

Parity occurs when return on capital **exactly matches** the interest rate (10 per cent). Low-geared Blue has twice as much profit to distribute to shareholders, but twice as many shareholders to distribute it to.

When return on capital falls **below** the interest rate, high-geared Red's return on equity falls below Blue's. Red has fewer shareholders to distribute to, but has spent almost all its profits on interest.

The lowest return on capital at which Red can meet its interest payments from earnings is 6 per cent. Blue has a safer rating: it need only achieve 2 per cent.

The situation can be shown graphically:

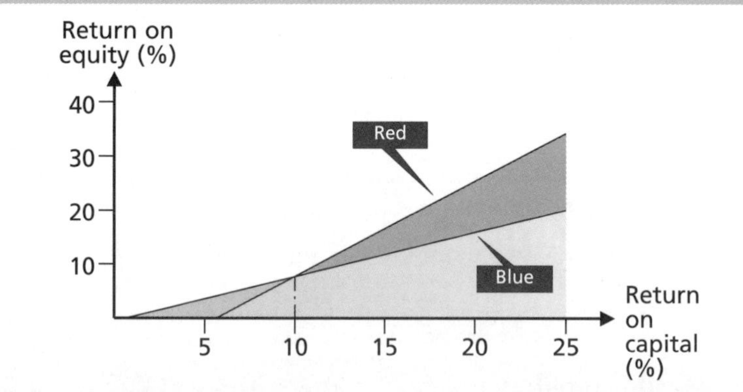

Figure 22.1
Return on equity and return on capital

Once interest cover sinks below 1, the firm can only meet its fixed interest obligations by using some part of its assets to fill the gap. In short, it is living on borrowed time.

Read case studies A and B and answer the questions below each.

A: Derby Designs Ltd

Derby Designs Ltd produces original designs and full-scale prototypes for the engineering industry. Rising costs and flat sales led to a depressed profit of £30,000 in 1995. This was in relation to £300,000 in owners' equity and £180,000 in long-term liabilities. Now Nick Woodthorpe, the managing director, has decided that a £120,000 investment in new computer equipment is the only way to improve performance. Jim Hance, the finance director, has arranged funding through a long-term loan, with interest on this and all other borrowing at 15 per cent.

1 Comment carefully on this decision.
2 The actual profit for 1996 showed a disappointing advance to £40,000. Explore the implications of this.

B: Fresco Fabrics Ltd

Fresco Fabrics Ltd has been producing original curtain fabrics on a small scale for five years. The managing director, Liz Bateman, has now obtained the offer of a breakthrough contract to supply the John Lewis Partnership. An expansion of capital is essential and Mr Kimber, the company accountant, estimates that £30,000 in new finance is required for additional machinery. At present the firm is funded by £50,000 in shareholders' equity and £20,000 in long-term loans. Being a small private company, none of the directors/shareholders are able to put forward any further finance of their own.

1 Make a checklist of all the sources of funds mentioned in this chapter.
2 From this list select three possible fund-raising strategies for Mr Kimber to investigate.
3 Assess the advantages and disadvantages of these options.

Evaluation

- The range of options in obtaining finance depends very much on the size and status of the firm and the nature of the intended investment. Large firms have major advantages in their access to public share subscription, institutional backing and international capital markets. They are regarded as a lower risk and can borrow at reduced rates of interest.
- In general, high-risk projects normally require equity finance, while investments with more predictable earnings may be funded by term loans. A need for additional working capital can be met by short-term bank loans, by retained profits or from other internal sources. However, each industry, each firm and each financial need is different and funding approaches vary widely.
- The relative cost of finance from different sources must be carefully assessed. Debt finance is loaded with an interest rate, which may be variable. Equity finance requires a reward to shareholders in dividends and should generate retained profits. Internal finance carries an opportunity cost which may be difficult to isolate.

- As the term, risk and relative size of a loan increase, so the conditions imposed by the lender are likely to become more demanding. Accordingly, indebtedness may cause management to sacrifice some part of its independence in decision making.
- High gearing is a high-risk strategy. It is advantageous while the rate of return on capital significantly exceeds the rate of interest. A reversal of this relationship will sharply depress profits available for distribution and may pose a potential threat to the solvency of the firm.

23 Investment decisions

Chapter objectives

After working through this chapter, you will:

- understand the meaning and importance of business investment
- be able to use the simple methods of investment appraisal
- know how to use discounted cash flow techniques
- recognize the non-numerate influences on investment decisions
- know the meaning of the following key terms: average rate of return (ARR), payback method, discounted cash flow (DCF), present/net present value, internal rate of return (IRR), required rate of return (criterion rate).

THE MEANING OF INVESTMENT

Every business has fixed assets. These remain in the firm from one trading period to another and represent the capacity of the firm to produce goods and services.

Fixed Assets as Investments

Bridgewater Biscuits Ltd is a small specialist producer of high-quality traditional biscuits. Its fixed assets include: land, office equipment, ovens, loading equipment, computers, processing machines, fixtures and fittings, buildings, vehicles, packing machines.

Unlike the working capital that circulates within the firm, the fixed assets are 'static'. This is the 'hard' structure of the firm, as opposed to the 'soft', more liquid assets that flow through it (see Chapter 29).

The balance sheet values each type of fixed asset and shows their progressive **depreciation** in value. Clearly a point is reached when an item needs replacement. Equally, the business may be expanding and need an extra machine, vehicle or computer. Then again, a new technology may tempt management to purchase equipment on the grounds of increased efficiency. In each case the firm is considering an **investment**.

▶ In 1995–6 British Telecom spent about £2.8 billion on an investment programme to modernize and expand its network.

Any investment will be expected to yield a stream of financial benefits over its life. The extent to which the value of these benefits

▶ Return on investment

exceeds their cost will determine the relevant level of profit - or **return on investment**.

Most firms have a large number of different ideas for investment that they would like to undertake. However, finance is limited and only those projects with the best returns can be selected. In order to identify these, the first step is to relate all the likely returns to the likely costs.

Returns *may include*	Costs *may include*
extra profits on goods/services produced by investment	initial outlay
costs saved	interest on external finance
government grants (if applicable)	depreciation
residual value	opportunity costs of internal finance

▶ **Investment appraisal methods**:
- average rate of return;
- payback method;
- discounted cash flow method.

Investment Appraisal

Analysis of the various costs and returns to show the overall gain or loss to a firm is called **investment appraisal**.

▶ Average rate of return (ARR)

Average Rate of Return and Payback Methods

Average rate of return (ARR) is a simple calculation of the average annual percentage return on the investment. Suppose Bridgewater Biscuits is considering the purchase of a new automated food-processing machine (machine A). Its purchase price is £10,000 and it is expected to produce returns over four years (we will ignore any scrap value in these examples).

Look at the table below. Do not be confused by the terms or layout. 'EOY' stands for 'End of year'. 'Year 0' means now, so 'EOY 1' means 'one year from now'. Remember that 'cash inflows' may represent **reduced costs** as well as additional revenues.

Investment Appraisal by Average Rate of Return

Machine A: ARR analysis

EOY	*inflows/outflows (£)*	
0	-10,000	
1	+3,000	
2	+4,000	
3	+5,000	
4	+6,000	(total inflows = £18,000)
net return	+8,000	(total outflows = £10,000)

$$\text{Average annual rate of return} = \frac{\text{average annual return}}{\text{original investment}}$$

$$= \frac{£8{,}000/4}{£10{,}000} \times 100 = 20\%$$

This means that for each year of its life the machine should make a 20 per cent average return on the original investment.

Now suppose a different machine (B) was also offered to the management. This has identical costs to machine A and will serve the purpose equally well, but its projected returns follow a different pattern.

Machine B: ARR analysis

EOY	*inflows/outflows (£)*
0	–10,000
1	+6,000
2	+5,000
3	+4,000
4	+3,000
net return	+8,000

The ARR equals 20 per cent, exactly as before. Apparently the two machines leave nothing to choose between them. But is this true? Machine B brings maximum returns much sooner than machine A. If the returns were invested each year in a bank account then it is clear that machine B would be preferable. Larger sums would be earning interest for a longer period. This raises a very important issue: **a sum of money to be received at a given date is always more valuable than that same sum received at a later date.**

▶ **ARR advantages:**
- a simple concept, familiar to all business managers;
- easy to calculate.

disadvantage:
- ignores the timing of cash flows.

The **payback method** means calculating the length of time taken by an investment to recover its original outlay.

▶ Payback method

Consider again machines A and B, each requiring an initial outflow of £10,000.

EOY	*inflows/outflows (£)* **Machine A**	**Machine B**
0	–10,000	–10,000
1	+3,000	+6,000
2	+4,000	+5,000
3	+5,000	+4,000
4	+6,000	+3,000
	+8,000	+8,000

Look first at machine A. At EOY 2, total inflows are £7,000; at EOY 3, the total is £12,000. The payback point – when total inflows are equal to the original investment – must occur during year 3. Assuming the inflows are evenly spread over each year, the exact payback point is calculated by interpolation as follows:

Inflows at EOY 2 = £7,000. We need a further £3,000 to reach the original outlay (£10,000). The period EOY 2–3 yields an inflow of £5,000. So £3,000 out of £5,000 should be received after three-fifths of one year:

i.e. $\frac{3}{5} \times 12 \text{ months} = 7.2 \text{ months}$

Therefore the payback period equals 2 years 7 months. The same

▶ **Payback advantages**:
- very simple and quick to use;
- whole focus is on timing of cash flows;
- reflects the risk factor by selecting projects with earliest payback.

disadvantages:
- disregards all cash flows beyond the payback period so fails to measure overall profitability;
- fails to recognize that money received early in the payback period is more valuable than money received later.

calculation for machine B shows a payback period of 1 year 10 months. Clearly there is now a preference for machine B.

▶ Discounted cash flow (DCF)

Discounted Cash Flow (DCF)

This concept is essential to understanding the other two methods of investment appraisal.

We start with an apparently simple question. If the interest rate was 10 per cent, which would you prefer to receive:

(a) £1 now;
(b) £1.15 in a year's time?

If you took the £1 now and invested it at 10 per cent, after one year you would have £1.10. So choice (b) at £1.15 is more valuable than (a). Now consider the option of £1 today or £1.10 in a year's time. It is clear that these two options have the same value: it does not matter which you choose. This establishes an important principle:

1 £1 today is worth £1.10 in a year's time, or
2 £1.10 in a year's time is worth £1 today.

In statement 2, we are saying that £1.10 in a year's time has a **present value** of £1. It is worth looking closely at the simple arithmetic involved.

To increase £1 to £1.10, we multiply by $\frac{110}{100}$ or 1.1

To decrease £1.10 to £1, we multiply by $\frac{100}{110}$ or 0.909

These multiplication factors are useful. Given a 10 per cent interest rate, we can make two further statements:

1 To find the value of any sum in one year, we multiply by 1.1.
2 To find the present value of any sum payable in one year's time, we multiply by 0.909.

We will focus on statement 2. When a sum of money is reduced, we refer to a discount. Thus, when we multiply a sum payable in one year by 0.909, we are using a **discount factor**.

Exactly the same principle applies to sums payable in two, three or any number of years' time. We continue to assume a 10 per cent interest rate.

To find the future value of a sum invested for two years we simply multiply by $\frac{110}{100}$ **twice.**

$$\left(\frac{110}{100}\right)^2 = (1.1)^2 = 1.21$$

So to find the present value of a sum payable in two years' time we multiply by $\frac{100}{110}$ **twice.**

$$\left(\frac{100}{110}\right)^2 = (0.909)^2 = 0.826$$

We can now calculate a series of discount factors:

Interest rate = 10 per cent

Number of years until sum is received	*multiply by*	=	*discount factor*
1	$\left(\frac{100}{110}\right)$		0.909
2	$\left(\frac{100}{110}\right)^2$		0.826
3	$\left(\frac{100}{110}\right)^3$		0.751
4	$\left(\frac{100}{110}\right)^4$		0.683
5	$\left(\frac{100}{110}\right)^5$		0.621

Given a 10 per cent interest rate, it is now easy to calculate any present value.

Examples

What is the present value of: (a) £100 payable in three years' time; (b) £1,500 payable in five years' time?

(a) £100 × 0.751 = £75.10
(b) £1,500 × 0.621 = £931.50

These discounts reflect the time value of money: the further payment is moved into the future, the lower its present value becomes.

Notice that the discount factors become more severe as the cash flows are placed further into the future. This is natural since the amount needed to yield £1 in five years' time will clearly be far smaller than that required to yield £1 in one year.

What would happen if the interest rate increased to 12 per cent? A new table could easily be constructed. To increase a sum by 12 per cent, we multiply it by 112/100. So to discount a sum by 12 per cent, the factor is 100/112, or 0.893. The rest of the arithmetic follows the identical pattern. Fortunately, these discount factors are readily available in a grid without any further calculation (see Appendix 1).

▶ The **present value table** is an appendix at the end of this book (see p. 397).

Now consider the significance of discount factors. Any sum of money to be received at any time in the future can be given a present value. So a firm that has estimated the future cash flows arising from an investment project can convert them to their **true** present value at any relevant rate of interest. This concept is known as **discounted cash flow (DCF)**.

Required Rate of Return
These examples derived the discount factors from a 10 per cent interest rate. In practice, a firm is concerned with the opportunity cost of capital. A project is only advantageous if it can earn more than the next best alternative. The 'next best' might be represented by the overall average rate of return the firm expects from its investments. When this discount rate (in this instance the opportunity cost) is applied to the cash flows, it is called the required rate of return or **criterion rate**.

NPV advantages:
• fully reflects time value of money;
• allows the application of different discount rates according to circumstances, expectations etc.
disadvantages:
• the net present value of a project lacks the clarity of, say, a 10 per cent return on capital. NPV has meaning, but it is not money in the normal sense;
• net present values are not directly comparable when the size of projects differs.

Discounted Cash Flow

Suppose Bridgewater Biscuits is considering two more costly but more highly automated machines, each using improved technology and each costing £15,000. Again, we will assume no residual values. The cash flow projections are as follows:

EOY	*inflows/outflows (£)*	
	Machine C	Machine D
0	–15,000	–15,000
1	+3,000	+11,000
2	+5,000	+8,000
3	+7,000	+4,000
4	+12,000	+2,000
	+12,000	+10,000

Machine C appears to be the best choice since it earns an extra £2,000 over the four-year period (ARR for machine C = 20 per cent, machine D = 16.6 per cent).

But we now know that simply adding up the cash flows is unsatisfactory. The sooner each £1 is received, the greater is its present value. DCF provides a more realistic valuation of projects through the calculation for a series of cash flows (arising from a project) of their **net present values (NPV)**. The arithmetic is simple:

Machine C: NPV calculation (@ 10% interest rate)

EOY	*cash flow (£)*	*discount factor*	*present value (£)*
0	–15,000	1.000	–15,000
1	+3,000	0.909	+2,727
2	+5,000	0.826	+4,130
3	+7,000	0.751	+5,257
4	+12,000	0.683	+8,196
	+12,000	net present value =	+5,310

Machine D: NPV calculation (@ 10% interest rate)

EOY	*cash flow (£)*	*discount factor*	*present value (£)*
0	–15,000	1.000	–15,000
1	+11,000	0.909	+9,999
2	+8,000	0.826	+6,608
3	+4,000	0.751	+3,004
4	+2,000	0.683	+1,366
	+10,000	net present value =	5,997

It is now clear that, contrary to appearances, machine D is the better choice (NPV is greater by £687).

Internal Rate of Return (IRR)

The internal rate of return (IRR) method uses the concept of discounting to give an exact percentage yield for an investment project. It is defined as the rate of discount that will reduce the net present value of a project's cash flows to be exactly equal to zero. This discount rate is called the **internal rate of return (IRR)**. To decide whether a project should go ahead, the IRR can be compared with the firm's required rate of return.

Internal Rate of Return Appraisal

Bridgewater Biscuits is now considering the purchase of a packaging machine (machine E). The estimated cash flows over a three-year life are:

Machine E: IRR calculation (@ 10% discount rate)

EOY	*cash flow (£)*	*discount factor (10%)*	*present value (£)*
0	-5,000	1.000	-5,000
1	+3,000	0.909	+2,727
2	+2,000	0.826	+1,652
3	+1,000	0.751	751
	+1,000	net present value =	130

At a 10 per cent discount rate, the investment rate is profitable. What rate is needed to make NPV zero? A trial and error method is necessary. We will try 12 per cent:

Machine E: IRR calculation (@ 12% discount rate)

EOY	*cash flow (£)*	*discount factor (12%)*	*present value (£)*
0	-5,000	1.000	-5,000
1	+3,000	0.893	+2,679
2	+2,000	0.797	+1,594
3	+1,000	0.712	712
	+1,000	net present value =	-15

A 12 per cent rate has led to a slight 'overshoot' and NPV = -£15. This error is small enough to disregard, though the true IRR is around 11.8 per cent (i.e. the discount rate at which NPV is exactly equal to £0).

A graph helps to clarify the process:

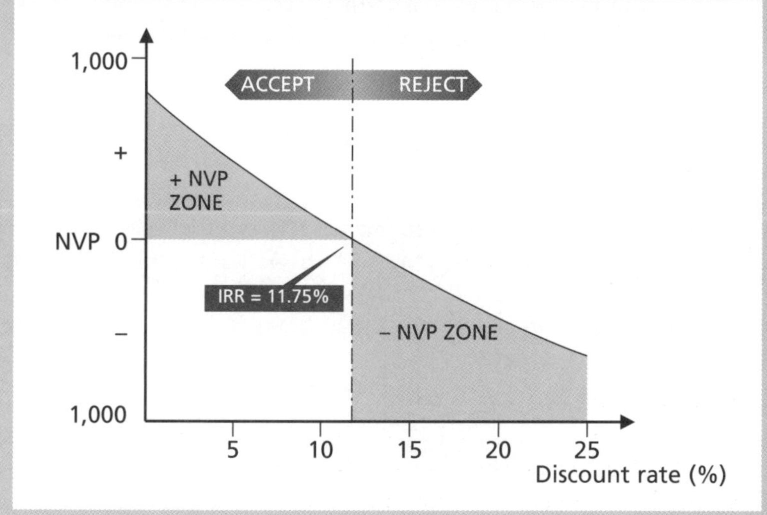

Figure 23.1
Investment appraisal by IRR

▶ **IRR advantages**:
- provides a clearly understood percentage rate of return;
- takes into account the timing of cash flows;
- makes projects of different sizes comparable

disadvantages:
- more complex in calculation.

Explanation

The horizontal axis shows a range of discount rates. At 0 per cent no discounting occurs and cash flows are 'worth' their full value. So NPV = £1,000 (see total of 'cash flow' column in the table above). As the discount rate increases, so the NPV must fall until it reaches zero. This is by definition the IRR – in this case 11.8 per cent. Up to this discount rate the project is profitable, since its NPV is positive. At any discount rate higher than IRR the project becomes unprofitable since its NPV is negative. For the packaging machine to be purchased, the company's required rate of return must not be higher than 11.8 per cent.

Look at the marginal notes on the advantages and disadvantages of different methods of investment appraisal. List the criteria by which these methods are judged. Use the criteria to construct a table – one column per criterion. Write the methods down the side of the table and use ticks or crosses to show how they compare.

Invicta Investments

Invicta Investments is considering project P, which carries an immediate cost of £50,000 and which is expected to yield a stream of returns as follows:

End of year	*1*	*2*	*3*
(£k)	75	15	5

The alternative is project Q, with the same initial cost and a single return of £110,000 at the end of three years. The firm's normal discount rate for investment appraisal is 10 per cent.

1 What are the ARR values of the projects?
2 Project Q does not yield 'payback' for three years. What is the payback period for project P?
3 For each project calculate (a) the net present value and (b) the internal rate of return.
4 What conclusions would you draw about the two investment proposals?

Evaluation

- The stream of future cash flows used in the appraisal methods may be highly inaccurate. It is derived from **expected** sales or cost savings, which may not actually occur. The relevant market research may have been flawed; the equipment or the product may develop faults; hidden expenses may emerge.
- Unexpected levels of competition may develop. Other firms may be about to make the same investment and may be more effective in their marketing.

- New technology always carries risks. 'Teething' problems are common but major failures are always possible.
- In the selection of a project, personalities in the management team may be important. Concealed rivalries and personal ambitions can play a large part in selecting investment projects.
- The human implications of an investment must be considered. Savings through job losses may be rational but any resulting loss of motivation and morale among staff could outweigh the gains. Trade unions might exercise significant power in accepting or rejecting the impact of change.
- Some investments are intangible assets whose benefit to the firm cannot be quantified. For example, the launch of a new logo and house colours may be highly beneficial, but no precise cash returns can be attached to the scheme.
- With the growth of knowledge-based industries, many firms make their biggest investments in **people** through recruitment, training and benefits packages. The financial advantages to the firm depend on the complex process of personnel development and cannot be tabulated in a cash flow statement.
- Interest rates are always important as the ultimate opportunity cost or as the price of borrowed funds. Sharp changes in the interest rate are always possible.
- A major underlying factor is the **economic outlook**. The prospect of recession, where demand for the firm's products may fall steeply, is very discouraging to investment. Managers may prefer to protect their liquid assets and to avoid any new risky exposure to interest rates and problems with interest cover.
- Instability in an industry, a country or in the world raises business risk. All future cash flows carry risk factors and their increase reduces the attraction of investment.

Monopolies, mergers and take-overs

▶ **Media Watch**
For this chapter collect news stories on monopolies, mergers and take-overs.

Chapter objectives

After working through this chapter, you will:

- appreciate how monopolies, mergers and take-overs may threaten the operation of competitive markets
- know how the government attempts to control this problem
- be able to evaluate the arguments for and against large dominant firms
- understand the phenomenon of concentration in industry
- know the meaning of the following key terms: monopoly, merger, demerger, disinvestment, asset stripping, concentration ratio, Monopolies and Mergers Commission, Office of Fair Trading.

MONOPOLIES, MERGERS AND MARKETS

▶ If competition in a market is such that every firm is equally efficient in producing the same product at one ruling price, then **perfect competition** exists.

What is to prevent any firm from raising its prices and profits, lowering its product quality and offering a reduced level of customer service? Always and everywhere the answer is **competition**. The more competitive the market, the less the opportunity exists for any firm to exploit the consumer through excessive prices or inferior quality. Indeed, competition tends to bring about the most efficient methods of production, the highest quality and the lowest prices.

Collect news stories on monopolies and mergers from the financial pages and annotate them to show what they illustrate.

The Problem of Monopoly

▶ In real markets firms are spread on a spectrum between perfect competition and pure monopoly.

Where one firm is literally the sole supplier of a product, then a **pure monopoly** exists. In the real world, however, there is generally some competition and only a degree of monopoly power occurs. This situation may work against the consumer by:

- keeping prices artificially high to yield excessive profits;
- protecting inefficiency and lack of quality;
- removing the incentive for research and innovation.

In Britain a monopoly is not illegal. But the force of law is available to break up an existing monopoly or to prevent a monopoly being formed if it is thought to be against the **public interest**. The term public interest is rather vague. Essentially, the law is hostile to monopoly unless special circumstances suggest that its drawbacks are outweighed by some wider benefit. For example, a monopoly might be necessary to achieve vital economies of scale or to compete effectively in export markets or to maintain employment in a development area.

▶ Where governments wish to ensure the fair and efficient operation of a free market economy, they must set the rules for business competition. The government acts in the market as a kind of 'referee'.

Monopoly Power

The essence of monopoly power lies in the exclusion of competition from a given market. This can occur in the following ways:

- **Resource concentration** in one geographical area may allow one firm to gain control over the major supply of a key product. This can occur with certain minerals and agricultural goods (e.g. diamonds from South Africa or certain wines from regions of France).
- **Minimum efficient scale (MES)** for an industry may be so high that there is only room in the market for one firm to harness the full economies of scale. Would-be competitors producing on a smaller scale face impossibly high unit costs.
- **Marketing barriers** occur when one or more dominant brands are heavily advertised and very widely distributed. Competitors may find it prohibitively expensive to launch a new brand and gain trade acceptance.
- **Transport costs** in supplying certain distant markets may prevent any competitive challenge to a local firm without such costs.
- **Small and captive markets** allow monopoly when the market is too small to support more than one firm (e.g. a taxi service in a small town) or when the market is 'captive' in a particular circumstance (e.g. a theatre bar or a train buffet).
- **Restrictive practices** create artificial monopolies through firms making agreements to restrict competition (see below).
- **Legal monopolies** exist where one firm is granted sole rights of supply. This occurs in state-owned industries (e.g. the Post Office), in issue of official licences (e.g. broadcasting franchises), and in patent protection.

▶ MES: see Chapter 13.

▶ In 1997 Grand Metropolitan and Guinness announced their intention to merge, forming GMG Brands, with an annual turnover of £13 billion.

It is important also to understand that virtually every firm tries to gain some monopoly power by being different from competitors. All brands, logos and trademarks establish a unique identity for a firm and its products. Such outcomes of marketing strategies create a form of monopoly. If consumers consider substitutes to be inferior, then the firm concerned will enjoy benefits such as higher margins or larger market share. But the pressure of competition remains and consumers can switch brands if they find better value for money elsewhere.

What are Anti-Competitive Practices?

So monopoly in itself is not necessarily a serious problem. But a threat to the public interest can arise from two or more firms using their combined market power to prevent fair competition in the market.

Typical anti-competitive practices include:

- **price agreements**, where firms deliberately maintain prices at an artificially high level;

▶ Anti-competitive practices 'jam' the price mechanism and prevent the efficient allocation of resources.

▶ The household detergent market is dominated by Unilever and Procter & Gamble. High fixed capital and marketing costs combine to form a barrier against competitors.

- **cartels**, where a group of firms agree on output or price, or collaborate to share out the market between them;
- **control of distribution or retail outlets**, where powerful firms threaten their customers with a block on supplies if competitor products are stocked;
- **excessive advertising or sales promotion**, when dominant firms allow battles between competing brands to add a major layer to their cost structures.

In some of these monopoly scenarios the law does not interfere. Only when the law is actually broken or where there is evidence of harm to the public interest do firms face the ultimate threat of legal action.

Monopoly Legislation

The major laws relating to monopoly and competition are:

- **Monopolies and Restrictive Practices Act, 1948**: This set up the Monopolies and Mergers Commission (MMC) to investigate actual or potential monopolies and to advise the government on necessary action.
- **Fair Trading Act, 1973**: This established the Office of Fair Trading (OFT) – headed by the Director-General of Fair Trading (DGFT) – to refer cases to the MMC and generally to protect consumer interests.
- **Restrictive Trade Practices Act, 1976** (original Act 1956): This requires registration of any agreement between firms to restrict competition (e.g. charging common prices or supplying only approved dealers) and provides for legal judgement on agreements by a Restrictive Practices Court.
- **Resale Prices Act, 1976**: This prohibits any agreements between suppliers and retailers to enforce a minimum price at which goods may be sold (books and medicines are exempted). **Recommending** a resale price is not illegal.
- **Competition Act, 1980**: This made any anti-competitive practices by firms subject to investigation and ultimate prohibition.

Mergers

It is inevitable that successful companies will grow. Their very success will attract resources. Growth may occur through:

- internal resources, e.g. ploughed-back profits or new share issues
- obtaining loans
- merging with other companies

▶ Mergers and take-overs are likely to bring a direct and immediate increase in market share.

A merger is the combination of two or more separate companies into a single business entity. The process can be by mutual agreement, where most of the owners exchange their shares for equity in the newly enlarged company. In many cases, however, one firm is clearly dominant and the merger becomes a take-over or acquisition. This involves one company making a bid for the other in order to gain a controlling interest (more than 50 per cent of the equity), often against the wishes of directors in the company acquired.

Many of Britain's largest firms were formed through mergers. This is evident in such names as NatWest Bank or Cadbury-Schweppes. In other cases one name embraces many formerly independent companies, e.g. Hanson, BTR, Trafalgar House. The record shows that mergers tend to occur in short periods of intense activity. The last two 'merger booms' occurred in 1967–72 and 1984–9. There has also been increased merger activity since the mid-1990s.

Why Do Mergers Take Place?

In each case there are usually several reasons and the importance of each depends on business circumstances. The main motives are:

- **Economies of scale**: a merger brings an immediate increase in the scale of business, often causing a fall in the average cost of production, marketing, administration and other functions (see Chapter 13 for details). The greatest economies are likely in capital-intensive flow production, where the high fixed cost of specialized plant can be spread over a larger output.
- **Market strength**: a merger usually increases market share and can reduce the pressure of competition.
- **Risk reduction**: a larger firm may be better able to survive downturns in the market or a more general recession. Mergers are also often a route to **diversification**, where a widened product and market range is expected to increase security or growth.
- **Defensive strategies**: mergers may themselves be defensive. A firm that is relatively small and weak may recognize that a merger is inevitable. The aim is then to secure the most favourable partner and the best terms for shareholders.
- **Complementary products and markets**: the products of two firms may be thought likely to make an effective match, so reducing costs and increasing strength in the market. Equally, firms may have complementary markets with strengths in different geographical areas or distribution networks.
- **Acquisition targets**: mergers may be driven by a firm's desire to obtain the markets, customers, brands, patents, technologies or staff of another competitor company.
- **Asset valuation**: one firm may bid for another on the basis that its market value (share price x issued shares) is below the true value of its assets. If successful in this strategy, the new owners may sell off unwanted divisions or subsidiaries of the firm taken over, so recouping part of the purchase price. There may also be opportunities for **asset stripping**, where the new owners sell certain items of property and plant, so yielding positive cash flow and a proportional capital gain.
- **Managerial motives**: managers may be encouraged in merger plans by the prospect of increased status and rewards. Expansion can become an end in itself as the ambitions of senior staff are fuelled by a succession of acquisitions.

▶ Economies of scale, see Chapter 13.

▶ It is important to notice that today's high standard of living in the industrial world is underpinned by a relatively small number of very large firms operating in world markets. Low unit costs achieved through their vast scale of production are supported by huge research budgets and an ethos of constant innovation.

The Merger Process

When one firm is bidding for another, it may offer the shareholders of the target firm one or a combination of the following:

- a cash price per share
- its own shares
- fixed-interest loan stock (i.e. IOUs or certificates of indebtedness bearing a fixed rate of interest).

The method of payment may have important consequences for the successful bidder's gearing ratio once the merger is complete.

▶ Gearing ratio, see Chapter 30.

An outright bid is often preceded by the predator building up a significant stake in the equity of the target firm. This might be purchased by a public company in a **dawn raid** – a surprise burst of buying activity on the Stock Exchange at the start of the trading day. Once an intention to bid is announced, the firm has twenty-eight days to make a formal offer.

▶ A famous dawn raid occurred on 13 April 1988 when the Swiss chocolate makers Suchard took thirty-five minutes to build a 35 per cent stake in Rowntree. This raised the curtain on a take-over battle in which Nestlé won the final victory.

The procedure for bids by public companies is regulated by the independent City Take-over Panel. This lays down an exact timetable through which bids may progress and is designed to protect the shareholders of all parties concerned. Time is allowed for the target company to make its case for rejecting the bid and for the bidder to revise its terms. The bid must either succeed or fail within sixty days of the original offer.

Control of Mergers

The main types of merger are:

- **horizontal**, when the firms have similar products (e.g. one brewery buying another);
- **vertical**, when the firms are in the same industry but at different stages in the production chain (e.g. a brewery buys a chain of pubs);
- **lateral**, when the firms are in a related area of business (e.g. a brewery buys a mineral water producer);
- **conglomerate**, where the firms produce unrelated products (e.g. a brewery buys a chain of newsagents).

▶ Monopolies and Mergers Commission (MMC)

Mergers are liable for referral to the MMC when they would create a market share of 25 per cent or higher or when they involve gross assets worth over £70 million. The DGFT assesses merger proposals and makes recommendations to the Trade and Industry Secretary, who then may make a formal referral to the MMC. In practice, the possibility of a referral often deters a planned merger.

▶ Since 1990 the European Union has had the power to investigate and control merger proposals when the companies involved have large-scale sales both worldwide and within the EU.

Mergers in Practice

In some cases mergers may fulfil their declared (and undeclared) aims. But do mergers really improve business efficiency? Do they benefit the shareholders? A significant report (Peacock and Bannock, 1991) finds no evidence that mergers have any positive effect on **overall** business performance. But behind this general judgement lie many successful mergers and many that fail.

▶ Contested take-overs normally increase the value of the target company's shares and this represents a premium to be paid by the bidders. The record suggests a likely fall in post-merger profitability and this premium cost may not be recovered.

All too often the high hopes raised by managers at the time of the merger are never fulfilled. The reasons include:

- **Compatibility**: every firm has a unique 'culture' – a style of action, an outlook, a complex web of loyalties (see Chapter 48). These cultures can be very difficult to merge and the effort may cause resentment, rivalry and general dislocation. Technically, too, different systems of management, accounting, research, sales and marketing may prove hard to combine. Often the expected synergy fails to occur.
- **Cost**: after the merger occurs, all aspects of the combined firm's policy, organization, products, operations and finance must be assessed, restructured and integrated. This carries real costs and may cause conflict and upheaval. In addition, the management time and energy expended have a heavy opportunity cost.
- **Industrial relations**: mergers are likely to cause redeployment and redundancy. Among employees a mood of uncertainty prevails. New teams of managers may wish to change established methods of negotiation and communication. Morale and motivation may fall, disputes may increase and key staff may leave.
- **Diseconomies of scale**: gains in efficiency are often less than planned, while the firm's increased complexity and scale can cause unexpected problems. Proportional administrative expenses may rise, the arteries of decision making may become clogged and responsiveness to change may diminish.

Demergers

Sometimes these factors lead to a **demerger**, when a previous merger is broken up. For example, the tyre makers Dunlop and Pirelli demerged in the 1980s. More recently, there has been a wider trend for diversified firms to break up into smaller units that serve specific markets. Smaller-scale demergers may take place when particular components of a merged business are sold off (this is called **disinvestment**). In their book *In Search of Excellence*, Peters and Waterman (1982) advised firms to 'stick to the knitting'. This meant that organizations should concentrate on certain core areas of excellence which were their real source of profitability and long-term competitive advantage. The result has often involved management buy-outs for those activities which fall outside the range of 'refocused' business (see Chapter 3).

▶ ICI demerged its pharmaceuticals division in 1993 under the name Zeneca. Hanson, a transnational conglomerate, began demerger operations to create four new companies in 1996.

Business Concentration

An industry whose output is dominated by a few very large firms is said to be highly **concentrated**. The degree of concentration is usually measured by a **five-firm concentration ratio**. This is calculated as follows:

$$\frac{\text{sales of 5 largest firms}}{\text{total industry sales}} \times 100$$

Five-firm Concentration Ratio

An industry includes ten firms with total UK sales of £550 million in 1997:

Firm	*Sales (£m)*	*Firm*	*Sales (£m)*
1	126	6	33
2	121	7	24
3	80	8	19
4	64	9	15
5	60	10	8

Five-firm concentration ratio

$$= \frac{126 + 121 + 80 + 64 + 60}{550} = \frac{451}{550} \times 100 = 82\%$$

It is clear that this industry is dominated by a few large firms – a situation that is called **oligopoly**. Suppose that firm 2 makes a take-over bid for firm 6. If successful, the result would be a rise in the concentration ratio to 88 per cent and an increase in firm 2's market share from 22 per cent to 28 per cent. Thus the bid would be liable for referral to the MMC.

▶ United Biscuits owns many major brands such as McVities biscuits, KP crisps and Ross frozen foods.

▶ In 1994 Unilever bought 56 companies which formed half the company's total growth that year.

The extent of actual concentration varies widely in British business.

UK five-firm concentration ratios

	%
Leather goods	13.1
Toys and sports goods	18.0
Footwear	38.8
Industrial chemicals	47.8
Soap and toiletries	54.3
Ice-cream and confectionery	65.3
Motor vehicles and engines	84.1
Synthetic fibres	93.2
Tobacco	98.8

Source: Central Statistical Office, Business Monitor *PA1002, 1991*

These ratios give only a general indication of an industry's competitive structure. Much depends on how we define the industry and on how many other firms exist apart from the five largest. The real issue is power in a particular market. The size of a firm alone does not necessarily correspond with market power. A conglomerate may be a very large firm yet lack a dominant share of any one market.

A common defence by firms in highly concentrated industries is to argue that the consumer benefits from producers large enough to exploit fully the technical economies of scale. Much depends on the minimum efficient scale (MES) for the industry concerned. The MES for industrial diesel engines is very high and represents over 50 per cent of the UK market. To split the market between, say, five firms would lead to inefficiency. In the case of washing powder, the MES is equivalent only to about 10 per cent of the UK market. This implies that ten firms could share the market without any necessary loss of efficiency.

Annual sales in a major consumer goods industry are as follows:

Firm	*Sales (£m)*	*Firm*	*Sales (£m)*
A	280	E	126
B	244	F	73
C	205	G	48
D	189	others	37

Firm A now announces a hostile take-over bid for Firm F.

1. On what grounds might the Monopolies and Mergers Commission object to this bid?
2. How might Firm A claim that the take-over was in the public interest?
3. Calculate the industry's five-firm concentration ratio, before and after the proposed take-over.

Evaluation

- Few MMC reports lead to any legal action by the government. Equally, even the threat of an MMC referral causes many firms to end anti-competitive activities. MMC recommendations are usually accepted on a voluntary basis.
- Only 1 to 2 per cent of all proposed mergers are actually prevented through the mechanisms of UK merger control. However, a major effect may be preventative, with many potential mergers never being proposed.
- Investigations by the MMC are very slow and often take two years or more. However, the MMC's thoroughness and attention to detail are valuable in combating monopolistic practices.
- The emphasis of UK monopoly and merger policy is traditionally on assessment of the public interest. But the balance has shifted towards **competition** as the key criterion. Referral of a merger proposal to the MMC is only likely if it threatens the consumer with higher prices or restricted choice.
- UK monopoly and merger policy has tended to make judgements in the context of the British market alone. Arguably, a merger giving market dominance in Britain may be in the wider national interest of competing effectively with large firms in Europe and the rest of the world.
- The most basic argument for mergers is that they can result in more efficient use of the resources involved. A bid by one firm for another is effectively a claim by the bidder that it could bring better management to bear on the other firm's resources.
- It is difficult to assess the performance of individual firms after a merger since published accounts do not yet demand any breakdown of results.

- There is widespread evidence that a **threat** to firms of being taken over can in itself act as a spur to greater efficiency. However, this can lead to short-termism among managers, who may, for example, cut the research budget in order to keep up apparent profits.
- Mergers carry both costs (e.g. reduced competition) and benefits (e.g. economies of scale) to firms and to society. A cost–benefit assessment would attempt to balance the positive and negative effects on the public interest.

Part 5

Accounts

 The meaning of accounts

Chapter objectives

After working through this chapter, you will:

- appreciate what is meant by the term accounts
- be able to outline the major accounting statements
- understand the key accounting concepts
- be able to distinguish the main users of accounts
- know the key contents of a company annual report
- know the meaning of the following key terms: balance sheet, profit and loss account, cash flow statement, assets (fixed and current), financial accounts, management accounts.

THE ACCOUNTING PROCESS

A business enterprise is a complex system with many resources involved, both material and human. These resources are managed by the directors on behalf of the firm's shareholders or legal owners. Naturally, the directors will be expected to keep accurate daily records to show how these resources were used and how they increased or decreased in quantity. For convenience, money is used as a common language to express these events and changes.

There are two aspects to the accounting process. The first is the recording of all financial transactions as they occur - purchases, sales, payment of wages, receipt of debts, etc. This task is called **book-keeping**, though with growing computerization it is more properly known as **data processing**. The second aspect is the periodic statements of account that summarize all the detailed financial events taking place from day to day.

▶ Book-keeping and data processing

▶ Financial accounts

The standards of company accounting are governed by the Companies Acts, 1985 and 1989, and by the Financial Reporting Council (FRC), whose members are appointed by the Bank of England and the Secretary of State for Trade and Industry. Answerable to the FRC is the Accounting Standards Board (ASB), which represents the major professional accounting organizations in Britain. Formed in 1990, the ASB issues Financial Reporting Standards (FRSs), which specify the required content and format of the published accounting statements.

▶ Until 1990, the ASB's predecessor, the Accounting Standards Committee, issued Statements of Standard Accounting Practice (SSAPs). Some of these are still in force.

▶ The balance sheet is dealt with in detail in Chapter 26.

▶ The profit and loss account is dealt with in detail in Chapter 27.

▶ The cash flow statement replaced the old funds flow statement in 1991 under FRS1.

The Major Accounting Statements

1 **The balance sheet**
This is a summary statement that shows a firm's sources of finance and their main corresponding uses at a given date.

2 **The profit and loss account**
This starts by stating the **sales revenue** from trading activity and then shows a series of deductions for each major type of cost until the trading profit (or loss) remains. After taking into account any costs or revenues arising from non-trading activities, the profit after tax is divided between dividends and **retentions** (funds ploughed back into the business). This figure is then transferred to the balance sheet.

3 **The cash flow statement**
This statement gives details of all cash inflows and outflows occurring over the accounting period. It opens with cash flows arising from ordinary operations and then summarizes those arising from financial investments and loans, taxation and capital investment. It ends by showing cash flow financing: how the firm used its net cash inflow or how it financed its net outflow.

Accounting Concepts

Separate Entity
This simply means that each business can be identified as existing in its own right, with corresponding assets, liabilities and shareholders'/owners' investment. We are able to define the affairs of the enterprise through its existence as a separate entity. This concept, which should not be confused with legal identity, is applied to any type of business organization.

Going Concern
When compiling accounts for a business enterprise, it is assumed to have the intention of continuing trading into the foreseeable future. If its liquidation was expected shortly, then the valuation of its assets would probably be different.

Money Measurement
Money is the common unit for the compilation of accounts. The single 'language' of money also allows accountants to make comparisons between one firm and another, and between different periods of time. Note that the changing value of money (inflation) presents special problems (see below).

Objectivity
Accounting always requires an element of human judgement. This may not involve any personal bias by the firm or its accountants. The consistent view of a detached observer must be adopted, i.e. an objective view.

Accruals
An accrual is an amount due that has not yet been paid. In any accounting period the firm must include all expenses incurred in

that period regardless of when they are actually payable. Likewise, it must include all income earned in that period irrespective of whether cash has yet been received. This principle ensures that costs and revenues are properly **matched**.

Materiality

Accountants must show all data that is material (i.e. necessary) to presenting a 'true and fair view' of the firm's affairs. This means that trivial detail may legitimately be left unspecified, while all significant (material) items must be disclosed.

Consistency

The potential to make valid comparisons is crucial to the value of accounting data. This is only possible if each set of accounts is based on consistent (the same) rules and definitions. If a firm changes its accounting rules, then this must be explained clearly to the user.

Prudence

Also called conservatism, the principle of prudence means that accountants will always adopt the least favourable estimate of likely outcomes. This means that any probable losses are acknowledged immediately, while expected profits are recorded only when actually realized (either as cash or as a sound debt).

Accounting and Inflation

Traditionally, accounting practice has been based on the assumption that money has a constant value. This is reflected in the practice of **historical cost accounting**, which treats all money quantities at face value regardless of the **time period** to which they relate. Until the late 1960s the UK annual inflation rate was under 5 per cent and the effect on accounts was probably not too serious. Far higher rates in some years since then have caused serious concern about their distorting effect on company accounts.

▶ Say the inflation rate is 5 per cent. A company announces profits of £700 million, up from £680 million last year. This apparent rise really represents a fall in profits since merely to keep up with inflation, a profit of £714 million would be necessary.

Accounting is based on money as a unit of value. Inflation reduces the value of money over time (see Chapter 41). Thus if the true value of the pound is constantly falling, then money values shown in accounts are potentially misleading. A range of problems emerges:

- How can previous years' profits be compared to the current year if the value of money has changed?
- How is the firm's profit on a sale affected if the replacement stock has increased in price?
- What is the true value of the firm's assets?
- How can a firm allow for depreciation (wearing out) of an asset when its purchase price is constantly changing?

Problems such as these led the accountancy profession to adopt a new system based on **current costs** in 1980 (SSAP 16). However, much lower inflation rates in the mid-1980s led to its abandonment (1985) and a return to traditional historical cost methods. In short, the problems have not been resolved.

Who Uses Accounts?

Accounting statements divide into two categories. **Formal financial accounts** are supplied in various forms to meet needs external to the firm's management. These needs arise from:

- **shareholders** who own the firm and wish to monitor the management of their investment;
- **employees/unions** who wish to assess the prospects in such matters as wage rises, working conditions and job security;
- **lenders/creditors** who need to know if the firm is likely to be a good risk in meeting debt repayments or settling outstanding bills;
- **customers** who need assurance that their supplies of particular products are secure;
- **local communities/councils** who need to consider such factors as employment changes, environmental planning and housing needs;
- **the government** when compiling national economic and business statistics that guide many decisions concerning the economy, tax revenues, assistance to regions, etc.

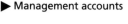

For needs internal to the firm's management, accounting statements are produced in much greater detail and with greater frequency. These **management accounts** (i.e. accounts to assist management) are normally confidential and relate to particular areas of the firm's operation. They are the vital data used by managers to control the firm and guide it towards agreed objectives. Careful analysis of detailed accounts will also provide warning signals of dangers ahead as well as indicating gateways of possible opportunity.

Coburn Castings plc

Coburn Castings plc manufactures aluminium components and is a major industrial supplier. The firm is located on an industrial estate on the edge of a medium-sized Midlands town. There is a substantial housing estate nearby and the firm is one of the largest local employers.

The company had enjoyed buoyant markets during the mid-1990s but lately there has been talk of difficulties. No one seems sure how serious these are.

For each of the following four scenarios, state who might wish to see the accounts and why:

1. Management announces that reduced demand means that redundancy notices will be served on 400 of the plant's 1,200 staff.
2. To assist in financing a new labour-saving technology, the firm proposes borrowing £8 million.
3. The firm accepts the need for pollution filters to be fitted to its two main chimneys. The cost will be £1.5 million. However, the board can only find sufficient funds for the work to be carried out in two years' time.
4. It is strongly rumoured in the City that a take-over bid is about to be announced for Coburn Castings by its main competitor.

Published Company Annual Reports and Accounts

All public companies issue an Annual Report and Accounts. These contain much interesting information and are very useful for students.

The best way to make notes on the following sections is to obtain your own copy of the published accounts of a company, then to look for the following nine features and annotate them.

▶ **Company accounts**
The published accounts and reports of companies are interesting documents. They are freely available from the head office of public companies. Addresses can be found in the trade directories in your public library. Make a selection of companies and request their annual report and accounts.
You can also find the accounts of some leading companies on the Internet (http:/www.bized.ac.uk/). The layout and information is specially designed for Business Studies students.

1 **Highlights**
Includes a summary of financial results, perhaps with brief reports of newsworthy events in company affairs.

2 **Chairman's statement**
Features an overview of the company's trading year. It normally adopts an upbeat and optimistic tone.

3 **Product and trading information**
Often a lengthy and glossy section, indicating the range of the firm's activities. It acts as a kind of showcase.

4 **Directors' report**
This serves as an introduction to the formal accounts. The material is factual, explaining the nature of the firm's business, its financial structure, its provisions for employees, and any legal or technical notices.

▶ Published accounts are only summary statements. The detailed financial data from which management accounts are prepared remains confidential.

5 **The accounts**
These include:

- the 'profit and loss account' (see Chapter 27)
- the balance sheet (see Chapter 26)
- the cash flow statement

6 **Accounting policies**

A summary of the firm's broad approach to matters of accounting practice, e.g. valuation of stock.

7 **Notes to the accounts**
Provide detailed explanation of items specified in the main accounting statements.

8 **Auditors' report**
A legally required statement from an independent external firm of accountants. This confirms that the published accounts have been checked and represent 'a true and fair view of the state of affairs of the Company'.

9 **Notice of meeting**
Gives the date and venue for the next annual general meeting, which all shareholders are entitled to attend to exercise their vote.

Disclosure of accounting information is required by the Companies Acts. Copies of accounts for all companies - private as well as public - may be inspected at Companies House in Swansea.

During the late 1980s there was a growing demand for companies to disclose more financial information, and to make it more comparable and more readily comprehensible. The Cadbury Report (1992) made detailed recommendations to this effect and, although it carried no legal force, has led to some real improvements.

However, it should be appreciated that published accounts are only summary statements. The detailed financial data from which management accounts are prepared remains confidential.

Evaluation

- Accounts organize vital financial data relating to firms within a logical and consistent framework. Useful analysis and comparisons can be made by external parties.
- In Britain, high professional standards are generally maintained. These are required by the law, the Accounting Standards Board and the professional associations.
- Accounts are expressed in money terms. This is convenient but cannot express all the variables affecting a firm, e.g. qualities in the staff.
- Despite appearances, accounts are only ever approximations. Human judgement plays a major part in their formulation.
- Although firms have major financial objectives, there is a risk of attaching excessive significance to accounting data alone. Non-financial factors can be critical to the firm yet easily be overlooked, e.g. staff morale, attitudes to change.

26 The balance sheet

Chapter objectives

After working through this chapter, you will:

- be able to make double entry changes in a balance sheet
- know precisely the meaning of items typically found on a balance sheet
- know how to convert T-form into vertical format
- know the meaning of the following key terms: shareholders' funds, long-term liabilities, current liabilities, fixed assets, current assets, net assets, goodwill, capital employed, net working capital, accruals, dividends, retained profits, depreciation, authorized share capital, called-up share capital, reserves.

THE SIMPLE T-FORM BALANCE SHEET

A balance sheet is simply a periodic listing of resources in use, with a corresponding list of how those resources were obtained. The two lists are therefore equal by definition (and are said to 'balance'). A balance sheet is always given an exact date, since in any active business the sources and uses of resources are continually changing (e.g. a bank loan is arranged, a new machine is purchased, more stock arrives, more sales are made, etc.). The basic pattern of balance sheet is called 'T-form' because of its outline shape.

▶ A balance sheet lists the sources and uses of a firm's funds. The total value of these two lists is automatically equal.

The Balance Sheet in Horizontal Format

The Big Bag Co Ltd
Balance Sheet as at 31 March 1997

Sources of funds	(£k)	Uses of funds	(£k)
shareholders' funds		fixed assets	
ordinary £1 shares	42	land and buildings	40
retained profits	24	machinery	22
		vehicles	17
long-term liabilities			
bank loans	30	current assets	
		stock	16
current liabilities		debtors	12
creditors	19	cash	8
	115		115

▶ **Assets**
Fixed assets with which the firm operates the production process and which remain continuously in the firm's possession, e.g. land, buildings, machinery.
Current assets that circulate quickly through the firm, e.g. stocks, money owing (debtors), cash.
Ordinary £1 shares represent the original value of the shares issued to finance the business.
Retained profits belong to the shareholders. This is the part of the profits from previous years not taken as dividends but ploughed back into the business.
Creditors: other firms (e.g. suppliers) whose bills have not yet been paid.
Debtors: customers who have not yet paid Big Bag Co.

▶ The finance of assets is divided between:
• **Long-term liabilities**: borrowings that need not be repaid for at least twelve months.
• **Current liabilities**: include any amounts owing that must be repaid within twelve months.

▶ Double entry rules do not exist in order to make the two sides balance but because the two sides balance by definition.

Double Entry Changes

A balance sheet is like a financial cross-section through a firm at a particular point in time. Although balance sheets are normally only drawn up at intervals, a new balance sheet could be published every day or even every hour! Each time it would be slightly different as events involving the firm's resources unfold. Each event requires a **double entry**.

The double entry principle is easy to apply in practice. All examples below relate to the Big Bag Co during the first week in April.

1 Issue extra 8,000 £1 ordinary shares and pay the money into bank:

Sources of funds	(£k)	Uses of funds	(£k)
shareholders' funds	+8,000	cash	+8,000

The money in the bank appears as extra cash and its source is an increase in the shareholders' funds.

2 Withdraw £8,000 from bank and buy a new machine:

Sources of funds	(£k)	Uses of funds	(£k)
		machinery	+6,000
		cash	–6,000

Cash has been turned into machinery. Sources of funds are not involved.

3 Sell surplus outbuilding for £5,000 and pay the money into bank:

Sources of funds	(£k)	Uses of funds	(£k)
		land and buildings	–5,000
		cash	+5,000

The use of funds in land and buildings falls, with a corresponding rise in cash. Again, sources of funds are unaffected.

4 Withdraw £5,000 cash and repay part of the bank loan:

Sources of funds	(£k)	Uses of funds	(£k)
bank loan	–5,000	cash	–5,000

The use of funds as a cash balance falls, allowing a reduction in the bank loan as a source of funds.

It is now useful to consider the effect of a trading transaction on the balance sheet. Exactly the same principle applies. Say the firm sells a consignment of bags that cost the firm £4,000 to a fashion retailer for £6,000 cash.

Step 1: reduce stock by £4,000
Step 2: increase cash by £6,000

At this point the balance sheet will not balance! The reason is the

£2,000 profit, which must belong to the shareholders and be added to retained profits. So:

Step 3: increase retained profits by £2,000

The result is shown below.

Sources of funds	(£k)	Uses of funds	(£k)
shareholders' funds			
retained profits	+2,000		
		current assets	
		stock	–4,000
		cash	+6,000
	+2,000		+2,000

▶ Now suppose that the transaction had not been for cash but on credit. This does **not** mean that creditors are affected! All entries are exactly the same, except that the £6,000 is entered as debtors (money owing to the firm) instead of cash.

The result of all these changes is:

The Big Bag Co Ltd
Balance Sheet as at 7 April 1997

Sources of funds	(£k)	Uses of funds	(£k)
shareholders' funds		fixed assets	
ordinary £1 shares	50	land and buildings	35
retained profits	26	machinery	28
		vehicles	17
long-term liabilities			
bank loans	25	current assets	
		stock	12
current liabilities		debtors	12
creditors	19	cash	16
	120		120

Make notes on the changes between the two balance sheets. Check your understanding by changing the second balance sheet to account for a further sale of bags costing £2,000 for a price of £3,000.

Items on the Balance Sheet

It is now necessary to look more closely at each section of the balance sheet.

1 Fixed Assets

Tangible Fixed Assets

Tangible fixed assets refer to all physical assets held by the firm to carry on production on a long-term basis ('tangible' literally means 'touchable'). These typically include land, buildings, machinery, equipment and vehicles. Items are generally recorded at their historic (original) cost. However, some assets can appreciate (rise) or depreciate (fall) in value. Thus property is periodically 'revalued' upwards or downwards, while such items as machinery are gradually 'depreciated' (marked down in value) over their useful life. This depreciation is shown as a cumulative total and is subtracted from the historic cost (see Chapter 28).

▶ In 1988 Rank-Hovis-McDougall (now part of Tomkins plc) became the first company to value its brands (Mother's Pride, Hovis, Mr Kipling, Bisto, Paxo and many more) on the balance sheet. These added £678 million to the final assets and to the shareholders' funds.

▶ Fixed assets are called 'fixed' because they remain within the firm. Assets are called 'current' if they are passing through the firm.

Intangible Fixed Assets

Intangible fixed assets mean other long-term sources of value that are not physical. When one firm buys another, it may pay a price in excess of the value of the assets concerned. This premium is called **goodwill** and arises from the value of customer loyalty and probable profits to be earned in the future. Goodwill is entered on the balance sheet, but usually written off quite quickly by an accountant. Patents (the legal right to exploit an invention without competition) and 'trademarks' may also have commercial value and appear on the balance sheet. Some firms now value their brands (e.g. Cadbury Schweppes, United Biscuits) – a subject of much current debate in the accounting profession.

Financial Fixed Assets

Financial fixed assets represent financial holdings of long-term value outside the company. These can include government and local authority stocks (see Chapter 22), debentures or holdings in other companies.

Holdings in Other Companies

If company A holds more than 50 per cent of the ordinary shares of company B, then company B is a **subsidiary** of A. If A holds between 20 and 50 per cent of B, B is an **associated company**. If A holds less than 20 per cent of B, this is simply a **trade investment**.

2 Current Assets

Stock

Stock is usually essential to the process of trading and includes raw materials, work-in-progress and finished goods. All stocks are valued at their cost or, if lower, at their realizable value (value for sale in the market). As stock purchase prices change, so stock value is affected. Firms must choose a consistent method of stock valuation.

Debtors

Debtors refers to amounts owed to the firm by its customers. This is a normal item for most enterprises since the provision of credit is often a competitive necessity in the marketing mix (see Chapter 9).

Cash

Cash includes balances at the bank plus any petty cash and cash not yet paid in.

3 Shareholders' Funds

Also called 'the equity', these resources are the foundation on which the business stands.

Share Capital

All firms have an upper limit on the ordinary or preference share capital that they may raise: this is the **authorized capital**. The **issued capital** is that part of the authorized capital that has already been allotted to shareholders. Initially, the firm may decide only to 'call up' part of the full value for each share. Hence the value shown on the balance sheet is the **called-up share capital**, i.e. that amount of money already paid to the company at a given time. Note that preference shares only feature in the capital structure of some companies (see Chapter 22); ordinary shares are always the major source of share capital.

Reserves

This is simply the name given to profits and surpluses generated over time and forming part of the company's long-term capital. These resources are **not** sums of cash being held back to meet future needs. Indeed, the funds represented by reserves are likely to be invested in buildings, plant and equipment.

▶ Reserves in accounting are not cash reserves.

There are three important types of reserves:

1 **Share premium**: the sale of a company's shares may be at a price above their face value. This surplus is indicated in the share premium reserve.
2 **Revaluation**: certain fixed assets often appreciate in value (e.g. land, buildings), and when revalued on the balance sheet the corresponding double entry is in the revaluation reserve. This adds to the shareholders' funds but cannot be distributed as a dividend.
3 **Profit and loss account (retained profits)**: this is normally the major reserve and represents the accumulated profits retained by the firm to finance the business. The retained profit from an accounting period is usually the largest source of new funding (see Chapter 22). This can be found as the last line in the profit and loss account itself (see Chapter 27).

4 Long-term Liabilities

A firm frequently wishes to obtain additional long-term finance without it becoming permanent in the form of a new share issue. Indeed, if earnings from loan capital exceed the cost in interest payments, then the shareholders' return can be dramatically increased (see Chapter 22). Loan capital may include:

- **Debentures**, which are certificates of indebtedness: the issuing company undertakes to repay the holder the amount specified at a future date and until then to pay interest at a fixed rate.
- **Bank loans** (and loans from other financial institutions) are normally available to businesses for periods of between one and twenty-five years. Both the availability of loans and the rate of interest depend on the amount requested, the period of the loan, the security available and the firm's business 'track record'. In the past, interest rates were often fixed, but the trend is now towards variable rate loans.
- **Mortgages** are long-term loans secured on land and buildings and are available from commercial banks.

5 Current Liabilities

All amounts that will become payable by the firm within twelve months are called current liabilities. They arise mainly through the process of day-to-day trading.

▶ Current liabilities are sometimes called 'creditors due within the year'.

- **Creditors** refers to unpaid bills from other firms (often suppliers). Between one and three months' credit is usually allowable between firms and this trade credit can be an important source of finance.

- **Bank overdraft** means any negative current account bank balance held by the firm. Overdrafts are intended for short-term financial needs and are legally repayable on demand.
- **Provision for tax** represents the size of any expected tax bill. Tax liabilities become payable to the Inland Revenue the year after they were incurred.
- **Dividends payable** are usually announced at six-month intervals as an interim and final dividend. A time-lag occurs between declarations of the final dividend and its payment following approval at the company's annual general meeting. It is treated as a liability from the time of declaration in expectation of its later payment.
- **Accruals** are accumulations of debt for a product or service when charges are not made until after the balance sheet date, e.g. charges for telephones.

Balance Sheet Formats

We will now look at a complete balance sheet, first in the T-form (traditional) format and then in the widely used vertical format.

▶ The left-hand side answers the question of where the resources came from, while the right-hand side answers the question of where the resources are now.

Balance Sheet: T-Form

Premier Paints Ltd
Balance Sheet as at 31st March 1997

Sources of funds	(£k)	(£k)	Uses of funds	(£k)	(£k)
shareholders' funds			fixed assets		
ordinary £1 shares			land and buildings	605	
fully paid	540		plant and equipment	730	
8% preference shares	165		goodwill	80	
share premium reserve	80		investments	120	1,535
revaluation reserve	90				
profit and loss account	475	1,350	current assets		
			stock	420	
			debtors	285	
			cash	110	815
long-term liabilities					
debentures	400				
other loans	210	610			
current liabilities					
creditors	200				
tax provision	115				
dividends payable	75	390			
		2,350			2,350

In practice, most companies today have dropped the T-form balance sheet in favour of a **vertical format**. Once familiar, this is quite straightforward. The data to be entered is unchanged. Only the arrangement of the various sections is different. The two 'sides' must still balance by the same logic. Look briefly through the following vertical format balance sheet. Then read the marginal notes alongside it and check each point for yourself.

Balance Sheet: Vertical Format

Premier Paints Ltd
Balance Sheet as at 31st March 1997

	(£k)	(£k)	(£k)
fixed assets			
land and buildings	605		
plant and equipment	730		
goodwill	80		
investments	120		1,535
current assets			
stock	420		
debtors	285		
cash	110	815	
current liabilities			
creditors	200		
tax provision	115		
dividends payable	75	390	
net working capital			425
net assets			1,960
financed by			
shareholders' funds			
ordinary £1 shares (fully paid)	540		
8% preference shares	165		
share premium reserve	80		
revaluation reserve	90		
profit and loss account	475		1,350
long-term liabilities			
debentures	400		
other loans	210		610
capital employed			1,960

▶ Notes on the vertical format.
1 The presentation of fixed and current assets is exactly as the right-hand side of the T-form.
2 Now current liabilities are subtracted from current assets. The value remaining is the **net working capital** – the net value of the assets circulating in the process of day-to-day business.
3 Fixed assets plus net working capital = **net assets**. This value amounts to the total assets less current liabilities.
4 Finally, add the shareholders' funds to the long-term liabilities to find **capital employed**. This balances with net assets but at a lower figure than the T-form balance. The difference is the current liabilities: this value has been subtracted from both sides of the T-form balance sheet.

Notice that net working capital is also called **net current assets**. Net assets are also called **total assets less current liabilities**.

1 Arrange the data below to form a horizontal balance sheet with clear subtotals for shareholders' funds, long-term liabilities, current liabilities, fixed assets and current assets.
2 Convert this balance sheet into a correctly presented vertical format.

The chief accountant has identified the following items for inclusion in the firm's balance sheet as at 31st March 1997.

	£
property	700,000
dividends payable	25,000
stock	290,000
subsidiaries	110,000
reserves	
revaluation	50,000
retained profits	620,000
cash	95,000
goodwill	45,000
debtors	200,000
issued ordinary £1 shares	444,000
provisions for tax	75,000
creditors	220,000
plant and equipment	
cost	500,000
less accumulated depreciation	160,000
loans (over 12 months)	350,000

Evaluation

- The balance sheet is a key accounting statement required from companies by law.
- Its format is now far more standardized than in the past, making comparisons easier.
- It is the raw material for calculating many key accounting ratios (see Chapter 30), assisting both management and external users.

However:

- Valuation of many fixed assets at historic cost can be misleading. Replacement costs are often much higher.
- Inflation more generally remains a problem. With the abandonment of inflation-adjusted accounting, the changing value of money is a real source of distortion.
- The valuation of intangible assets is an increasing problem. While goodwill is hurriedly written off, some firms are introducing brand valuation, yet others are not.
- Firms in the service sector may indicate low tangible fixed asset values yet have a very high market value. The difference is the value in human assets (e.g. creative designers), which does not appear in any balance sheet.

The profit and loss account

Chapter objectives

After working through this chapter, you will:

- understand the construction and logic of a published profit and loss account
- know the principles that underlie the recording of revenues and costs
- recognize the distinction between profit and cash
- know the meaning of the following key terms: trading account, trading/operating profit, non-operating income, profit before/after tax, gross/net profit, retained profit, realization concept, matching principle, exceptional items, liquidity.

A SPECIMEN PROFIT AND LOSS STATEMENT EXPLAINED

A major objective of most companies is to generate profit as a reward for their investors and as a source of funding for investment. The profit and loss account summarizes a firm's trading results over a period and shows how the resulting profits were used (or how the losses were funded).

Copy down the profit and loss account for Megasound, leaving a usable space to one side. Then read through the explanation, making notes on what the various items in the accounts mean.

Megasound Ltd is a Berkshire-based firm that manufactures high-quality loudspeakers. It had a good year in 1996, with sales revenue reaching £2 million for the first time.

▶ The opening item on the profit and loss account is always the **sales revenue**. From this all the direct costs relating to production are subtracted. This gives the **gross profit**. Then all overhead costs are subtracted, leaving the **operating profit**. To this non-operating income is added. With subtraction of the interest charges, this becomes the **profit before tax**. Subtraction of tax gives the **profit after tax**. Finally, subtraction of dividends leaves the **retained profits**, which are added to the **reserves**. Remember that all references to profit may also be to loss.

Megasound Ltd

Profit and loss account for the year ending 31 December 1996

	(£k)	(£k)
sales revenue		2,000
less: cost of goods sold		
direct materials	450	
direct labour	630	
manufacturing overheads	150	1,230
gross profit		770

less		
distribution costs	190	
administrative expenses	160	350
operating (trading) profit		420
add		
non-operating income		15
		435
less		
interest payable		35
profit before tax (net profit)		400
tax on profit		140
profit after tax		260
dividends		100
retained profit		160

Together, the items down to gross profit are known as the **trading account**. Its specific contents are not normally disclosed by firms.

The uses of the profit before tax are called **appropriations**. These include taxation, dividends and retentions of profit in the reserves.

Explanation of Terms Used

▶ Revenue minus costs equals profit.

▶ Revenue minus costs of goods sold only equals gross profit.

▶ Revenue minus all costs equals net profit or profit before tax.

1 **Sales revenue less costs = profit** is the most basic equation in business. We therefore start with the total revenue generated from ordinary trading activity. This must exclude any VAT element.
2 **Cost of goods sold** is the first group of subtractions. This includes all costs related to the product (often called **product costs**) rather than to the operation of the firm as a whole. So we include direct materials, direct labour, plus all overhead costs that can be allocated to the production process.
3 **Gross profit** is the sum remaining.
4 Next we subtract all other running costs (except the cost of finance). These relate to the firm rather than to the specific product and are charged for a period (often called **period costs**).

   Distribution costs include all outlay on selling and marketing.

   Administrative expenses feature all remaining overheads including office costs and management salaries.
5 **Operating or trading profit** is the amount remaining after these deductions. It is the surplus achieved through the firm's normal trading activity when all operating costs have been deducted.
6 **Non-operating income** means any earnings arising from outside the firm's normal trading activity. This could be derived from financial fixed assets such as investments in other firms.
7 **Interest payable** on the firm's loan finance is deducted next. This is permitted before profits are subject to any taxation.
8 **Profit before tax** (also called **net profit**) is the profit remaining and is liable to corporation tax. Corporation tax is charged at a standard rate of 33 per cent. Small firms (profits less than £250,000) pay tax at a reduced rate of 25 per cent,

but on a scale of 25 to 35 per cent if profits fall between £250,000 and £1,250,000.

9 **Profit after tax** is subject to subtractions/additions arising from exceptional items (see below, p. 210), dividends to preference shareholders and payment of dividends to minority interests (shareholders outside the firm with holdings in its subsidiary companies). Profits remaining are available to the ordinary shareholders.

10 **Dividends** may be recommended by the directors at any rate (e.g. 8p per £1 ordinary share) and must be approved by the shareholders at the annual general meeting. The total distributed profit may be any proportion of profit after tax, although usually more than half is retained.

11 **Retained profit** is that part of the final profit ploughed back into the firm. This will be added to the reserves on the balance sheet.

If a firm makes a loss for a period, then it may pay no dividend and the reserves will be **reduced**. This would reflect the real loss of resources (assets) from the firm. A dividend can still be paid from the retained profit of previous years. Any loss can be deducted from future profit for the purpose of tax liability.

PRINCIPLES OF PROFIT AND LOSS

The principle of prudence is applied by accountants to the calculation of profits and losses. A firm's confident expectation that sales will occur is not sufficient. For sales revenue to be recorded (i.e. **realized**), the product must have been delivered to the customer and either cash received or a debt accepted. This is called the **realization concept**.

To work out a firm's profit over a stated period, it is necessary to decide which revenues and costs to count. The two vital guiding points are:

1 Allow all revenue earned by products sold in the period.
2 Subtract all costs incurred by the firm in achieving those sales.

Suppose a firm starts its financial year on 1 January. At the beginning of February a payment is received from a customer who accepted delivery in December. This sales revenue will be included in the previous year's accounts. Only sales realized during the current year can be counted in that year.

Now suppose the firm buys a large consignment of stock for the Christmas market. By the new year half is still unsold. Only the cost of the stock that was sold before 1 January would be charged to that year's accounts. The cost of unsold stock will be carried forward into the next year. Similarly, a bill for rent to cover the three months from November to January would be charged $^2/_3$ to the previous year and $^1/_3$ to the following year.

▶ To calculate profit and loss, all revenues must be matched to their corresponding costs.

This insistence on linking or matching the sales of a period with their corresponding costs is called the **matching principle**. It applies equally to the purchase of fixed assets. Suppose that towards the start of its financial year a firm takes delivery of a new and expensive machine. This does not mean that its profits are immediately reduced by the cost of the machine. Instead, only one year's depreciation (loss of value) will be charged to the profit and loss account. The remainder of the machine's cost will be spread over the future years of its life (see Chapter 28).

The distinction here is between **capital expenditure** and **revenue expenditure**. That part of a firm's expenditure that can be shown as an asset on the next balance sheet is called capital expenditure. This is because it has added to the value of the firm's fixed capital. It does not appear as a cost in the current profit and loss account. All other expenditure (e.g. wages, administration) that does not create any future asset is called revenue expenditure. This is because its purpose is to obtain revenue for the firm. It **does** appear as costs in the current profit and loss account.

▶ WH Smith Group plc allowed £124 million to reflect exceptional losses in 1996, mainly due to its disposal of the Do It All DIY chain to Boots.

Exceptional Items

The goal of all accounts is to convey a 'true and fair' picture of the organization's affairs. Thus any special items that significantly affect the results are highlighted and explained in the **notes to the accounts**.

Any significant cost that is not part of a firm's normal trading activity is called an **exceptional item** and must be disclosed in the accounts. This might be a cost that has become much larger than usual (e.g. bankruptcy of a major customer and write-off of their debts) or a cost that is 'one-off' and unlikely to recur (e.g. a legal claim against the company).

Most 'exceptionals' are simply explained in the notes to the accounts, but items arising from closure of an operation are shown on the published profit and loss account, directly below operating profit.

▶ Profit and cash are different.

Profit and Cash

A highly profitable firm may go bankrupt for lack of cash. A firm awash with cash may announce heavy losses. There is no contradiction in either of these statements.

Liquidity means nearness to cash. Cash therefore represents perfect liquidity. All firms need adequate cash to meet their expenses (e.g. wages or rent). Equally, too much cash is wasteful since it earns little or no return (see Chapter 29). An expanding, profitable firm may quickly spend its cash earnings on, say, stock, wages or new fixed assets. If unexpected bills arrive, it may run short of cash. At the opposite extreme, a declining firm could be trading unprofitably yet accumulate large sums in cash. These may be unused for fear of incurring further losses.

Cash and profit are therefore distinct. Cash is merely a totally liquid form in which to hold resources. Profit is a surplus earned by the use of resources and may be invested in any form of asset.

Draw up a profit and loss account for 1996–7 from the following data.

Portcullis Locks Ltd

Portcullis Locks Ltd is a Midlands firm manufacturing locks and mechanical security equipment. During 1996–7 sales revenue was £2,590,000. Stock at the start of the year was worth £430,000 and by the end of the year had fallen in value to £360,000. Materials cost £610,000, while direct labour expenses amounted to £805,000. Production overheads have been calculated at £250,000, while total selling expenses reached £195,000. Administration of all kinds cost £300,000. The long-term loans on the firm's balance sheet stood at £420,000, with interest rates at 8 per cent, while tax on profits was payable at 30 per cent. It was the directors' policy to retain three-fifths of the profit after tax and to distribute two-fifths in dividends.

Evaluation

- The profit and loss account is the key operating statement showing how a firm made a profit or a loss with the resources that it controlled.
- Taken with the balance sheet, the profit and loss account makes an analysis of performance possible.
- Notes to the accounts may clarify the nature of revenues and costs. However, most of the detail is missing from the published accounts.
- No rigid rules exist for defining every heading. Much depends on discretion. Caution is needed in comparing data between firms.
- The appropriations show how any final profit was divided between tax, dividends and investment in the firm.

28 Depreciation

Chapter objectives

After working through this chapter, you will:

- know the meaning and causes of depreciation
- be able to apply simple numerate methods in accounting for depreciation
- understand the recording of depreciation on the balance sheet
- know the meaning of the following key terms: depreciation, straight-line method, reducing balance method, net book value.

WHAT IS DEPRECIATION?

▶ **Depreciation**: fall in the value of a fixed asset over time.

A good quality family car bought new might cost £10,000. One year later its value could have fallen to around £7,000. After three years it might only be worth £4,000, while five years are likely to reduce the value to £2,500. Even after ten years its value will still be falling and it might be likely to fetch around £1,000. This process of falling value year by year is called **depreciation**. It is a real cost and a major part of the expense of owning a car.

▶ Depreciation is caused by:
- wear and tear;
- new technology making an asset obsolete;
- changes in fashion or style that reduce an asset's market value.

Although land and buildings often **appreciate** in value, most durable consumer or producer goods suffer from depreciation. Typical fixed assets for a firm – machines, computers, trucks and vans – will all depreciate over time. Just as the private car owner must recognize depreciation as an expense, so the firm must allow for depreciation in its accounts. This allowance has two clear aspects:

1. Most fixed assets will be recorded with a falling value over time. This will be shown on the balance sheet.
2. The loss of value in the fixed assets is a cost to the firm, directly reducing the profits. This will be shown in the profit and loss account.

The Depreciation Cycle

▶ A business computer system typically depreciates rapidly over a short useful life. This is due to the speed of technological innovation. The residual value is generally low.

▶ **Historic cost**: the price that the firm originally paid for an asset.

The speed at which depreciation occurs may be fairly constant, or it may vary. 'Useful life' may not end until the physical exhaustion of the asset, but it is more likely to end at the firm's discretion, when it is judged to be more efficient to purchase a replacement. The 'useful life' can usually be estimated in advance fairly accurately. When the asset is discarded, it generally has some remaining (**residual**) value. When allowing for depreciation in the accounts, the sum to be depreciated is the historic (original) cost 'less' the residual value.

Depreciation Methods

The firm must choose a fair and consistent method by which depreciation of its fixed assets can be recognized.

▶ There is no single correct way of calculating depreciation, but the accountant must ensure that the same methods are used throughout the firm.

Depreciation: Action Fashion

Action Fashion is a newly established company making a distinctive range of leisure and sports clothing. It has decided to purchase a computerized fabric-cutting machine at a cost of £16,000. The new machine is expected to have a useful life of four years and a residual value of £4,000. Two different methods of depreciation are being considered.

1 **Straight-line method**

This is a very simple method. It treats the asset as though it will lose value at a constant rate over its useful life. To find the annual depreciation charge we take the original cost, subtract the residual value and divide by the useful life in years, i.e.:

$$\text{annual depreciation} = \frac{\text{original cost less residual value}}{\text{useful life (years)}}$$

$$= \frac{\text{£16,000 less £4,000}}{\text{4 years}} = \text{£3,000}$$

The pattern of depreciation can now be shown in a table ('End of year 0' means the time of purchase):

End of year	*Depreciation charge (£)*	*Balance sheet value (£)*
0	nil	16,000
1	3,000	13,000
2	3,000	10,000
3	3,000	7,000
4	3,000	4,000

The constant annual depreciation charge would form a straight line on a graph.

▶ At the end of an asset's useful life, its net book value will equal the residual value.

Sketch the graph for the data above (number of years on x-axis, balance sheet value on y-axis). Write your notes on the straight-line method of depreciation alongside.

2 **Reducing balance method**

This method reduces the balance sheet value each year by a fixed percentage rate. This rate is exactly sufficient to reduce the balance sheet value to equal the residual value by the last year of useful life. Action Fashion will use a rate of 29 per cent:

End of year	*Depreciation charge (£)*	*Balance sheet value (£)*
0	nil	16,000
1	4,640	11,360
2	3,294	8,066
3	2,339	5,727
4	1,661	4,066

▶ Now the balance sheet value falls rapidly at first, but more slowly later.

You will notice that the balance sheet value is still £66 above the residual value at the end of year four. This is because 29 per cent was not quite a high enough depreciation rate. The exact rate can be calculated with the formula below.

If RV = residual value
C = original cost
n = number of years useful life

then annual depreciation rate $= 100\left(1 - \sqrt[n]{\frac{RV}{C}}\right)$

for Action Fashion the rate $= 100\left(1 - \sqrt[n]{\frac{4{,}000}{16{,}000}}\right)$

$= 100\ (1 - 0.701)$

$= 29.29\%$

Sketch a graph to show depreciation by the reducing balance method and write your notes on the method alongside.

Despite the constant percentage rate, the actual annual depreciation charge falls steadily from a high initial level. This contrasts with the constant charge using the straight-line method:

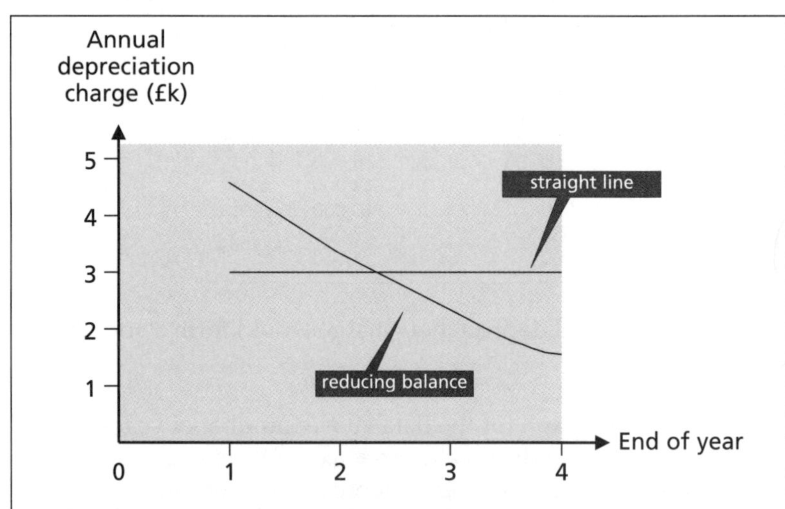

Figure 28.1
The straight-line and the reducing balance methods of depreciation

Depreciation and the Balance Sheet

▶ Net book value

Fixed assets that depreciate are recorded in the balance sheet after the accumulated depreciation has been subtracted. The resulting figure is called the **net book value**.

Fraser Fabrication Ltd
Balance Sheet as at 31 December 1991

fixed assets	*at cost* (£)	*accumulated depreciation* (£)	*net book value* (£)
tangible assets			
land and building	220,000	–	220,000
plant and machinery	140,000	55,000	85,000
vehicles	82,000	28,000	54,000

▶ Depreciation and the balance sheet: an example.

Depreciation and the Profit and Loss Account

Consider a machine costing £50,000 with a four-year life and a residual value of £10,000. In each year of its use its value falls by £10,000 on a straight-line basis. '£10,000 worth' of machine is 'used up' in a year's operation. Thus it is a cost that must be entered in the profit and loss account.

▶ If depreciation relates to production equipment (e.g. a machine), it will be entered as part of production overheads and so counted before gross profit.
If depreciation relates to office equipment, computers etc., then it will be entered as part of administrative expenses and counted after gross profit, but before operating profit (see Chapter 27).

Depreciation and Cash

Although depreciation is a very real cost to firms, the profit and loss account entry does not mean that an actual cash outflow has occurred. The literal payment for the asset was made at the time of its purchase. At that point there was a single cash outflow but no expense was recorded in the profit and loss account. Since then no corresponding cash outflows have taken place, but a series of expenses (i.e. depreciation charges) have been recorded. These depreciation charges in the profit and loss account represent costs like any others. The only difference is that they have been paid for in advance.

So when purchase of a fixed asset occurs, the firm is that amount worse off in cash-flow terms than its profits suggest. However, each year of depreciation then works in the opposite way. Recorded profits allow for an expense that is not being paid in cash. Therefore the firm is better off in cash-flow terms than its profit suggests – to the extent of the depreciation charge.

▶ **Replacement costs**
Firms could set aside an amount each year in a 'savings account' that would yield the funds for replacement (a few firms do so). Most firms choose to keep the funds for their own use, believing it to be more profitable to invest in themselves. However, this means careful planning of cash so that the money to replace fixed assets is available when needed.

Read the following case study and answer the questions below.

Polden Potteries
Polden Potteries, a small business in Somerset, is drawing up its profit and loss account for 1996–7. Part of this is summarized below:

	(£)	(£)
sales revenue		40,000
less: cost of goods sold		
direct materials	9,000	
direct labour	16,000	
production overheads	3,000	28,000
gross profit		12,000

However, Hannah Lacey, the owner, had failed to make any allowances for the depreciation of a key asset – a new electric kiln.

This had been purchased at the start of the current financial year for £15,000. It was expected to have a useful life of five years, when it should have a second-hand value of about £5,000.

Calculate the gross profit of Polden Potteries using:

(a) the straight-line method of depreciation;
(b) the reducing balance method of depreciation.

Evaluation

- Straight-line is a simple depreciation method widely used in Britain for much industrial and commercial equipment.
- Reducing balance has the advantage of writing off the value of the asset quickly while it is fairly new and slowly as it approaches the end of its life. This matches more closely the real decline in market value over time. Reducing balance is especially suitable for vehicles and electrical equipment.
- When considering the net cost of using a fixed asset, the reducing balance method can again be more realistic. In its early years the asset has a high depreciation charge but low maintenance costs. Later, the depreciation charge falls but the maintenance cost rises. Thus the overall cost recorded might be fairly constant.
- However, in the long run the firm may receive a fairly constant stream of benefit from a fixed asset which is periodically replaced. The straight-line method ensures a constant charge and avoids the risk of deflating and inflating profits merely because of an asset's age.
- The accountant must use discretion in choosing the most appropriate method for different assets. The aim is a 'true and fair view'. Consistency is essential.
- Depreciation is a real process by which a fixed asset loses value over time. The reduction in value must be shown on the balance sheet and entered as a cost on the profit and loss account.
- Inflation is a complication. If the cost of an asset rises during its useful life, then the depreciation charges become too small, accounting only for the original cost. This means that profit is overstated while the balance sheet value is understated.

29 Cash flow and working capital

Chapter objectives

After working through this chapter, you will:

- understand the concept of liquidity
- be able to construct a cash-flow forecast
- appreciate the distinction between profit and cash flow
- recognize the working capital cycle in a typical firm
- be able critically to analyse working capital requirements
- know the meaning of the following key terms: petty cash, liquidity, spectrum of liquidity, insolvency, net cash flow, cash-flow forecast, cash-flow crisis, cash mountain.

WHAT IS CASH?

Money exists as either notes and coins or codes in the memory of bank and building society computers. In itself it has no value. It is wanted only for its purchasing power – in other words, its exchange value for goods and services. Thus money is really an official token, representing a claim on resources. To a business, a £10 note represents, perhaps, a small sheet of steel, a pane of glass, a bag of screws or an hour of labour. It is the general acceptability of money – or cash – to settle almost any kind of debt that makes it so useful.

All firms hold varying amounts of cash during their trading year. The balance sheet shows the cash balance on one particular date. But throughout the year a small amount of **petty cash** will be kept in the office for minor day-to-day expenditures. It will be kept to a minimum since it is a security risk and carries no interest. Most of the cash total will be held in the firm's bank accounts: in a current account for short-term needs and in a deposit account for longer-term requirements. Large firms may also have substantial deposits with merchant banks and other city institutions, which can be released given appropriate notice.

Liquidity

▶ Liquidity

Liquidity simply means closeness to cash. Pure liquidity is cash. Turn to Chapter 26 and look at the typical headings down the right-hand side of a T-form balance sheet. The value of the assets is recorded after each heading. But value is not the same as cash. The land and buildings may be very valuable, but it would be difficult and time-consuming to turn them into cash. Vehicles would be easier to convert into cash, stock easier still, while debts can usually be factored for ready cash. Thus the assets represent a **spectrum of liquidity**, the structure of which should be planned and monitored by the firm. A large need for cash and a low level of liquidity would cause serious problems.

Why is Cash Important?

Any active firm receives a continuous flow of demands for cash. These are to meet many different expenses. Unless the firm is able to meet these demands, it will become **insolvent** and could potentially face liquidation. The frequency and pattern of cash demands varies widely. Some expenses recur every week or month, for example wages and materials. Others such as rents, rates or insurance premiums are regular but occur at longer intervals. Yet others are irregular needs, but may involve large sums when they do occur, for instance new buildings or machinery.

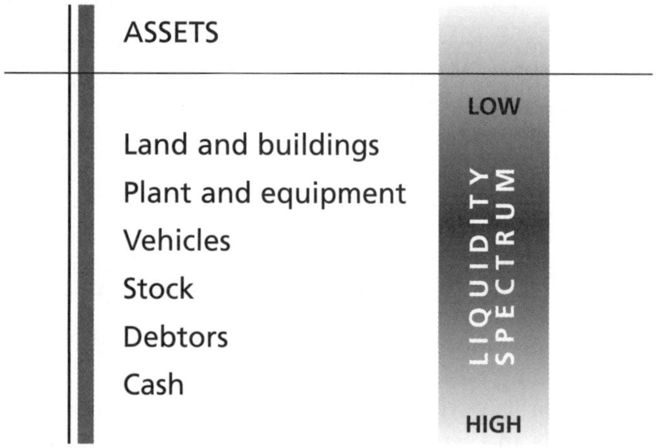

ASSETS	LIQUIDITY SPECTRUM
	LOW
Land and buildings	
Plant and equipment	
Vehicles	
Stock	
Debtors	
Cash	
	HIGH

Figure 29.1
The liquidity spectrum

Because cash is so important, managers could be tempted to ensure an excess of cash over projected requirements. A safety margin is wise planning, but a significant excess is wasteful. Cash holdings earn little interest and therefore carry an opportunity cost relative to funds being used profitably in the business. For example, a firm could use its surplus cash to invest in labour-saving machinery.

Sometimes a firm may hold large sums of cash for a special reason. This may be to finance a major project or even to make an offer for another firm. A **cash mountain** within a firm should occur only as part of a calculated management strategy.

CASH-FLOW FORECASTING

▶ The cash-flow forecast is an important part of the firm's budget; see Chapter 31.

The **cash-flow forecast** is a month-by-month statement of expected inflows and outflows of cash.

The Cash-flow Forecast

New Flame Ltd

Annabel and Chris Pugh decide to start in business, making and selling candles. They hope to begin trading on 1 April 1997. With savings of £3,000 as starting capital, they approach their local bank for an overdraft agreement. The manager asks for various business projections, including a cash-flow forecast. Annabel first draws up a statement of key financial estimates:

1 The average selling price of the candles will be £2. Half the customers are likely to pay in cash, the other half with a month's credit.
2 Sales are expected to be 500 candles in the first month, 1,000 in the second month and 2,000 in each month thereafter.
3 2,000 candles will be made each month at a cost of £1,000 in materials. The labour costs will be £1,500 per month.
4 Rent for some small premises will be £600 per quarter, payable in advance.
5 Other overhead expenses are likely to amount to £300 per month.
6 At the beginning of the first month it will be necessary to spend £1,000 on fixtures and fittings.

This information enables her to construct a projected cash-flow statement for the first six months' trading.

Look briefly at the items below and the columns of data. Then check carefully through the explanatory notes and verify the reasoning for each column.

Item	*Apr*	*May*	*Jun*	*Jul*	*Aug*	*Sep*
cash inflows						
owners' capital	3,000	–	–	–	–	–
cash sales	500	1,000	2,000	2,000	2,000	2,000
credit sales	–	500	1,000	2,000	2,000	2,000
total inflows	3,500	1,500	3,000	4,000	4,000	4,000
cash outflows						
materials	1,000	1,000	1,000	1,000	1,000	1,000
labour	1,500	1,500	1,500	1,500	1,500	1,500
rent	600	–	–	600	–	–
overheads	300	300	300	300	300	300
equipment	1,000	–	–	–	–	–
total outflows	4,400	2,800	2,800	3,400	2,800	2,800
Net Cash Flow	(900)	(1,300)	200	600	1,200	1,200
Balance Brought Forward	–	(900)	(2,200)	(2,000)	(1,400)	(200)
Balance carried forward	(900)	(2,200)	(2,000)	(1,400)	(200)	1,000

▶ **Explanatory notes**

1 The cash inflows are listed first. When originally received, the owners' capital represents an inflow.

2 Notice that for each month's sales, half the value is received in cash immediately and the other half, on credit, is received one month later.

3 Materials, labour and overhead payments are straightforward. The rent appears at the start of trading and again three months later (in July). Payment for the equipment is a single outflow, in April.

4 Subtract the total outflows from the total inflows to find the **net cash flow**.

5 Add the **balance brought forward** to give the **balance carried forward** to the next period.

It is clear that New Flame Ltd will need an overdraft in order to begin trading. This will peak at £2,200 by the end of May, followed by a steady return to credit. Annabel and Chris will need to negotiate overdraft facilities for more than £2,200 (£3,000 could be ideal) so that any adverse variances in the budget can be financed.

Make your own notes to explain the cash-flow forecast, but raise the labour costs to £2,000 per month and the rent to £800 per quarter.

▶ If cash reserves are about to be exhausted, the firm will need some source of short-term finance such as a bank overdraft. If no immediate credit can be negotiated, a **cash-flow crisis** exists. It may be possible to sell some stock cheaply, to factor some debts or to dispose of a surplus fixed asset quickly. If even these measures prove inadequate, then the firm is insolvent and could be forced into receivership.

The Cash-flow Crisis

Inaccuracy in a cash-flow forecast may arise through lower than expected cash inflows or higher than expected cash outflows. Some possible reasons are shown below:

Cash inflows down	Cash outflows up
depressed sales reduced prices increased debtors bad debts failure of an asset sale	increased wage settlement rise in material costs higher overheads intensified marketing unexpected repairs unforeseen events, e.g. legal action

PROFIT AND CASH FLOW

Some of the most acute cash-flow crises occur in profitable firms. Consider a firm that has discovered a really successful business formula. Projected sales – as reflected in the cash-flow forecast – are expected to be highly profitable. Naturally, the management wishes to expand and exploit the market more fully. To do this requires an increase in output. More property, increased investment in plant and equipment, and higher levels of working capital are all necessary. Perhaps bids for other less successful firms will speed expansion. **More cash is needed**. Every decision to commit more cash could be justified in the long run. But the profits are in the future and cash is needed now. This phenomenon is called **overtrading**. It is extremely tempting when a firm has a winning product, especially if this coincides with a time of economic expansion. The flaw – and it can be fatal – is the mismatch between cash flow and profit.

▶ Cash and profit are not the same. Very profitable companies can have cash-flow crises. Cash-rich companies can be unprofitable.

Cash and profit are not the same. Cash is simply the holding of assets in a perfectly liquid form; it is no more than a statement at the bank. Profit is a trading outcome, a surplus of revenues over costs for a given period. The surplus itself is most unlikely to be stagnant in the form of cash. Probably it will have been invested in new fixed assets and distributed to the shareholders as dividends.

It follows that a **cash-rich** firm could be unprofitable. Plentiful cash could exist for many reasons, including an inability to use it in the business profitably. Cash alone no more implies profit than, say, stock alone. For profit to occur, there must be a recorded surplus of revenue over costs.

Read the following case study and answer the questions below.

Julie and Elizabeth Thorlby make reproduction nineteenth-century porcelain dolls dressed in period costume. The business is about to expand and will enter a proper workshop on 1 July at a quarterly rental of £750 (payable in advance). Each doll costs £1.50 in materials. Labour costs are £2,000 per month. Monthly overheads amount to £500. Output will be a constant 50 dolls per week, while sales are projected as follows:

July	80
August	100
September	120
October	180
November	320
December	400

Dolls are sold for cash at £20 each.

1 If the cash held at the end of June is £1,000, draw up a cash-flow forecast for July–December.
2 Comment briefly on the situation of the business.

WORKING CAPITAL

Working capital is simply the amount of resources that a business needs to operate on a day-to-day basis. Business involves the purchase of resources which are then transformed into a product that is sold to customers. No firm can achieve this process instantaneously. There will always be a gap between obtaining the resources for production and the sale of the eventual product. In financial terms, we are concerned with the gap between payment for resources and the receipt of sales revenue for the corresponding product. However, the burden of this gap is cushioned by the firm's current liabilities. These provide short-term (less than twelve months) credit for the finance of current assets. For example, **trade creditors** are effectively financing part of the firm's stock. Therefore:

▶ When a firm orders and receives supplies but does not pay for them immediately, the supplier becomes a **trade creditor**.

Net working capital = current assets – current liabilities

The cash that is finally realized as a sale is recycled to provide the cash necessary to purchase more materials and to pay the other costs of production. Provided that unit price exceeds unit cost, then a profit is also generated.

▶ Profit as a percentage of the resource flow is the **profit margin**.

Make notes on net working capital, showing each item involved in its calculation.

Working Capital Management

Working capital requirements must be carefully budgeted and actual levels closely monitored. Working capital is essential for two major reasons:

▶ A firm cannot afford to run short of working capital. It is the 'life-blood' of the business.

1 **Trading:** stocks to meet consumer demand; debtors to provide customer credit; cash to meet expenses.
2 **Liquidity**: taken together, current assets provide the potential cash to meet all current liabilities that require payment.

Stock is necessary for any business to function (see Chapter 17). Manufacturers need raw materials, work-in-progress and finished goods; wholesalers and retailers trade in finished goods; even service industries carry consumables (such as stationery).

▶ Stock is necessary for production and for the satisfaction of consumer demand (marketing) but carries a high opportunity cost.

▶ Working capital circulates through the fixed assets

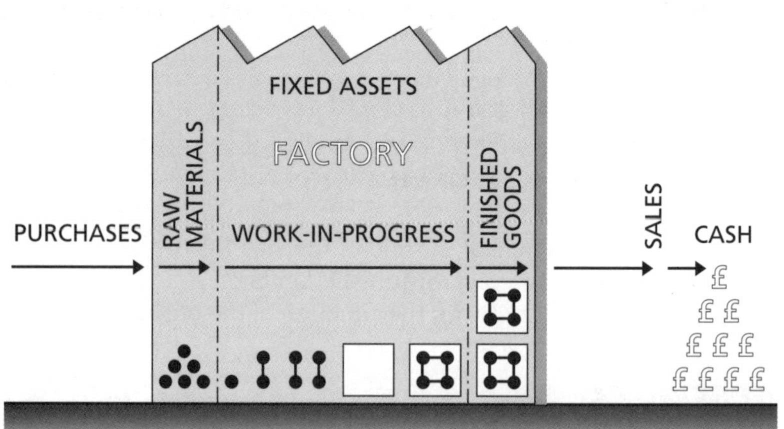

Figure 29.2
The circulation of working capital

▶ To cut stockholding costs, many firms now operate just-in-time stock systems. These depend on computerized real-time information and close relationships with suppliers.

▶ Debtors are expensive. Waiting for customers to pay for goods/services involves a minimum opportunity cost of interest earnings foregone.

▶ Cash flow control

▶ Creditor control

▶ The value of debtors will normally exceed the value of creditors because the goods and services received are only one element in the final selling price, which includes labour, overheads and a profit margin.

Stock has two critical interfaces. The first is with **production** in ensuring sufficient raw material to meet schedules and to allow flexibility in speeding or advancing output or in adjusting the product mix. The second is with **marketing** in keeping distribution channels filled and in responding rapidly to changes in demand. However, stock carries a high opportunity cost. It often represents as much as 40 per cent of the net assets and keeps resources tied up that could be used profitably elsewhere in the business.

Debtors are unavoidable in many lines of business since customers expect a period of credit. This may vary from one week to two months or more. Competition is a key factor in determining the 'going' credit period.

Credit control is a vital operation and effective pressure must be put on customers who exceed the agreed credit terms. Initially this will take the form of polite reminders, but progressively firmer measures may be necessary, culminating in legal action. In extreme cases, where the amount involved is very large and a trade customer is probably unable to settle, an application may be made for their compulsory liquidation. Management must balance the gains from pressurizing late payers against administrative costs and the negative effects on customer relations.

Many firms try to build a trustworthy credit relationship with customers and to assess carefully their credit risks. Sometimes a discount is offered for immediate or prompt payment, e.g. 2 per cent discount if the invoice is settled within twenty-eight days. This, though, can be a costly tactic which slices back the firm's profit margin.

Cash is essential in running any business and needs particularly careful budgeting using a cash-flow forecast. The firm must balance carefully its cash (and liquidity) needs against the corresponding opportunity cost.

Creditors refers to all sums of money owed by a business and falling due for repayment within twelve months. **Trade creditors** is frequently the most important item. When one firm supplies goods to another there is normally an allowable time-lag before payment. The period of trade credit extended by suppliers is usually between thirty and ninety days. This period of credit helps to compensate a business for the time-lags in payments represented by their own debtors. For most firms, the credit periods applying to suppliers and customers are similar.

Trade creditors can be a major source of finance, especially in retailing, where debtors are small and goods received may be sold for cash before the corresponding payment is due. Managers will attempt to obtain favourable credit terms from their suppliers. Firms that are large-scale purchasers have market power and may drive a hard bargain with smaller companies. However, reliable long-term relationships with suppliers are also important.

Liquidity is crucial to a firm's financial health. Although current liabilities represent a valuable source of finance, they remain liabilities, i.e. subject to early payment. Generally, the firm must ensure that the liquidity constituted by its current assets exceeds by a safe margin the level of its current liabilities. This is measured by the current and acid test ratios which show the number of times the firm could settle its current liabilities using its current assets.

▶ Current liabilities may include bank overdrafts and provisions for taxation and dividends (see Chapter 26).

$$\text{Current ratio} = \frac{\text{current assets}}{\text{current liabilities}}$$

$$\text{Acid test ratio} = \frac{\text{current assets} - \text{stock}}{\text{current liabilities}}$$

The acid test is a more severe assessment of liquidity and strips out stock, since this is the least liquid current asset (it may be hard to sell and its market value may have fallen).

A wider picture of liquidity can be obtained by using the ratio:

$$\frac{\text{net working capital}}{\text{sales}}$$

The actual value may vary widely between firms and industries. These ratios are most meaningful when compared over a period of time.

Read the following case study and answer the questions below.

Midland Models

Midland Models supplies good quality plastic models in kit form to the UK and overseas markets. Sales in the last financial year reached £1.2 million, while profit before interest and tax was £120,000. Net assets at the end of the same period were valued at £1.4 million.

The firm's audited accounts are being considered. The managing director believes that the present level of working capital is excessive.

Raw materials are valued at £160,000, while work-in-progress is worth £120,000. The company holds finished goods to the value of £210,000. Debtors are shown at £310,000 on the balance sheet, with £110,000 in the bank. Meanwhile, creditors total £350,000 and there is a provision for tax of £30,000. There are no other current liabilities.

The finance director feels that the criticism is unfair. The production department needs ample stocks to meet an unpredictable order pattern, while export customers are always slow to pay. The balance in the bank is needed to avoid a repeat of the cash-flow crisis experienced three years ago.

The managing director is unconvinced and proposes a 50 per cent reduction in all types of current assets to be achieved without delay.

1 Does Midland Models appear to have an excessive level of working capital?
2 How could the managing director's proposal be carried out? How would it affect financial ratios in the firm?
3 Could the finance director's argument be justified?

Evaluation

- Managers must always ensure that sufficient cash is available to meet labour costs and regular bills. Forward planning is needed to ensure that enough cash can be obtained to pay for major investments and to cope with unexpected events.
- Adherence to the cash-flow forecast must be carefully monitored. The forecast depends on accuracy in predicting sales and costs. Internal changes (e.g. increased waste) and external changes (e.g. increased energy prices) can seriously affect actual against forecast data. Managers must be ready to adjust or revise the forecast as events unfold.
- An adequate supply of cash is essential, but it carries a real opportunity cost. The firm's purpose is not to hold funds but to use them in business to generate profit.
- The faster the expansion of a firm, the greater the likely pressure on cash flow. The costs of acquiring, equipping and operating new business units usually outpaces the corresponding increase in sales revenue. A cash-flow crisis may develop even though the business is trading profitably.
- Apparently excessive cash holdings – a cash mountain – may be held for a strategic purpose (e.g. a bid for a rival firm) or for tactical flexibility (e.g. in wage negotiations).
- The value of cash held by a firm does not necessarily represent the cash available. Other assets such as debtors, stock or surplus fixed assets are **relatively** liquid and can be converted to cash if necessary. However, this liquidation of assets may be time-consuming, involving significant losses through selling at a discount, and could disrupt those areas of the firm affected.
- The allowance in the firm's accounts for the depreciation of fixed assets (see Chapter 28) represents a real cost but not a cash outflow.
- Working capital means the net assets within a firm that are continuously circulating or being 'turned over'. A business aims to operate with as little working capital as possible.
- Managers must plan their working capital requirements for the trading period ahead. This is formalized in the master budget, which shows a projected balance sheet and profit and loss account. Variance from budgets should be investigated for the working capital implications.
- All elements in the working capital cycle need to be monitored constantly. For any given profit margin, the faster the working capital can be driven round the cycle, the greater the return on net assets.

- The ratios used to measure working capital need recalculation on a regular basis. In practice, they may vary considerably over a year. This will reflect the fluctuating requirements for working capital according to season, sales trends, competition etc.
- One of the commonest causes of business insolvency is overtrading, where the rate of sales expansion is too fast relative to the working capital available.

30 Ratio analysis

Chapter objectives

After working through this chapter, you will:

- appreciate why ratios are useful
- understand the meaning of all key accounting ratios
- be able to investigate a firm's accounts using ratios
- know how to interpret interfirm comparisons using ratios
- know the meaning of the following key terms: RONA, profit margin, asset turnover, stock turnover, interest cover, return on equity, earnings per share, dividends per share, dividend yield, dividend cover.

WHY ARE RATIOS USEFUL?

▶ Applied to the main financial statements, ratios are vital in assessing the performance and prospects of a business.

We have been concerned to this point with understanding the main financial statements and the principles on which they are based. Now we will see how the accounts might be used to assess the performance and prospects of a business.

Think about the two major accounting documents. The balance sheet (see Chapter 26) tells us – at a stated date – all the resources held by a firm and how these resources have been financed. The profit and loss account (see Chapter 27) links one balance sheet date to the next. Remember that sales revenue less costs yields a profit (or loss). Payments of tax and dividends are then indicated, followed by the amount retained within the business. This last sum appears on the new balance sheet as an addition to reserves.

All this data now needs bringing to life. A **ratio** simply relates one quantity or number to another. For instance, in a school, the head will want to know the number of GCSE passes. On its own this figure means very little. As a percentage of all entries it becomes more meaningful. However, a thoughtful head might also want to know the proportion of passes at grades A*, A and B relative to all passes. He or she might further explore how this ratio varied between, say, maths and English and how it had changed over the previous three years. This would be a ratio analysis of exam results.

▶ Ratios themselves are easy to calculate. They provide a powerful means of investigating a firm's affairs. But the results are only pointers or clues; decisions, as always, require judgement.

It is very similar with a firm. 'Sales increased to £10 million, net assets fell to £8 million and profits rose to £2 million'. This data has very limited meaning when stated in absolute terms. Expressed in relative terms using ratios, it begins to be interesting (e.g. return on net assets = 25 per cent). Compared with the ratios of previous years, or with the ratios of competitors, it becomes vital evidence for managers.

The best way to store the formulae for ratios is on index cards. However, as you work through the following list of ratios, keep referring to the data for Quist Electronics below to see how its accounts provide the source figures.

▶ Refer back to this page for each of the examples that follow.

Data for Ratio Analysis

Quist Electronics plc is based near Cambridge and has become a leading manufacturer of advanced micro-electronics circuits. It became a public company in 1993 and its 80 million 25p ordinary shares are currently priced at 250p.

Balance Sheet as at 31 March 1997

	(£m)	(£m)
fixed assets		
land/buildings	28	
plant and equipment	15	43
current assets		
stock	30	
debtors	36	
cash	6	
	72	
current liabilities		
creditors	33	
tax provision	5	
final dividend provision	2	
	40	
net working capital		32
net assets		75
financed by:		
shareholders' funds		
ordinary 25p shares	20	
reserves	30	50
long-term liabilities		
loans		25
capital employed		75

Profit and Loss Account for the period 1 April 1996 to 31 March 1997

	(£m)	(£m)
sales revenue		225
direct materials	72	
direct labour	56	
production overheads	25	153
gross profit		72
distribution overheads	24	
administration overheads	30	54
operating profit		18
interest payable (@12%)		3
profit before tax		15
tax on profits (33%)		5
profit after tax		10
dividends		4
retained profit		6

Efficiency Ratios

▶ All the ratios below are calculated on data from Quist Electronics. Most £ signs have been dropped for convenience.

Efficiency ratios analyse the efficiency of the firm in its use of resources to generate profit.

Return on Net Assets (RONA)

▶ **RONA** = return on net assets; also called the **primary efficiency ratio**. RONA may also be measured as return on capital employed (ROCE). This makes no difference to the data used or the resulting ratio.

$$\textbf{Return on net assets (RONA)} = \frac{\text{operating profit}}{\text{net assets}} \times 100$$

$$= \frac{18}{75} \times 100 = 24\%$$

This is the most basic of all ratios and is sometimes called the **primary efficiency ratio**. It is the task of business management to use resources to create new wealth. RONA measures its success. Typical performance in the UK at present is 18–25%.

The next two ratios are closely related. Each opens a different pathway of investigation into efficiency.

Profit Margin

▶ Profit margin

$$\textbf{Profit margin} = \frac{\text{operating profit}}{\text{sales revenue}} \times 100 = \frac{18}{225} \times 100 = 8\%$$

This means that for every £1 in sales, 8p is profit.

Asset Turnover

▶ Asset turnover

$$\textbf{Asset turnover} = \frac{\text{sales revenue}}{\text{net assets}} = \frac{225}{75} = 3 \text{ times}$$

This means that total sales are equivalent to three times the value of net assets. In other words, the net assets have been 'turned over' three times.

There is now an important relationship to recognize:

▶ The profit margin depends on the relationship between sales revenue and costs. Further analysis can therefore relate sales to the various costs on the **profit and loss account**.
The asset turnover depends on the relationship between sales revenue and the various items on the **balance sheet**.

$$\text{profit margin} \times \text{asset turnover} = \text{return on net assets}$$

$$\frac{\text{operating profit}}{\text{sales revenue}} \times \frac{\text{sales revenue}}{\text{net assets}} = \frac{\text{operating profit}}{\text{net assets}}$$

$$8\% \times 3 = 24\%$$

Stock Turnover

▶ Stock turnover

$$\textbf{Stock turnover} = \frac{\text{sales revenue}}{\text{average stocks}} = \frac{225}{15} = 15 \text{ times}$$

If stocks are too low then sales may suffer. But stocks are expensive to hold and the firm wants to minimize costs. So a balance is required. If the ratio gets too low, it suggests excessive stock levels. But the ratio could get too high, with an unacceptable risk of stock-out.

Days' Sales in Debtors

▶ Days' sales in debtors

$$\text{Days' sales in debtors} = \frac{\text{debtors}}{\text{sales}} \times 365 = \frac{36}{225} \times 365 = 56.8 \text{ days}$$

This value measures the debtors in terms of the number of average days' sales that they represent. Most firms specify the length of the credit period allowed to customers. If the actual credit period is much longer, then it suggests a need to tighten credit control.

Liquidity Ratios

▶ Liquidity ratios measure the firm's safety from risk of cash-flow problems.

Remember that liquidity means 'nearness to cash'. The firm's current liabilities are really pending demands for cash. The creditors must be paid, tax bills settled, dividends distributed. Even an overdraft can be recalled at short notice. The value of the current assets is therefore vital. These assets are 'current' precisely because they are short term and designed to be turned into cash. **Liquidity ratios** measure the firm's **safety** through the balance between current assets and current liabilities.

Current Ratio

▶ Current ratio

$$\text{Current ratio} = \frac{\text{current assets}}{\text{current liabilities}} = \frac{72}{40} = 1.8$$

Traditionally, this ratio should be between 1.5 and 2, but it can vary widely depending on the type of business.

Acid Test Ratio

▶ Acid test ratio

$$\text{Acid test ratio} = \frac{\text{cash + debtors}}{\text{current liabilities}} = \frac{(6 + 36)}{40} = 1.05$$

This is a more severe test of liquidity. Stock is the least liquid current asset. A firm cannot be sure how quickly or how easily cash can be raised from stock. The acid test is the current ratio with 'stock stripped out'. Its typical value is 1, but again what is considered satisfactory will depend on the particular business.

Debt Ratios

▶ Debt ratios measure the risk involved in the firm's level of debt.

Essentially there are only two sources of funds for a firm: the shareholders' money and borrowed money. These are very different. The shareholders' money is not repayable and although a dividend is desirable, it is not obligatory. Borrowed money is repayable and the payment of interest is obligatory. The risk involved in a firm's level of debt can be measured by ratios.

▶ Gearing ratio – see Chapter 22.

Gearing Ratio

$$\textbf{Gearing ratio} = \frac{\text{long-term liabilities}}{(\text{shareholders' funds} + \text{long-term liabilities})}$$

$$= \frac{25}{(50 + 25)}$$

$$= 33.3\%$$

This ratio simply shows the proportion of long-term funding that is debt and interest bearing. While RONA is greater than the rate of interest, the highly geared firm will enjoy greater than proportional returns to the shareholders' funds. But if RONA falls below the interest rate, then the profit available to the shareholders falls sharply. The risk is that profits will be insufficient even to pay the interest charge, with insolvency as the final threat.

▶ Interest cover ratio

Interest Cover

$$\textbf{Interest cover} = \frac{\text{operating profit}}{\text{interest charges}} = \frac{18}{3} = 6 \text{ times}$$

This value measures the number of times the profit would pay or 'cover' the current interest charges. The higher the value, the safer the firm. Interest cover is often regarded as a clearer indication than gearing of a firm's exposure to the risks of indebtedness. It has the advantage of relating the actual profits to the actual interest payable.

▶ **Investors' ratios** measure the attractiveness of a firm to investors.

Investors' Ratios

The ultimate owners of a company are the shareholders. Their reward takes the form of dividends and any increase in value of their investment (i.e. a rising share price).

▶ Return on equity ratio

Return on Equity

$$\textbf{Return on equity} = \frac{\text{profit after tax}}{\text{shareholders' funds}} \times 100$$

$$= \frac{10}{50} \times 100 = 20\%$$

This percentage uses the profit remaining after interest and tax payments to show the return on shareholders' funds alone.

▶ Earnings per share

Earnings per Share

$$\textbf{Earnings per share} = \frac{\text{profit after tax}}{\text{number of shares}} = \frac{10\text{m}}{80\text{m}} = 12.5\text{p}$$

Since the crude number of shares is not significant, this value only has meaning when compared over time.

Price–Earnings Ratio

$$\textbf{Price–earnings ratio} = \frac{\text{market price of share}}{\text{earnings per share}} = \frac{250p}{12.5p} = 20$$

▶ Price–earnings ratio: P/E ratio

This ratio relates the market value of a share to its level of return as a unit of investment. The ratio is widely used in City analysis. A high ratio shows confidence in the share, while a low ratio suggests doubt about future prospects. The ratio can be distorted by short-term market abnormalities, e.g. a take-over bid.

The next measurements all relate to the payment of dividends.

Dividends per Share

$$\textbf{Dividends per share} = \frac{\text{dividends}}{\text{number of shares}} = \frac{4m}{8m} = 5p$$

▶ Dividends per share

As with earnings per share, this value only has meaning when measured over a period.

Dividend Yield

$$\textbf{Dividend yield} = \frac{\text{dividends per share}}{\text{market price of share}} \times 100 = \frac{5p}{250p} \times 100 = 2\%$$

▶ Dividend yield

This value relates the return on a share – expressed as a dividend – to the value of the investment (share value).

Dividend Cover

$$\textbf{Dividend cover} = \frac{\text{profit after tax}}{\text{dividends}} = \frac{10m}{4m} = 2.5 \text{ times}$$

▶ Dividend cover

This multiple shows the number of times the directors 'could' have paid the dividend.

RATIOS IN ACTION

Imagine a town centre where a large imposing shop is in the process of closing down. Notices announce 'Final Reductions', 'Everything Must Go!'. Perhaps it was a traditional firm, a landmark in the town. What has gone wrong? Where are the directors now? Was there no warning? Did they study their accounts a year ago? And what action did they take? Were their prices too high, or too low? Was the product mix right? Did they borrow too much, did they invest enough?

This is what accounts for management – or **management accounting** – is all about. We can analyse accounts rather as a doctor would examine a patient. For temperature, blood pressure and pulse-rate we may substitute profitability, efficiency and liquidity. The aim is **diagnostic**: what is going wrong – and right?

▶ Firms should watch key ratios continuously. Computerized accounts make this possible and **target ratios** can be set for the period ahead. Actual performance can be compared with targets (see Chapter 31).

The 'readings' are simple to make. But skill is required in spotting the vital connections. For example, Lucifer Lighting Ltd, a firm manufacturing table lamps, has a low 'acid test' ratio at 0.6. However, its current ratio is an overweight 2.4. The accountant finds that the stock turnover ratio is falling at 3.1. There is now a strong suspicion that the firm is carrying excessive stock.

As a means of analysis, ratios are most powerful when compared over time. For instance, Gloucester Glass Ltd finds that its RONA has fallen from 28 per cent to 21 per cent over three years. Asset turnover has been fairly constant at around 3, but the profit margin has fallen from 9 per cent to 7 per cent. Closer analysis of the internal accounts shows that the gross profit margin is steady but the value for expenses: sales revenue is rising sharply. Distribution and marketing expenses relative to sales have not changed significantly, but administrative expenses: sales revenue has nearly doubled. The accountant decides to explore further. Suppose each administrative expense is related to sales? Is the culprit paperwork in the office, or could it be management expense accounts? It is a management accountant's job to find out.

Interfirm Comparisons

Managers may also find it revealing to make ratio comparisons with other firms, or with industry averages. These could provide a valuable means for assessing the firm's own performance.

Interfirm Comparisons

Wigtown Woollens Ltd

Mr Crane, the company accountant, is examining his firm's ratios at the end of the financial year. The following data is included:

RONA	= 18.8%
profit margin	= 8.2%
asset turnover	= 2.3
stock turnover	= 4.9
days' sales in debtors	= 68 days

Considering a year of difficult trading conditions, results seem reasonable.

Now look at the data below for a comparison with three other firms in the woollens industry.

It can readily be seen that Wigtown's performance is **relatively** weak, although it does not have the worst ratios on every criterion.

	Wigtown	*Cheviot*	*Kielder*	*Swaledale*
RONA	18.8%	20.6%	36.2%	27.8%
profit margin	8.2%	7.9%	11.3%	9.9%
asset turnover	2.3	2.6	3.2	2.8
stock turnover	4.9	8.8	6.0	5.6
days' sales in debtors	68	55	48	72

How would **you** assess Wigtown's performance in the light of this information? Check each ratio with the earlier part of this chapter to make sure you know what each implies for Wigtown's performance.

Even more valuable are interfirm comparisons over a number of years. These enable management to analyse its own firm's progress relative to that of others and to spot both encouraging and worrying trends.

In practice most of the data needed for useful interfirm comparison is confidential and published accounts are limited in their scope and comparability.

▶ The Centre for Interfirm Comparisons in London enables firms to submit their accounts anonymously and then to receive a detailed comparison with the data for other firms in their industry.

Window Dressing

When companies use legal methods to give an artificially favourable appearance to the ratios in their published accounts, it is called **window dressing**. There are many highly specialized ways of giving accounts an optimistic gloss. Some are quite simple. The balance sheet can be 'strengthened' by placing a valuation on brand names. This leaves the real value of a company unchanged but may make any hostile take-over bid more difficult. The profit and loss account can be brightened by including profits made on the sale of fixed assets, which has no relationship with the firm's real trading activity. Many firms also choose a date for the publication of accounts that is at a helpful stage in their annual financial cycle. For example, stock might be 'reduced' or 'increased' by selecting a reporting date either side of Christmas.

▶ The manipulation of data from published accounts to justify mergers or take-over bids was a source of growing concern and a factor in the reforms of the early 1990s.

Read the following case study and answer the questions below.

Carlton Carpets Ltd

In 1996 total sales at Carlton Carpets Ltd amounted to £800,000, with a profit before interest and tax of £32,000. The summarized balance sheet as at December 31 1996 is shown below:

	(£k)	(£k)	(£k)
fixed assets			
land and buildings		205	
plant and equipment		83	
investments		40	328
current assets			
stock	36		
debtors	210		
cash	6	252	
current liabilities			
bank overdraft	69		
creditors	111	180	72
			400
financed by:			
shareholders' funds			
ordinary £1 shares		100	
reserves		120	220
long-term liabilities			
mortgage		95	
other loans		85	180
			400

Now calculate the ratios of your choice to answer the following questions:

1 Does the firm appear to be efficient?
2 Assess the firm's liquidity.
3 How stable is the firm's financial structure?

Evaluation

- Ratios should not be understood as financial signals. They provide **indications**, not answers. Ratio analysis highlights areas for investigation.
- Ratios on their own have very limited meaning. They are valuable when compared with those of previous years, internal targets, or competitors. However, there remains the possibility of window dressing.
- Return on net assets (RONA) or return on capital employed (ROCE) are widely used as indicators of efficiency. But what exactly is the definition of 'net assets'? Clearly it depends on what is counted. For example, which intangibles? At what price? John Kay (1993) offers the idea of calculating added value after all costs - including those of equity capital - have been deducted.
- Interfirm comparisons must be treated with caution. Each company has different assets, products and markets. There is no single 'correct' or 'standard' pattern.
- The most valuable use for ratios is the analysis of trends over time, both within and between companies.
- Ratios relate by definition to results from the past. They do not predict the future, which is always liable to be different.
- Different firms use different accounting definitions. Great care must be taken to ensure that ratios are calculated on a common basis.
- For some ratios, such as RONA/ROCE, the higher the value the better. For most ratios, there is no single 'ideal' value. Often a range of values is considered satisfactory and only movement outside the range boundaries is cause for concern.
- Abnormal or worrying ratios may be a **quantitative** signal indicating a **qualitative** problem. For example, falling turnover ratios might be traced to a troubled relationship between the sales manager and sales team.
- All business activity is subject to external forces. Changes in the law, the national economy or world conditions may radically affect ratios.

31 Budgeting

Chapter objectives

After working through this chapter, you will:

- recognize the nature and purpose of a budget
- know how budgets are drawn up in a company
- understand the master budget and its links with sub-budgets
- be able to analyse budget variances as a technique of management control
- know how a pyramid of ratios may be constructed and applied
- know the meaning of the following key terms: standard costing, budget variance.

BUDGETS IN BUSINESS

A budget is simply a financial plan. Many families use a simple budget to plan their income and expenditure for the coming period. Allowance is made for day-to-day spending, regular outlays (e.g. housing, electricity) and one-off items (e.g. buying a car). There may be provision for unexpected events and for savings. The budget enables the household to know its financial limits and responsibilities and to achieve those goals that depend on money. If income falls unexpectedly or spending rises above planned levels, then the problem can be tackled and the budget adjusted if necessary.

▶ 'The Budget', produced by the government every November, is a national plan for raising and spending money.

Budgets for a business are very similar. They involve a specific financial plan to achieve the firm's objectives. Since money represents resources, a budget is a set of decisions concerning the use of scarce resources that have many possible uses.

▶ Business is about adding value to scarce resources. Budgets plan the addition of that value and the use of those resources.

Preparing the Budget

Well ahead of the start to the relevant financial year, a firm begins work on constructing its budget. In larger firms a task group or budget committee is often formed. In smaller firms the company accountant or the owner may be responsible for the job.

The starting point must be the firm's objectives as translated into a business strategy. This may involve targets expressed in terms of accounting ratios (see Chapter 30), market share, total sales or any other relevant criteria. The detailed budget may then be based on historical cost information and forecasts for the year ahead. Alternatively, some firms use **zero budgeting**, where every manager starts

▶ The advantage of zero budgeting is that it avoids the tendency of managers to plan a repeat of the current year – often plus some increase in their expenditure. Instead, they are encouraged to plan for each target and its financial implications.

with a budget of zero and must justify all plans as though making a completely fresh start.

Traditionally, budgets are set for a year ahead, which is a relatively short time horizon. Consequently, they are detailed and practical plans which amount to the next realistic steps on the longer journey towards corporate objectives. The year's budget is often broken down to give monthly data, which is important in keeping plans on target.

Budget Structure

▶ Managers will feel responsible for meeting budgetary targets only if they have been genuinely involved in setting those targets.

▶ A budget is not a forecast. It is a statement of 'what will ...' rather than 'what might ...'

▶ Areas of the firm that generate sources of income are called **revenue centres**, while areas that are sources of expense are called **cost centres**.

What is called the firm's budget is actually a whole series of sub-budgets covering all areas of operation. Often managers will involve as many staff as possible in setting their own element of a budget. This not only makes the budget more realistic but also encourages a sense of ownership of the budget itself. This is important because a good budget is not a target but a **commitment**. The level of performance required by the budget should be neither 'ideal' nor 'soft' but a real intended standard.

The essential pattern is easy to understand. The simple profit and loss account format indicates the basic sequence of budgets. Each element is planned through the months ahead to create a satisfactory overall outcome.

The starting point is sales, pricing and corresponding sales revenue. The marketing department will project sales levels by product, customer and outlet types on a month-by-month basis. The estimates depend on market research, analysis of trends and the detailed opinion of sales staff.

As a likely 'key factor', the **sales budget** usually has special importance. Clearly it must be tightly interlocked with the **production budget**, which must be based on budgeted sales levels plus or minus any planned changes in stock levels. It will be necessary to plan the scale and timing of output around available capacity. A **plant utilization budget** will allow machine time and identify any peaks or troughs around the normal utilization level. The **materials budget** will indicate the flows of raw materials, components and finished goods needed to meet the production schedule. Similarly, the **staffing budget** must specify the direct and indirect staff required, by department and grade. The personnel manager can then plan necessary recruitment, training and deployment. The **production overhead** budget attempts to allocate the fixed overheads (e.g. rent, rates, insurance) that can be directly related to production. Finally, these various production budgets can be expressed in financial terms through the **production cost budget**. In profit and loss terms, this is the vital total that, subtracted from sales revenue, gives gross profit.

The **administrative expenses budget** embraces a wide range of items, including management salaries, office expenses and non-production overheads. The **selling expenses budget** is drawn up by the marketing department and represents the cost of the marketing mix. It will include costs of advertising, sales promotion, distribution and the sales office.

The cost elements that are used to calculate operating profits have now been budgeted and the vital step then is to draw up the

master budget. This includes a projected profit and loss account and balance sheet and so commits the firm to an overall level of performance that should be in accord with corporate objectives.

There are two other financial budgets that relate specifically to the balance sheet. First, the **cash budget** or the **cash-flow forecast** is a month-by-month estimate of all cash flows and the aggregate cash balance. This is essential to ensure solvency (see Chapter 29). Second, the **capital expenditure budget** will depend on the level of funding provided by senior management. This will then be distributed between rival projects seeking financial backing (see Chapter 23). **Investment budgets** normally extend over a number of years and planning in any one year must take account of costs incurred by projects in progress.

▶ In smaller firms the budgetary process will be simplified but still follows the same underlying logic.

Functions of Budgets

The functions of the budget are:

- to create a coordinated strategy to reach corporate objectives;
- to generate communication and interaction among managers in setting budgets;
- to identify costs, question their necessity and sharpen efficiency;
- to assign responsibility for financial decisions and commitments;
- to assist delegation of responsibility while retaining effective means for monitoring performance;
- to represent a system of control over operations and cost centres;
- to provide yardsticks against which actual outcomes can be compared, so pinpointing where management action is required;
- to motivate the organization in meeting budgetary demands.

▶ The importance of budgeting can hardly be overstated. It is the resource control system for the firm and a basis for managerial responsibility.

Variances and Control

As soon as the budgetary period starts, managers can begin to monitor actual outcomes for **variance**. Favourable variances are shown as positive and unfavourable variances as negative. The relative size of a variance is shown by its expression in percentage terms.

▶ **Variance** is the difference between what is budgeted for and what actually happens.

Example of Budget Variance

Bournemouth Bakeries Ltd
Sales budget report

White loaves to external outlets:

April (month 4)				**Cumulative (4 months)**			
budget (£k)	*actual (£k)*	*variance (£k)*	*%*	*budget (£k)*	*actual (£k)*	*variance (£k)*	*%*
16	17.1	+1.1	+6.9	65.4	68.2	+2.8	+4.3

▶ **Standard Costing**
Standard costing takes a given production process and calculates the exact value of its materials, labour and allocated overheads per unit of output. Budgets can then be built up using the standard cost.

The accountant or budgeting manager in a firm should supply senior management with full monthly budget reports. These will include all the major budget statements, with variance shown for monthly and cumulative data. Modified reports may be prepared for specific managers. It is essential that the information is clearly presented, speedily distributed and promptly analysed. Consequent action should be triggered by the variances.

Example of Sales Budget Report

Bournemouth Bakeries Ltd
Sales budget report: April (month 4)

	budget			**actual**			**variance**					
	own shops	*other outlets*	*total*	*own shops*	*other outlets*	*total*	*own shops*		*other outlets*		*total*	
	(£k)	(£k)	(£k)	(£k)	(£k)	(£k)	(£k)	%	(£k)	%	(£k)	%
white	22	16	38	22.4	17.1	39.5	+0.4	+1.8	+1.1	+6.9	+1.5	+3.9
brown	10.5	12.5	23	9.9	8.8	18.7	−0.6	−5.7	−4.3	−29.6	−4.3	−18.7
cakes	28	13	41	27.3	13.3	40.6	−0.7	−2.5	+0.3	+2.3	−0.4	−1

It is clear from Bournemouth Bakeries' sales budget report that sales are proceeding broadly to budget, with one major exception. Sales of brown bread to other outlets are nearly 30 per cent below budget. This problem requires urgent investigation. What was the January variance? What action was taken? What is the real trouble? Was the budget unrealistic? Has a supermarket account been lost? Is competition greater than predicted? Have deliveries failed?

It would be impossible for manufacturers to explore the background to every result with which they are presented. The general rule is to focus investigation only on sources of significant variance. Since budgets are by definition estimates, small variances are usually acceptable. Management attention should be attracted once a variance moves outside a reasonable margin above or below budget.

▶ Management by exception

Management by Exception

The concentration by managers on abnormal features of a firm's operation is called **management by exception**. The principle is based on the assumption that there is no purpose, or time, for managers to examine systems that are functioning normally.

Note that it is not only negative variances that matter. A positive variance may indicate a rich new opportunity: a chance to reduce costs or a sudden gap in the market. Managers will aim to increase such a variance and learn from its implications.

Variances are not only caused by unexpected changes in **volume** (e.g. increased sales) but also arise from changes in **price**. An accountant investigating a positive sales variance would wish to know what proportion was due to increased volume and what proportion to increased price.

Analysis of Variance – Volume or Price?

Firm A is selling a single product.

Budgeted sales: 100 items at £10 each = £1,000
Actual sales: 110 items at £11 each = £1,210

Of the +£210 variance, how much is due to higher volume and how much to higher price?

The rule for analysis is:

volume variance × budget price
price variance × actual volume

So:

volume variance =	10 × £10 =	£100
price variance =	£1 × £110 =	£110
		£210

The same principles are used to analyse a cost variance.

▶ Information technology has made variance analysis faster and cheaper to undertake.

Analysis of Cost Variance

Firm B is selling a single product.

Budgeted cost: 1,000 items at £5 each = £5,000
Actual cost: 950 items at £4.80 each = £4,560

Of the –£440 variance, how much is due to lower volume and how much to lower unit costs?

The same rule for analysis as above is used:

volume variance =	50 × £5 =	£250
cost variance =	£0.20 × 950 =	£190
		£440

The manager of Ace School of Motoring Ltd is examining the company's results for April. The sales budget had projected 2,700 one-hour lessons at £15 each. In reality, a disappointing March had promoted a cut in fees to £13.75. Even so, the number of one-hour lessons taken was only 2,400.

Calculate (a) the volume variance and (b) the price variance from budget targets.

Flexible Budgets

Variance may arise from controllable or non-controllable factors. For example, a positive production cost variance may be due to increased efficiency or a reduction in sales/output. If the firm uses standard costing then the exact sources of the variance can be analysed. In some cases **fixed budgets** with rigid sales assumptions are inadequate and a **flexible budget** is needed. This means that a budget is produced in a range of versions for different levels of potential output relative to budget, for example 80 per cent, 90 per cent, 100 per cent. Thus if sales are 10 per cent below budget the '90 per cent version' can be used to check on controllable variances.

Pyramid of Ratios

▶ The apex of the pyramid is the return on net assets or capital employed. This breaks down into: (1) profit/sales – an analysis of the profit and loss account; (2) sales/net assets – an analysis of the balance sheet.

We know that a budget specifies certain levels of sales and costs. It is therefore also a plan for a range of accounting ratios, which in turn often express key management objectives. The analysis of variances can also be applied to accounting ratios. Because ratios express financial relationships, the investigation of ratio variances may lead an accountant to the heart of a business problem. The analysis becomes even more penetrating when we recognize that ratios form a logical pattern or hierarchy. This can be represented as a 'pyramid of ratios':

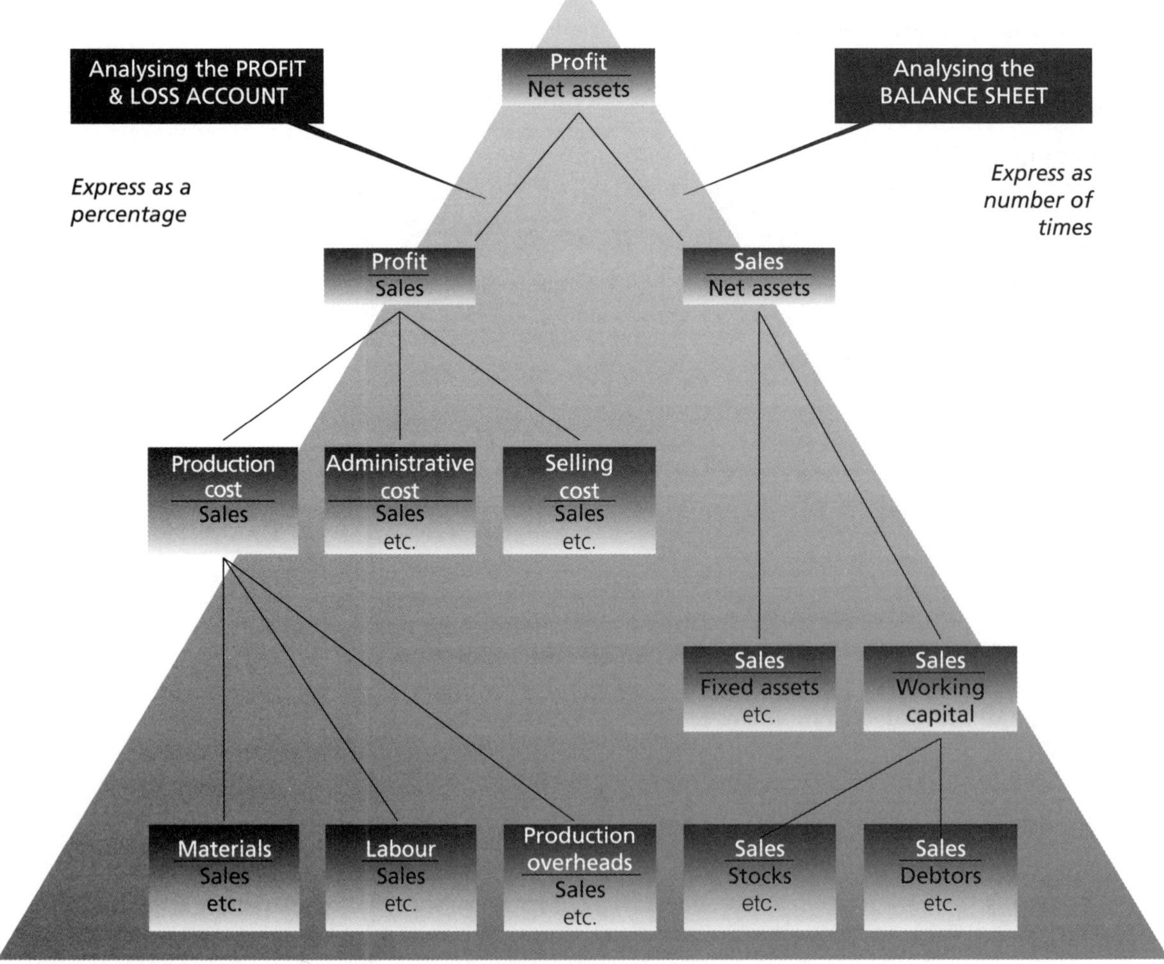

Figure 31.1
The pyramid of ratios

Each arm of the pyramid can be broken down further through the various items on the profit and loss account and balance sheet. Using the master budget it is simple to produce budgeted ratios. Actual results and actual ratios then allow detailed variance analysis to proceed.

▶ Remember that:

$$\frac{\text{profit}}{\text{sales}} \times \frac{\text{sales}}{\text{net assets}} = \frac{\text{profit}}{\text{net assets}}$$

Evaluation

- Budgeting is essentially a planning and control system. It enables managers to translate goals into detailed commitments at every operational level.
- Often the process of setting budgets is as valuable as the budget itself. How does this cost arise? How great is the benefit derived? How could we sell to this customer? Such questions can lead to reduced costs and increased sales.
- Budgets must be realistic. They are effective in human terms only if genuinely negotiated and not simply imposed. In this way staff feel a sense of ownership for their particular budget and respond to it with commitment.
- Variances should work as a management alert system. Progressively higher levels of percentage variances trigger correspondingly more urgent management action.
- Information technology has made the operation of budgetary systems cheaper and more effective. Managers can depend on rapid and frequent access to data.
- A budgetary system must not incur costs greater than its benefits. Budgeting itself works within a budget – for time and money.

Part 6

Human Resources

32 Recruitment, selection and training

Chapter objectives

After working through this chapter, you will:

- know the meaning and scope of personnel management
- be able to analyse the role of personnel management within the business organization
- understand the 'human resources' approach
- be aware of current trends in personnel management
- understand the principles of human resources planning
- appreciate why and how jobs can be analysed
- know how firms recruit potential employees
- be able to evaluate methods for selecting staff
- know the meaning of the following key terms: labour turnover rate, internal recruitment, external recruitment, head-hunting, performance appraisal.

THE FUNCTIONS OF PERSONNEL MANAGEMENT

▶ **Personnel management**: making and implementing decisions that will provide the firm with the human resources necessary for its optimum performance.

Personnel departments vary widely in prestige, size and functions. In some firms they are merely providers of staff and problem solvers when personnel matters go wrong. In other firms the personnel department is at the centre of all people-related decisions and comes even to represent the essential ethos of the company.

▶ The pattern and functions of personnel or human resources management vary widely according to the size and type of enterprise.

Typical major functions fulfilled by the personnel department are:

- **human resources planning**, which analyses all labour grades and skills in terms of projected demand and supply;
- **recruitment and selection**, which involves attracting and identifying the best candidates for posts available;
- **training and management development**, which includes assessing and fulfilling training needs (in accordance with any manpower plan);
- **terms of employment**, which is a wide area of concern including the observance of business laws; disciplinary matters; implementation of redeployment, redundancies and dismissals; maintenance of health and safety at work, plus welfare and social functions;
- **pay and benefits**, which must be assessed and structured to attract, retain and motivate staff of the necessary calibre; there must also be efficient administration;

▶ See Chapter 33.

▶ Personnel management has tended to operate within a 'caring culture', at a distance from the main business functions. There is a trend towards its reintegration into mainstream business decision making.

- **industrial relations**, which means ensuring effective communications between representatives of management and the workforce, not only to resolve grievances and disputes but also to benefit from employee ideas and suggestions.

Depending on its status and importance, the personnel department may also address some broader corporate goals, such as employee motivation (see Chapter 35), communications within the firm (see Chapter 36), the reputation of the firm, the management of change and the development of the corporate culture of the company (see Chapter 48).

Personnel Management Within the Firm

Small firms do not employ personnel specialists and tend to cope with personnel matters on an informal day-to-day basis. Once a business has grown in size to between 150 and 200 employees, a personnel manager becomes necessary, at least to ensure fair and legal practice, but also to recruit staff of the required quality, to organize proper training programmes and generally to bring expertise to 'people problems' throughout the firm.

The basic **policies** of the personnel department are decided by the personnel manager or director in conjunction with the other directors or senior management. Policy statements set the direction and priorities of the department, for instance: 'levels of pay and rewards will be above the industry average to attract and retain a high quality of staff'. Policies must then be reflected in **strategies** for action. These will have a fairly long time horizon, be broad in scope and be subject to revision as events unfold, for instance to adopt pay systems that better reflect individual performance. Such strategies are translated into detailed **tactics** and **operating plans**. These will be much more specific, with a short time frame and expressed as measurable targets, e.g. introduction of a new staff grading system.

The Human Resources Approach

▶ The human resources approach regards people management as a mainstream profit-driven activity rather than a specialist service.

Some firms have renamed their personnel function using the title 'human resources'. This is significant and marks a shift away from the idea of personnel as a free-standing specialist department towards its integration as a player in the mainstream business activity. The **human resources** approach means regarding people as an economic resource that requires combination with other resources to achieve organizational goals. Many personnel departments grew in size and importance during the 1960s and 1970s, but faced sharp retraction in the 1980s. The rise in unemployment reduced the traditional need for recruitment, while the rapid decline in trade union power made industrial relations less prominent in management thinking. Since then many firms have reduced the size of their head offices, decentralized many functions and adopted the concept of focusing all resources – human included – on profit-led objectives with closely measured results. Human resource managers are not just independent professionals or specialists but 'people strategists' and facilitators who are tightly integrated members of the management team. This fits in with the growing idea of more flexible, proactive organizations that are less hierarchical and bureaucratic.

Explain briefly how a personnel manager might contribute to tackling the following problems:

1 The managing director at Steel Box plc is considering relocation of the firm's main steel-cutting and fabrication plant from Birmingham to South Wales.
2 The marketing manager at Tryfan Tents Ltd is alarmed by a sharp rise in returned goods from retailers. Apparently the stitching in the lightweight hiking range is failing and causing the tents to leak.
3 The sales team at MicroEngineering plc must combine all the usual marketing skills with advanced technical knowledge of the firm's hi-tech product range. Salaries and conditions are excellent, with most staff in their mid- to late twenties. Why, then, do sales teams keep losing their best personnel to rival companies?

HUMAN RESOURCES PLANNING

▶ Human resources or personnel planning is often called 'manpower planning', even when the majority of staff are female!

The essence of human resources planning is to match and synchronize the firm's demand for and supply of labour. The demand for labour depends on:

▶ Labour demand

- staff being promoted, leaving, retiring, etc.
- projected expansion, reorganization, etc.
- changing skill requirements
- technological change

These are all complex variables and the firm must attempt to estimate demand as accurately as possible. Often management will make these estimates using its own judgement and experience. Decisions may be taken by senior management alone or based on reports from the line managers of each department, division, branch, etc. Greater accuracy may be obtained by using statistical techniques for forecasting requirements or by using work study to assess the staff-hours for the projected level of activity.

The supply of labour likely to be available depends on:

▶ Labour supply

- the current workforce: its size, skills, qualifications, productivity and potential;
- the external labour market: its size, age structure, availability and mobility, skills and qualifications.

In analysing the current workforce, management should be able to use staff records. It is helpful to calculate the **labour turnover rate**, which is defined as:

▶ Labour turnover rate

$$\frac{\text{number of employees leaving in one year}}{\text{average number of employees during year}} \times 100$$

A moderate staff turnover rate is desirable as it brings 'new blood' into the organization and opens promotion prospects. But a high turnover rate would be adverse, suggesting staff dissatisfaction and causing instability, dislocation and high costs in recruitment and training.

1 Make a list of all the factors you can think of which might lead to a high labour turnover.
(a) Regard the items on your list as possible causes and work out a plan for researching the situation to decide which are the most important causes for a particular firm.
(b) Choose two of the items on your list and write down what the firm might do to reduce labour turnover caused in these two ways. Try to think through the wider implications for the company of your suggestions. For example, if you decide to put up wages, then this cost will have to be paid for.

The external labour market is chiefly influenced by:

- **demographic factors** such as the age structure of the population, which determines the number of school and college leavers;
- **macroeconomic factors**, especially the overall level of demand, which is a key determinant of the employment level;
- **competition** from other employers which may cause shortages of particular skills;
- **education and training**, which affects the availability of younger age groups and the skills and qualifications offered.

From all the data collected regarding the projected levels of labour demand and supply, the human resource plan will be constructed. Although always subject to amendment, it is an important guide in both recruitment and training.

▶ Job analysis is essential to maintaining efficient deployment of staff – often the firm's greatest source of cost.

Job Analysis

Most people are employed by firms only for the tasks which they undertake to complete. These sets of tasks – or jobs – each form interrelated parts of a firm's total productive process. Jobs are the building blocks of business activity. Sound construction of jobs is vital to operating efficiency.

Job Analysis

'Chief Dogsbody' was how Lucy Barrett described her job at Farnham Foods. In theory she was employed as assistant sales manager, but Chris, her boss, was usually out meeting supermarket buyers or chasing contracts in Germany. She was left answering the phone, showing round customers, tackling the post and sorting out distribution failures. She'd given up on 'small UK accounts', which were meant to be her 'special responsibility'. The real irony was that Liz, the new export accounts clerk in the other office, was bored with not enough to do.

In the case in the box above, the lack of job analysis is causing serious inefficiency as well as dissatisfaction among staff. Effective job analysis enables management to construct and define jobs and to place them for greatest efficiency in the organizational structure. A **job description** provides detailed factual information about the position under headings such as:

- title
- grading
- location
- immediate superior
- purpose
- duties
- responsibilities
- special features
- skills and qualifications
- promotion prospects
- pay and benefits
- conditions of employment

▶ The danger of job descriptions is that, rather than being definitions, they become **limitations.** Staff can be led by them to adopt a static and inflexible approach to their role. People grow into jobs and may be carried by their enthusiasm and imagination far beyond their job's original boundaries. Some firms are scrapping formal job descriptions and offering statements of broader objectives instead.

If you are employed yourself, write a job description for the job you do. If you are not employed, interview someone who is and compile a job description using the headings above.

A **job specification** states the requirements made by a job on its holder. The component tasks of the job are listed and matched with necessary knowledge, skills and attitudes.

Job Specification

A company seeks a clerk in the accounts department who will be chasing small debts by telephone. This job may require **knowledge** of elementary accounts, **skills** in the use of both telephone and information technology, and the personal qualities of confidence and courtesy towards others.

It is important that job analysis should provide for regular revision and re-analysis, since jobs are constantly changing. Particular skills diminish and increase in importance, while departments and sections shrink and expand in their workload.

In the previous activity you drew up a job description. Write a corresponding job specification by listing the characteristics and the skills a suitable applicant for the job should have.

THE TASK OF RECRUITMENT

The most basic task is to establish the vacancies that the firm wishes to fill and then to confirm or construct the job description. Most vacancies exist through staff leaving or retiring, but expansion and reorganization may also demand recruitment. When vacancies occur they are not always filled or the opportunity may be taken to make major alterations in the job description.

▶ Recruitment means attracting the most suitable applicants for job vacancies in an organization.

Recruitment Methods

▶ Organizations should be wary of breeding inward-looking or convergent cultures where appointments only confirm the corporate self-image. Injections of unfamiliar assumptions and ideas may be essential to growth and innovation.

The methods of recruitment used must try to achieve the best balance between cost and time against choice and suitability of applicants. The first possibility is **internal recruitment**, where the post is advertised within the firm or a particular person is invited to apply (or even appointed directly). This saves expense, while the performance of the applicant is already well known. The applicant is also likely to be familiar with the organization's style and culture. Internal recruitment keeps open career pathways for existing staff and is a source of motivation. However, it will trigger a chain reaction of vacancies within the firm and loses the advantage of new ideas and new perspectives brought in by outsiders.

In most cases **external recruitment** will be necessary and a range of ways of advertising the vacancies may be used:

- **local press**, which is widely used for clerical and manual positions;
- **national press**, which is used for managerial and professional positions;
- **specialist magazines and journals**, which reach particular groups of professional and technical staff;
- **job centres**, which are run by the Department of Education and Employment and provide a free service mostly used for manual and junior positions;
- **local careers service, schools, colleges and universities**;
- **private employment agencies**, which may be general, covering lower grades of staff, or specialist, supplying managerial, professional and higher grades.

▶ To fill some senior posts, a firm may use **head-hunting**. This means that a potential candidate who works for another employer is asked to apply for or is offered a post. The process may be through informal channels but agencies also offer a head-hunting service.

The use of private employment agencies has sharply increased in recent years. Firms are relieved of the need to advertise and the agency may have a wide range of candidates on its register. Agencies will also carry out all or part of the selection process. But these services are expensive and, although agency selection is often expert and impartial, it cannot take account of the firm's working culture or networks of human relationships.

Recruitment adverts are usually abbreviated interpretations of the job description and job specification. It is essential that they provide candidates with the main details of the job and the qualifications, experience and personal qualities required.

Recruitment advertising is, of course, marketing of jobs. Look back to Chapter 9 and write notes to show the parallels between promoting products and services and recruitment advertising. You may well find it helpful to take cuttings of job adverts from the newspapers to illustrate your notes.

Application Procedure

Look at the job advertisements in the newspapers and select a few. Ring up and ask for application forms and further details. When these arrive, evaluate them according to the following criteria:

(a) Do the further details give the applicant the necessary information about the job?
(b) Is the application form well designed to collect the information the employer will need to shortlist applicants?
(c) Do both together serve to make sure that only suitable people apply and that the employer can judge that those who have applied are suitable?

Interviews

The interview is still the most widely used selection procedure. The evidence suggests that it is not a very good predictor of candidate suitability, but the importance of meeting a potential employee face to face remains. The main purposes of an interview are to assess:

- candidate's likely competence in the job;
- any personal qualities that are an additional advantage or disadvantage;
- general character and personality.

▶ Many managers are amateurs when it comes to interviewing. A personnel department can offer useful advice and assistance.

The firm may adopt a one-to-one or panel approach to the interview (a panel is a group of people who take turns to ask questions). Panel interviews tend to be highly formal and are used most in the public sector and for some senior positions. One-to-one interviews allow for an informal approach. To gain the advantage of several opinions, a sequence of short one-to-one interviews may be arranged. It is important that interviewers have familiarized themselves in advance with candidate details and have agreed any special strategy or allocation for questions.

Candidate Testing

Some firms set tests to complement the interview process. The main types are listed below.

Knowledge/Skills Tests

These aim to establish the candidate's competence in specific tasks, e.g. keyboarding speeds or proficiency in a foreign language.

Aptitude Tests

These are intended to indicate the candidate's potential to gain skills or pursue a particular career. These would include general intelligence tests. More specific tests - say for an engineering apprenticeship - might assess manual dexterity and spatial reasoning. Generally, aptitude tests are most important when the costs of training are particularly high.

▶ Selection tests carry ethical implications. There is a risk that tests can discriminate against candidates with non-European cultural backgrounds. Tests may also violate personal privacy. Individuals may object to a firm wanting to explore and pass judgement on their inner thoughts and feelings.

Personality Tests

These may be used if a particular personality type is thought necessary for the job or found to be particularly unsuitable. Such **psychometric** tests aim to detect introversion or extraversion, convergent or divergent thinking, creative potential, likely behaviour under stress, etc. For example, **Cattell's 16PF (Personality Factor)**

▶ Most personality tests are easy to administer. The skilled task is to interpret the results.

Test works through responses to a series of questions and allows a 'personality profile' to be constructed for comparison with the profile thought most appropriate in the job concerned. More complex projective tests need the expertise of psychologists to be effective. But even a simple list of the candidate's leisure interests may be revealing of personality type.

▶ Because most employees work as members of teams, performance in a group situation can be an important indicator of suitability.

Group Situation Tests

These bring groups of candidates together and their performance is closely observed in a variety of challenging tasks and situations.

▶ The selection process must be very careful to comply with the law concerning sexual and racial discrimination. The law should be a minimum requirement of every selection procedure.

Limitations of Candidate Testing

All tests are subject to serious limitations. They are difficult to apply objectively and results are frequently distorted by candidates either feeling overstressed or attempting to supply 'favourable' responses. Tests may allow valid inferences about candidates' skills or aptitude when the tests are taken, but they have a poor record for predicting actual candidate performance in the job.

1 How might the personnel department of an international construction company recruit:
   (a) experienced surveyors;
   (b) crane operators?
2 What might be the most suitable selection methods for an airline wishing to appoint:
   (a) trainee pilots;
   (b) cabin crew?

TRAINING

▶ Offering high-quality training with effective career planning is more likely to retain key staff and to attract outstanding recruits. People who are well qualified and ambitious look critically at a firm's training opportunities.

▶ Britain arguably suffers from too sharp a divide between academic and vocational study. Many commentators suggest that we need to give much greater status to vocational and technical achievements.

For the great majority of major business enterprises, training is not an optional extra. It is a key means by which firms can gain competitive advantage and sustain or expand their market share. Specific benefits of training include:

- increased labour productivity (output per person-hour);
- ability to use new technology;
- greater flexibility from a wider skills base;
- improved product quality and customer service;
- greater motivation and commitment.

However, many firms still perceive training as an expensive investment where the returns are unknown and unmeasurable. By its nature, training brings long-term rewards and managers tend to be driven by their immediate problems. When a business needs to reduce its costs, training can be an obvious choice for cutbacks. Firms may also fear the loss of expensively trained staff to rivals who have not made any comparable investment.

Large firms will have a formal training policy and this will determine whether the training function is regarded as a short-term supplier of needs or a longer-term investment. The practical forms of training will depend on the nature of the business and its distinctive quality. In a hotel chain it would be customer based, while in an engineering firm it would be technically based.

Before any training plan can be constructed, the firm must identify its **training needs**. These exist wherever the value of an improvement in employee performance is greater than the cost of its achievement through training. Training needs arise both through the demands of the job itself and through changes in the structure and activities of the enterprise. They can be analysed for:

- the company: its labour requirement projections, its introduction of new technology, its changing structure and product base;
- the department: its changing workload and demand for skills;
- the team and the individual: any gaps between existing knowledge and skills and those needed for optimum performance.

In two previous activities you drew up a job description and a job specification. Take the same job and consider what training needs the job holder has in order to improve performance and adjust to changing circumstances. How could these training needs be satisfied?

Evaluation

- Personnel excellence is essential for achieving the levels of quality required in modern business. Recruiting and nurturing this excellence makes personnel management indispensable.
- The nature of the personnel department is shifting from being 'product led' – concerned with employing people – towards being 'market led' – concerned with supplying staffing requirements.
- The human resources approach blurs the old distinction between shop floor and management staff and binds personnel management into the main productive activity of the firm.
- The personnel department has to justify its expenditure like any other cost centre. Its total performance is becoming more strictly accountable.
- Personnel management is finding an increasingly important role in communicating the firm's objectives and values to employees.
- Macroeconomic pressures are a key influence on personnel management. The business cycle impacts directly on recruitment, rewards and employee relations.
- Human resources planning provides a good opportunity to assess critically the real value of jobs performed. Sometimes posts continue to exist after their justification has largely disappeared.
- Selection decisions should meet the long-term interest of the firm as well as immediate staffing needs. Some candidates represent an investment whose value will not be fully realized until long after their appointment.

▶ **Performance appraisal**: regular, individual interviews with employees to assess their performance in the job, to set targets for improvement and to discuss the means for reaching those targets. It helps to discover and clarify training needs.

▶ During and after training it is important for staff to be given the opportunity to use their new knowledge and skills. It is very discouraging if these are ignored or even rejected by line managers.

- The continuous process of restructuring and filling jobs is a vital means by which an enterprise can respond to change. Often resignations and appointments are a key source of adaptation and renewal.
- If the quality of a firm is represented by the quality of its staff, then recruitment and selection is not a routine task. Major firms are increasingly recognizing that employment is not merely a matter of exchanging money for time or tasks completed. It is a deeper relationship between a human organization with its own culture and values, and a human being with his or her own needs, abilities and aspirations.
- Skill shortages are a serious threat to expansion in British industry. Such shortages may discourage use of the most advanced technology and while weakening competitiveness, encourage some firms to locate elsewhere in Europe.
- Low levels of skill among the workforce mean lower levels of value added to the product and lower real wages. This may attract 'screwdriver factories', where assembly only is taking place, but fail to secure 'sunrise industries' and hi-tech manufacturing.
- Employers have a direct economic motive in providing their employees with training for job-related skills. They do not have the same incentive to give training for **transferable skills** – skills that have a wider application across a number of different jobs. Yet these skills are essential to achieve a more flexible and sophisticated workforce.
- Some large firms provide all levels of training, but smaller employers too often regard training for more than their immediate needs as too costly and likely to encourage good staff to leave.
- Training should not be regarded as an occasional or specialized activity. It must be a continuous function that is integral to the firm's life and growth.

33 Employment

Chapter objectives

After working through this chapter, you will:

- know how pay structures and pay rates are decided
- understand redundancy and dismissal procedures
- be aware of employment law and its impact on staffing decisions
- know how the health and safety and the welfare of employees are promoted
- know the meaning of the following key terms: time rates, payment by results, measured day work, salaries, Health and Safety Executive.

PAY STRUCTURES

Pay and benefits are key factors in recruitment, a prime source of motivation and the greatest source of cost in business. Consequently, most firms develop a policy for pay and benefits at the highest management level. This is likely to address:

- the balance of pay against other benefits;
- the mix of fixed rates against piece rates or commission;
- the variation of rewards between different jobs;
- the extent to which rewards-related decisions will be decentralized;
- the relative level of rewards the firm will offer (e.g. a high-pay, high-expectation policy).

▶ There is a growing trend towards individually negotiated rewards packages that reflect the added value likely to be derived from particular staff.

It is usually the task of the personnel department to devise a formal pay structure. This often roughly corresponds to the levels of the hierarchy for each department or branch. Any such system raises questions of fairness, which larger firms may try to resolve through **job evaluation**. A common method is to use a form of grading system, which ranks jobs by some interpretation of the skills, responsibilities and qualifications required. For example, a simplified structure for an administrative office might be:

▶ Job evaluation

grade 1: simple clerical duties
2: dealing with public enquiries
3: junior supervisory
4: section manager

It is traditional to operate separate structures for manual and non-manual work. In addition, some firms also maintain different grading structures for technical and managerial positions.

Analytical job evaluation is a more precise approach. It involves breaking down certain jobs into their component parts and allocating 'points' according to such factors as effort required, skill, responsibility and working conditions. The jobs that have been broken down become 'bench-marks' for all others, which are then slotted into the resulting scale. Such a method is costly but may be more widely acceptable in a large organization.

Rates of Pay and Rewards

▶ Grading structures often include sub-grades. These act as the rungs in the pay and promotion ladders which staff climb. The pay scales within grades often overlap to allow for differences in experience or age.

Pay for a job may be at a fixed or 'flat' rate, or it may be incremental according to length of service or merit.

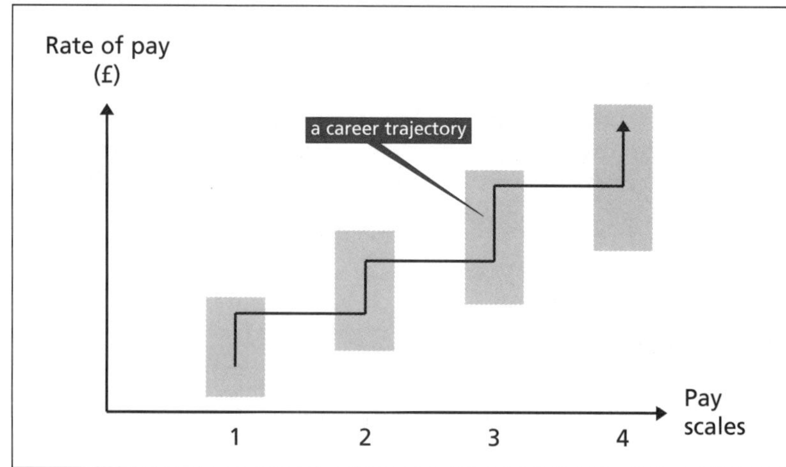

Figure 33.1
A grading structure

Traditional payment systems distinguish between wages for manual jobs, which are paid on an hourly or weekly basis, and salaries for non-manual jobs, which are paid monthly. The main methods of payment are:

1 Wages

- **Time rates** are fixed and paid on an hourly or weekly basis regardless of the worker's output (e.g. £5.75 per hour for a thirty-eight-hour week = £218.50 per week).
- **Payment by results** is often called piecework. Its simplest form involves payment directly related to output or the time taken to achieve a certain level of output.

▶ **Commission**: a form of piece-rate payment. Sales staff often receive a basic salary plus a percentage rate of commission on sales achieved.

Some systems combine time and piecework rates by paying a basic rate up to a standard level of output, beyond which payment is by results.

Time Versus Piece Rates

Time rates are widely used where the nature of the output makes measurement difficult or impossible (e.g. most services). Their drawback lies in failure to make a clear result/payment connection, allowing employees to 'time-serve' or 'coast'. Staff who work to a high standard may resent being paid at the same rate as those who are less efficient or less conscientious. Payment by results (piece rates) provides employees with a direct incentive to maximize output. In practice, workers may adopt restrictive 'norms' for production to protect easily attainable targets. In addition, new work practices may be resisted and quality can suffer.

- **Measured day work** involves setting a level of performance (the 'incentive level') for the worker which is agreed in advance and paid at a fixed rate. The employee has the responsibility to reach this level and may progress to higher levels at higher rates.

2 Salaries

Salaries can be paid on a fixed rate for all staff doing the same job, with individual increases only available through promotion to a different job. Usually, however, there is scope for personal progression through the salary grade according to age, length of service or merit.

Single Status

Some firms have abolished the distinction between their manual and white collar (non-manual) staff to adopt **single status**. All staff then enjoy the same payment systems and benefits (e.g. pensions and holiday rights), often bringing a much improved package for manual workers. Apart from simpler administration, the aim is to dissolve the barriers between management and manual workers in order to give all staff a unified sense of responsibility and commitment in the organization.

▶ Single status may also involve abolition of social divisions between management and staff. For example, everyone may share the same staff restaurant or adopt first-name terms.

Bonus and Share Option Schemes

Some firms use bonus schemes to supplement earnings. Bonus payments may be made according to:

- time of year (usually Christmas)
- personal merit
- productivity on plant-wide basis
- profitability

A more recent development has been employee share option plans (ESOPS), where staff receive their bonus in the form of ordinary shares in the company, sometimes at a preferential rate. Such schemes have certain rules concerning the sale of shares and tax liability. The aim is to encourage greater employee identification with the firm and its need for profitability.

Overtime

Many companies provide opportunities for employees to work overtime at higher rates of pay (e.g. 'time and a half', or one and a half times the normal rate), especially for manual staff. This normally arises because of a short-term need for increased output. In some firms it becomes a regular occurrence and a substitute for

▶ **Flexitime**: employees must attend work for some stated 'core time' but can complete their working hours when they choose.

additional full-time staff. Although this can be cheaper and more flexible than recruiting new staff, there are dangers in relying on the arrangement. A withdrawal from overtime by either side can cause serious problems: resentment among employees or short-staffing for the employer.

▶ Increasingly competitive labour markets have led to widening differentials in levels of reward. Like firms, people with skills in high demand and short supply can earn very high rewards. Conversely, those without special skills – especially in periods or areas of slack labour demand – often earn very little.

Setting the Rate of Pay

Labour exists in a competitive market like any other resource. The firm has a demand for labour while its value to the firm is greater than its cost (pay and benefits). The worker will supply labour while his or her valuation of the rewards is greater than the opportunity cost – no one will take overtime indefinitely: sleep becomes more valuable! These forces of demand and supply are reconciled in the real labour markets through recruitment, pay bargaining and redundancy. The actual level of pay and benefits offered depends mainly on the following factors:

- **Demand for the product**: affects output and hence the need for staff.
- **Elasticity of product demand curve**: rewards for staff are the major cost affecting price, in turn bearing on the level of sales.
- **Demand for particular skill or qualification**: some types of staff are more sought after than others.
- **Supply of labour type**: there are always shortages and surpluses of different skills.
- **Nature of the job**: the attractiveness of the job, the training necessary, the occupational hazards, etc.
- **Trade unions and professional organizations**: the greater their power relative to the employer, the higher the likely level of rewards (see Chapter 37).
- **Benefits**: pay depends partly on the value of the benefits package that is offered.

Benefits

▶ Flexible benefit systems allow staff to choose up to a certain value from a 'menu' of different benefits. This increases the value of benefits to the individual employee at no extra cost to the firm.

Most jobs carry some benefits in addition to wages or a salary. These are variously called 'fringe benefits' or 'perks', or are included in the concept of a 'rewards package'. Some range of benefits is now widely expected by employees and can be an important factor in retaining their loyalty and in increasing motivation. There are also tax advantages that make benefits cheap relative to their value for employees. The most common benefits are:

- **Pensions**: all employees contribute to the basic state pension scheme, but firms can opt out of the earnings-related element and provide their own more generous scheme.
- **Holidays, hours and leave**: the amount of paid holiday granted by firms is tending to increase (four to six weeks is common). Flexible working hours are valued by employees, especially if they need to fit work around domestic commitments. Paid or unpaid leave of absence may also be available.
- **Loans, grants**: these are provided by some firms to assist with season tickets, buying a car, house purchase or relocation. Loans may be at reduced interest or interest free.
- **Expenses**: more senior positions often include entitlement to

refund of expenses (or a company credit card) for travel, meals, hotels, etc.
- Subsidized **canteen and social facilities**, company cars, health insurance, discounts on the firm's products.

Look through the employment advertisements in the local or national newspapers to discover modes of payment and other benefits of employment. What kinds of jobs seem to be associated with what kinds of benefits?

REDUNDANCY AND DISMISSAL

▶ Unemployment, see Chapter 40.

There are many reasons why a firm may need to eliminate jobs and reduce certain inputs of labour:

- new technology replaces manpower
- the cost of labour increases
- a merger leads to rationalization (see Chapter 24)
- the firm relocates

Efforts are usually made to avoid compulsory **redundancy** by using natural wastage (non-replacement of staff leaving), redeployment and retraining, early retirement and voluntary redundancy. If compulsory redundancies are unavoidable, then management must take great care in handling the procedure in order to minimize ill effects on all concerned. To be made redundant is a great personal blow to many people and the event may create a deep sense of insecurity in them and other staff. If trade unions are recognized, then proper consultation must take place. A fair basis for selecting staff to be made redundant must be chosen – often the 'last in, first out' principle. Notification of the individual concerned should be sensitive and prompt after the decision is made in order to avoid destabilizing rumours.

A firm may wish to dismiss an employee who is incapable of reaching an acceptable standard in the job, or whose conduct is unsatisfactory. Both these grounds for dismissal are legally considered to be 'fair'. However, the relevant manager will usually make efforts to assist the employee to become competent or to improve his or her conduct before resorting to formal dismissal. If dismissal does become necessary, the firm must be careful to check the terms of the employee's contract and to follow the formal disciplinary procedure that has been agreed. Under the **Employment Protection Act** there are various grounds for dismissal that are automatically 'unfair', such as joining or refusing to join a trade union or becoming pregnant. Any dismissed employee is entitled to claim unfair dismissal and to take his or her case to an industrial tribunal. Efforts will then be made to settle the matter through the Advisory, Conciliation and Arbitration Service (ACAS). If this fails, and if the tribunal finds in favour of the employee, then reinstatement or compensation may be ordered.

▶ Employment Protection Act, 1978
This specifies the minimum periods of notice and scale of redundancy payments. In practice, many employers offer more generous terms, which may be embodied in agreements with unions.

Sex and Race Discrimination

It is illegal for employers to discriminate on grounds of sex or race. The key legislation is as follows:

- **Equal Pay Act, 1970** requires employers to offer equal pay and conditions of service to men and women for equal or broadly equal work, or for work of 'equal value'. An employee with a grievance under the Act will take the case to an industrial tribunal for judgement.
- **Sex Discrimination Acts, 1975 and 1986** prohibit discrimination in such matters as recruitment and selection, promotion and retirement ages. Two kinds of discrimination are banned. Direct discrimination occurs when a person is treated unfavourably because of his or her sex (e.g. a man taking precedence in promotion). Indirect discrimination means setting conditions which are applied equally but which favour one sex (e.g. unnecessary regulations regarding physique). Again, discrimination claims are taken to an industrial tribunal. The 1975 Act created the Equal Opportunities Commission, which promotes equal opportunities and can instruct an employer to end a form of discrimination,
- **Race Relations Act, 1976** prohibits discrimination on grounds of race, with the same pattern of application as the sex discrimination laws. Complaints can be brought to a tribunal, which has the right to award compensation. The **Commission for Racial Equality** promotes fair and harmonious race relations. It can bring a complaint to a tribunal on its own initiative.

▶ Many major firms have active equal opportunities programmes.

▶ With few exceptions, job advertisements must not specify race or gender as necessary for the job.

HEALTH AND SAFETY

▶ In Britain, about 340 people are killed in accidents at work each year and around 130,000 people are injured badly enough to need three or more days off work. Many other people – some retired – suffer from long-term industrial disease.

Many jobs involve activities where failure to follow the correct procedure can cause death or serious injury. Almost every workplace has the potential to endanger health and safety.

Health and safety can be put at risk through a work environment that is badly designed, ill equipped or poorly maintained. Work practices – official or unofficial – may be inherently dangerous. Training may be inadequate. The attitude among employees may be casual or dismissive towards safety, while the final responsibility for all safety factors must rest decisively with management.

▶ The number of accidental deaths at work has halved since 1974.

The **Health and Safety at Work Act, 1974** states that every employer has a duty to ensure, as far as is reasonably practicable, the health and safety at work of all employees. This means making the workplace physically safe, and then ensuring its safe use through the design of work practices and by proper training, supervision and leadership.

For employees, a recognized trade union has a legal right to appoint **safety representatives** and require the formation by the employer of a safety committee. The safety representatives will carry out checks and investigations into safety and liaise with both the employer and the safety inspectorate. The safety committee will study safety reports, make proposals for improvements and promote safety awareness. The terms of the 1974 Act are enforced by the **Health and Safety Executive (HSE)**, which maintains a range of specialist inspectorates. HSE inspectors can examine business premises at any time and order improvement or, if necessary, launch prosecutions.

Hartlepool Hydraulics

Hartlepool Hydraulics was close to liquidation in late 1993 owing to an excessive cost structure and the impact of foreign competition. A major restructuring followed, with investment in new technology and concentration on specialist hi-tech markets. A single-status agreement was accepted by all staff in 1994.

Year	*Total employees*	*Labour turnover (%)*
1994	4,000	28
1995	2,800	36
1996	2,000	15

Classification by skill (%)	*1994*	*1996*
unskilled	52	20
semi-skilled	20	14
skilled	15	40
administrative and professional	13	26

1. What would be the likely changes in the pattern of rewards offered by the company?
2. How might the firm have achieved the personnel changes indicated?

Evaluation

- Firms with the best results and reputations tend to offer above-average rewards and have above-average expectations of above-average staff.
- The choice of payment system must depend on the nature of the work. Where commitment to the organization is important, time rates are appropriate. If the firm is merely purchasing a discrete labour process, then piece rates may be suitable.
- Payment-by-result schemes, with their direct link to output, can be inappropriate during a recession.
- Although pay is important, employers can gain a good reputation and a highly motivated staff through the quality of their benefit schemes, their training and their concern for individuals.
- Firms are tending to develop a smaller core of well-rewarded permanent full-time staff. Part-timers and contract staff will receive payment at the market rate and without the full rewards package.

- Enforcement of employment law in Britain tends to be by advice and warning, with formal prosecution used only as a last resort. Large firms are highly sensitive to criticism that might become public.
- Like quality, safety needs to be 'in-built' rather than 'added on'. It needs to be an automatic factor in every decision.

34 Leadership

Chapter objectives

After working through this chapter, you will:

- understand the qualities and functions of leaders
- be able to evaluate the major leadership styles
- know the key theories that analyse leadership in organizations
- know the meaning of the following key terms: autocratic leadership, democratic leadership, laissez-faire leadership.

THE MEANING OF LEADERSHIP

▶ 'Leadership is the process of influencing others to work willingly towards an organization's goals.'
Koontz, O'Donnell and Weihrich

Turn on the television or the radio and you will almost certainly see or hear leaders – leaders of countries, political parties, local councils, churches, sports teams, trade unions, major companies. Human affairs seem to be expressed through leaders. There appears to be a natural need for leadership (even groups of small children have leaders ...) and a process by which leaders emerge.

A leader is able to mobilize the energy and ability of other people and to create in them an urge to reach stated objectives. A business manager is responsible for setting objectives and efficiently deploying resources to fulfil them. It follows that leadership is a key management quality. All tasks are ultimately achieved through people. Without leadership the talents of people as well as physical resources are wasted and an organization will rapidly lose ground to its competitors.

Leadership Qualities

Given its great importance, many studies have attempted to identify the vital qualities of a good leader. This has proved very difficult, since different leaders in different situations seem to have different qualities. It may be better to suggest some key pointers to the **potential** of leadership.

1 **Competence**: This means skill in a particular type of task, usually combined with experience. It includes flair and instinctive ability.
2 **Analysis and synthesis**: The potential leader is receptive to both events and ideas. He or she readily uses these to form patterns with **meaning** (analysis), and this leads to new actions and ideas (synthesis).
3 **Social interactivity**: The person is highly sensitive to how

▶ The rising importance of teamwork makes these qualities valuable in almost all staff.

others involved are thinking and feeling. He or she is effective in gaining the support of people, often using fluent and persuasive language.

4 **Self-belief**: A strong, even passionate, self-belief in at least some respect provides the conviction and confidence for leadership. This self-belief may range from a quiet assurance to a burning sense of mission.
5 **Energy and drive**: A need is felt for activity and achievement. There is a sense of restlessness and urgency. The person often tires less easily than average.
6 **Charisma**: This is the innate ability to inspire others with confidence and hope. People with charisma are somehow naturally admired and sought after by those around.

There is now an important question: does leadership arise from the **qualities of the person** or the **demands of the situation**?

The 'scientific school' of management believes that business managers must be tough and determined in making their own decisions and enforcing them among the workforce. Certain people were thought to be born with leadership qualities, and that made them able to use power effectively. 'Great men' were born and not made.

During the twentieth century the 'human relations school' of management rejected this view, arguing that each situation demands a different **style** of leadership.

The Functions of Leadership

A leader aims to reach goals through the efforts of the people available. People working together towards a common goal – formally or informally – make a group or a team. John Adair (1973) presents the leader working in three overlapping areas of concern:

▶ Effective leadership involves judging the relative importance of task, group and individual needs.

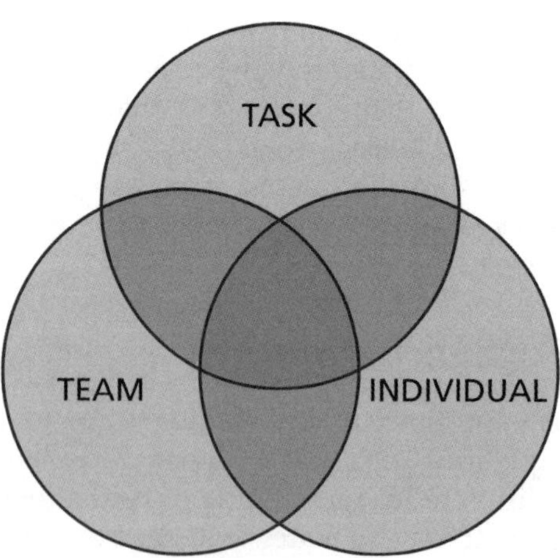

Figure 34.1
The functions of leadership

- **The task**: The leader needs clear strategic objectives and the ability to set the right tactical goals at the right time. Delegation will be necessary but proper standards must be maintained and targets set. It may be necessary to obtain expertise from other sectors of the organization, or from outside consultancies, contractors etc.
- **The group**: The leader decides and/or enforces formal group structures. The leader must recognize **informal group norms**, at the same time working constantly in shaping them

towards task objectives. Motivation is maximized through recognition and rewards. However, disciplinary action can be necessary and individual needs may need to be sacrificed in the interests of the group. In maintaining morale and commitment, the leader's personal example is most important. The leader will take credit for the group's success – and responsibility for its failure.

- **The individual**: Support for a leader is strongly related to his or her skill in satisfying personal needs within the group. The leader must understand what motivates his or her subordinates at a psychological as well as contractual level. Rewards and penalties are distributed to individuals. Protection may be given to those in difficulties, but the final threat of dismissal remains.

These 'need' areas overlap one another, but each also exists in its own right. According to the situation, the relative size of each circle will vary. For example, a fire officer in action would recognize a very large 'task' circle and a very small 'individual' circle. Equally, the manager of a taxi firm would face a large 'individual' circle but a fairly small 'group' circle. The effective leader uses judgement in each **situation** to set the **priority** of each need.

Leadership Styles

Interest in the personal qualities of leaders has shifted towards the style of leadership. This view first gained ground in the 1950s, influenced by a famous study of leaders in a boys' camp described by Lewin, Lippitt and White in 1939. Three types of leadership were identified:

▶ **Styles of Leadership**
• **autocratic**: decisions imposed by the leader;
• **democratic**: the group shares the decision making;
• **laissez-faire**: members of group are left to make their own decisions.

▶ Autocratic leadership is most effective when there is a need for immediate action within precise rules.

1 Autocratic leadership

The leader aims for personal control. He or she is clearly separated from the group, who must obey orders. Virtually all decisions are made by the leader, who releases only a minimum of information to subordinates. Communications are 'top-down', with little chance for feedback. Working methods are strictly specified and little allowance is made for individual preferences. Praise and promotion are difficult to anticipate or understand: the leader's motives remain unknown.

▶ Democratic leadership is most effective when the ideas and agreement of all staff are important.

2 Democratic leadership

The leader involves the group in decision making and aims to work by **consent**. Argument and discussion are normal and, although the leader makes final decisions, members of the group are all able to contribute freely to debate. Formal communications have open pathways, with a variety of routes both 'down' and 'up' the hierarchy. Subordinates decide their own methods of work, often checking output and quality themselves. Individual needs are actively considered and the distribution of rewards is according to clear criteria.

▶ Laissez-faire leadership can be effective when individuals are highly qualified and are working on very creative projects.

3 Laissez-faire leadership

'Laissez-faire' means literally 'leave to do'. The leader is present and may make known some broad objectives, but otherwise he or she has a very limited role. The group members are allowed to make their own decisions and follow their own individual wishes. Communications are very varied in pattern, liable to conflict and largely informal. Powerful informal groups may develop with their own widely differing 'norms'. Rewards will be unpredictable.

Decide on the optimum leadership style relative to the situations below and tick the columns accordingly.

Situation	*Autocratic*	*Democratic*	*Laissez-faire*
Senior fire officer tackling warehouse blaze	☐	☐	☐
Leader of team at advertising agency generating new themes for client	☐	☐	☐
Experienced social worker responsible for inner-city team	☐	☐	☐
Office manager organizing company social outing	☐	☐	☐

Fred Fiedler

In 1967 Fred Fiedler, a professor of psychology and management at the University of Washington, published *A Theory of Leadership Effectiveness*. He wanted to discover the leadership factors likely to achieve maximum performance in a group. He describes two styles of leader:

1 Relationship-motivated leaders, who gain most job satisfaction in relationships with people.
2 Task-motivated leaders, who get most job satisfaction through successful completion of the task in hand.

Fiedler argues that either style can be the 'right' style depending on the situation. This, in turn, depends on the extent to which the circumstances are favourable to the leader. The key factors are:

- leader–member relations – quality of leader–group and leader–individual relations;
- task structure – the degree to which the task is clearly described and structured;
- leader's position-power – the rights and powers of the leader, for instance, to reward or discipline staff.

▶ Fiedler balanced emphasis on the relationship or the task according to the circumstances prevailing.

Fiedler then related leadership styles to the extent to which the situation was favourable or unfavourable. This analysis showed that the task-motivated leader was more effective if the situation was very favourable or very unfavourable. In the intermediate situations a relationship-motivated leader was more effective.

Blake and Mouton

Robert Blake and Jane Mouton are psychologists who have led an American behavioural science consultancy. They assume that the goal of management is to generate both efficiency in the task and a creative, innovative climate. Their managerial grid (1962) relates a manager's concern for production and concern for people.

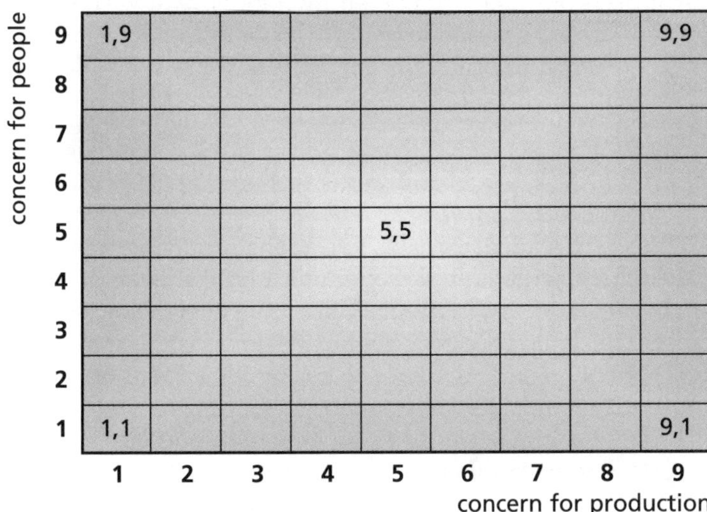

Figure 34.2
The management grid

Adapted from R. Blake and J. Mouton, The Managerial Grid: advanced management office executive, *1962*

A large range of possible managerial patterns can now be examined. The five key combinations are:

1,1 **Impoverished management**: responsibility is avoided both for tasks and for people.

1,9 **The 'country club' management style**: the emphasis is on people and a sense of cosy 'togetherness'. The task is very secondary.

5,5 **The 'dampened pendulum' style**: this is the compromise position. Extremes of the pendulum (1,9 or 9,1) are avoided and adequacy is the goal.

9,1 **Task management**: authoritarian leadership focuses on the task and treats people as mere tools.

9,9 **Team management**: demands high concern for both production and people. Human needs are satisfied within a team that is motivated by excellence in the task.

▶ Position 9,9 represents the ideal location on the grid.

Blake and Mouton argued that maximized concern for both people and production is always the most effective management style.

Charles Handy

In his *Age of Unreason* (1989), Charles Handy looks again at leadership, given the trend towards greater delegation and federalism. Leadership should be a quality that exists throughout the organization. Each leader must help to shape and transmit a clear vision that gives purpose to work and stretches staff towards their potential. Correspondingly, the model of the leader as a teacher, counsellor or friend is more appropriate than the model of the leader as guardian, inspector or judge.

▶ Handy sees organizations becoming more like intelligent networks where leadership is more widely spread.

In a modern organization, the leader should support a learning culture within the firm where staff are colleagues and co-learners. Learning will occur only if staff can make mistakes and know that they will be forgiven. In this supportive atmosphere, risks can be taken and creative ideas proliferate.

Evaluation

- The team under autocratic leadership is likely to depend heavily on the leader for any success and to lack development in self-discipline or self-motivation. Efficiency may be high when objectives are clear and the supervision level is high. Pro- and anti-leader factions are likely to divide the team.
- Democratic leadership leads to a strong group that is more self-reliant, with multiple communication pathways between members. Individuals are more likely to be self-disciplined and efficiency is probably good without being exceptional. The leader has a lower profile and his or her authority causes little resentment.
- The laissez-faire leader has very limited importance to the group, whose members participate vigorously in all decision making. Efficiency is very variable and self-discipline is essential. Conflict between group members is likely to be a constant problem.
- It is debatable to what extent effective leadership depends on the person or the task/situation.
- Some theorists such as Fiedler stress the importance of the right leadership style for the right situation. The effectiveness of the various leadership styles depends on the situation in terms of the task and the people involved.
- Handy's more radical idea of leadership as a basic human quality exercised by everyone is gaining ground. Firms are moving away from a 'culture of command' towards a 'culture of consent'. Decision making 'ripples' through 'flatter' federal organizations that show intelligence at every level.

35 Motivation

Chapter objectives

After working through this chapter, you will:

- appreciate the meaning and importance of motivation in business
- know some major theories of human motivation
- be able to classify and evaluate these theories
- understand how motivation theory can be applied to practical management
- know the meaning of the following key terms: Hawthorne effect, informal groups, motivation factors, valence, expectancy.

THE MEANING AND IMPORTANCE OF MOTIVATION

Motivation means a human being's strength of desire to act in a particular way. A person who is highly motivated is keen to start an activity and works at it with a sense of urgency and personal commitment. A poorly motivated person is relatively unconcerned about the activity and approaches it with a lack of energy or direction. You will know from your own experience the importance of motivation in getting things done. Achievement in any field of human effort – academic work, art, music, sport for example – depends critically on the level of motivation.

▶ Everyone is motivated by private needs of some kind. These may be tangible, such as money, or intangible, such as a sense of pride or self-respect. It is a vital task of management to understand these needs and attempt to harness their power through the rewards offered by jobs in the organization.

This is equally true in business. Only the highly motivated entrepreneur is likely to succeed in starting a new business. Only the motivated salesperson will convince customers. And only the motivated worker will achieve quality and efficiency. Motivation affects nothing less than the whole network of human forces that animate the organization and enable it to meet objectives. The productivity of every person in the firm depends centrally on their level of motivation. Even more than this, motivation determines the vitality of the organization and its ability to anticipate and respond to the forces of change. It is a kind of electricity in the air. There is no substitute for it.

▶ Motivation is the human key to productivity.

NM As you read through this chapter, note down how each theory highlights a source of motivation and how each theory could be applied to improve employee motivation.

Theories of Motivation

F.W. Taylor

During the 1880s Frederick Taylor worked at the Midvale Steel Company, Philadelphia, where he rose from shop floor labourer to chief engineer. Here he evolved the concept of 'scientific management', which simply means the application of scientific principles to the process of management. From 1889 he worked at the Bethlehem Steel Company, where he conducted famous experiments in labour productivity. The resulting ideas were formalized in his *Principles of Scientific Management,* published in 1911. His work focused on the concept of **cost effectiveness** in the labour force. Taylor assumed that all individuals are motivated by personal economic gain and that in their behaviour they closely resemble machines. His approach was therefore mechanical in maximizing cost effectiveness. This involved a scientific analysis of the task to find the most efficient methods. Workers could then be trained accordingly and motivated through 'scientific' payment according to effort and results.

▶ 'What the workers want from their employers beyond anything else is high wages and what employers want from their workmen most of all is low labour cost.'

F.W. Taylor

Taylor's ideas have been very influential. Indeed, 'Taylorism' became a philosophy of management, active across the industrialized world. The very real productivity gains it brought to the Bethlehem Steel Company went on to occur in most major industries and fitted well with increased mechanization and the development of assembly-line methods. But Taylorism also has serious limitations because it is an **inadequate view of human beings**. The motivational power of money is limited.

Elton Mayo

Elton Mayo was professor of industrial research at Harvard University. Over the period 1924–32, he carried out what became a world-famous research project at the Hawthorne plant of the Western Electric Co. in Chicago. The results were published in *The Human Problems of an Industrial Civilization* in 1933. Before Mayo arrived at Western Electric, the company had conducted the 'optimum illumination investigation', which used control and test groups of workers to determine the effects of changes in lighting intensity on efficiency. The mysterious outcome was a sharp rise in output by all groups regardless of lighting. Mayo started with similar assumptions to Taylor and further explored this phenomenon in the 'relay assembly test room' experiments. These involved altering rest breaks, lunch times and working hours for one group of women workers. Again, output increased whether conditions were made better or worse. The explanation has become known as the **Hawthorne effect**. Western Electric was a dreary, anonymous place to work and the tasks were repetitive and boring. Output in experimental groups was rising for **human** not physical reasons. It was the personal attention and recognition of research teams that was the source of the Hawthorne effect.

▶ The **Hawthorne effect** refers to an improvement in efficiency as a result of better human relations rather than better technology or working conditions.

Later the 'bank wiring room' investigation closely analysed how fourteen male workers behaved as a group. The men quickly established their own sub-groups with social and working 'norms' that cut across the company's rules and incentive systems. These

informal groups with their own leaders were very powerful in determining productivity.

Mayo's work established the 'human relations' approach to management and motivation. It revealed that human needs were far more complex than the simple desire for money and that human relationships vitally affect how hard and how well people work.

▶ Mayo founded the 'human relations' approach to management.

Abraham Maslow

Maslow was an American psychologist who studied human motivation. In 1954 he published *Motivation and Personality,* which proposed a hierarchy of needs.

▶ Once a level in Maslow's hierarchy is fulfilled, it loses its power to increase motivation.

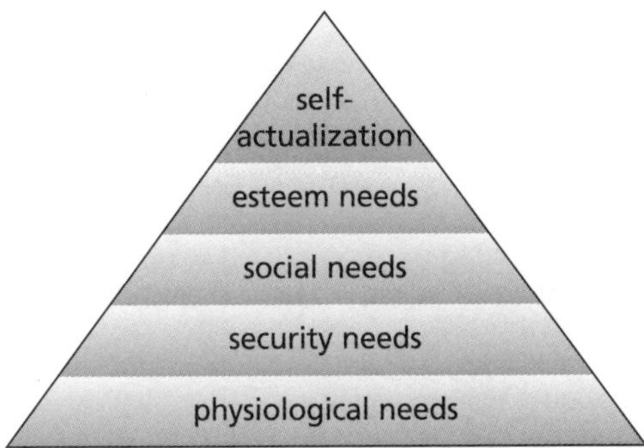

Figure 35.1
Maslow's hierarchy of needs

- **physiological needs**: the basic physical requirements of food, shelter, warmth and sleep;
- **security needs**: the need to know that physical safety is assured;
- **social needs**: the need for rewarding relationships with other people;
- **esteem needs**: the need for self-respect and the respect of others;
- **self-actualization needs**: the need for fulfilment of inner potential.

Frederick Herzberg

Frederick Herzberg was professor of management at the University of Utah and carried out a survey of engineers and accountants in Pittsburg during the late 1950s. The respondents were asked to describe sequences of events that had made them feel very dissatisfied and very satisfied in their jobs. The results were published in *The Motivation to Work* (1959). Two distinct sets of factors emerged: **maintenance or hygiene factors** (see Figure 35.2), which were the dissatisfiers, and **motivation factors**, which were the source of satisfaction.

It can be concluded that the presence of motivation factors is a key source of job satisfaction, but their absence is a very minor source of job dissatisfaction. The conclusion for management is that, while it is important to get the hygiene factors right, they are only a baseline from which the motivators can operate.

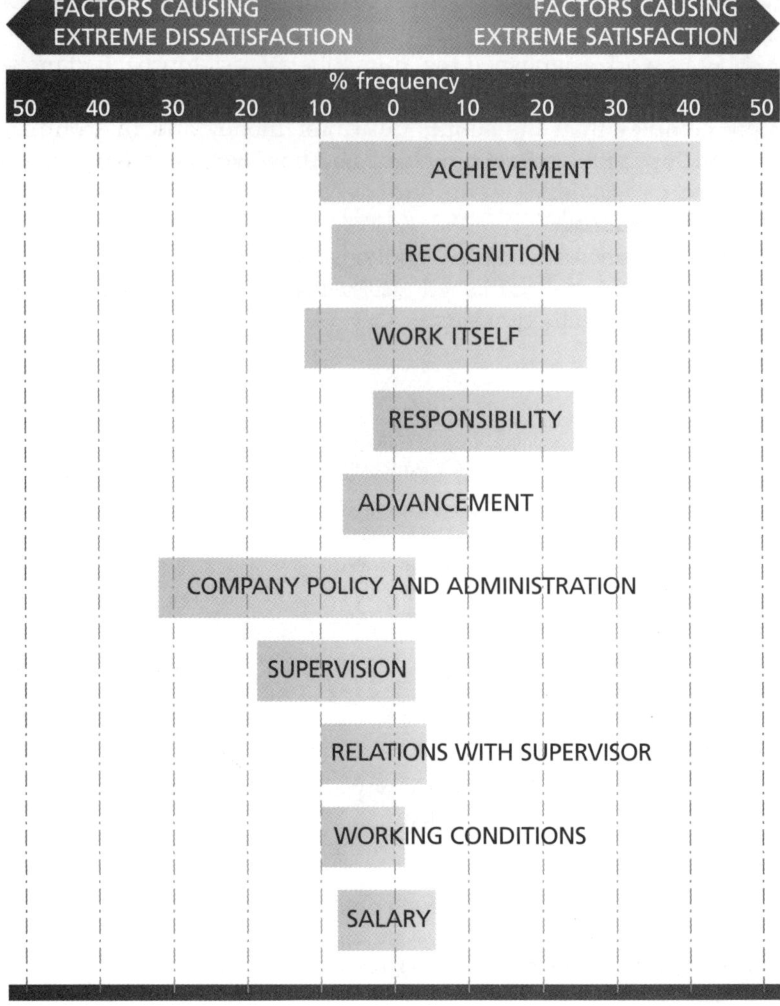

Figure 35.2
Dissatisfiers and satisfiers: Herzberg's theory

▶ McGregor argued that many people behave in accordance with Theory X because their managers have Theory X assumptions.

Douglas McGregor

Douglas McGregor was professor of management at the Massachusetts Institute of Technology and is best known for his celebrated **Theory X and Theory Y** analysis described in *The Human Side of Enterprise* (1960). Two sharply opposed interpretations of people at work are offered:

Figure 35.3
McGregor's Theory X and Theory Y

Theory X	Theory Y
• The average person dislikes work and will avoid it. • Most people must be pushed, controlled and threatened by punishment if they are to work adequately hard. • The average human being wants to avoid responsibility. • Such people are unambitious and have security as their greatest need.	• Work is natural to humans and is not fundamentally disliked. • People can use self-direction and self-control towards objectives to which they are committed. • The average person grows first to accept and then to seek responsibility. • The greatest human need is self-actualization, for which most people have large funds of creative potential – mostly unused at present.

McGregor argued that the Theory X pattern is indeed widespread, not as a natural condition but as a **consequence of management**. The Theory Y scenario will not always be attainable, but the task of good management is to create the conditions where it can prevail. Enormous reserves of hidden potential in the workforce can be released in this way. Theory Y is not 'soft' management: it is a highly exacting vision of what people at work might become.

Victor Vroom

Victor Vroom worked on the psychology of organizations in Canada and the USA. His expectancy theory was published in *Work and Motivation* (1964). The essential idea is that a motivation towards any course of action depends on:

- the value of the anticipated reward;
- the perceived likelihood that it will be forthcoming.

More precisely, Vroom asserts that:

force (motivation) = valence × expectancy

where **force** is strength of the urge to act, or degree of motivation; **valence** is the expected value of the outcome; and **expectancy** is the subjective estimate of probability that the outcome will occur.

▶ Notice the parallel between Vroom's theory and the concept of expected value in decision trees (see Chapter 46).

The concept is based on the individual's personal perception of reality. The valence of any outcome will vary both between individuals and over time. Expectancy depends on the behaviour of the organization and on the experiences and prejudices of the person concerned.

The Expectancy Effect

A marketing manager of a textile company is told to expect promotion if she can increase market share for a key product. Although she would value promotion very much, she has heard such promises before and seen them come to nothing. She therefore opts for a quiet life. Conclusion: high valence and low expectancy does not produce high motivation.

Edgar Schein

In his *Organisational Psychology* (1970), Edgar Schein argues for a theory of **complex man**, in which people are motivated by a range of needs from lower to higher levels. In each individual these needs form a complex pattern that is dynamic and constantly evolving through growth and experience. Needs at all levels change in their nature and intensity over time, and managers of people must try to optimize the motivational forces acting on their staff. This means maintaining a constant awareness of:

▶ Schein emphasized that the pattern of individual needs changes with time and experience.

- individuals and their inner needs;
- the demands and rewards of jobs and the corresponding performance of staff;
- the relevant styles of leadership and the prevailing organizational culture.

This view coincides with the concept of the organization as a kind of living organism, where managers are not just occupying positions of command but are nurturing configurations of human energy.

MOTIVATING FACTORS

Pay as a Motivating Factor

▶ Pay may be the main reason for holding a job yet not the major source of motivation when working within that job.

F.W. Taylor regarded pay as the only motivational factor. Human relations theorists regarded pay as meeting only lower-order needs and therefore limited its value as a source of motivation. Herzberg's research confirmed pay as a weaker motivator or source of job satisfaction. Yet most people in most jobs would undoubtedly name pay as their major reason for going to work. In this no doubt they are telling the truth, but as a fact it fails to explain the springs of motivation while they are actually at work.

An important distinction must be made between the motivation to **hold a job** – where pay is a key factor – and motivation **within a job**, where money is far less important. This explains the apparent contradiction between Herzberg's findings and the attitudes of most people towards their job. Indeed, for most people with permanent employment on time rates, the motivational force of pay applies primarily to the maintenance of their livelihood rather than to how hard they work. However, a rate of pay that is perceived to be unfairly low for the demands of the job would be demotivating. The prospect of a higher pay rate is often associated with promotion and responsibility. Where pay becomes a badge of status and a factor in this sense of recognition and self-esteem, then it is a significant motivator.

For workers paid by piece rates or commission, or who are dependent on bonus schemes, pay is much more directly motivational. It is noticeable that such jobs tend to offer less scope for meeting higher-order human needs and the simple incentive of money becomes a general substitute.

Job Satisfaction

▶ It is often possible to redesign jobs in order to meet a fuller range of human motivational needs.

Research into the sources of human motivation has produced a powerful case for making job satisfaction much more widely attainable. The work of Herzberg in particular points to the importance of enabling employees to experience achievement, recognition, responsibility and satisfaction in the work itself. It is a popular observation that many jobs are inevitably dull and unrewarding. This is a view that modern human resources managers would reject. Using the logic of McGregor's attack on Theory X, it can be argued that jobs are not inevitably dull but are made dull by the way in which they are constructed. There are several important methods by which some firms have attempted to increase job satisfaction:

▶ Job rotation and job enlargement increase the horizontal (same-level) range of responsibilities. Job enrichment and autonomous work groups extend the vertical (higher) reach of responsibility.

1 Job Rotation

A group of workers may all be performing relatively simple but different specialized tasks. The tasks and the group are formed into a carousel system, where each individual performs each task for a limited time before moving on to a period at the next task, in a continuous rotation. The method does not make the work itself more satisfying, but it gives the worker greater variety with a wider range of competencies. From a managerial viewpoint, labour flexibility is also increased.

2 Job Enlargement

This simply involves increasing the range of tasks included within a worker's job description. The additional tasks do not in themselves increase responsibility and are on a similar level to the existing job. The aim is not to increase the **amount of work** for the individual but its **variety**.

3 Job Enrichment

▶ Job enrichment works against the phenomenon of employee alienation.

This is a more radical approach that means the vertical extension of a job to allow the worker access to greater responsibility and the satisfaction of higher-level motivational needs. With the support of training, more demanding tasks are specified and the worker is granted greater independence in decision making. Where possible, staff are enabled to take charge of a complete process, section or area in the organization of work. This can provide the necessary sense of empowerment so that staff feel responsible for the quality of their work and the effectiveness of their relationships with other people in the organization.

Jobs can be deliberately designed to provide scope for fulfilling the higher human needs that are most strongly motivational. For some types of job this is obviously difficult to achieve, but once a commitment to enrichment exists, there is usually some potential. However, managers may find that job-enrichment schemes can carry demands for higher pay and that resentment can be caused if skill boundaries are too freely crossed.

4 Autonomous Work Groups

The principles of job enrichment can be applied to a number of related workers whose responsibilities are combined to form an **autonomous work group**. This means that the group takes responsibility for a particular department, process or product, often only with broad supervision from a superior manager. The planning and allocation of work, with such functions as maintenance, quality and safety, may all be brought within the authority of the group. Provided that the trust of management is real, this is likely to intensify the experience of empowerment.

▶ Famous experiments of this type began at Volvo and Philips in the 1970s.

The concept has been refined and has spread to many firms, some of whom organize production on a cellular model (see Chapter 18). This involves reconfiguring the traditional production line to form areas or discrete stages, responsibility for each of which is taken by a 'cell' of workers. There is often job rotation within the cell, but also greatly increased potential for job enrichment. Participation in a complete stage of production enables each employee to see the **meaning of his or her work**, which in itself encourages a sense of involvement and responsibility. The informal group dynamics first analysed by Mayo can then be orchestrated to coincide more fully with organizational objectives. Similar strategies have been developed in service industries, where 'family groups' of staff take responsibility for complete units of work.

Take any job with which you are familiar. Either analyse it for the job satisfaction it creates, and/or suggest how it could be restructured to be more satisfying.

▶ See also Chapter 48.

Organizational Culture

If an organization is serious about moving its relationship with staff beyond a simple exchange of work for money, then a real shift in its values will be necessary. Efforts to meet a wider range of employees' needs are only likely to succeed if management assumptions are reasonably close to McGregor's Theory Y. Otherwise staff may be understandably suspicious of enrichment schemes that only seem to be a technical ploy to improve short-term productivity. In some firms new ways of organizing work to increase motivation have been part of a wider transformation in attitudes throughout the enterprise.

Read the following case study and answer the questions below.

Southern Office Supplies (SOS) Ltd

'Roll on Friday.' Paul Scobie had arrived for work. This was his favourite remark.

'Another week. And forty more till Christmas.' Vickie Reader was an invoice clerk. She looked at her watch. 'Never mind, five minutes of today have gone already.' The phone rang. She groaned. 'Here we go ...'

SOS Ltd was a large regional office supplies wholesaler that also dealt with major corporate customers. Andy Fraser was manager of the main warehouse. His thirty-five-strong staff had been attracting critical attention from senior management. How did Mr Fraser account for so many dissatisfied customers? Unexplained delays and omissions in orders? Incorrectly addressed packages? He spoke frankly to Christina Mardle, the senior despatch clerk. 'Why can't staff follow simple instructions to do a simple job?' he enquired. 'They all know the procedure back to front. It should be a well-oiled machine. What's going wrong?'

'It's not lack of instructions. And it's not lack of common sense.' She paused. 'It's sheer boredom. Order after order. Package after package. Hour after hour. Day after day. The customers are just names off the computer. They could be anyone.'

Fraser interrupted. 'But the staff are well paid. They've got good working conditions. A subsidized canteen. What more do they want?'

1 Answer Mr Fraser's last question, making specific reference to the theories of Maslow and Herzberg.
2 Look through the various theories of motivation in this chapter. Make two suggestions for improving motivation in this warehouse, showing how the particular theories relate to your suggestions.

Evaluation

- The real value of employees in terms of both the quantity and quality of their output depends on the level of their motivation.
- A century ago motivation was assumed to depend on little more than the receipt of wages in exchange for labour. Research in the social sciences has revealed the wider range of human needs that demand satisfaction at work. Instead of paying people to fit jobs, the emphasis has shifted to designing jobs that fit people.
- Where work fails to meet the full range of human emotional needs, the result is boredom, frustration, alienation and waste.
- The development of Taylorism and scientific management runs parallel to the rise of Fordism – mechanical mass production for uniform mass markets. The shift towards people-centred management and the recognition of the needs of employees has an interesting echo in the phenomenon of post-Fordism: new flexible technology making diverse products for complex, fragmented markets.
- Pay is likely to remain the key motivator for the growing numbers of part-time, contract and temporary staff. For those with a career in an organization, meeting more complex inner needs becomes the most powerful source of motivation.
- By adding new vertical scope to the responsibilities of employees, job enrichment schemes tend to cut through the lines of traditional hierarchies. This may imply a flatter and more flexible organizational structure.
- The importance of making staff feel that their views are taken seriously can hardly be overstated. Personal consultation and recognition are essential to any strategy for motivation.
- Proper training demonstrates to employees that their jobs are important. It encourages higher standards and makes the individual feel more involved with the organization.
- Motivation to improve performance is much strengthened by continuous high-profile feedback on progress to date. This may even be most effective if made public and competitive.
- The careful extension of increased trust to employees breeds motivation. Most people are keen to accept responsibility and justify the trust shown in them.
- The growing use of autonomous work groups to improve motivation represents a kind of micro-decentralization. The equivalent trend in organizational structures (see Chapter 45) is to decentralize authority to the lowest management level at which it can still be effectively exercised. This principle is also called **subsidiarity**.

36 Communication

Chapter objectives

After working through this chapter, you will:

- understand the theoretical basis of communications in an organization
- know the main methods of communication and why they are used
- be able to assess the typical barriers to communication
- appreciate the role of informal communications
- know the meaning of the following key terms: intention, encoding, transmission, filters, reception, feedback.

THE IMPORTANCE OF COMMUNICATION

▶ **Communication**: the transmission and receipt of messages between people.

A business is a social organization embedded in the human world. Its dependence on **communication** is both

- internal, for information, motivation and coordination;
- external, with the shareholders, bankers, suppliers, customers, markets, the community and the government.

Any firm is a maze of communication pathways along which messages are travelling. Imagine the endless conversations and meetings, the filing baskets filled with memos and letters, the flicker of computers and VDUs, the receipt and transmission of e-mails and faxes, the coloured lights that flash on and off across the telephone switchboard. A business is only 'live' when communicating.

The Communication Model

▶ The same message is interpreted slightly differently by every individual. Differing personalities, beliefs and experiences all combine to add to and subtract from the intended meaning of the message.

Communication means the transmission and receipt of messages between people. The word 'transmission' suggests the world of telecommunications, which is the basis for the best known and most useful communications model:

1 **Conception**
The person becomes aware that he or she has a message to communicate and establishes the outline of its content. For example, the sales manager recognizes that the sales team need further briefing on the unique selling points of a new product.

2 **Encoding**
The message is translated into words, symbols, diagrams or images. For example, a text is prepared regarding the product.

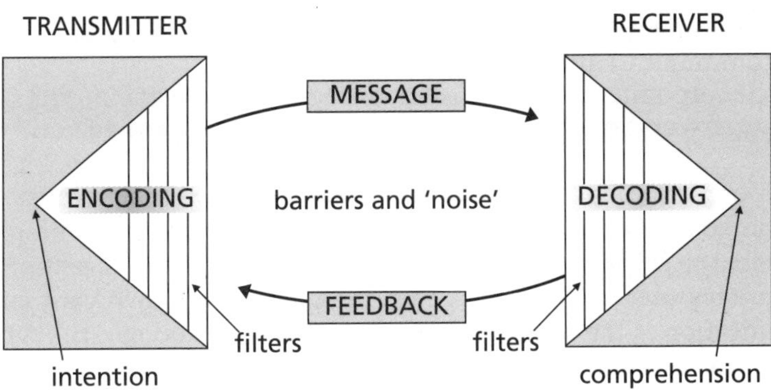

Figure 36.1
A model of communication

3 **Transmission**
A medium is selected and the encoded message is directed towards the receiver. Distortion is liable to arise from two sources: failings in the act of transmission, or external barriers between the transmitter and the receiver. For instance, the sales manager addresses the sales team in a soft monotone after a lingering pub lunch.

4 **Filters**
The human brain acts as a filter on incoming messages, many of which are rejected or highly coloured by beliefs or emotional needs. For instance, the salesperson for the West Midlands has just been criticized for under-performance and whispers to the London rep that the whole talk is time-wasting propaganda.

▶ The spoken word is the most personal and flexible form of communication.
Written communications tend to be more formal and provide a direct permanent record.
Electronic communications are very fast and allow access to large stores of information.

5 **Reception**
To prompt any response, the message must be understood and processed by the receiver. For instance, the salesperson for Yorkshire understands the message and relates it to recent customer enquiries.

6 **Feedback**
Communication is made two-way when a response to the message is sent back to the transmitter. For instance, the West of England salesperson asks if the product can be delivered in smaller quantities and at more frequent intervals.

Draw your own version of the communication model and annotate it using an example drawn from your own experience.

Selecting Communication Methods

The object of communication is to achieve understanding in the receiver and an appropriate response. Much depends on the choice of media and the route by which the message travels.

The choice of communication method will be influenced by:

▶ A shift from paper-based towards electronic communications is increasingly well advanced in many firms.

- the nature of the message, e.g. complex ideas or simple facts;
- the importance of feedback;
- the degree of formality, i.e. a chat in the canteen or a formal memo;

- the importance of speed in transmission and response;
- the relative cost, including the opportunity cost of time used;
- the need for a permanent record (mainly lacking in spoken communication);
- the corporate culture, which may be bureaucratic (favouring paperwork) or organic (favouring a personal approach).

The organization chart of a firm (see Chapter 45) indicates the basic structure of formal communication. In any pyramid-type model the emphasis will tend to be on vertical communication, i.e. messages that move down or up the hierarchy. Downward communication is the basic structure for command and control, while upward communication is the vital feedback channel. Lateral communication is designed to provide coordination for different objectives and activities within the firm. Mechanistic systems with tall pyramids have long communication lines, which may be very slow or become blocked. Feedback is likely to be limited and late. More organic systems, often using 'flat' or matrix models, sacrifice some unity of command for shorter, faster links and greater use of lateral connections.

▶ The use of five-person networks is purely illustrative. Groups may be larger or smaller, and the networks may interlock with others of the same or a different type.

Communication Channels

Alex Bevalas (1948) carried out research into the properties of five well-known models of communication network. Notice the condition that communication can only occur when a line directly connects two members of the group.

Figure 36.2 Communication channels and networks

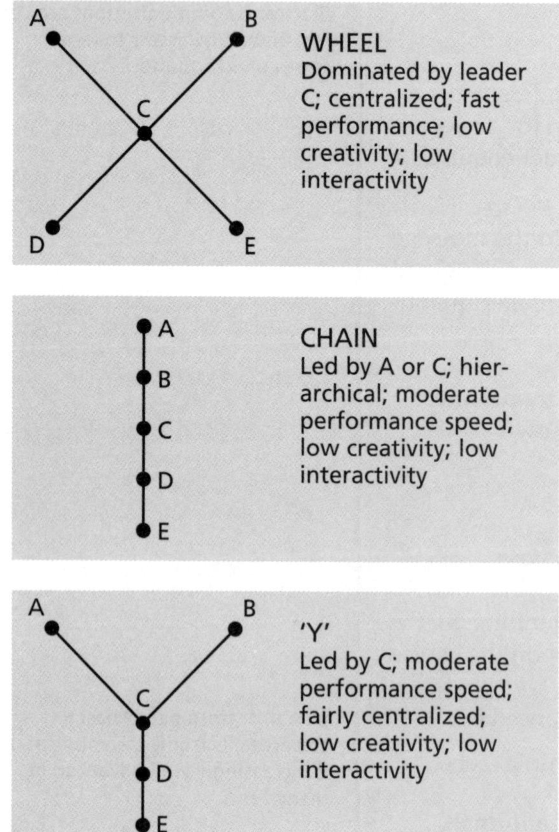

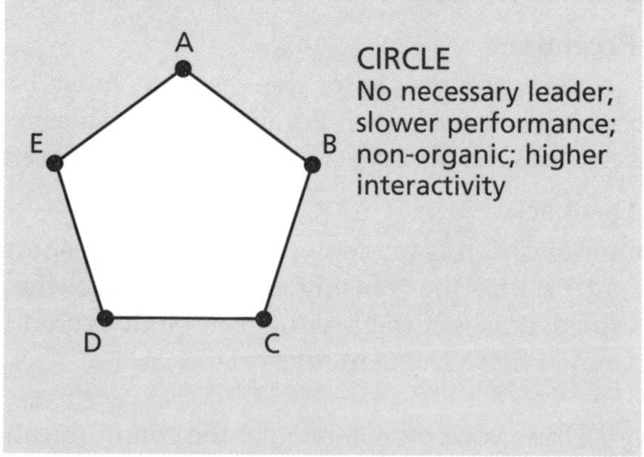

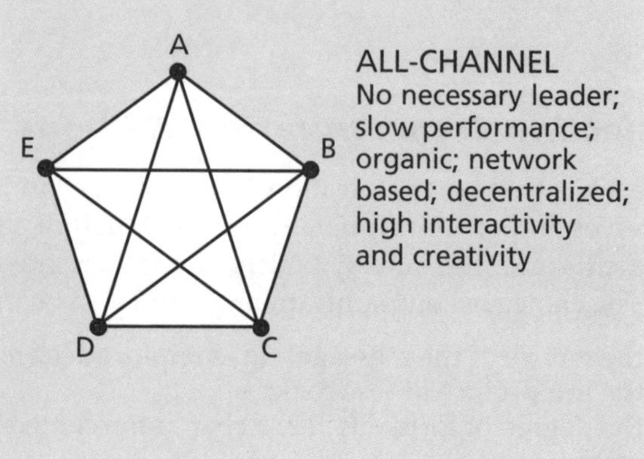

Look at each kind of communication network. From your own experience identify a situation which had that kind of network. Did it aid or hinder communication?

Barriers to Communication

▶ The structure of an organization can become encrusted with barriers to communication. This leads to reduced motivation and trust, weaker coordination and slower responses to change.

The perception of human beings is too complex for any communication to be received exactly as intended (even 'yes' or 'no' can convey hidden meanings).

> Anna Jenks wanted to do an art foundation course but felt she had been virtually forced to join Shield Insurance by her father. The company's northwestern claims bureau was in Manchester and her uncle had helped her to get a job in the motor department. It was very boring, but she was supposed to be grateful. Mr Hammond (the section leader) was conducting her first appraisal interview. He was a dull, middle-aged man who spoke very quickly in a fussy voice and ended each sentence with a suggestion of mirthless humour.
>
> 'So, are you enjoying your new job?' he asked with a short, official-sounding laugh.
>
> 'Er, yes.' Anna gazed at the poppy in his lapel.
>
> 'Only, "er, yes"?' He smiled.
>
> 'No, er, I mean ... yes.' Somewhere she could see a whole field of poppies.

Barriers to communication exist:

in the transmitter:
- poor presentation fails to hold attention
- lack of credibility in the eyes of the receiver
- badly structured or unfocused message
- wrong timing
- complexity of message pitched too high or too low
- excessive use of jargon
- lack of empathy with the audience

between transmitter and receiver:
- wrong route of message
- poor choice of media
- excessive bureaucracy
- uncongenial environment
- 'noise' from distracters
- 'Chinese whispers' effect as message is retransmitted
- deliberate manipulation of message in retransmission

in the receiver:
- attitudes or bias filter the message
- hostility towards the transmitter or the message
- low motivation
- personality differences
- inadequate background knowledge
- overload of information
- limited concentration span

Other Problems in Communication

Many other more complex difficulties can reduce or distort the flow of communication:

- Social or educational differences between the two sides can cause misinterpretation of messages, while stereotyping of 'workers' or 'management' can be a problem.
- Emotional energies such as fear, anger or insecurity can grossly distort communication and lead to the message being given interpretations that are entirely unintended.
- 'Group-think' occurs when an individual becomes submerged in a group identity and loses the capacity to think independently.
- 'Halo/horns' effect occurs through people tending to swing in their response from extremes of acceptance or rejection of what they hear and then projecting this judgement onto all else they hear from the same source.
- Previous experience of life and at work creates a 'picture' of the world that makes sense to the individual. Messages that do not fit into this picture are often simply rejected (this is called cognitive dissonance).
- Organizational pressures may lead to management or staff feeding only the information that they think would be found acceptable.
- Lack of confidence prevents many people from communicating their views or feelings. This is a particular problem in large groups.

Informal Communications

▶ 'We aim to kill the grapevine.' This was the recent comment of a manager at a Lucas car components factory, where the goal is open communications.

Formal organization structures do not reveal the complex, invisible networks of informal contacts and alliances. Many staff obtain advice from anyone but their supervisor and know good 'sources' for all kinds of information. A network of gossip, rumour and intrigue can easily develop in which more is to be learned in the canteen or the cloakroom than from senior staff. Some informal off-the-record communication is inevitable and can be a catalyst to the achievement of official goals. But a busy grapevine is usually a symptom of communication failure and can deeply undermine morale and motivation.

From your experience of any organization, identify the kinds of messages that travel through the formal communication channels and those that travel through informal channels. How would it affect the organization if messages now travelling only in informal channels were transmitted through formal ones?

Non-verbal Communication

▶ 'One look was enough.'
'His eyes went straight through me.'
'I could see she was nervous.'
'He patted me on the shoulder.'
'I didn't like the way you came in.'
'We've still heard nothing.'

There is a complete sub-text to much communication in a non-verbal form.

The main types of non-verbal communication are as follows:

- **gestures**, e.g. wagging of the forefinger

- **body contact,** e.g. handshakes
- **posture**, e.g. refusing to sit down
- **eye contact**
- **critical space**, e.g. standing over a person
- **silences**, adding impact, creating uncertainty
- **dress and accessories**, e.g. a dark suit and a large fountain pen suggest power.

Read the following case study and answer the questions below.

Klockwise

Klockwise was a young firm in the novelty gift business. Its first product remained a particular success: ceramic-faced clocks customized with the buyer's name and logo. The original team of owner-managers were all aged in their twenties when they started the company and had worked closely together. Even today, decisions were often reached through informal chats and general agreement.

Deborah looked desperately through her diary. She was company secretary and administrator. Holding the receiver, she stared hard at 24 November. 'We agreed to deliver last Friday? Sixty clocks?' she faltered. 'Yes, of course. I'll check that right away.'

The following morning a letter arrived from the personnel manager of the life assurance company in question. Since gifts to clients had to be posted in good time for Christmas they would not now require any clocks. The specimen clocks were accordingly returned.

Nicholas, the marketing director, was aghast and furious. 'Our largest single order. And with huge potential. I made three visits to clinch the deal. I thought we had a production team?'

'We did.' Deborah spoke in a flat voice. 'Tim says he's leaving. And David says that if Tim goes, he goes too.'

'But why didn't you tell me?' Tim later appealed angrily to Deborah. 'You must have known it was an exceptional order. How could you even think we would deliver by 24 November? I could have told you that was impossible. Nicholas doesn't even know how the clocks are made. He takes orders and seems to think the products will appear by magic.'

Deborah felt unfairly criticized. 'I simply did my job,' she countered. 'To me it was just another order. I put it through like any other. No one said anything. It wasn't my responsibility.'

1 What went wrong at Klockwise? Where does the responsibility rest?
2 What changes would you recommend to prevent such a failure occurring again?

Evaluation

- The pattern and style of communication in a firm accurately mirrors the values and culture of the whole organization. For example, a secretive and formal system would reflect a rigid mechanical organization. Open and informal communications are typical of more organic systems with a flatter organizational pyramid.
- Firms need a balance between vertical and lateral communication. Lateral communication is the least emphasized in conventional management models, yet it is essential to flexibility and proactivity in an organization.
- Communications with employees are gradually becoming

less confrontational and more participative, i.e. managers and workforce are tending to work more in partnership and less in opposition.

- Failures in communication are a classic diseconomy of scale. Too often a 'brontosaurus' principle operates: the organizational brain is remote from the muscles of an ungainly body (and there may always be a Tyrannosaurus Rex in the form of a rival firm ...!).
- In too many firms only lip service is paid to the concept of bottom-up communication. Not only is motivation vitally affected by the sense of being heard and taken seriously, but staff at lower levels are the best source of ground-floor 'intelligence'.
- No one pattern or system of communication is invariably superior to another. Different objectives and different situations can call for different styles of communication. For instance, management of a traditional, stable market has needs that are different from the management of a radically new and expanding market.

37 Employee relations

Chapter objectives

After working through this chapter, you will:

- understand the nature and functions of trade unions and employers' associations
- know how the process of collective bargaining operates
- be able to analyse the sources and resolution of conflict in business enterprise
- be aware of the key contemporary trends in industrial relations
- know the meaning of the following key terms: convenor, productivity deal, picketing, secondary action, pendulum arbitration, company council.

WHY TRADE UNIONS?

Employees generally have many common interests such as fair treatment, proper training, secure employment and improved pay and benefits. Inevitably, these aspirations will not always be fulfilled by employers in pursuit of objectives such as profitability. It is to assist employees in defending or advancing their shared interests that trade unions exist. Quite literally, they are a 'union' of employees in one or more 'trades'.

Unions vary widely in their character and in the nature of the services they provide. However, six main subjects of trade union negotiation or activity are:

▶ The modern trade union movement has its origins in the industrial revolution, when terms of employment were extremely harsh and no 'welfare state' existed.

1 Pay rates and productivity agreements.
2 Working hours, staffing levels, training, redundancy.
3 Conditions of work, health and safety.
4 Grievance procedures; suspensions and dismissals.
5 Communications with management, the media and the government.
6 Employee services, e.g. insurances and mortgages, clubs and social facilities.

If possible, contact a local branch official of a trade union and interview him or her to discover what he or she does in this capacity. Use the points one to six above as a checklist for your interview.

Alternatively, write to one of the major trade unions and ask for information on its services to members.

▶ Types of Trade Union
Craft unions: skilled workers in a particular trade, e.g. printers in the Graphical, Paper and Media Union (GPMU).
General unions: workers across a wide range of industries; mass membership of semi-skilled or unskilled staff, e.g. Transport and General Workers Union (TGWU).
Industrial unions: workers of all skill levels in one particular industry, e.g. National Union of Railwaymen (NUR).
White-collar unions: administrative, clerical and technical staff, e.g. Manufacturing, Science and Finance (MSF).

Trade Union Structures

The number of trade unions in Britain has fallen from 453 in 1979 to 267 in 1994. This has been due to a series of mergers designed to increase both bargaining strength and efficiency. Each union is entirely independent and self-governing, but most unions belong to the **Trades Union Congress (TUC)**, which provides coordination and national representation for the trade union movement.

The internal structure of unions varies widely but there is a typical pattern. Each union has a **president** or **general secretary** and a national headquarters with full-time officials, who carry out the policies decided at the national conference. Larger unions have a regional or district structure, also with full-time officials whose task it is to assist the local branches. The foundation of a union is its branches, which may cover a particular place of work or all members in a wider locality. Each branch elects a secretary and holds regular meetings, but these may often be poorly attended. They also elect delegates to the national conference. To conduct day-to-day union business in the workplace, **shop stewards** are elected. The duties of stewards have tended to expand and include representing the views of members to management and negotiating many aspects of pay, conditions, hours and staffing levels. In addition, there is the duty to ensure constant feedback to the shop floor and to recruit new members.

Within a place of work the various shop stewards may form a committee and elect a **convenor** to negotiate on their joint behalf with management. The committee might be limited to one union, but often it is a joint committee including stewards from all the unions involved. It is important to realize that management is often actively supportive towards all of these arrangements. Industrial relations need a proper structure with well-developed channels of communication.

The Closed Shop

Also called a 'union membership agreement', this means that all the workers within a given industry or workplace must be members of a stated union. This tends to increase union bargaining strength and enables agreements with the employer to be enforced without giving benefits to any non-union members. It is also supported by some employers as creating a more stable environment for negotiation and avoiding conflict between unions. The closed shop has also aroused strong opposition. Staff may have genuine objections to joining the union and, if expelled, may lose their jobs. Under the **Employment Act, 1982**, at least 80 per cent of the workforce, in a ballot, must support a new closed-shop agreement, or 85 per cent be in favour of one continuing. Exceptions to the principle of dismissal for non-union membership were introduced, including personal conscience, non-membership of the union before the agreement and unreasonable expulsion from the union.

Decline in Union Membership and the 'New Unionism'

In recent years there has been a very significant decline in the total membership of trade unions, from 12.2 million in 1979 to 8.2 million in 1993. This has been caused by:

- large-scale closures in manufacturing industry where unions were traditionally strongest;
- new technology eliminating unionized jobs;
- employment growth occurring fastest in service industries where unions are traditionally weaker;
- marked increase in contract and part-time employment;
- the more restrictive legal framework;
- a trend for firms to negotiate directly with individuals and smaller work groups;
- some shift in public attitudes away from trade union values.

With long periods of high unemployment and a shift in the balance of power towards greater management authority, a 'new unionism' has emerged. This involves a clearer belief that the success of the business will further the interests of union members (more jobs, more security, higher wages, better conditions) and can lead to a stronger sense of partnership. Some firms (e.g. Nissan in Tyne and Wear) have negotiated **single-union agreements**, where only one union is recognized and allowed to represent the workforce. This can be associated with a **no-strike agreement**, where the union undertakes not to withdraw labour during disputes, which are settled by pendulum arbitration (see p. 291). Such agreements often also involve single status and labour flexibility (no restrictions on tasks that members will accept).

▶ Research shows that strike activity is highly concentrated in a few plants in a few industries. Even during the years of highest strike activity 98 per cent of workplaces remained strike free. The vast majority of trade union members never experience a strike during their working lives.

Employers' Associations

These are organizations representing the interests of employers for a particular industry. There are about 1,300 associations in Britain, but many are very small. Local associations may form a national federation (e.g. the Engineering Employers' Federation), with a national committee and a range of specialist sub-committees. A major function is to negotiate on a national basis with trade unions, but they also provide an important range of commercial and other advisory services.

Employers' associations and individual employers can join the **Confederation of British Industry (CBI)**, which represents employer interests at a national level. It has a director general and its own specialist committees. As well as providing advice to members, it communicates employer interests to the media and government.

COLLECTIVE BARGAINING

To negotiate separate agreements between each employer and each employee can be inefficient and unfair in its outcome. A system where agreements are made on a collective basis is often to be preferred. In Britain **collective bargaining** is 'free', in that agreements reached are not normally subject to any state control. This allows for market forces to operate but risks polarized confrontations where the monopoly power of one side in the labour market may unjustly prevail.

There are many subjects for collective bargaining, but the question of pay and other rewards is the most central and will serve best to illustrate the process. The traditional outline of a bargaining situation is clear. While the firm will seek to minimize the cost of its labour inputs, the workforce will aim to maximize the value of its rewards.

▶ When you take your car to a garage for repairs, the mechanic is paid significantly less per hour than you are charged for labour. The difference is a source of profit to the company.

Collective Bargaining Scenario

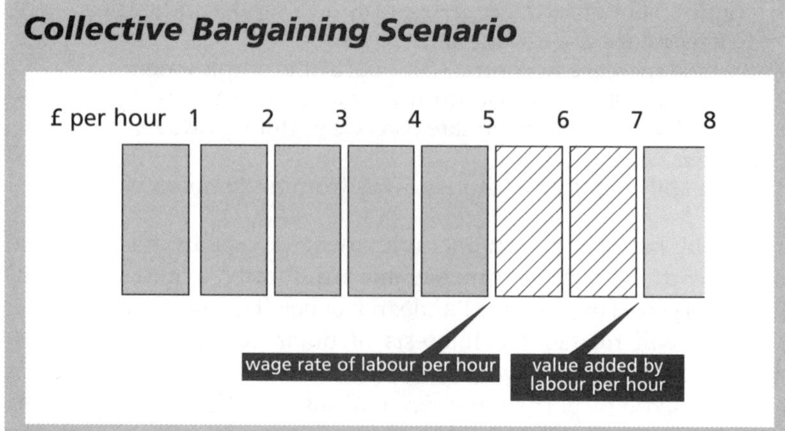

Figure 37.1
Basis for wage bargaining

There is clearly a zone between £5 and £7 per hour which represents a surplus for the employer. Employees will wish to narrow this zone with a higher wage, while the employer will wish to widen the zone with a higher rate of value added by labour.

Bargaining can be of two types:

1 **Distributive**, where the employer's loss is the employee's gain, or vice versa (e.g. the wage rate rises to £6 per hour with no change in the value added by labour).
2 **Integrative**, where the goal is an outcome that benefits both sides. In pay bargaining this would involve a **productivity deal,** where the workforce gains a pay increase and the firm gains from increased output per man-hour, e.g. the wage rate rises to £6 per hour and the value added by labour rises to £8.50 per hour.

Before the actual bargaining begins, both sides will need to prepare their case and ensure that their negotiators are armed with all necessary information and arguments. A vital factor will be the relative bargaining power of the union in making its claim. This depends on:

- **Supply of labour**: employers will be influenced by skill shortages or surpluses, while the union will need to consider the rate of unemployment.
- **Demand for the product**: the firm's need for labour is derived from demand for the product; employers are influenced by short- and long-term prospects.
- **Capital substitution potential**: if pay rates rise, the firm is more likely to invest in labour-saving machinery.
- **Relative labour cost**: the ratio of labour cost to total cost will determine the effect of pay rises on final price and hence sales.
- **Structure, funding and solidarity of unions**: the strongest position that will be enjoyed when bargaining is by a single union that is well funded and solidly backed by members.
- **Negotiation skills**: the skills of either side in framing demands and in conducting negotiations can be decisive.

- **Macroeconomic trends**: union power is weakened by recession and strengthened by a boom. The general level of demand for labour is related to the current level of output and the economic prospects ahead.
- **The state, media and public opinion**: public sector claims may be constrained by government pay 'norms' or cash limits. In high public profile industries (e.g. transport), media and public opinion can be significant.

The Bargaining Cycle

Negotiations between the two sides will follow an agreed agenda. Usually both sides make an opening statement setting out their position and emphasizing their expectations and demands. This stage is sometimes called the 'battle cry', as both management and unions stake out their ideal terms, on which they know a compromise is likely. The differences between the two sides are now clarified. The main negotiations follow, in which issues are explored in detail and some element of compromise begins. Bargaining techniques and interpersonal skills become very significant. A careful balance must be struck between concessions and demands, between objective and subjective argument, between speeding and slowing the negotiations. A crucial point will come - normally during an adjournment - when decisions must be made and the management team will emerge with an offer. In pay negotiations, both sides will have a private scale of responses and expectations.

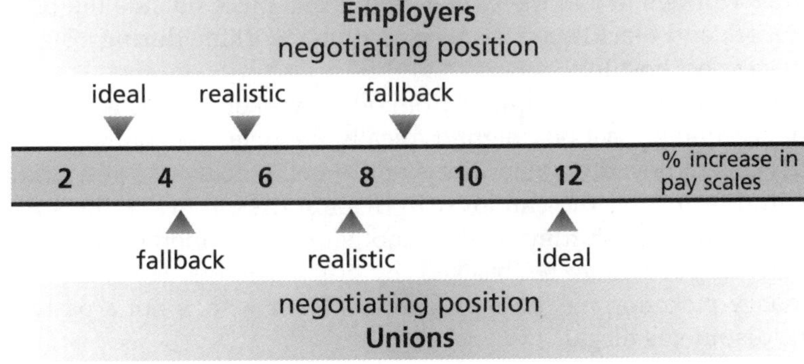

Figure 37.2
A wage bargaining model

The situation shown in Figure 37.2 offers good prospects for reaching agreement; a settlement in the range of 6 to 8 per cent looks likely. It is clearly important that there is at least some overlap between the two scales. If not, non-pay factors may bridge the gap, or else - under pressure - a fall back position may begin to slide. Eventually, either a settlement will be reached or deadlock will prevail and a dispute begins.

Look for news cuttings of employer/employee negotiations to illustrate your notes on collective bargaining.

INDUSTRIAL DISPUTES

When negotiations fail, a state of dispute may smoulder for a time, with further meetings, restatements of position and drawing up of deadlines. If industrial action follows, there are various sanctions that the union may take:

- **withdrawal of cooperation**, e.g. ceasing to attend joint meetings;
- **work to rule** or **go-slow** will both reduce output;
- **overtime ban** may disrupt production;
- **token strike** is of short duration and serves as a warning to management;
- **strike**, which may be partial or total for a fixed, repeated or indefinite period.

▶ The code of practice associated with the Employment Act of 1980 suggests six pickets as a maximum for the entrance to a workplace. Pickets may not use threatening or violent tactics.

▶ It was popularly believed that Britain is subject to frequent strikes and industrial disruption. In fact, most unions rarely organize industrial action and in many large firms strikes are virtually or wholly unknown. Even in Britain's period of greatest unrest (the 1970s), the record was better than in the USA, Canada or Italy.
The underlying trend of the 1980s and 1990s has been a steady decline in the frequency of strikes. Working days lost through stoppages averaged 12.9 million per year during the 1970s and 7.2 million in the 1980s. In 1994 there were 0.3 million days lost – and there were 205 strikes, the lowest figures for a century.

A strike becomes official when it has trade union backing. Under the **Trade Union Act, 1984,** this can only be given when a ballot among members has shown majority support. In practice, about 95 per cent of all strikes are unofficial but these tend to be less serious and shorter in length.

A strike clearly places immediate and strong pressure on employers, who are normally unable to continue their main operations. Orders will be lost and relationships with important customers may be endangered. Meanwhile, the union members will suffer from loss of earnings and the union's funds will be depleted by strike pay or other campaigning action. Solidarity among strikers is practically and psychologically important. **Picketing** (persuading other workers to join the strike) often takes place outside the place of work and **blacklegs** (staff who continue working during a strike) may expect hostility.

A union may seek support from other workers. If this is successful, secondary action might typically involve persuading truck drivers employed by other firms not to make deliveries at a strike-bound factory. If the employer in dispute tries to evade the strike by, for example, shifting work to another plant or another company, then the goods may be 'blacked' by other workers. However, secondary picketing (i.e. picketing an employer who is not a party to the dispute) is illegal.

As the strike continues, the employer may re-enter negotiations or make an improved offer. Alternatively, he or she may be more resolved and maintain or even withdraw the previous or final offer. In extreme cases, the employer may dismiss striking employees for breach of contract or decide to close down the workplace, making the staff redundant.

Conciliation and Arbitration

▶ **Arbitration**: the settlement of a dispute by an independent third party (person or organization).

If all efforts to resolve a dispute through collective bargaining fail, then **arbitration** may be requested from an independent third party. Some industries have their own built-in arbitration procedures. Particularly important are the services of ACAS (Advisory, Conciliation and Arbitration Service), which is government financed but strictly independent. If requested, ACAS officials will conciliate and mediate in a dispute, bringing the two sides together and helping them to find sufficient common ground for a settlement. Where a dispute has reached deadlock, and with the consent of both sides, the arbitration service will give a judgement that must then be accepted by all concerned. In recent years the device of **pendulum arbitration** has been used, especially as part of single-union agreements. This means that the arbitrator is presented with the final positions of the two sides and must make a straight choice between them with no further compromise. The effect is to encourage a 'pendulum effect' on the two sides as they compete to occupy the most 'reasonable' position in the centre ground.

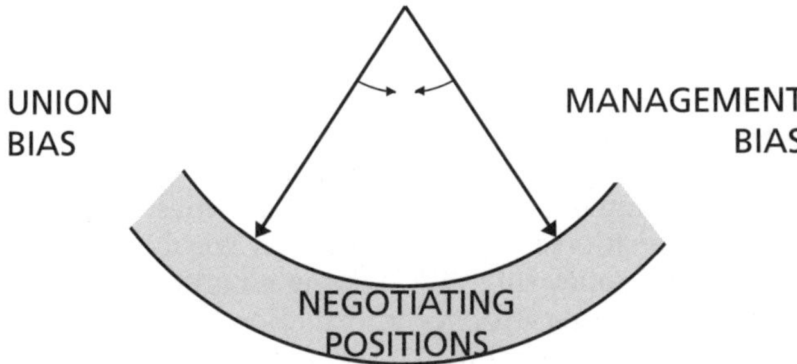

Figure 37.3
Pendulum arbitration

Often the final arbitration is unnecessary as the pendulum effect brings an earlier settlement.

Conflict in Business Organizations

Strikes and major disputes are only the high profile part of conflict in organizations. Conflict has many other less obvious but still very damaging symptoms. For example, high or rising rates of labour turnover, absenteeism, accidents or customer complaints can all be signs of excessive conflict. Ultimately, an organization can become paralysed by conflict and thus highly inefficient – and fatally unable to respond to change. Formal grievance and dispute procedures are important but do not touch the real sources from which conflict springs. Examples of these might include:

- rigid and authoritarian management with a lack of bottom-up communication, causing a build-up of frustration;
- rapid or poorly planned change, causing dislocation and a decline in the status and prospects of some employees;
- decline in the firm's markets or market share, causing the threat of redundancy;
- lack of involvement, boredom and alienation (see Chapter 35) among staff;
- badly designed organizational structure (see Chapter 45) that divides the workforce, distorts communication and overloads some staff.

▶ High levels of motivation and a vigorous two-way communications network help to reduce conflict.

The really vital task for management is to **create rather than assume** a unity of purpose. This is not the same as requiring everyone to act in the same way. The firm may get the best from its staff by tolerating many different methods of moving in the same direction. Broad strategies include the following.

- **Worker participation** means involving staff in the machinery of decision making. This might be through a **Joint Consultative Committee**, which brings together managers and worker representatives on a regular basis, with a formal constitution. Meetings may tackle many subjects of mutual importance (e.g. job security, working conditions), so improving the flow of communication and tending to build understanding and trust. A danger lies in crossing wires with the process of collective bargaining. Some firms have set up a **company council**, with representatives of all grades, which is free to address major planning issues. A very few firms have introduced employee directors, who have seats on the main board.
- **Profit sharing** is designed to encourage a unitary view of the firm and to motivate employees in such areas as quality, sales or customer service (see Chapter 35).
- **Open styles of management** involve cultivating a more unified and less conflict-prone culture in the organization. Single status often brings all-staff social facilities, common eating and relaxation areas and less hierarchical privileges. An 'open door' policy (literally keeping all office doors open where possible) and a stronger information flow to employees can also be helpful.

▶ In 1981, the Japanese firm Toshiba took over from Rank a loss-making television plant in Plymouth. A single-union no-strike agreement was reached with EETPU and single status was introduced throughout the factory. Ten years later, employment had trebled, output had increased eightfold to 600,000 sets per year – and not one day had been lost through strikes.

Industrial disputes are only one, rather rare, symptom of conflict in a business. List all the other symptoms of conflict you can think of and make notes on how worker participation, profit sharing and more open styles of management might alleviate conflict.

Read the data below and answer the questions.

Transport and General Workers' Union (TGWU)

Membership
main industries
transport: air/roads/docks
manufacturing: cars; engineering; chemicals; food processing; textiles
energy
hotels/catering/cleaning
water, health and public services
agriculture

Membership numbers
1979 2.1 million
1981 1.7 million
1983 1.5 million
1985 1.4 million
1987 1.3 million
1989 1.3 million
1991 1.2 million
1993 0.9 million

Unions amalgamating with TGWU
National Union of Agricultural and Allied Workers
National Union of Dyers and Bleachers

1 How would you account for the TGWU's membership data?

2 Why might other smaller unions wish to amalgamate with the TGWU?
3 How might a decision by a company's workforce to join the TGWU – in a single-union agreement – benefit the employer?

Evaluation

- The geographical, occupational and social mobility of the labour force is increasing with wider educational and training opportunities and accelerating technological change.
- In the past fifteen years there has been a major decline in male-dominated blue-collar manual employment due to de-industrialization and new technology. This has greatly weakened some sectors of the trade union movement.
- To retain members and to attract new recruits, unions are tending to stress the specialist services they can offer while placing greater emphasis on partnership with management.
- The emphasis on productivity in collective bargaining is likely to remain. There is increasing recognition that improvements in real rewards – and job security – depend on a competitive level of value added by labour.
- The need for legal restraints in industrial relations is now widely accepted: the issue is the balance of advantage provided by the law.
- The concept of involving the labour force in decision making is gaining ground both through joint committees and in more autonomous work groups, project teams and 'cells' where all members participate in problem solving.
- As hierarchical pyramid structures become flatter and even begin to dissolve into open 'networks', so the traditional opposition between 'management' and 'workers' loses force. The emerging trend for the future suggests an organic kind of unity in which common purpose is achieved less by confrontational bargaining and more by mutual consent.

Part 7

Economic Environment

National income

Chapter objectives

After working through this chapter, you will:

- appreciate the link between business and the economy
- know how the output of the economy is measured
- understand the basic models that explain how the economy works
- know how economic growth occurs
- know the meaning of the following key terms: factors of production, national income, national output, national expenditure, standard of living, withdrawals and injections, disposable incomes, the multiplier, aggregate demand and aggregate supply.

▶ No understanding of business is complete without an understanding of the economy and the key principles by which it operates.

NATIONAL INCOME

Economists identify four **factors of production**. These are:

Factor	Reward
land	rent
labour	wages
capital	interest
enterprise	profit

The chief factor input of most households is labour, rewarded by wages (or salaries). However, it is quite common to let a room or a garage for rent, to hold deposits in a bank or building society for interest and, by owning some shares, to receive dividends (profits). Now imagine making a list of these income sources for every person in the UK to cover one year. The grand total is called the **national income**. It is calculated in exactly this way by the government in the **national income accounts**.

Consider the total value of all the goods and services produced in the UK over one year, i.e. the **national output**. By definition this has been yielded by combining the factors of production. It follows that the cost of these factor inputs – wages, rents, interest and profits – must equal the value of total output. In fact, national income and national output are just opposite sides of the same coin.

▶ UK total income in 1995 = £609 billion.
wages and salaries: 73.2 per cent
profits: 15.7 per cent
rent: 10.3 per cent
The profits shown here are a gross value, which means that they include interest payments.

▶ Analysis of the economy as a complete system is called **macroeconomics**.

▶ Note the sum of the items does not add up to the stated national output because of adjustments and residual error in official statistics.

UK national output for 1995 = £603.5 billion

	(£bn)	%
agriculture, forestry, fishing	11.9	2.0
energy and water	30.4	5.0
manufacturing	131.7	21.8
construction	31.8	5.3
transport and communication	50.8	8.4
distribution, hotels, catering	84.7	14.0
banking, finance, insurance, etc	158.2	26.2
public services	112.5	18.6
other services	23.3	3.9

Source: ONS, Annual Abstract of Statistics

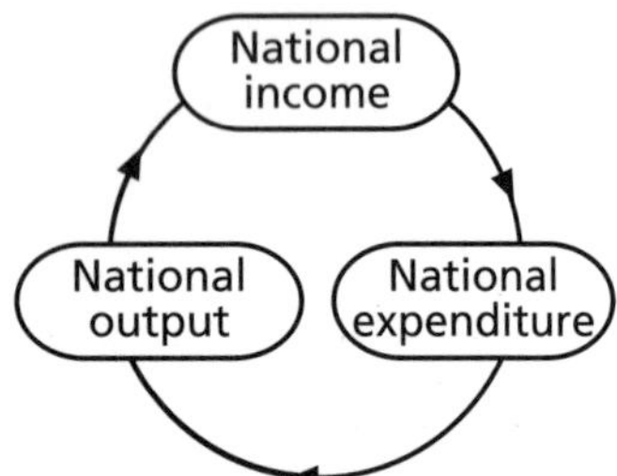

The next step is simple. All output must either be purchased or added to stocks. It follows, therefore, that total expenditure in the economy must equal total output after allowing for net changes in stocks. We now have the identity:

national income ≡ national output ≡ national expenditure

We can see that the value of national expenditure is also equivalent in value to national income. Of course, households save as well as spend, but their savings are used by firms and the government for investment, i.e. expenditure on capital goods (long-lasting durable goods, e.g. machine tools). Thus the identity holds good.

▶ No reference has been made so far to taxation or foreign trade. They qualify but do not alter the identities and will be explained on p. 300.

▶ A higher standard of material living does not always mean a higher quality of life.

The Standard of Living

This term is much used – and abused. It is generally taken to mean the rate at which goods and services are consumed by the average household or individual. The population of the UK in 1995 was 58.6 million, so the average income per person was:

$$\frac{\text{£603 billion}}{\text{£58.6 million}} = \text{£10,299}$$

▶ Rising national income changes the size and character of markets.

Ten years earlier, in 1985, the value of national income was only £308 billion. But, before making any comparisons, we must:

- allow for the change in population size;
- adjust money values to take account of inflation (see Chapter 41).

Inflation from 1985 to 1995 amounts to 58 per cent. In 1985 national income is therefore worth £308 billion × 1.58 = £487 billion in 1995 terms. The population in 1985 was 56.7 million. Thus income per head was:

$$\frac{\text{£487 billion}}{\text{56.7 million}} = \text{£8,589}$$

▶ **GDP = gross domestic product** – the total money value of all final goods and services produced in an economy over a one-year period.

The true increase over ten years is therefore from £8,589 to £10,299 per person, or about 19.9 per cent. In terms of living standards, gross domestic product (GDP) statistics must always be treated with caution. Significant factors to consider are:

- the proportion that is investment rather than current consumption;
- the nature of expenditure, e.g. defence costs;
- the distribution of income among the population;
- the social and environmental costs of production.

The Circular Flow of Income

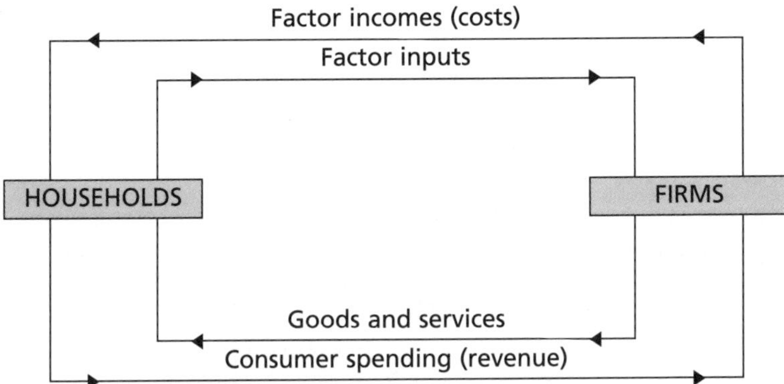

Figure 38.1
The circular flow of income: a simple model

Begin by imagining a simple economy where households and firms are in a direct relationship: all incomes are spent without savings, there is no government or public sector, and no foreign trade. Households express demand for goods and services. Firms meet this demand by employing the factors of production: land, labour, capital and enterprise. For these services they make payments that form their costs and the factor incomes that reach households. These households (or consumers) now spend their incomes, receiving goods and services in return, and supplying revenue to firms. This revenue can then be used to employ further factor services, and the cycle begins again. Notice that in terms of money there is a circular flow between households and firms.

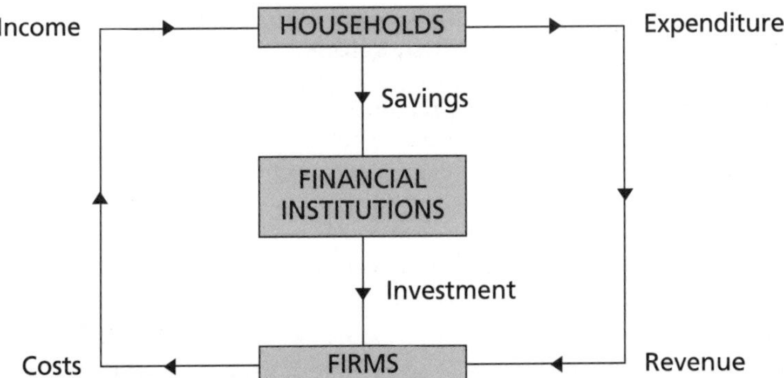

Figure 38.2
The circular flow of income: showing money flows

This is a model of the same simple economy except that only **money flows** are now shown, and the assumption that all income is spent has been dropped. Clearly, households do not spend the whole of their incomes: part is saved and deposited in a range of financial institutions (commercial banks, finance houses, pension funds etc.). These savings represent a diversion or **withdrawal** from the circular flow and mean that the spending by households is correspondingly less than the factor incomes paid by firms. However, firms do not rely solely on demand from consumer spending. They obtain an additional **injection of demand** through the financial institutions that lend for investment in industry. In this sense the banking system acts as a kind of 'clearing house' between the savings intentions of households and the investment intentions of firms (see Chapter 42). The relationship between the resulting withdrawals and injections is of crucial importance.

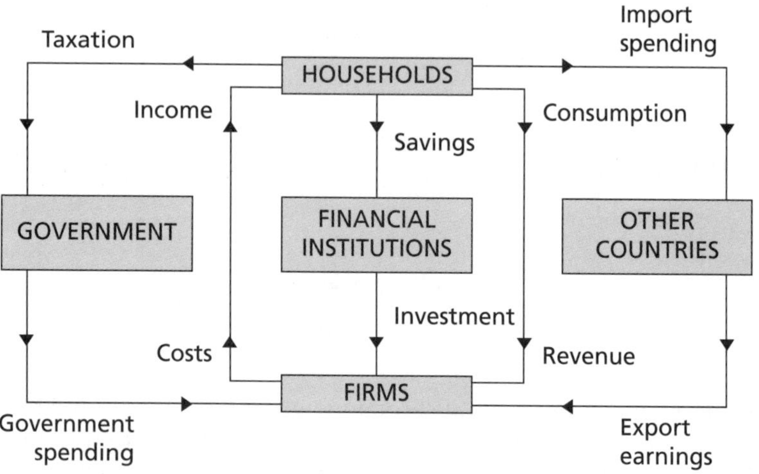

Figure 38.3
The circular flow of income: financial institutions, government and overseas trade

In the real economic world there is a government sector and there is overseas trade: both exert an important influence on the circular flow. To finance the goods and services that it provides, the government levies taxes on incomes (and on spending), which means that the **disposable incomes** of households are considerably lower than their gross earnings. As this is more money diverted from the circular flow, it represents another withdrawal. However, when government spending takes place, it represents another injection of demand for firms.

The sale of imported goods diverts a part of households' spending to other countries and is therefore a withdrawal. But exports also yield extra revenue from overseas, representing an injection into the UK circular flow. Therefore:

total withdrawals = savings (S) + taxation (T) + imports (M)

and

total injections = investment (I) + government spending (G) + exports (X)

Economic equilibrium always exists when total demand equals total supply. In our model, this means that total planned withdrawals must equal total planned injections. If withdrawals exceed injections, the revenue received by firms is less than the value of total output (or factor incomes). The result is increasing stocks of unsold goods, causing firms to reduce output, which in turn reduces incomes. If injections exceed withdrawals, the reverse process occurs: effective demand is greater than the value of current output. Firms expand production and incomes increase. It is clear that the relationship between withdrawals and injections is vital in determining the size of national income.

To make notes on the circular flow of income, draw your own diagram and annotate it.

The Multiplier

This is one of those concepts that can look very difficult but is actually quite simple. You should now have a clear picture of injections and withdrawals. Consider an economy in equilibrium. There is no net force to cause expansion or contraction. Then suppose that a large firm decides to increase its investment by £1 million. What will be the consequences? In the first place, other firms will enjoy extra orders for their capital goods, worth £1 million. But that is not all. Where does the extra £1 million actually go? To produce the extra capital goods the other firms will need to employ additional factors of production and pay out additional factor rewards, which take the form of increased incomes for households. This extra money will then be spent again, creating another rise in demand for the output of firms. This second round of spending will not increase demand by a full £1 million, since it will be reduced by our three sources of withdrawal. Suppose that for every extra £1 that households receive:

▶ This analysis was first developed by J.M. Keynes in his *General Theory of Employment, Interest and Money* (1936).

30p is paid in taxes
10p is saved
10p is spent on imports
= 50p in total withdrawals

It follows that the extra demand on the second round of spending will be £500,000. When this spending creates a yet further increase in output and incomes, the same withdrawals will occur again and demand will rise by £250,000. The cycle continues like a fading echo through the economy. The final increase in demand will be:

£1 million + £500,000 + £250,000 + £125,000 + … n = £2 million

You can see that an initial £1 million increase in injections has had an end value of £2 million in terms of extra demand and extra output. In other words, it has been subject to a **multiplier effect** of 2. The value of the multiplier is easily calculated for any data. In the above example the total rate of withdrawals was 50p in the £. This is called the **marginal rate of withdrawal** since it refers to any extra £1 spent.

▶ The multiplier can operate internationally, nationally, regionally or even locally in causing the level of demand to expand or contract.

$$\text{The multiplier} = \frac{1}{\text{the marginal rate of withdrawal}}$$

Or in the example:

$$\text{The multiplier} = \frac{1}{0.5} = 2$$

It is clear that the smaller the rate of withdrawal, the more powerful the multiplier effect. However, the multiplier can also operate in the reverse direction. A decrease in any source of expenditure (e.g. a cut in investment or government spending) will be subject to the same multiplier effect in reducing demand and output.

Summarize in simple terms how the multiplier works. Work out for yourself the decrease in demand created by a reduction in investment of £2 million with a multiplier value of 1.5.

Aggregate Demand and Aggregate Supply

▶ The diagram relates the overall level of prices (on the y-axis) to the real level of national income or output (on the x-axis). 'Real income' means that the value is measured at constant prices, undistorted by inflation.

We have already explored basic demand and supply curves for individual products (see Chapter 11). It is also possible to extend the principle to the whole economy.

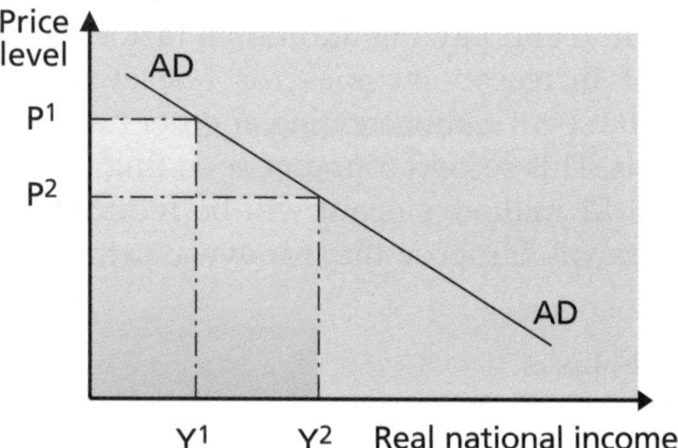

Figure 38.4
The aggregate demand curve

The aggregate demand curve is downward-sloping since a reduction in the price level increases the purchasing power of incomes and wealth, so enabling consumption to increase. Thus, a fall in the price level ($P^1 - P^2$) causes a rise in national income/output ($Y^1 - Y^2$).

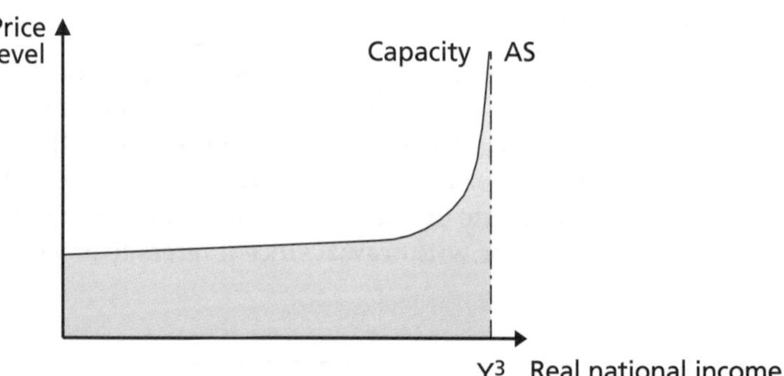

Figure 38.5
The aggregate supply curve

But just as firms have a limit to their productive capacity, so does the economy as a whole. At first the aggregate supply curve is virtually flat (i.e. perfectly elastic), since there is spare capacity in all firms and an increase in output will not cause costs to rise. However, as capacity is approached, the curve sharply steepens owing to an increasing number of firms running short of factor inputs (especially skilled labour) and being forced to offer progressively higher rewards (e.g. higher wages). These higher costs are passed on to the consumer in a higher level of prices. When capacity is reached, it follows that output cannot rise and so any attempt to expand output can only cause a corresponding rise in prices.

▶ National income level Y^1 can be achieved at price level P^1. A higher level of demand (AD^2) pushes up prices to P^2, while AD^3 hits capacity and causes a sharp rise in prices to P^3. This problem is explored in Chapter 41.

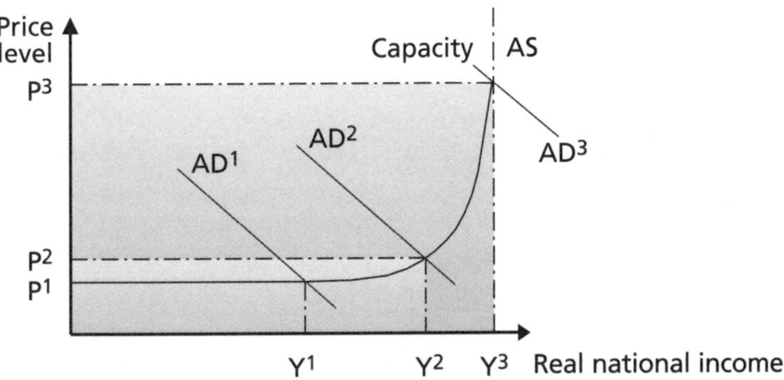

Figure 38.6
Demand, capacity and price

Draw your own versions of the graphs illustrating aggregate demand and aggregate supply and annotate them.

Economic Growth

▶ Economic growth can carry serious environmental costs (see Chapter 49).

This means an increase in the level of real national income. Important ways by which this can be achieved include:

1 **Increased factor inputs**
- net investment in capital goods, e.g. building new factories;
- a rise in the working population;
- the discovery of new natural resources, e.g. North Sea oil.

2 **Increased factor productivity**
- new and more efficient technologies, e.g. computer-aided manufacturing systems;
- increased education and training, improving skill levels in the workforce;
- economies of scale (see Chapter 13);
- improved management in combining factor inputs.

Such changes have the effect of shifting the aggregate supply curve to the right, enabling real national income to increase without any sharp rise in the level of prices.

It is found that for every pound earned, 8p is saved, 20p is paid in taxes and 12p is spent on imports.

1. What is the value of the multiplier?
2. If an extra £100 million is spent on investment, by how much will national income be expected to increase?
3. What would you expect to be the business effects of the following events:

(a) a rise in the rate of VAT to 22 per cent;
(b) a reduction in business rates;
(c) an environmental tax placed on all industrial goods liable to cause pollution;
(d) a surge in economic growth in countries that are major trading partners;
(e) a cut in the rate of income tax to 15p in the £ with unemployment at a record low level?

Evaluation

- The performance of all firms is affected by changes in the economy as a whole. Even a profitable and well-managed enterprise may fail as a result of adverse economic conditions, such as a combination of falling demand, higher interest rates, increased taxation or greater competition from imports.
- It is essential for managers to pay close attention to economic trends and forecasts. These may provide some advance indication of dangers or opportunities ahead. For instance, many investment decisions are dependent on longer-term economic prospects.
- There is no necessary equality between the planned savings of households and the planned investment by firms. Their actual values must balance, since the resources saved by a society become resources available for use in a future period – the economic definition of investment. But these resources are not necessarily devoted to spending on capital goods. They may simply become increasing stocks of unsold goods, so causing firms to cut output, with downward multiplier pressures on national income. Eventually, equilibrium will be reached with planned savings equal to planned investment, but at a reduced national income level. The sequence works in reverse if planned investment exceeds planned savings and the eventual equilibrium will be at a higher level of national income.
- The actual marginal rates of withdrawal in the UK are approximately 32p in the £ for direct taxation, 10p in the £ for savings, 18p in the £ for indirect taxation and 32p in the £ for imports. This gives a rough multiplier value of 1.33.
- In the short run, economic growth tends to depend on increased factor inputs generally. In the longer run it is increased investment and factor productivity that are significant.
- An interesting feature of economic growth is its tendency to push the largest source of income and employment from the primary to the secondary to the tertiary sector over the long term. These stages are sometimes described as pre-industrial, industrial and post-industrial.

The business cycle

Chapter objectives

After working through this chapter, you will:

- be able to analyse the business cycle and its main stages
- understand the causes of the cycle
- know the recent history of the cycle in Britain
- be able to assess its impact on business decisions
- know the meaning of the following key terms: boom, recession, slump, recovery, upper and lower turning points, multiplier-accelerator theory, inventory cycle, income elasticity of demand, indicators (leading, coincident, lagging).

BOOMS AND SLUMPS

In business there have always been good and bad times. Unfortunately, good times don't last. For a while every result improves. Sales increase, margins improve, output rises, more staff are recruited and ambitious plans are launched to increase capacity. Cash seems strangely plentiful and optimism abounds. Then, for no apparent reason, the boom ends, sometimes slowly with a gentle sinking, sometimes suddenly like a burst bubble. The symptoms are familiar. Trade slackens, customers seem less certain, the order books empty. Margins have to be squeezed, costs cut back, staff laid off. Profitability falls and plans for expansion are shelved. A slump has arrived.

Yet this pattern is not the experience of one firm alone. It is virtually the simultaneous experience of thousands of firms all over the country - and often in other countries as well. The slide into slump is not caused by errors of management but by huge impersonal forces beyond its control. These forces exist both in the national and the global economy. Their interpretation involves some interesting ideas in economics.

▶ The only years of negative growth between 1967 and 1997 in Britain have been 1975, 1980, 1990 and 1991.

The Business Cycle and its Stages

Over the past hundred years in Britain, economic growth has averaged around 1.5 per cent per annum. The figure for the past ten years has been higher at about 2.5 per cent. These values represent the trend path of output. But the actual level of business activity weaves above and below the trend path in a cycle of booms and slumps. Although irregular in its intensity and in the duration of its phases, the cycle has a distinct pattern.

▶ **Stages of the Business Cycle**

Boom: business expectations high; sales high; stocks low; output near capacity; profits and investment high; unemployment low with labour shortages; prices rising.

Recession: optimism fades; sales start downwards; stocks begin to build; profits are lower; investment cut; unemployment begins to rise; prices usually rise more slowly.

Slump: pessimism dominates; sales low; de-stocking is widespread; output is low with extensive spare capacity; profits and investment are depressed; unemployment high; prices often tend to stabilize.

Recovery: expectations rising; sales increase; re-stocking beings; output increases and spare capacity is brought back into use; profits and investment rise; unemployment starts to fall; prices begin to accelerate.

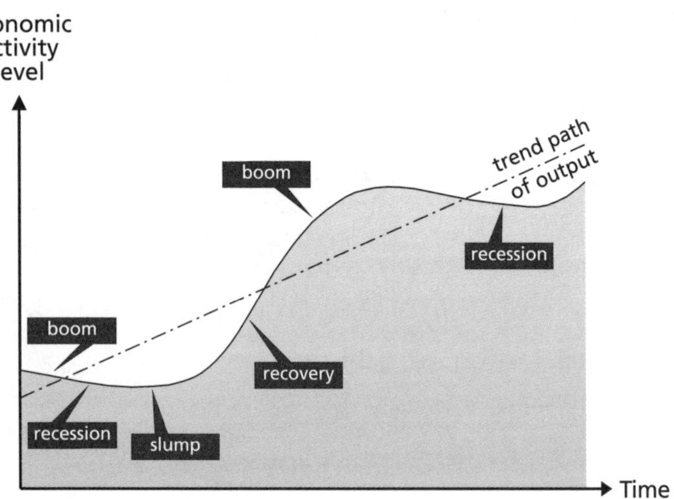

Figure 39.1
The business cycle

The average length of the modern cycle is about four to five years (the peaks and troughs are called the **upper** and **lower turning points**).

▶ On 24 October 1929 – 'Black Thursday' – Wall Street experienced a spectacular crash. Within one week, American investors had lost $40,000 million.

The Cycle in Practice

Reality is more complex than the classic four-phase pattern suggests. Not only can the boom-to-boom length of the cycle vary widely, but the exact profile of each phase is unique. Booms and slumps can be prolonged, while recoveries and recessions can be shallow or steep. Deceptive upturns or downturns can occur, which fail to lead to the next boom or slump. The cycle is also influenced by government policies and by wider world economic and political events.

With the Wall Street crash in 1929, the booming US economy moved into a steep recession which then spread rapidly all over the world. Britain was already in a long slump, which worsened to become the Great Depression of the 1930s. After the Second World War, the cycle was far milder and faster moving, with a strong underlying growth trend. But in 1973–4 the quadrupling of world oil prices pushed the economy into a sharp recession and unprecedented inflation. Unemployment began a long climb which continued through the next recovery. In 1979 a second oil crisis ushered in the deepest recession since the 1930s: unemployment soared and inflation surged again. Large numbers of manufacturing firms were forced out of business. A slow recovery from 1981–4 led to a long boom, with abundant new business start-ups and the rapid growth of service industry. The new pattern of high growth was broken by a serious trade deficit and renewed inflation. Another severe recession began in 1989 and sustained recovery did not begin until 1993.

Draw a timeline 1973–97 and on it mark the periods of boom and slump.

Causes of the Cycle

Many theories have been advanced to explain the business cycle. The most important ones will be briefly explained.

1 The Multiplier-Accelerator Theory

We have seen how the multiplier (see Chapter 38) amplifies the upward or downward effect of any change in the level of aggregate demand. In practice the theoretical state of equilibrium never actually occurs and the economy is always in the process of expansion or contraction. Suppose demand and output are rising as a result of increased investment. This involves not just one investment project with multiplier effects but a continuous flow of additional investment spending, with continuous multiplier effects. This might represent a recovery phase turning into a boom. We now meet the **accelerator**.

The Accelerator

A truck operator delivering consumer goods to retail outlets owns ten trucks, each costing £50,000, and needs to replace one vehicle each year. However, demand for his services then expands by 20 per cent in one year, making necessary the purchase of two extra vehicles. His order to the manufacturers is thus for three vehicles - one for replacement and two for expansion - costing £150,000 in all. Next year the economic climate is still good and demand increases by around another 10 per cent. The firm therefore orders two vehicles costing £100,000. In the following year the boom flattens out and demand is steady. No extra trucks are needed and one replacement vehicle is ordered at £50,000. A slight downturn begins in the succeeding year and demand falls by 10 per cent. No extra vehicles are needed and no replacement is needed either. No vehicle order is placed.

Year	*Change in demand*	*Vehicles ordered*	*Value (£k)*	*Change in order value*
1	+20%	3	150	+200%
2	+10%	2	100	-33%
3	0	1	50	-50%
4	-10%	0	0	-100%

▶ The accelerator makes investment and production planning in capital goods industries particularly difficult.

This simple example has serious implications for the producers of capital goods. Compare changes in demand for consumer goods to the resulting changes in demand for capital goods. A 20 per cent rise in demand for consumer goods causes a 200 per cent rise in demand for capital goods. Just a **slowing in the rate of expansion** in consumer goods industries then causes a major contraction in capital goods industries. Stable demand for consumer goods inflicts a further 50 per cent fall in orders for capital goods. A 10 per cent fall in demand goes on to cause a collapse in demand to zero for capital goods. These changes in demand all carry multiplier effects and, when repeated across the country, help swing the economy into booms and slumps.

▶ Retailers may resort to frequent 'sales' during periods of recession.

2 The Inventory Cycle

In America, stock is called 'inventory' and the concept of a cycle is based on the pattern of orders placed by retailers. If a fall in demand – and hence retail sales – occurs, then stock starts to build up, with a mounting opportunity cost. Retailers (and wholesalers) respond by targeting lower stock levels. This means that orders to manufacturers for new stock are severely reduced or even stopped altogether. Output and incomes fall as a phase of de-stocking takes place. Once stocks are sufficiently low it is necessary to start ordering again at a moderate rate even to meet depressed demand. This is often experienced by manufacturers as an increase in demand, so starting a modest expansion in output and incomes. This continues to grow as re-stocking keeps ahead of sales. But the relationship is volatile. Any decline in sales – or even a slowing of sales growth – may cause a sharp fall in orders.

3 Government Intervention

During the Great Depression of the 1930s the government claimed that there was little it could properly do to initiate recovery. At exactly the same time, John Maynard Keynes was writing his *General Theory* that led later governments to become actively involved in trying to influence the business cycle. In recent times, government policies have included:

- changes in public spending which increase or reduce aggregate demand;
- changes in direct and indirect taxation designed to affect consumer demand and factor supply;
- changes in the rate of interest which affect business investment, consumer borrowing and the rate of saving;
- exchange rate policy which affects the demand for imports and exports.

These 'levers' of economic policy are often used in combination, but their accuracy is doubtful and there can be unintended effects. There is also a significant political cycle at work. Governments face elections every four to five years and often aim for a recovery or boom to be in progress at the end of their term of office. Tax and interest rate cuts are possible tactics in the pre-election period.

1 Take your previous notes on the multiplier effect and add notes on the accelerator.
2 Make notes to show the effect of the inventory cycle and government intervention on the circular flow of income.

Impact of the Cycle on Business

▶ The retail chain Next crashed from a pre-tax profit of £62 million in 1988 to a £41 million loss in 1990. Its share price slumped to 6p in December 1990. Yet by 1996 pre-tax profit was back up to £142 million, with the share price at over 700p.

The business cycle is beyond the control of any one firm. For some firms the cycle provides only a gentle ebb and flow in the underlying pathway of growth. Such firms are called 'recession proof' and tend to trade in necessities (e.g. supermarkets). At the opposite extreme, the business cycle can create new business opportunities, which may then be seriously undermined only a few years later. As so often, risks and rewards are very finely balanced.

Decision areas where the business cycle makes a particular impact include:

- **Investment decisions**, which are based on expectations of future sales. When forecasting the cash flows arising from an investment project, it is essential to allow for cyclical changes in the economic climate. Basing decisions on performance during a boom can lead to grossly over-optimistic business expansion.
- **Capital structure**, which needs to be appropriate and sustainable over the course of a complete cycle. A particular danger is allowing a boom to prompt excessive borrowing and the development of very high gearing. During a recession sales fall and interest rates may rise (as over 1988–90), leaving the firm very vulnerable to falling interest cover and difficulties with repayments.
- **Market exposure**, which means the structure and nature of markets on which the firm is reliant. Some markets are low risk where sales and profit margins may be unspectacular but can safely withstand any economic downturn. Other markets are far more volatile and prone to dramatic expansion and contraction as the economy shifts from phase to phase. A useful guide is **income elasticity of demand**. This measures the change in quantity of a product demanded relative to a change in incomes:

$$\text{income elasticity of demand} = \frac{\%\ \text{change in quantity demanded}}{\%\ \text{change in income}}$$

▶ **Income elasticity of demand**: change in demand for a product in relation to changes in income.

  Broadly, income elasticity below 1 indicates a necessity and values above 1 indicate a luxury. During a boom, demand for luxuries can increase very quickly, causing fast growth in 'frothy' business opportunities, which can then subside suddenly with the onset of recession. Many service industries are prone to this effect. For example, a product with an income elasticity of 4 may find that a 10 per cent rise in disposable incomes within its target market leads to a 40 per cent rise in sales. Hasty expansion can then be very dangerous if, two years later, the same arithmetic moves into reverse.
- **Labour flexibility** in terms of employee skills, numbers and hours, which vitally affect the firm's ability to adapt in a changing economic climate. Flexible skills enable management to vary its product mix at short notice. The use of part-time temporary and contract staff enables the total labour input – and costs – to be varied without the disruption and expense of redundancies.

Make notes to show which kinds of firms are most and least vulnerable to the business cycle. What implications does this have for the marketing mix?

Large firms make use of **business forecasting**, which takes careful account of economic trends. In this task, managers can use their internal sales and market research data together with macroeconomic forecasts issued by the government and a range of external organizations. Various statistical series provide indicators of movement through the business cycle:

- **Leading indicators** point to changes in economic activity around six to twelve months in advance. Examples include the CBI survey of business optimism and the FT-SE share index.
- **Coincident indicators** directly represent the cycle itself. They include real GDP, the volume of retail sales and the CBI index of firms working below capacity.
- **Lagging indicators** reflect the state of business activity about a year earlier. The key examples are investment and unemployment.

Economic indicators are frequently quoted and commented on in the financial news. Collect examples and make your own notes on the way in which commentators use indicators as evidence of the state of the economy.

Look at the diagram and answer the questions below.

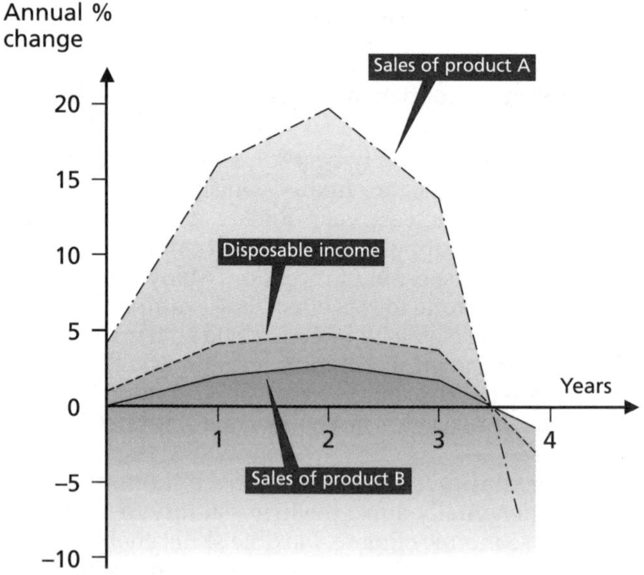

Figure 39.2
Sales and incomes changes

1. Suggest possible identities for products A and B, giving your reasons.
2. Indicate ways in which a firm selling product A only might be affected by the information given.
3. What is the probable income elasticity of demand for products A and B?

Evaluation

- The effect of the retail inventory cycle can be dampened by manufacturers' stock. As retailers cut their orders in a recession, so manufacturers tend to increase stocks. When orders begin to increase, manufacturers can initially supply from stock without increasing output.
- However, the development of just-in-time delivery systems is tending to connect demand and production more directly and to reduce the effect of stock levels on the business cycle.
- The growing integration of European economies is tending to mean that movements in the business cycle are no longer so dependent on economic events in one country - or on the policies of one government.
- The business cycle can be very uneven in its impact on the regions within a larger economy. In the 1980–1 slump, the manufacturing parts of the Midlands and northern Britain were far more severely affected than the south. But in the sharp downturn of 1990–1, construction and service industries were worst affected, with disproportionate impact in the south-east.
- Sudden changes in the output of one particular firm or industry can cause local business cycles that strongly exaggerate or counteract national patterns. Contrasting recent examples include pit closures in the South Wales valleys and the oil industry-led expansion in the Aberdeen area of Scotland.
- Economic forecasting is still liable to be inaccurate and misleading, despite the use of increasingly sophisticated computer models. Not only are there many internal and external variables involved, but their interactivity can be very complex.

40 Unemployment

Chapter objectives

After working through this chapter, you will:

- understand the significance of employment and unemployment
- be able to distinguish the causes and types of unemployment
- understand the strategies and problems of governments in their efforts to reduce unemployment
- know how the level of unemployment affects a firm's human resource function
- know the meaning of the following key terms: cyclical unemployment, frictional unemployment, structural unemployment, regional unemployment.

WHAT IS UNEMPLOYMENT?

▶ In common usage unemployment refers to labour, but it can also apply to idle land or capital.

Employment means the use of a resource. In a market economy this means use at a price, i.e. the use of a resource in return for payment. We can distinguish three types of resources:

1 labour or human resources;
2 land or natural resources;
3 capital or human-made resources.

In theory, any accessible resource that has an economic value will always be employed. Falling demand or rising supply simply causes a falling price. If this price is low enough then it will always be profitable to employ the last unit of any resource. *In practice*, all resources require some rate of minimum return for their supply. Unless the market rate of reward is above this minimum for every resource, then some unemployment is inevitable.

In common use, the term **unemployment** is applied to **labour** and refers to those among the working population who are unable to find paid work. However, the term is equally applicable to land and capital which also fall idle when the gap between their price and earnings fails to represent an adequate rate of return.

Unemployment is a subject about which feelings run high and it has always been a major political issue. The non-use of land and capital carries what seems a wasteful opportunity cost, but the non-use of labour – or people – increases the social security burden and carries additional human costs in poverty, social decline and psychological damage. Work is a fundamental human need and for many people it is an important source of identity and self-respect.

The Great Depression

As the British economy followed the USA into a dramatic downward spiral, so unemployment soared. By 1932, 23 per cent of the working population were without a job. In the regions of heavy industry the rate was 38 per cent and locally up to 75 per cent. Factories closed and stood empty, ships rusted in estuaries and farmers left crops to rot in the fields. National income fell and social hardship became acute. This is the paradox of a slump. People are in great need and wish to work. Natural and human-made resources are ready and available. The wheels of business simply fail to turn.

The reason is lack of demand. Resources will not be employed unless there is a demand for their output at a price that sufficiently exceeds their costs. When this condition is not met, unemployment is the result.

An increasing level of demand from the circular flow of income draws resources into employment. The higher the level of aggregate demand, the higher the proportion of the labour force that will be employed. **Thus demand is the motor of employment**.

However, there is an important qualification. In the 1960s when the economy was working at or near capacity, about 300,000 people remained unemployed. It is now clear that the current equivalent figure is around 1.5 million. If demand were to be increased further during a boom, then inflation (and the trade deficit) would rise very sharply indeed, with unacceptable consequences (see Chapter 41). The reasons for this change are complex, but possible factors include:

- Employers tending to reward their permanent 'core' staff above the market rate to ensure loyalty and motivation. Workers outside the 'core' are employed casually or not at all.
- The effective 'dismissal' of the long-term unemployed from the labour market so that the active labour market operates only above a certain base level of unemployment.
- Bottlenecks in the economy, meaning that as demand increases, some industries reach full employment long before others. Rising inflation then quickly forces the government to curb demand.

Make notes to explain why unemployment sometimes remains high when demand is high.

Although we speak of the labour force as a whole, every worker in the market is unique. People vary in qualifications, skills, experience, motivation, where they live, age and sex. For some groups of workers there is always a very high level of demand and virtually no unemployment. For other groups the reverse is true.

Unemployment statistics are usually presented both as a national average and on a regional basis. Regional unemployment rates are affected by:

- level of demand in specific industries;
- local levels of aggregate demand;

▶ In 1988, at the peak of a boom, the unemployment rate in parts of Northern Ireland was 30 per cent, yet in the more prosperous towns of the south-east of England the rate was under 3 per cent.

- technological developments affecting particular jobs or processes;
- trade union influences;
- 'going rate' for local wages.

UK unemployment rates (% of working population)

	1966	*1978*	*1990*	*1993*	*1995*
North	2.5	8.2	8.7	11.9	10.6
Yorkshire	1.1	5.5	6.6	10.2	8.8
East Midlands	1.0	4.7	5.1	9.5	7.7
East Anglia	1.4	4.7	3.7	8.1	6.4
South-East	0.9	4.0	3.9	10.2	7.9
South-West	1.7	6.1	4.3	9.5	7.0
West Midlands	0.8	5.1	5.7	10.8	8.4
North-West	1.4	6.9	7.6	10.7	8.8
Wales	2.8	7.6	6.7	10.3	8.3
Scotland	2.7	7.6	8.2	9.7	8.2
Northern Ireland	5.3	10.5	13.0	13.8	11.4
UNITED KINGDOM	1.4	5.7	5.8	10.3	8.2

Economists classify unemployment in a range of types:

- **Cyclical unemployment** is caused by the general lack of demand during a recession and slump (e.g. early 1990s).
- **Frictional unemployment** is caused by the short-term pattern of workers changing jobs as a result of the contraction and expansion of labour demand in different firms and industries.
- **Structural unemployment** is a severe frictional type as whole industries face long-term decline (e.g. coal mining or shipbuilding).
- **Regional unemployment** is often the result of structural change since industries tend to be geographically concentrated (e.g. textiles in West Yorkshire).
- **Technological unemployment** occurs when new technology makes a certain type of worker unnecessary or uncompetitive with machinery (e.g. computerization of typesetting and printing in the 1980s).
- **Seasonal unemployment** exists when demand fluctuates sharply between seasons and workers become jobless during slack periods (e.g. winter in seaside resorts).
- **Residual unemployment** refers to those workers who lack the personal skills to retain any paid job.

Government Policies

▶ Post-war levels of unemployment were extremely low. In 1950 the national rate was 1.6 per cent and in the West Midlands the rate was only 0.5 per cent. Even by 1970 the overall rate was still only 2.6 per cent. Yet since 1980 the rate has never been below 7 per cent.

Governments aim for 'full employment' but this does not mean zero unemployment. A certain base level of unemployment appears to be necessary to allow structural change to take place in the economy and to avoid the risk of inflation caused by the 'bidding up' of wage rates.

Measures to prevent or reduce unemployment can include:

- **Increased public spending**: higher spending on schools, hospitals, housing, defence, transport and other projects increases demand in the economy and creates jobs.

- **Reduction in tax and interest rates**: lower taxes leave consumers with a larger net income to spend, so raising demand. Cutting interest rates helps mortgage borrowers, encourages consumer credit spending and makes it cheaper for firms to invest.
- **Improved training**: more and better training tends to make workers more productive and therefore more valuable to firms (see Chapter 32). It also helps workers to adapt to technological and structural change, equipping them with skills needed for new jobs.
- **Regional policy**: in areas of high unemployment, a range of government incentives is available to attract business enterprise and so to create more jobs (see Chapter 12).
- **Assisting labour market efficiency**: job centres, careers services and a variety of job awareness initiatives help people to fill the vacancies that exist.

Make notes to show the possible effects of the different kinds of government intervention on the various types of unemployment listed earlier on p. 314.

▶ The ideas of John Maynard Keynes were a major factor in the achievement by successive governments of low unemployment for 25 years after 1945.

To put government policies in perspective, it is necessary briefly to consider the past. The 1930s had demonstrated the evils of mass unemployment. Governments after the Second World War used Keynesian demand management to maintain full employment. This involves the government in using public spending and interest rates deliberately to hold aggregate demand at a level yielding full employment. The approach was successful for about twenty years, but eventually broke down as increases in demand brought rising inflation and increased imports without any lasting impact on unemployment. Meanwhile, the oil crises of the 1970s, the recession of the early 1980s and widespread de-industrialization brought the unemployment rate to 14 per cent (or 3.2 million jobless) by 1983. The problem was largely left to market forces as the Conservative government made the defeat of inflation its priority. However, with declining union power, wage rates tended to become more flexible, while a significant expansion of youth training took place. After the upswing/boom of 1985–8, the unemployment rate had fallen to 8.1 per cent but rose again with the recession of the early 1990s. Since then a general recovery has pushed down the rate once more.

▶ Since the 1980s government policy has shifted away from stimulating the demand for labour towards the **supply side**. The emphasis has been on better training, increased mobility and reduced trade union power.

Add the historical facts above to your timeline.

Effects on the Firm

The level of employment directly affects all firms and has particular importance for the human resources:

- Labour turnover normally falls with increasing unemployment. Staff are less able to find alternative jobs and tend to value their existing employment more highly. This can cause a rising average age and increasing conservatism among staff.

- Recruitment of staff becomes easier with higher unemployment and the selection process is likely to become more exacting. When labour shortages occur the reverse pattern applies and firms need to market themselves as attractive employers.
- Pay and benefits are strongly influenced in their movement by the tightness of the labour market. As the supply of labour in the market increases, so firms feel under less pressure in negotiating pay and benefits. But labour shortages are usually quick to bring improved rewards, especially if in the context of a general business upturn.
- Industrial relations depend partly on relative bargaining strengths which, in turn, depend on the prevailing demand for labour. Generally, unions tend to moderate their claims as unemployment rises, with less chance of disputes leading to industrial action.
- The human resources department can find that its apparent importance and actual influence increases during periods of labour shortage. Conversely, as a provider of manpower, its role may be diminished by unemployment and a plentiful labour supply. Recruitment, in-house training, rewards and employee relations all move up the agenda when the labour market is tight.

Draw up a two-column table. Head one column 'high unemployment' and the other 'low unemployment' Use the table to summarize the situation of firms under the different circumstances.

Read the following statistics and answer the questions below:

Unemployment rate (% of working population)

	1989	*1991*	*1993*	*1995*
North-West	8.4	9.3	10.7	8.8
South-East	3.9	6.9	10.2	7.9
UK	6.2	8.0	10.3	8.2

1. Why has unemployment been persistently higher in the north-west than in the south-east?
2. Why might the unemployment rate in the south-east have risen relatively faster to 1993 than in other regions?
3. How would you account for the trend in the UK unemployment rate over the period shown?

Evaluation

- Before 1980 governments attempted to maintain 'full employment' by influencing the level of demand. As this proved increasingly to cause inflation, policy shifted to the 'supply side', with more emphasis on freer labour markets, more training and controls on trade union power.

- The greatest source of new jobs is in the small firms sector, but this can be vulnerable to recession.
- High regional rates of unemployment have been essentially structural as traditional heavy industries have declined. This problem may be less acute in the future, as much adjustment has now taken place.
- A balanced and diversified local economy has been most effective in resisting recent rises in unemployment. An area is vulnerable when it depends heavily on one industry or one employer.
- The rapid expansion of service industry in the 1980s created much new employment but it is clear that many jobs in consumer services can disappear during an economic downturn.
- A human resources department may enjoy long-term status and influence in a firm only if contributing directly to business and financial performance.

41 Inflation

Chapter objectives

After working through this chapter, you will:

- understand the meaning of inflation and how it is measured
- know the difference between nominal and real prices and be able to convert sums of money between them
- be familiar with the main causes of inflation
- recognize and be able to interpret the key government policies for its control
- know how inflation affects decision making in firms
- know the meaning of the following key terms: inflation, deflation, real and nominal values, cost-push, demand-pull, monetary theories of inflation, wage-price spiral.

THE MEANING OF INFLATION

▶ **Inflation** means a fall in the purchasing power of money.

Inflation means a persistent rise in the general level of prices – or, put another way, a steady fall in the purchasing power of money. It is important to remember that £1 has no fixed value; indeed, its value changes every day. As the level of prices rises, so the value of money falls. In 1914 – the outbreak of the First World War – £1 had the equivalent buying power of £49.42 by 1995; or, put another way, 2 pence then was roughly equivalent to £1 now.

▶ With **hyper-inflation** the annual rate becomes first hundreds, then thousands per cent. The value of money collapses, savings are wiped out and all business confidence is lost. The most famous hyper-inflation was in Germany in 1923, when the inflation rate reached millions per cent and thick wads of million-mark notes were needed to buy even a loaf of bread.

From 1920 to 1935 prices in Britain were actually falling in a **deflation** that amounted to about 70 per cent over the period. Since 1935, the price level has risen in every year. Almost all western industrial countries have experienced rising prices, mostly in the form of a 'creeping inflation' at an annual rate of below 10 per cent. Low inflation rates are often seen as a sign of steady economic growth, as aggregate demand keeps slightly ahead of aggregate supply. Britain's inflation rate averaged just over 3 per cent during the 1950s and 1960s. A rapid acceleration into **strato-inflation** then occurred as rates soared to peaks of 25 per cent in 1975 and 18 per cent in 1980. The rate since 1982 has been fluctuating in a band between 2.5 per cent and 10 per cent.

Add the historical facts to your timeline.

Measuring Inflation

The government measures movements in the rate of inflation through the retail price index (RPI). A representative sample of household goods is used to establish a typical spending pattern. This provides 'weighting' factors to reflect the relative importance of the selected items (clearly, a 5 per cent rise in the price of gas has a far bigger impact than a 5 per cent rise in the price of matches). Price levels for the chosen products are then checked across the country and combined according to their weights at a 'base' date. This value is given the index number of 100. Prices of the same products are then researched each month and expressed as a percentage of the base prices. Their weighted average forms the monthly index. The last base date was January 1987 and the value in January 1997 was 154.1. This means that the price level over the period had risen by 54.1 per cent.

Real and Nominal Values

Nominal prices are those actually quoted by firms. **Real prices** measure the purchasing power represented by a nominal price.

▶ The £1 coin was introduced in 1983. In the terms of that year its value has already slumped to 55p (1997).

Real and Nominal Values: Prices

A retail price index was as follows:

year	*index*
1	100
2	106
3	112

Suppose that product X sold for £10 in year 1 and for £11 in year 3. The nominal price has risen by 10 per cent. But has the price really risen? Prices generally have risen by 12 per cent over the same period. Now convert the year 1 price into year 3 terms:

$$£10 \times \frac{112}{100} = £11.20$$

We can now see that product X is actually **cheaper** today in real terms, i.e. after allowing for inflation.

This concept is very useful. With an index of inflation it is simple to convert the prices of any year into the terms of another year. Consider the prices of a pint of milk and a litre of petrol:

	1977	*1987*	*1997*
pint of milk	11½p	26p	32p
litre of petrol	17p	37p	67p

The prices for milk and petrol can now be converted into 1997 terms. The method involves:

▶ A retail price index for these years is:
1977 = 100
1987 = 220.9
1997 = 333.8

using the price index (see margin):

multiply 1977 prices by $\frac{333.8}{100}$ and multiply 1987 prices by $\frac{333.8}{220.9}$

In constant 1997 prices, the table now reads:

	1977	*1987*	*1997*
pint of milk	38½p	39p	32p
litre of petrol	57p	56p	67p

▶ Interestingly, when the 50p coin was introduced in 1969, its value in today's terms was £5!

Make notes on calculating constant prices. For your own example, use the fact that a Mars Bar was selling for 11p in 1977 and 32p in 1997.

Exactly the same principle can be applied to the published results of companies or any other financial data spread over time.

Real and Nominal Values: Company Accounts

Morley Motors plc

The firm's annual report and accounts for 1995 included the following bar chart:

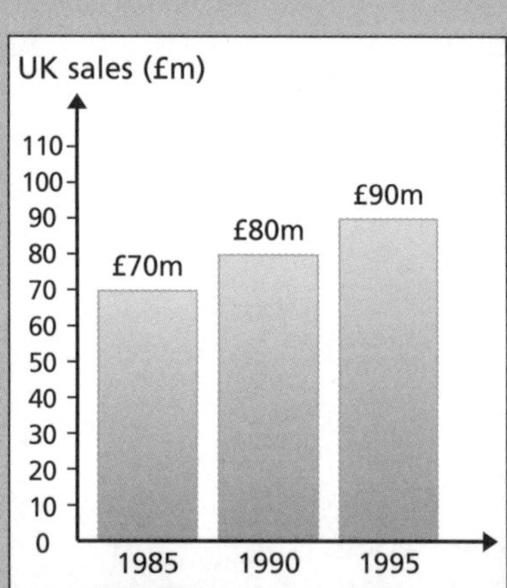

Figure 41.1
Morley Motors: a decade of progress

At first glance, a shareholder might indeed perceive 'a decade of progress'. However, a price index for the period shows:

1985 = 100
1990 = 133.3
1995 = 157.6

When corrected to constant 1995 prices, the bar chart is rather different:

▶ Notice, too, that sales alone are not a sign of progress. To make any judgement, we would need data for profits and net assets.

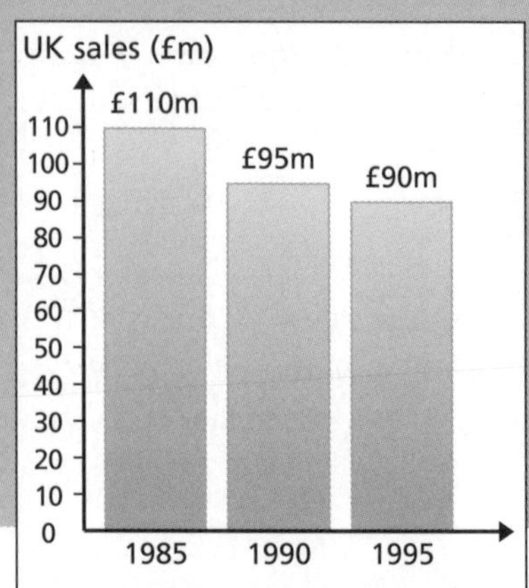

Figure 41.2
Morley Motors: a decade of progress?

CAUSES OF INFLATION

This is a hotly contested subject and many theories exist. The major contenders are described below.

Cost-push Theories

Cost-push theories propose that inflation is essentially caused by rises in the market prices for the factors of production. Wage increases, especially when negotiated by powerful unions, are the most important source of cost pressure. Rents similarly may rise sharply. Material costs can also increase rapidly, especially for imports, and movements may be exaggerated by changes in the exchange rate (see Chapter 43). Rising costs from any source drive up prices through pressure on profit margins. Initially, in difficult trading conditions, firms may absorb increased costs. Eventually a target return on capital must be achieved and prices rise.

▶ The cost-push theory seemed most relevant when trade unions were more powerful and raw materials were surging in price.

Demand-pull Theories

Demand-pull theories consider that price levels rise when aggregate demand approaches the limits of aggregate supply (see Chapter 38). While firms have unused capacity, increasing demand leads to increased output. But with rising output, bottlenecks develop in the economy as more and more firms approach capacity. The result is a slower increase in output and a faster increase in prices. This is because the factors of production - especially labour - run into short supply. Costs are being 'bidded up' by the pressures of demand.

Monetary Theories

Monetary theories essentially propose that inflation is caused by the supply of money increasing faster than output. Money depends for its value on the goods and services that it will buy. Assuming that the speed of circulation remains roughly constant, it must follow that expanding the money supply faster than output will mean a fall in the buying power of money. This is exactly the meaning of inflation. Money is created through the extension of credit by the banking system. It is argued that to control inflation the government must target and limit growth in the money supply. This used to be attempted through the control of interest rates (see Chapter 42) and restrictions on public sector borrowing.

▶ Since the 1980s, controlling inflation tended to be the dominant factor in the Conservative government's economic policy.

There is no agreement over the causes of inflation. The problem has a chicken and egg quality. For example, an existing rate of inflation may cause higher wage increases, which expand demand and increase the rate of inflation. This process is called a **wage-price spiral**. Similarly, it can be argued that increases in the money supply are not the cause but the effect of inflation.

CONTROLLING INFLATION

Different theories to explain the causes of inflation mean different policies for its control. These include the following:

1 Taxes and Government Spending

An increase in direct taxation cuts disposable incomes and hence demand. But an increase in indirect taxation, while choking off demand, directly raises the inflation rate (by adding to retail prices) and may only fuel the pressures for higher wages. Cuts in government spending reduce aggregate demand and also help to avoid growth in the money supply.

2 Incomes Policy

This means a public policy to control the growth of incomes and demand. Compulsory and advisory policies ended with serious industrial unrest in the 1970s and the Conservative government abandoned the whole principle. However, control of public sector pay can represent an indirect incomes policy.

3 Control of the Money Supply

This was most intensively applied during the early 1980s. The government attempts to manage the money supply through setting time-related targets for its growth. However, it has proved very difficult to define the money supply, while the nature of its link with inflation has been widely questioned.

4 Interest Rates

Increases in the rate of interest are not only important in controlling the money supply. They also reduce demand through their effect on mortgage payments and interest on consumer credit, loans and overdrafts.

Set up a three-column table. In the first column make notes on the theories to explain the causes of inflation. In the second column note the kinds of policy which the theory implies. In the third column write the limitations of the theories and their associated policies.

▶ Inflation raises the level of risk in business.

IMPACT OF INFLATION ON BUSINESS

Inflation has a number of negative effects on business.

- **Planning and budgeting** are undermined by uncertainty over the value of money in the future. A varying inflation rate means that all future financial flows are unknown in real terms. This creates instability and increases the risk of business enterprise.
- **Investment** may be reduced by a climate of business uncertainty. Real rates of return on investment become very difficult to predict.
- **Profits** are often depressed by cost inflation as attempts by firms to increase their prices may cause unacceptable reductions in sales.
- **Pricing decisions** are complicated by inflation. Nominal price increases which are only in line with the general price level may be perceived by consumers as real increases. Frequent price changes meet particular consumer resistance,

yet periods of a 'steady' price mean periods of continuous price reduction in real terms.

- **Export sales** can be badly hit if UK inflation rates exceed those in competitor and customer countries.
- **Industrial relations** may worsen as the workforce makes increasing pay demands to keep up with the rate of inflation. These demands may be unrelated to the financial realities of the business.

Some firms benefit from inflation, since part or all of their costs increase more slowly than the rate of inflation. The result is a fall in real costs and a potential increase in profits. In the medium term many fixed costs do not rise with inflation, leading to an advantage of this type.

Read the following data and answer the questions below.

Bettabox Ltd

Bettabox Ltd manufactures plastic storage boxes in a range of colours. The table below shows average cost and price data for three consecutive years:

	year 1	*year 2*	*year 3*
Average total cost	£3.00	£3.15	£3.60
Price	£4.00	£4.20	£4.50
Retail price index	100	105	115

1. How has the firm's profit margin changed between year 1 and year 3?
2. How has the real price of a box changed over the period?

Evaluation

- Various governments have tried to 'fine-tune' the economy. This means regulating demand so that growth occurs without causing inflation. In practice, adjustments to tax, government spending and interest rates have complex time-lagged effects and may anyway overshoot their targets.
- Fairly stable rates of inflation are less damaging to firms than erratic rates which create instability in the business environment.
- The effect of inflation on the overall output of business is difficult to judge. Policies to reduce or control inflation often cause sharp falls in demand that can cut output and investment.
- Inflation results in winners and losers among consumers. Those on fixed incomes lose, while those in employment often gain, especially if strongly unionized or if in a buoyant sector of the economy. Firms whose market is mainly among 'winners' or 'losers' will find their sales affected accordingly.

42 Interest rates

Chapter objectives

After working through this chapter, you will:

- understand the meaning of interest rates
- know how consumer demand is affected
- understand the relationship with investment decisions
- be able to analyse the impact on a firm's sources and uses of funds.

▶ An **interest rate** is a hire charge for money.

THE MEANING OF INTEREST RATES

If a firm or an individual wants the loan of a car or a piece of machinery, then they expect to pay a hire charge. This is reasonable since the owner of the car or machine is deprived of its use for a period, knows that the value will depreciate and risks the borrower's failure to ensure its safe return. Exactly the same principle applies to lending money. A sum of money represents a certain quantity of resources. Indeed, money is in effect an open-access entitlement to resources of the holder's choice. Thus interest is simply the hire charge for money. The rate of interest must be high enough to compensate the lender for:

- the period without the use of their money and the postponement of their consumption;
- the likely fall in the value of money caused by inflation;
- the risk that the borrower will fail to make repayment.

Demand for Loans

It is attractive to borrow money when the benefits of its use are judged likely to outweigh the cost of borrowing. For example, you might take a bank loan to buy a new car so that you could accept a new job with a longer journey. The benefits of this job might easily outweigh the cost of interest payments: the car, in other words, is a good investment. A firm makes decisions in the same way, balancing the interest rate on additional funds against the projected rewards.

Tyne Taxis Ltd

Tyne Taxis Ltd is operating profitably but needs an additional car to meet growing demand from railway station forecourts. The firm obtains a business loan after estimating that the return from this investment will comfortably exceed the bank's rate of interest.

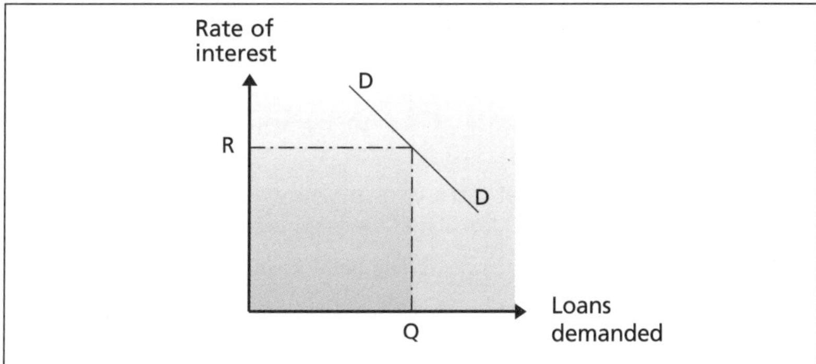

Figure 42.1
The demand for loans

The demand curve for loans is downward-sloping. As rates of interest rise, demand for loans falls.

Supply of Loans

Money for loans is made available through savings, i.e. postponement of present consumption. The rate of savings tends to rise with the rate of interest but also depends on other factors, e.g. financial expectations about the future. However, the largest source of loan finance is credit created by the banking system on the strength of its existing deposits. This is also how the money supply expands and is subject to some indirect government control through the Bank of England.

The Rate of Interest

There is no single rate of interest. Instead, a range or grid of rates exists, with the actual rate charged depending on such factors as:

- the size of the loan
- the duration of the loan
- the risk factor presented by the borrower
- the security offered to cover any default

Mortgage finance is relatively cheap since the lender has the security of the house. Credit card finance, by contrast, is expensive, being both risky and costly to administer.

▶ Base rates

The grid of lending rates rests on a **base rate**, which is the absolute minimum interest rate payable. When the base rate changes, the whole grid of rates is shifted upwards or downwards. Base rates in turn are determined by the Bank of England, whose decisions became independent of government control in 1997.

Real and Nominal Rates of Interest

The nominal rate of interest is that actually charged. As an annual rate, however, its real value depends on inflation. Thus:

real rate of interest = nominal rate - inflation rate

Suppose you borrow £100 for one year at a 10 per cent interest rate, during which time the price level also increases by 10 per cent. After one year you repay £110, which now has a purchasing power of exactly £100 one year ago. In real terms your lender has received no interest at all. Real interest rates in the UK were actually negative through most of the 1970s, transferring resources from lenders to borrowers. From 1980 there was a sharp change, with positive real interest rates varying between 4 and 8 per cent.

Impact on Demand

▶ The Conservative government (1979–97) was increasingly inclined to use interest rates as a way of attempting to regulate the level of aggregate demand and to control inflation.

The level of interest rates is a very important factor affecting the demand for goods and services. It works in two ways:

1 Interest payments by households make up an increasing proportion of total spending. The growth of home ownership through easy mortgage availability and the explosion of consumer credit mean that the spending power of many households is sharply affected by the rate of interest.
2 Credit sales of goods and services are affected by the rate of interest charged. This is particularly important for consumer durables (e.g. cars), where a high proportion of total sales are on credit. Firms may offer favourable credit terms as part of their marketing mix (see Chapter 9).

Investment Decisions

The discount rate used by firms in investment appraisal (see Chapter 23) may be influenced by the rate of interest. In addition, changes in the rate of interest will determine the cost of investment for many firms. Thus, an increase in interest rates will make investment more expensive and rule out previously viable projects. However, the benefits of investment usually accrue in the longer term and large firms may be fairly insensitive to short-run fluctuations in the interest rate.

Sources of Funds

Changes in the rate of interest also affect firms through their gearing ratio (see Chapter 30). Loans to business may carry either fixed or variable interest rates. A highly geared firm with variable-rate loans will be sharply affected by any rise in the rate of interest. The increasing burden of interest charges may come at exactly the time when sales and profits are squeezed. The result is falling interest cover and the ultimate risk of insolvency. Meanwhile, creditors are likely to increase the pressure for prompt payment as the finance of unpaid bills becomes more expensive.

Asset Management

The rate of interest represents the ultimate opportunity cost for all the assets in any business. If the available rate is 8 per cent and an asset is earning a return of less than 8 per cent, then in theory at least, the shareholders would be better off selling the asset and investing the proceeds in a bank. A rise in interest rates should make managers look more critically at every asset category. The feasibility of cutting underperforming assets usually depends on their liquidity. Typical questions might be:

- Could a surplus strip of land be let or sold?
- Might the size of the vehicle fleet be reduced?
- Can stock levels be cut, especially for slow-moving items?
- Should credit control be tightened?
- Could cash or liquid assets be shifted into higher interest-bearing investments (financial fixed assets)?

▶ The minimum opportunity cost of holding non-interest-bearing assets rises with higher interest rates.

Interest Rates

In less than a year the bank base rate is increased from 6 per cent to 12 per cent. How would you expect the following to be affected and why?

1 A retailer of curtains, carpets and home furnishings.
2 A firm planning to use loan finance for the construction of a new warehouse complex.
3 (a) The total number of titles held in stock by a large bookshop.
(b) The period of credit allowed to customers by a computer supplier.

Evaluation

- Changes in interest rates have powerful effects on aggregate demand and can be used as part of an anti-inflation strategy.
- Increases in interest rates are effective in reducing demand but also cut business investment, which may be harmful to future growth prospects.
- High interest rates increase the opportunity cost of liquid assets and put pressure on managers to reduce their working capital.
- Small firms may find fixed-rate loans a safer choice, enabling them to plan realistic levels of interest cover.
- Rising interest rates generally depress demand most severely for luxury consumer services and durables. Necessities and single-use goods are less affected.
- The increase in mortgage finance means that many households are now highly geared. The effect of interest rates on mortgage payments has been a key factor in homeowner spending patterns.

43 International trade

Chapter objectives

After working through this chapter, you will:

- know the advantages of international trade and the reasons why countries may restrict its flow
- be able to interpret the balance of payments
- understand how exchange rate movements affect business decisions
- appreciate the significance of multinational firms
- know how trade and debt affect Third World nations
- know the meaning of the following key terms: current account, visible/invisible trade, current balance, external assets.

ADVANTAGES OF INTERNATIONAL TRADE

Trade has taken place for thousands of years. In essence, the principle is that of swapping. Exchange bargains are struck so that both sides gain. This is most likely to occur through natural advantages (e.g. the climate for growing citrus fruits in Mediterranean countries), or through specialization (e.g. the production of watches in Switzerland). Clearly, modern financial systems make literal swapping unnecessary and the use of money enables complex patterns of trade to take place.

Exactly the same principle applies to the towns or regions within a country. The West Midlands specializes in car production and Cornwall specializes in the production of butter. It is internal trade that makes this specialization possible. The result is that cars made in the West Midlands are used in Cornwall, while Cornish butter is eaten in the West Midlands. Similarly, it is international trade that allows international specialization, which is a major source of increased wealth throughout the world.

▶ Over the period 1960–90, the volume of world output increased three times, while the volume of world trade rose by nearly five times.

Each country has a unique pattern of comparative strengths and weaknesses in producing the goods and services demanded in the world. The vital benefit of trade is that it enables each country to concentrate its resources on the output combination for which it has the greatest **comparative advantage**. In this way, each country can achieve the most efficient allocation of its resources and the value of every country's output is greatly increased.

Arguments for Protection

Despite the advantages of international trade, countries often have reasons for wishing to restrict its flow. These chiefly relate to the **protection** of home industry:

- **New industries** may need time to become established before confronting the full force of foreign competition. In their early stages average costs [illegible] still be relatively high and markets only weakly secure[illegible] otected, firms may find the transition t[illegible] very difficult.
- **Structural change** [illegible] through shifting patterns of deman[illegible] An industry in decline may need protecti[illegible] adjustment and investment in rest[illegible]
- **Unemployment** [illegible] sult of foreign competition as fir[illegible] bour through falling market share.
- **Dumping** can oc[illegible] r country exports goods at prices below thei[illegible] n in order to liquidate a surplus or seize [illegible] ad. Such tactics are recognized as fa[illegible] tion.
- **Balance of payn**[illegible] ow) may prompt short-term protection [illegible] take effect.
- **Strategic indus**[illegible] steel, electronics) may be protect[illegible] rity.

With the exceptio[illegible] the case for protection is essentially sho[illegible] t is to featherbed inefficient industries [illegible] benefit of competitive world prices.

Barriers to Tra[illegible]

The main metho[illegible]

- **Tariffs** are a tax on imports by value or volume.
- **Quotas** limit the quantity of an imported product entering the country over a given period.
- **Exchange controls** limit the availability of foreign currency to buy imports.
- **Subsidies** involve government financial assistance to home industries.
- **Voluntary agreements** mean that one country agrees to limit its exports to another.
- **Administrative restrictions** create technical and bureaucratic obstacles for particular imports.
- **Counter-trading** means that a country makes certain import orders conditional on the other country buying an equivalent value of its exports.
- **Buy-back agreements** involve import of capital equipment on condition that part of its subsequent output is bought by the exporter.

The trend since the late 1940s has been a steady reduction in trade barriers, assisting the rapid growth in world trade. The use of trade barriers by any country invites retaliation by others. There is always the risk that retaliatory actions can escalate, causing mutually damaging reductions in the flow of trade.

▶ In the slump of the 1930s, many countries tried to protect home industries by raising tariffs. The results were reduced flows of trade, more factory closures, more redundancies and further twists in the downward spiral.

▶ The World Trade Organization (WTO) brings countries together for the negotiation of reductions in the barriers to trade.

The British textile industry has been very severely affected by imports of textiles from cheap labour areas in Asia. Both manufacturers and unions have lobbied Parliament to impose higher duties on cheap imports. Draw up a case for protection of the British textile industry and then draw up a case against it.

THE BALANCE OF PAYMENTS

A country's international accounts, showing a summary of all financial transactions with the rest of the world, is called the balance of payments. This will be explained by referring to the following specimen accounts:

UK Balance of Payments 1995
Summary Statement

	(£m)	(£m)
CURRENT ACCOUNT		
Visible trade		
exports	+152,346	
imports	−163,974	−11,628
Invisible trade		
exports	+144,528	
imports	−135,792	+8,736
Current balance		−2,892
CAPITAL ACCOUNT		
External assets		−124,245
External liabilities		+125,194
Net transactions		+949
BALANCING ITEM		+2,446

▶ All accounts in the balance of payments record inflows and outflows of money – not literal goods or services. A British family taking a holiday in France creates an invisible import – i.e., it has bought a range of services (e.g. accommodation) from France. The family's payments involve an outflow of money from the UK.

The **current account** is essentially a record of the financial flows arising from exports and imports of goods and services. **Visible trade** refers to tangible goods (e.g. motor vehicles), while **invisible trade** refers to a broad range of services such as tourism, transport, banking and insurance. Also included are interest and dividend payments received in Britain or paid abroad. The **current balance** is simply the net balance of visible and invisible trade.

The capital account shows the inflows and outflows of investment between the UK and the rest of the world. Short-term capital flows represent movements of money between countries to maximize the financial gain – through changing interest or exchange rates. Long-term flows occur when international investment takes place in the purchase of shares or fixed assets, or when governments agree long-term loans. Changes in the UK's **external assets** refers to net outflows of sterling (e.g. UK residents buying securities abroad) and it is therefore shown as **negative**. Conversely, changes in the UK's **external liabilities** refers to sterling inflows (e.g. foreign residents buying UK securities) and is therefore shown as **positive**.

Balance of Payments and Inward Investment

The Japanese car firm Toyota recently built a new car plant at Burneaston, near Derby. The cost began as a **positive** item on the **capital account**. Notice, however, that once profits began to be remitted back to Japan, they appeared as a **negative** item on invisibles in the **current account** (check that you understand).

Which item in the UK balance of payments would be affected by each of the following business decisions?

1 A north of England manufacturer sells six heavy electric motors to a firm in Spain.
2 A timber merchant in Hampshire buys a consignment of pine planks from a Swedish company.
3 A Belgian chemicals company takes out fire insurance with a major London firm.
4 A West Midlands steel fastenings company sends its sales executives to a conference in Paris.
5 During one year, a Japanese-owned car company sells 30,000 vehicles from its UK factory to dealers in Germany.
6 A Californian electronics firm builds a factory in South Wales.
7 A British metals conglomerate buys a copper mine in Zambia.

Taken as a whole, the capital and current accounts must **always balance**. The reason is simple. Any deficit (i.e. a net outflow) must have been financed by borrowing (an inflow), selling assets abroad (an inflow), or using foreign currency reserves (counted as an inflow). The same principle applies to a household. If you spend more than your income, then you must have either borrowed, sold off assets or used savings. By the same reasoning, a country with a surplus can repay debts, increase its assets abroad or add to its reserves. In practice, the accounts do not actually balance, since many transactions inevitably go unrecorded. However, the principle is not affected and the **balancing item** is simply an accounting device to ensure a technical balance.

Clearly, a country's current account balance is an important sign of economic health. A deficit in some years, balanced by a surplus in others, is satisfactory. But repeated or increasing deficits mean that a country is either running down its reserves or becoming progressively more indebted. This cannot continue indefinitely without a collapse in the country's currency. Consequently, governments adopt policies to keep the pattern of trade in broad balance. These can directly affect business:

▶ Only structural (long-term) deficits on the balance of payments normally require corrective government policies.

- **Trade barriers** (against non-EU countries) may be raised, perhaps increasing the cost of imports but protecting UK firms.
- **Aggregate demand** may be reduced by increasing tax levels,

or – at the discretion of the Bank of England – by raising interest rates. This should cut demand for imports but will increase unemployment and reduce investment.
- **Depreciation of the exchange rate** will increase exports and will also reduce imports by making them more expensive. This runs the risk of increasing the rate of inflation.

In the early 1980s, Britain had a large balance of payments current account surplus. Since 1986 there has been a deficit, which peaked at £22 billion in 1989. This was a factor in government efforts to reduce aggregate demand from 1988 to 1990. Significant improvement followed, with the deficit down to £3 billion in 1995.

EXCHANGE RATES

When goods or services are purchased by one country from another, it is necessary to settle the debt in the currency of the seller. For this reason, a worldwide foreign exchange market exists, with electronic dealing between financial centres. An exchange rate is really the price of one currency in terms of another. These prices vary with the forces of demand and supply like any other price:

▶ The demand for pounds might increase (DD – D¹D¹) through growth in UK exports or high UK interest rates attracting investors' funds to London. As a result, the equilibrium value of the pound rises from X – X¹.

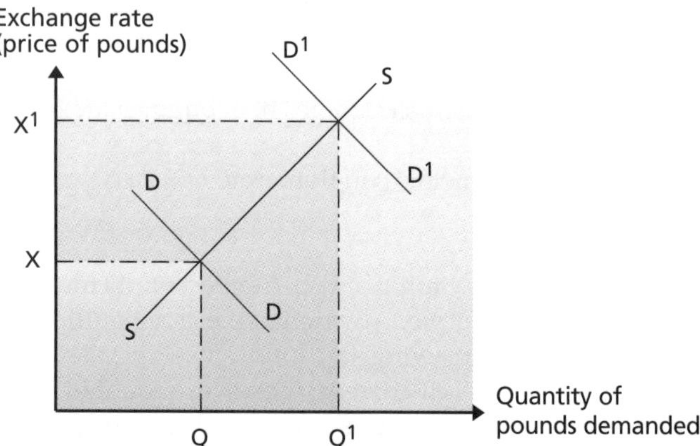

Figure 43.1
Exchange rates and the demand for sterling

From 1971 to 1990 the pound 'floated' on market forces, although there were often government policies to influence its value. From 1990 to 1992 Britain was a member of the European Exchange Rate Mechanism (ERM). This means that the currency must remain within a narrow range of values against any other EU currency. Any risk of breaking these boundaries is counteracted by the Central Bank deliberately buying or selling its currency on the foreign exchange market, so adjusting the equilibrium of demand and supply. In 1992 efforts to support the pound at its fixed rate foundered and Britain left the ERM. Since then the value of the pound has depended on market forces.

The exchange rate has a vital effect on the effective price – and hence volume – of UK exports and imports.

The Effect of Exchange Rates on Demand

Britannia-Marine Ltd sells deep-sea pumps to US oil companies, competing with leading Japanese suppliers. Each basic pump costs £10,000. The exchange rate stands at £1 = $1.60, so the American importers pay $16,000 per pump. Sales amount to 1,000 units each year, with an estimated price elasticity of 2. The following year, the pound strengthens to an average rate of £1 = $2. The American importers must now pay $20,000 for each pump, or a rise in the effective price of 25 per cent. The result is a switch to Japanese suppliers and a slump in sales to 500 units (down 2 x 25 per cent = 50 per cent).

Exchange rate fluctuations are a real hazard to many firms. A UK manufacturer importing components or raw materials will suffer cost increases if the pound falls in value. Of course, the mechanism can operate in reverse. For exports, a fall in the pound's value will boost sales. A major argument for ERM membership has been that more stable exchange rates assist business planning and greatly reduce the risks of European trade.

▶ Economic and monetary union (EMU) – as planned by some EU member states – will eliminate exchange rates between those countries as all transactions become denominated in terms of the euro.

Obverse Ltd

Obverse Ltd imports American baseball boots at $27 per pair to sell at a 25 per cent mark-up through sports outlets in Britain. The exchange rate has been £1 = $1.50, but suddenly it strengthens to $1.80. The mark-up remains the same but sales rise by 33 per cent.

1 What was the old and what is the new selling price of boots in Britain?
2 Calculate the price elasticity of demand.
3 If the firm was selling 6,000 pairs per month under the old exchange rate, what is the increase in the total profit caused by the strengthening of the pound?

MULTINATIONALS

When a firm owns or controls business facilities in more than one country it is called a **multinational enterprise**. Such firms vary from industrial giants with global operations to many medium-sized enterprises with a few branches abroad. Multinationals are increasingly important and 313 of the FT's top 500 firms operating in Britain are now foreign owned. Multinationals generate about 30 per cent of Britain's GDP and account for nearly half Britain's manufacturing employment. Significantly, Britain's foreign-owned firms tend to be found in the fastest-growing business sectors and over half are American. Worldwide, multinationals are extremely important - and powerful - in the business world.

▶ The American firms Ford, General Motors and Exxon each have sales values greater than the GDPs of all but fourteen countries in the world. The dominance of multinational firms is still increasing as their output grows at 10 to 15 per cent annually – well ahead of most national growth rates.

The multinational form of business organization has certain distinct advantages:

- Achieving control over raw material supplies in multiple locations (this was the origin of many multinationals).
- Exploitation of scale economies, including greater access to capital and ambitious research and development programmes.

- Attraction, accumulation and full development of technical and managerial skills.
- Ability to place different stages of production in low-cost locations. The use of cheap labour in developing countries is particularly important.
- Potential to qualify for government assistance, e.g. capital or training grants, in a range of host countries.
- Capacity to develop international products and yet to produce different versions in different countries with accurate targeting of national markets. These are often supported by valuable patents and trademarks.
- Gaining monopoly power both in buying the factors of production and in selling end products.
- Ability to minimize tax liabilities using transfer pricing techniques. This means selling semi-finished goods between subsidiaries at prices which ensure high accounting profits where tax rates are low and low profits where tax rates are high.
- Opportunity to avoid trade barriers between countries.
- Diversification of risk by operating in a range of production centres and markets.

Complex combinations of these factors determine the multiple locations that are actually selected by multinational managements.

There has been heated argument over the rights and wrongs of multinational enterprise from the point of view of host countries. The major advantages are:

- new jobs are created in host countries which are often relatively well paid;
- modern investment and new technology is transferred from the home country;
- foreign exchange earnings may be considerable and balance of payments deficits reduced;
- local management may be improved through the example set by multinationals;
- tax receipts of governments are increased and foreign aid may become politically more likely.

However, the criticisms are also serious:

- the risk of closures and withdrawal when more profitable locations emerge or when government grants expire;
- some investment is only for assembly purposes (known as 'screwdriver' factories), with limited value added locally;
- prestigious and highly skilled functions (e.g. research and development) remain based in the home country;
- actual tax payments may be very slight as a result of transfer pricing;
- economic and even political independence is reduced as decisions taken at corporate headquarters may come to overshadow national policy.

Poorer countries usually welcome the employment and investment potential from multinational enterprise, but they face particular problems. The company may bring capital-intensive production methods that create relatively few local jobs. Its output may consist of luxuries inappropriate to the country's needs, yet still marketed to the population. Raw materials may be rapidly exhausted, with the risk of long-term environmental damage. Traditional ways of life may be undermined and the rural–urban population drift accelerated.

Make notes on the advantages and disadvantages of multinationals to the host country.

LESS DEVELOPED COUNTRIES (LDCS)

▶ The North–South divide

The term 'less developed countries' includes many nations in Latin America, Africa and Asia. Despite rich and vital cultures, they face a range of economic problems which often include:

- small endowments of natural resources;
- a dependence on labour-intensive primary production;
- a small industrial base with limited availability of newer technology;
- very basic and incomplete infrastructures of power, communications, transport, education and health care;
- rapid population growth;
- low or very low GDP per capita.

▶ Ethiopia has a population of 55 million compared with the UK's 58 million, yet the UK's GDP is about 195 times greater.

Developing countries often suffer from a cycle of poverty and deprivation from which it is difficult to escape. Low and unstable incomes mean a lack of saving and investment. Governments have limited tax revenues, while export earnings from primary production are overspent on essential imports and interest on debt. The potential for economic growth can thus be very restricted, with constraints on per capita incomes from population growth. Problems are often further compounded by political instability, unfavourable climates and low standards of education, nutrition and health.

▶ South Korea achieved an average growth rate of 9 per cent over the period 1980–8. Thailand's economy was growing at 12.5 per cent in the late 1980s.

The economic problems and achievements of LDCs vary very widely. The least developed countries have the very lowest incomes (less than $400 GDP per capita) and are usually the most severely constrained by the poverty cycle. By contrast, the newly industrialized countries (NICs), especially in the Pacific Basin, have achieved high rates of economic growth and increasingly compete with western countries in industrial markets.

All of the wealthier western nations have **aid programmes** for LDCs. The official United Nations target is for aid to represent 0.7 per cent of GDP. In practice, aid as a percentage of GDP (1995) varies widely but is a relatively small item in national budgets:

Denmark	0.96
France	0.55
Britain	0.28
USA	0.10

Source: Overseas Development Institute

Some of the aid programmes have been immensely valuable, but problems have been:

- the failure of some Third World governments to channel aid towards the poorest sectors of the population;
- the tendency to favour urban projects when the greatest needs are in rural areas;

- a bias towards large-scale prestige projects (e.g. airports) when small-scale local projects would be more cost effective.

There are two particular areas of difficulty for the developing world in its relationship with the industrial western countries:

1 Primary Produce Markets

Some LDCs have depended excessively on a single primary product (e.g. coffee from Kenya or copper from Zambia) so that a fall in its price disrupts the national economy. Price instability among primary products generally causes damaging fluctuations in producer incomes. Meanwhile, real prices themselves have tended to fall since 1980, yet some essential imports for LDCs have become relatively more expensive. The developed world's demand for many primary products is in long-term decline as usage becomes more efficient and synthetic substitutes are found for natural materials (e.g. rubber).

▶ Brazil owed $121 billion in 1992.

▶ By 1992 Nigeria's debt represented 108 per cent of annual GDP with interest payments costing 30 per cent of total export earnings.

2 Debt

Large-scale lending by western countries to LDCs took place during the 1970s. The subsequent sharp rise in real interest rates left some countries with a vast burden even to service, let alone repay, their debts. The result was that for most of the 1980s the outflow of interest and repayments substantially exceeded the inflow of new loans and official aid. The position has eased somewhat in the 1990s.

Make notes on the problems Third World countries experience in the pattern of international trade.

Evaluation

- The downward trend in trade barriers since the Second World War has been interrupted by recent recessions. The pressure on countries to protect their home industries against competition increases when sales are falling and unemployment is rising.
- Often trade barriers only delay inevitable changes in a country's industrial structure. The postponement may actually intensify the consequences of competition by enabling firms to avoid the necessary development of new technologies, new products and new markets.
- Although the relative importance of manufacturing industry has declined, it remains a vital sector. Services lead proportionally to fewer exports and are more vulnerable to recession.
- Economic expansion in Britain is very prone to causing a faster growth in visible imports. This is partly due to the wide range of goods that are no longer domestically produced. It is also caused by a tendency for consumers of durables and luxuries to prefer imported brands.
- Inward industrial investment has increased since the late 1980s. Japanese and American firms have been attracted by Britain's relatively low costs and the opportunity to produce inside the single European market.

- Since the 1980s there has been a rapid growth in joint ventures, where companies enter into partnerships for research, production or marketing purposes. The trend has been strongest within Europe and between Europe and Japan. Many deals fail but joint ventures can be an effective way to match differing strengths or to compete successfully with larger rivals.
- Despite the very real criticism of multinationals, it must be remembered that they have sponsored enormous progress in new technology and business techniques. A real part of our living standards depends on their strength and vigour.
- British aid programmes often have 'strings attached', in the form of requirements to purchase British goods.
- Quite apart from ethical considerations (see Chapter 49), it can be argued that through assistance to raise incomes in poorer countries, western firms will benefit by finding new markets for their goods and services.

The European Union

▶ **Media Watch**
For this chapter, look out for news stories on the debate over Britain's policy in the European Union.

Chapter objectives

After working through this chapter, you will:

- understand the objectives and structures of the European Union (EU)
- be aware of EU policies as they affect business
- know the implications of the Single European Market
- be able to analyse the current response of firms to EU membership
- know the meaning of the following key terms: European Council, summit meetings, Social Charter.

WHAT IS THE EUROPEAN UNION?

▶ The European Union (EU) was founded by the **Treaty of Rome**, 1957.

The Second World War began in Europe, during which 22 million lives were lost. When the war ended there was a very strong feeling that the countries of Europe should never go to war with one another again, and instead should build a new unity that would embody their shared culture and common goals. A step in this direction was taken in 1951, when France and Germany brought their coal and steel industries under joint control. More radical progress came in 1957, when the **Treaty of Rome** formed a community of six nations: France, Germany, Italy, Holland, Belgium and Luxembourg.

The main economic goals were:

- to eliminate customs duties and quotas on trade between member states;
- to charge a common external tariff on imports from non-member states;
- to ensure fair competition between community firms;
- to operate a common agricultural policy;
- to achieve the free movement of people, capital and services within the Community.

In addition – and as a natural consequence – there was a commitment among members to increasing coordination and unity at a political level.

At first Britain chose to remain outside these initiatives, given its close links with the Commonwealth (ex-colonies of the British Empire) and the United States. Instead, the European Free Trade Association (EFTA) was formed to include Britain and smaller countries outside the Community. However, during the 1960s, the economic importance of the Community increased and Britain applied to join. After initial rebuffs, serious negotiations began in 1969 and membership was achieved with Ireland and Denmark in 1973. The European Union has continued to grow. Greece joined in 1981, followed by Spain and Portugal in 1986 and then Austria, Sweden and Finland in 1995. Future expansion looks likely to include a number of eastern European countries.

EU Members (1995)

Country	*Population (millions)*	*GDP per capita*		*Growth % rate (av. 1992–5)*	*Unemployment. % rate (1995)*	*Inflation % rate (av. 1992–5)*
		Money[1] *($)*	*PPP*[2] *($)*			
Austria	8.0	28,870	21,000	1.8	3.8	3.1
Belgium	10.1	26,400	20,990	1.1	9.9	2.4
Britain	58.3	18,740	18,480	2.0	8.8	3.3
Denmark	5.2	33,080	21,440	2.2	7.1	1.4
Finland	5.1	24,070	na	0.9	16.6	2.7
France	58.0	26,450	20,040	1.2	11.6	2.1
Germany	81.6	29,570	20,510	1.4	8.2	3.4
Greece	10.4	10,717	na	0.7	9.1	12.2
Holland	15.4	25,630	19,400	1.8	7.0	2.2
Ireland	3.6	17,040	16,760	5.6	12.4	2.3
Italy	57.2	18,990	19,690	1.1	11.9	3.3
Luxembourg	0.4	na	na	3.7	2.9	2.7
Portugal	9.9	9,949	na	0.6	7.3	6.8
Spain	39.2	14,260	14,310	1.1	22.9	5.3
Sweden	8.8	25,930	18,360	0.5	9.2	3.4

[1] measured in direct money terms
[2] adjusted so that money has equal purchasing power in each country, called purchasing power parity (PPP)

RUNNING THE EUROPEAN UNION

The supreme decision-making body in the EU for setting broad long-term policy is the **European Council**, comprising the heads of state from each member country. Their **summit meetings** take place in different European cities at least twice each year. Because the Treaty of Rome created a community of nations in an evolving and permanent relationship, a number of formal institutions exist:

- The **Council of Ministers** decides detailed EU policy on each issue. Each member state is represented by its foreign minister or minister responsible for the subject concerned.
- The **European Commission** makes proposals to the Council of Ministers and is responsible for carrying out policy as finally decided.
- The **European Parliament** is directly elected by the people of the member states. It has a right to be consulted about Commission proposals and has an important role in drafting the EU budget. However, it does not possess the law-making power of a national parliament.
- The **Court of Justice** has fifteen independent judges and passes judgement on EU disputes.

▶ The EU incorporates a common market: barrier-free trade between member states and a common tariff against imports from non-members.

▶ The main EU institutions are based in Brussels, Luxembourg and Strasbourg.

▶ The last elections for the European Parliament were in 1994. The next are in 1999.

The European Union Budget

The EU is financed by contributions from each country, which include the proceeds of the Common External Tariff, a percentage of

VAT receipts and an additional percentage (up to 1.2 per cent) of GDP. Total revenue in 1996 amounted to 82 billion ECUs (European Currency Units).

The ECU is the EU's own currency which will become known as the euro when the single currency is launched. It is used to denominate the budget and is of growing importance. Its value is based on placing a quantity of each member state's currency – weighted according to the size of its economy – in a 'basket'. This can then be valued in terms of any national currency on the basis of current exchange rates. In mid-1997, the ECU was worth 70p.

The major items of budget spending finance the following:

▶ Efforts are in progress to reduce the real level of European farm subsidies and to encourage environmentally sensitive farming.

▶ The purchase of surplus farm output has caused the accumulation of food 'mountains' for some products.

- The **Common Agricultural Policy** (CAP) aims to ensure relatively stable and fair incomes for farmers within the EU. The 'guidance fund' attempts to improve agricultural efficiency and the 'guarantee fund' supports farm produce prices. This involves purchasing any surplus output of farmers at guaranteed minimum prices. The CAP accounts for a substantial 48 per cent of the total budget.
- A **Regional Fund** provides grants to finance improvements in the infrastructure of the EU's least prosperous regions (e.g. construction of roads and bridges). These are designed to encourage business investment.
- A **Social Fund** provides grants to assist in creating employment, with particular emphasis on training schemes. Aid is targeted towards people and areas with special needs.

UK MEMBERSHIP OF THE EUROPEAN UNION

▶ The European Union used to be called the European Community.

In 1951, at the time of the coal and steel initiative, Britain's GDP was higher than those of the Union's founder members added together. In 1958 when the European Union was established, Britain still had a higher GDP per capita than any major member. Yet by 1973 when Britain finally joined, its GDP per capita was the lowest in the enlarged Union except for Italy and Ireland. It was partly Britain's economic decline relative to continental countries that spurred the government into joining. Unfortunately, the first decade of membership was a period of sharp recession and instability. Some British firms were ill prepared for the export opportunities of membership, with their export marketing geared towards the Commonwealth countries rather than Europe. In many consumer goods industries there was increasing import penetration of the British market by European firms. Meanwhile, the Union's rules and budget – and especially the support for farming – had been designed without thought for British interests. The result was a long dispute over fair budget contributions, eventually settled in 1984.

▶ Britain's most important trading partner is Germany, not the USA.

More fundamentally, Britain has never shared the continental desire for a progressive political union of member states. However, the EU has become increasingly important to the British economy. Over the period from 1972 (the year before joining) to 1995, the proportion of Britain's exports taken by the EU has risen from 34 per cent to 58 per cent, and the proportion of imports that are purchased from the EU has risen from 34 per cent to 55 per cent.

The Business Arguments for British Membership of the EU

There has always been overwhelming support from British industry for EU membership. The major arguments in favour of membership are:

- **Economies of scale**: the potential is increased by the open European market. The population of the UK is 58 million, while the total EU population is now 371 million. Firms can develop products for a European rather than purely UK market. There are further advantages in combined European research projects and in the growth of joint ventures.
- **Specialization** of business shifts towards a Europe-wide pattern, allowing the principle of comparative advantage to be amplified in its benefits. In theory, market forces drive resources in each member state towards their most efficient use.
- **Export potential** is increased within the EU by the removal of any trade barriers. Sales to other countries may be increased through greater efficiency and hence lower prices.
- **Competition** between firms in Europe should provide a greater spur to both innovation and efficiency.
- **Investment** is stimulated by competition and the enlarged sources of finance in Europe. Inward investment from non-EU states (e.g. Japan) is made more attractive by a unified market. Poorer regions within EU states gain grants from the Regional Fund.
- **Synergy** (or the 2 + 2 = 5 principle) can be generated by the dynamism of an expanding market and the rise in business expectations for the future.

▶ The UK population is only 15.7 per cent of that of the European Union.

However, these arguments are mostly about potential and not automatic advantages. Economies of scale may fail to materialize or may even become diseconomies. Competition may be obstructed by monopoly power. European export potential may reverse into national import penetration. Investment may flow towards the most prosperous countries and regions, causing unemployment and decline elsewhere.

THE SINGLE EUROPEAN MARKET, 1992

All of the arguments above were sharpened in importance by the **Single European Act, 1985**. This set in motion a programme of removing the remaining barriers to trade and fair competition within the EU. It amounted to a final fulfilment of the Treaty of Rome, customs duties and quotas having already been abolished between members. The result was a **Single European Market** from 1992, whose features include:

- **technical regulations** relating to many products becoming standard throughout the EU;
- **free trade in services** (e.g. banking and insurance) achieved by harmonizing relevant regulations;
- **public sector purchasing** opened to competition from all member states (e.g. in defence contracts);

- **elimination of subsidies** by governments for home industries that distort competition;
- **indirect tax rates** (especially VAT) broadly standardized to ensure fair price competition;
- **free capital movements** between countries by abolition of exchange controls (see Chapter 43);
- **free movement of labour** ensured by agreeing on EU-wide validity of vocational and professional qualifications;
- **unrestricted physical movements** of goods and people through the abolition of border controls and simplification of paperwork for goods in transit.

▶ Increasingly, firms are developing a European marketing mix with modifications for each national market.

The Single Market provides major opportunities for UK firms to increase their sales and European market share. However, it remains necessary to strengthen and broaden management skills, especially in the areas of strategic planning and marketing for Europe. There is also still a need for better understanding of European national cultures and greater proficiency in the main European languages.

In 1989 a European Social Charter was approved by all EU countries excluding Britain and was appended as the **Social Chapter** to the Maastricht Treaty, 1992. This gives all employees a range of social rights including a minimum wage and representation on European Works Councils at the firms for which they work. Britain opted out of the Social Chapter until 1997, when it was accepted by the incoming Labour government.

ECONOMIC AND MONETARY UNION

Plans for Economic and Monetary Union (EMU) date back to the late 1960s. Some of the motives are political but one major economic aim was to eliminate exchange rate uncertainties for trade between member states. Cooperation in the 1970s to reduce fluctuations in exchange rates led to the launch of a European Monetary System in 1979. This established the ECU and Exchange Rate Mechanism (ERM) – from which Britain withdrew in 1992 (see Chapter 43).

The Maastricht Treaty of 1992 represented a major step towards further European economic, social and political integration. Its most immediately important implication has been a timetable for the implementation of EMU. By building on the continuing existence of the ERM, a series of inter-governmental conferences is planned to culminate in the locking of exchange rates in 1999 and the introduction of the euro as a single currency. This will be issued only by a new European Central Bank. However, the current schedule allows until 2002 for the final elimination of national currencies and the release of euro-denominated notes and coins.

The key arguments for these changes are based on the need for a European zone of complete currency stability. This will enable firms to know exactly the costs and selling prices of all products within EMU member states without the uncertainty and distortion created by national rates of exchange. In addition there will be direct pressure on all EMU members to avoid excessive rises in business costs or in government borrowing.

Public and political opinion in Britain is divided on the issue of EMU and the single currency. Participation is criticized on the grounds that it will reduce political sovereignty and severely restrict Britain's freedom in making macroeconomic decisions. The reverse arguments stress the benefits of currency stability and the risk of sliding into a 'second division' Europe that is less influential and less attractive to international investment. UK business leaders have always been largely pro-European and a significant number believe that Britain should indeed be among the first group of countries to adopt a single currency.

Make notes on the opportunities and threats to British firms arising from EU development.

Kent Conserves Ltd

Kent Conserves Ltd is a medium-sized firm producing a wide variety of fruit jams at its factory near Ashford in Kent. With well-established success in the UK, the marketing director now aims for export orders from other countries in the EU.

1. State one important factor that should be considered by each of the following departments before launching the export initiative: (a) production, (b) finance, (c) personnel.
2. Suggest three problems – apart from price – which might arise from the firm's European marketing mix.

Evaluation

- Certain UK business sectors have particular comparative advantages and are well placed to benefit from the Single Market. These include electrical engineering, pharmaceuticals, food and precision equipment in the manufacturing sector, and banking, insurance and aviation in the service sector.
- The Single Market also offers opportunities for all EU companies. There is the risk that a new wave of assaults on some UK markets could occur.
- The removal of remaining trade barriers may tend to increase the importance of price in the European marketing mix.
- With their heavy reliance on equity finance, UK companies will be vulnerable to take-over bids from American and Japanese firms seeking access to the European market
- Income and prosperity remain very unequal within the EU. The benefits of membership have probably been strongest within a 'golden triangle' linking London, Milan and Paris. On the geographical fringes of the EU, major regional problems continue to exist (e.g. in southern Italy, Northern Ireland and Portugal).
- Britain has found it psychologically difficult to identify with European Union membership. Physical separation from the continent, language barriers and historic links with the USA and the Commonwealth have made integration difficult.

- It must be recognized that greater economic and political integration in Europe is likely to happen regardless of British objections. Meanwhile, aspects of the EU may change with the likely accession of new members from both Western and Eastern Europe.
- It can be argued that the EU forms an exclusive and inward-looking 'club' for rich nations. However, the Union accounts for nearly 20 per cent of all world trade, even when excluding transactions between EU members. It offers favoured trading terms to the poorer countries that were formerly part of the European empires and provides by far the largest proportion of world foreign aid.
- Opposition to the EU is often based on the belief that membership is eroding the sovereignty of the British Parliament and the independence of national policy. On the other hand, the EU can exert greater influence in world affairs than Britain alone, while the business world is increasingly integrated on a European basis.

Part 8

Management Challenge

45 Organizational structures

Chapter objectives

After working through this chapter, you will:

- know the main theories of how organizations work
- be able to interpret organization charts and recognize different structure types
- understand the significance of a firm's span of control and its use of delegation
- grasp the concept of centralization and decentralization
- know the meaning of the following key terms: scientific management, human relations approaches, systems theory, contingency theory, formal and informal organization, management hierarchy, span of control, line management, chain of command, delegation, 'virtual corporations', functional, divisional, matrix and federal structures.

THEORIES OF ORGANIZATION

▶ An organizational structure is the agreed network of responsibilities that makes possible the coordinated use of resources.

Most people find a completely unstructured day - never mind a week or month - surprisingly difficult to use well, or even to enjoy. They do not thrive on aimlessness. They need goals with some structure and commitments through which to achieve them. Look around the room in which you are sitting - or through the window at the world outside. Nothing that you see would be possible without an intricate organization of people and resources. Indeed, the most remarkable human achievements - from building cathedrals to constructing the space shuttle - have depended on the most exceptional levels of commitment and coordination between people.

Business activity is the organization of human and material resources to achieve an agreed objective. This will almost certainly require:

- **leadership** to provide direction and coordination;
- **specialization**, which is the acceptance by people of defined tasks and duties for which they are responsible;
- **hierarchy**, which is the arrangement of people in layers of authority;
- **communication and coordination** to ensure that the work of specialist staff in the hierarchy combines to achieve objectives;
- **motivation**, which means the will among people to fulfil their agreed tasks.

In a small enterprise these features are often fairly informal. A small bakery, for example, will have an owner or manager who provides leadership. There will be some kind of hierarchy or 'pecking order' among staff, who will specialize in, say, food preparation or counter sales. Communication will be verbal and direct, while motivation will depend on a team spirit and the 'atmosphere' of the shop.

As an enterprise grows, these features need more precision and planning. The alternative would be confusion, inefficiency and waste.

Large business organizations first appeared in the nineteenth century as the industrial revolution made possible mass production and distribution. Theories evolved in the twentieth century to explain how organizations work. There have been four broad approaches.

1 Classical

Early theories tended to regard human organization rather as if it were a machine. These **mechanistic** views emerged in the work of F.W. Taylor (1856–1917), who developed the principles of **scientific management**. This meant defining a task and then carrying out a scientific style of research to find the most efficient methods of operation. The worker was trained to follow precise instructions and paid according to the results achieved. Soon after, Henri Fayol (1841–1925) described the operation of a **formal organization**. This included:

- clear direction or objectives for all activities in the organization;
- a chain of authority running down the organization where each employee has a superior to whom he or she is responsible;
- specialization in responsibilities of staff and functional departments.

▶ **Bureaucracy** does not necessarily mean inefficiency and 'red tape'. It means operating according to rules rather than in a whimsical and idiosyncratic way.

Formal organizations also construct systems of rules and procedures. Called **bureaucracy**, this phenomenon was first analysed by Max Weber (1864–1920), who stressed the importance of officials behaving in accordance with known rules rather than personal preference.

▶ The theories of Mayo, Maslow and Herzberg are described in Chapter 35.

2 Human Relations

Elton Mayo and his Hawthorne experiments (1924–36) showed the importance of human relationships in the workplace as a key factor in the efficiency and motivation of staff. He also revealed the significance of hidden informal structures of power and influence at work. It was clear that regarding organizations as machines did not achieve the best results and that management should respond to human needs. His analysis was developed further by Maslow in the 1940s and Herzberg in the 1950s.

3 Systems Theory

A system is an arrangement of parts that work together to form a whole. An organization is a complex social system containing a range of sub-components such as social systems, technical systems and internal structures. Each of these entities has a separate existence, but they are also interdependent. Greater than the sum of its component systems is the organization itself, which interacts with the wider economic, technological, social and political environment.

A famous application of systems theory was in the study by Trist and Bamforth (1951) of the coal industry in Durham. Underground coal cutting had just been mechanized, yet the expected productivity gains had not occurred. The research found that the miners had previously worked as small, closely knit social groups. The new mechanized 'long-wall' method placed the men in large anonymous shifts, each completing only one stage in production. It was proposed that the **socio-technical systems** had been unbalanced. The answer was a 'composite long-wall method', which retained the new technology but enabled shifts to tackle different tasks with stronger group identities. The key measures of performance all improved.

4 Contingency Theories

▶ **Contingency** means pressure to meet a particular need.

The 'contingency approach' to organizations comes from research by Lawrence and Lorsch (1967) into a range of American firms. They found that different firms and different departments within firms adopt widely differing structures to suit their particular needs. The most successful firms had the best methods of resolving the tensions created by their own (necessary) diversity of inner structures.

In Britain, Burns and Stalker (1961) studied the structure of firms in the electronics industry. They found two major types of management system:

1 **Mechanistic systems** were machine-like in their emphasis on rigid hierarchies, specialized work roles and the obedience of subordinates.
2 **Organic systems** were more like a living organism where control and communication operate in a network, with emphasis on mutual assistance and achievement of goals.

THE FORMAL ORGANIZATION

▶ An organization chart shows the **formal** pattern of authority and responsibility.

The best way to understand the structure of an organization is to draw a map or model. This is called an **organization chart**, and we will look first at its basic principles. A highly simplified example is shown in Figure 45.1 (page 350).

ABC Ltd has a traditional pyramid structure, spread out like a family tree from the top towards the bottom.

This top–bottom dimension represents **authority** and **responsibility**. The highest position of authority is held by A, to whom B, C and D are responsible. Below this point only part of the structure is shown, but B, for example, controls the work of E, F, G and H. Similarly, F has authority over staff M–Q.

The pyramid structure of authority in an organization is called a **hierarchy**. The layers in the structure are called **levels in the hierarchy**. The number of subordinates for whom each manager is responsible is called the **span of control**. For example, the span of control for A is three, for B four and for F five. The top-down pathways of authority are called **line management**. Say B is the

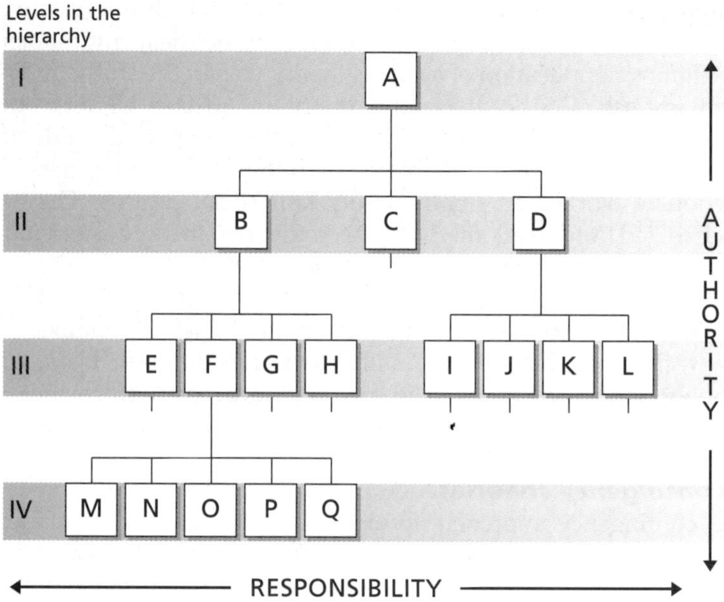

Figure 45.1
Organization chart for ABC Ltd

production manager. Then B to F (supervisor) to P (foreman) is a pathway of line management authority. Such a pathway is called a **chain of command**. Production and marketing are typical **line functions** within a company, which means that they are primary to the purpose of the organization. By contrast, accounting and personnel are called **staff functions**, meaning that they are secondary in purpose (the primary purpose of a firm is not to draw up accounts). Often there are direct links between staff functions and line managers: for instance personnel may advise on health and safety requirements. Notice that communication generally can take three directions:

- top-down, e.g. instructions down line A to D to K;
- bottom-up, e.g. request on route Q to F to B;
- lateral, e.g. discussions between F and J.

So far we have been discussing the formal structure of ABC Ltd. This assumes that the authority and communication between people in an organization follow the official pattern. In reality, most organizations also experience an invisible and informal structure. Suppose F is regarded as a weak supervisor. Then N may find it more effective to bypass his authority and deal directly with B. However, H may have some lingering grudge against B and happens to know C socially. And since C has specially favoured relationships with A, H feels able to disregard B, taking pride at having hidden influence within the firm. Some lightly drawn hidden pathways are probably inevitable in any organization, but managers must treat them with great caution. Too easily they lead to an inbreeding of mistrust, speculation and rumour, which in turn cause misunderstanding, inefficiency and weakening of team effort. Informal structures can be symptoms of faulty staff selection or weaknesses in the formal structure.

Delegation

Delegation means a manager passing part of his or her authority to a subordinate while retaining full responsibility for the consequences. Most managers know that they could not possibly fulfil the whole of their jobs without delegating some tasks to those for whom they are responsible. The ability to delegate the right tasks to the right staff is a key quality in a good manager. Certain core parts of the manager's job require his or her particular expertise, skills and status, and these tasks must not be delegated. But to ensure concentration on such core elements, delegation of other tasks is essential.

Other advantages of delegation are:

- the development of specialized skills is encouraged;
- subordinate staff gain valuable experience and a track record on which to base their future promotion;
- motivation is increased as staff feel more important and more trusted;
- the subordinate can make immediate decisions in the light of circumstances at the time.

Delegation always carries a risk. If a task delegated is not properly performed, then the manager is still to blame. Typical problems in delegation include:

- the subordinate proving to have inadequate expertise or training;
- abuse of the manager's trust through carelessness or incomplete work;
- the subordinate exceeds the boundaries of delegated authority;
- insecurity in the manager, who fears the implications of holding ultimate responsibility.

The extent of delegation in an organization varies widely. It particularly depends on:

- the consequences of errors (the higher the risk factor, the more difficult it is to delegate);
- the experience and quality of staff;
- the confidence of management;
- the leadership style and traditions of the organization.

▶ Effective delegation requires the right balance between **trust** and **control**.

Span of Control

The span of control – or number of subordinates reporting to a superior – is closely related to the extent of delegation. As a superior's span of control increases, so the demands on him or her by subordinates will increase. For this reason, the larger the span of control, the greater the extent of delegation likely. There is no perfect span size, but studies suggest that for general management a range of five to eight is typical. In very complex work the span may be under three, while for routine work lower in the hierarchy spans often rise to twenty or thirty or higher. The optimal span depends on the complexity of the work, the experience and calibre of management and staff, and the potential seriousness of errors.

Narrow spans of control require more levels in the hierarchy and a taller pyramid structure. Wider spans allow fewer levels and a flatter pyramid.

▶ When BP announced a new structure for the 1990s it was a 'flat' organization, cutting at a stroke its layers of management from eleven to only five.

Tall pyramids allow a high degree of supervision but have a tendency to be rigid and bureaucratic in their behaviour. The trend in the 1990s is towards 'delayering': that is, cutting out layers of middle management and creating a flatter structure with wider spans of control. This reflects:

- the need to be more responsive to change, with shorter chains of command and more sensitive bottom-up communication;
- the advance of market orientation and the need for all managers to be closer to the market interface;
- the growth of teamwork using laterally linked staff in flexible patterns;
- the pressure to cut administrative overheads and achieve a leaner organization.

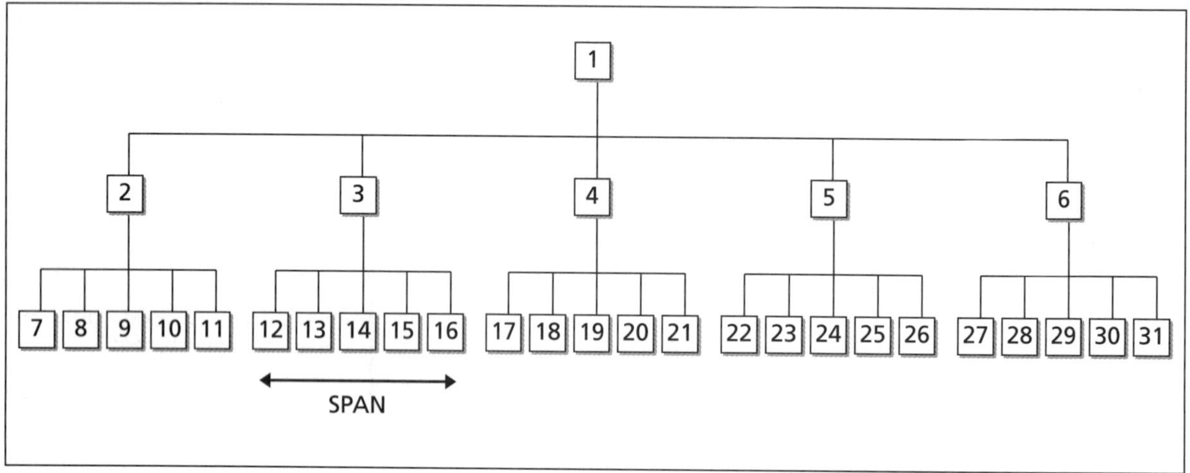

Figure 45.2
ABC reconstructed

Five levels in the hierarchy are necessary when using a span of two, while only three levels are needed when the span is increased to five.

The principle of 'flattening' the organization has interesting possibilities. If delayering is taken to its logical conclusion, the apex of the pyramid touches the floor and a hierarchy no longer exists. The firm becomes a kind of network or configuration of functions and expertise. This has given rise to discussion of the '**virtual corporation**', in which the organization becomes a completely flexible network of productive possibilities. In this 'Lego-like' vision of the firm, connections and structures are built according to market need. The assets of the 'firm' are almost entirely people-based and practically all added value is knowledge.

Read the data below and follow the instructions.

Papyrus Ltd
Zoe Ashby was managing director of Papyrus Ltd, an expanding company in the specialist paper business. Her production director was Ian Thompson, who had four works supervisors each responsible for a team of eight skilled operatives. The marketing director, Matthew Collis, had two strands of responsibility. His promotions manager was Toby McNeill, with six regional representatives. Rachel Smithers was export sales manager, with representatives in Frankfurt, Paris, Milan and Madrid. As finance director, Shahid Khan had two section heads, each of whom was assisted by five office staff.

1 Draw up an organization chart for Papyrus Ltd.
2 State the span of control for each of the four directors.

Structure Types

The actual structures chosen by organizations vary enormously in pattern and style. However, four broad types can be distinguished:

1 Functional

Each major business function (e.g. production, marketing, personnel) has its own department and hierarchy of management authority.

▶ Functional models are based on management responsibilities.

Advantages

- specialized departments can offer higher levels of expertise;
- clear vertical chains of command assist control;
- coherent career pathways exist for staff.

Disadvantages

- functional departments tend to pursue their own sectional interests;
- lateral communication and coordination may be difficult;
- the model is not suitable for diversified companies or multiple locations.

2 Divisional

When a firm has several product types, physical locations or distinct markets, then it may create corresponding divisions: in effect mini-companies coordinated by top management. Usually, functions such as strategic planning and finance remain at head office level.

▶ Divisional models are typically based on products, locations or markets.

Advantages

- increased flexibility to respond to particular conditions of product type, location, market;
- greater motivation for managers in running a semi-autonomous division;
- distinct profit centres assist closer monitoring of performance;
- enables policy and major strategic decisions to be freed from day-to-day management.

Disadvantages

- the danger that divisions operate without regard to the interests of the whole organization;
- divisions may resent central management, causing a sense of 'distance' between the divisions and head office.

3 Matrix

This is a newer type of structure that combines both vertical and horizontal lines of responsibility. Typically, the vertically structured specialist functions remain, but across them is superimposed horizontal lines of **project responsibility** forming **project teams**. This means that an accountant, for example, might have conventional hierarchical responsibility while also belonging to a project team

▶ Matrix models are based on both management responsibilities and project goals.

and answering to a project manager. The aim is to align the specialist functions into an integrated system for the fulfilment of specific goals: for instance a special order for a key customer.

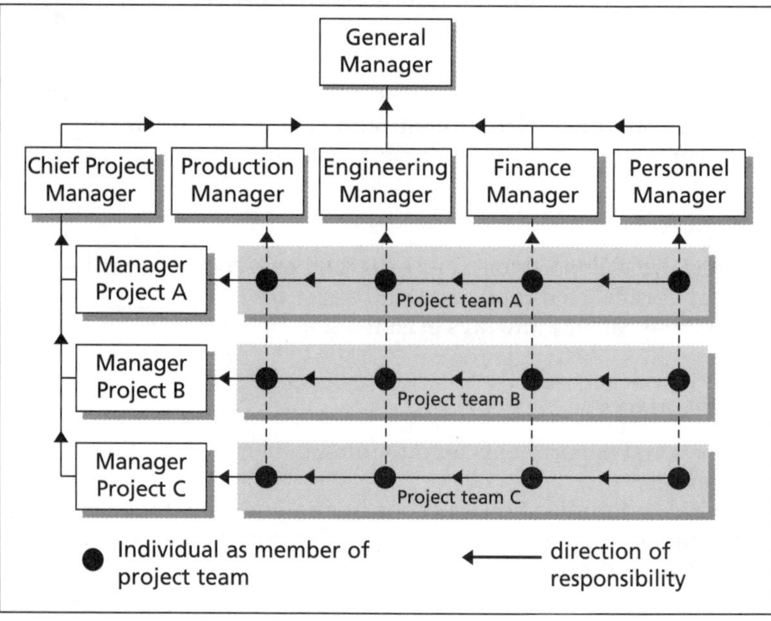

Figure 45.3
Matrix structure

Advantages

- overcomes isolation of departmental hierarchies;
- focuses resources on meeting the project in hand;
- project management is market oriented in giving large customers direct management access.

Disadvantages

- the risk of conflicting line and project responsibilities;
- the more complex structure may lead to confused and wasteful use of resources.

▶ Federal structures are based on a range of separate business entities.

4 Federal

Some firms consist of virtually free-standing businesses, with headquarters providing only coordination and some element of control. The balance of power between headquarters and the federation members varies, but headquarters usually operates some key financial controls. Charles Handy (1989) observes that to be truly federal, it must be the component business needs that grant power to the federal culture and not the other way round. Federal structures can arise from take-over bids that form conglomerates (see Chapter 24).

Advantages

- an entrepreneurial spirit can flourish in each business;
- bureaucracy is minimized;
- layers of middle management are avoided;
- access remains to the financial resources of headquarters.

Disadvantages

- the authority of the headquarters may be resisted;
- only possible to achieve limited economies of scale;
- risk of 'organizational sprawl', with loss of direction and focus.

Draw up a table to summarize the advantages and disadvantages of the different structures described above.

Centralization and Decentralization

Many firms centralize some functions while decentralizing others. For example, finance and accounts may be controlled from head office, while personnel and production may be managed locally. Similarly, within a single location decision making may be centralized at the top or dispersed down the hierarchy.

Centralize or Decentralize?

Centralization can encourage efficiency as the managerial overview may enable all resources to be put to their optimum use. Scale economies are fully harnessed, planning is easier and administration is streamlined.

However, mistakes become magnified. Branches or small departments may lose their incentive to work through a lack of independence, with 'orders' being sent from head office. Decisions may be slow and poorly suited to local circumstances.

Decentralization allows faster and more flexible decision making that can respond readily to circumstances. Red tape is reduced, while creative thinking and initiative are increased. Motivation among management and staff should improve with greater personal commitment to work.

However, decentralization risks a loss of coordination as the operating units of the firm pull in different directions - perhaps wasting resources or undermining top management's goals. Work may be duplicated at lower levels and managers may busy themselves 'reinventing the wheel'.

▶ **Centralization**: the concentration of decision making among the most senior management at the 'centre' of the organization.

▶ **Decentralization**: dispersion of decision making throughout the organization, with greater independence in the firm's operational units, e.g. factories, departments, branches.

▶ There is no perfect degree of centralization. The approach varies by industry, by firm and by period. Centralization was popular in the 1960s as very large firms began to use mainframe computers and to present a corporate identity. Since the 1980s the trend has been to decentralize, aiming for flatter structures and increased delegation.

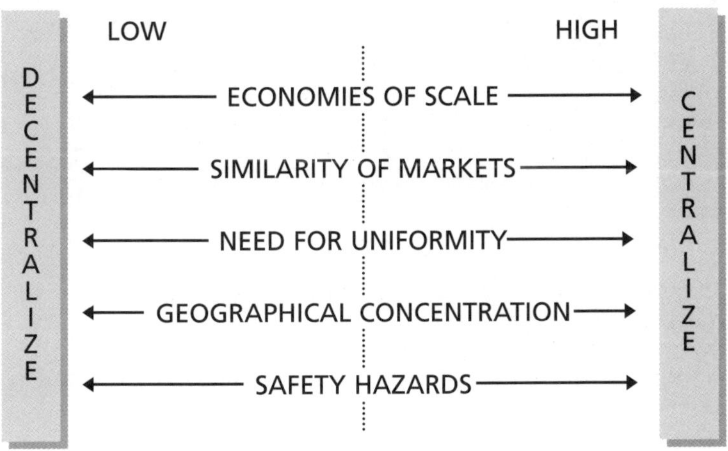

Figure 45.4
Centralize or decentralize?

To what extent would you expect the following enterprises to have a centralized or a decentralized structure? Give your reasons.

(a) a mass-production manufacturer of injection-moulded plastic products for the consumer market, with a single large factory;
(b) a chain of health food stores;
(c) a fire brigade.

Evaluation

- Organizational structures are maps of resource mobilization. They should reflect clearly the firm's objectives. For example, a divisional structure might reflect selling as the firm's central activity, or a matrix structure could suit a construction firm with complex projects.
- The wrong structure can cause many problems such as over- or understaffing, slow decision making, poor communications or conflicting loyalties.
- Tall, rigid hierarchies are often product driven. Flatter, more flexible systems are usually market oriented.
- The traditional manufacturing organization with a mass workforce (often called **Fordist**) tended to be hierarchical, with high supervision levels. With the growth of new technology and customer-related services, the shift has been towards smaller, flatter, 'core' organizations that are networks rather than pyramids (**post-Fordist**).
- Flatter structures imply wider spans of control, more delegation, increased trust and greater staff autonomy. The corresponding trend in the 1990s is towards decentralization.
- The management's role is changing from supervision of subordinates towards the leadership of teams. Teams tend to be project- or goal-focused.
- Effective structures are in a state of constant change. Small firms must be particularly careful to update their structure as they grow. Adjustment to change is easier for organic than for mechanistic structures.
- The first emergence of the firm as a networked system is being made possible by information technology. Skill and judgement are replacing much physical labour, while electronic transmission and memory replaces many physical events.

46 Decision making

Chapter objectives

After working through this chapter, you will:

- know the meaning and nature of decision making
- understand the use of a simple decision model
- appreciate the role of intuition and creativity in the decision process
- recognize the problems and realities of decision making in organizations
- know the meaning of the following key terms: objectives, mission statements, environmental constraints, decision trees, scenario planning.

WHAT ARE DECISIONS?

To make a decision, there must be a choice. Only when there is no option is there no decision. Usually there is at least the option of saying 'no' or of doing nothing. How do you decide? Consciously or subconsciously, you consider your objectives. You then evaluate the available options and assess to what extent they are likely to fulfil your goals.

Often the final choice is not easy. Options can seem equally attractive. The cost of making one choice is forgoing another. This **opportunity cost** may be uncomfortably high and we may try to postpone the decision in the hope that one option will take a decisive lead, or that another will lose its attraction. But in the end a choice must be made. Excessive delay can often prove to be the worst decision of all.

DECISIONS AND MANAGEMENT

Management is the art of making the best use of available resources to fulfil agreed objectives. This means:

- recognizing problems and opportunities;
- responding by making decisions;
- ensuring that decisions are efficiently implemented.

Objectives

Objectives are a statement of what an organization wants to

▶ **Objectives**: a statement of what an organization wants to achieve.

▶ The aims of most public companies do not merely express the narrow financial interests of the shareholders. Employees, customers, the community and the environment are all often quoted as interests to be satisfied.

achieve through its operation. A firm's formal objective is given in its Memorandum of Association (see Chapter 3), and larger firms may publicly state their general philosophy and values in a list of aims. For most plcs, profit is only one goal among others.

Objectives provide specific criteria for decision making. They are intended to drive the organization – or parts of the organization – forwards in a chosen direction. Objectives are most effective when expressed in unambiguous, quantified terms, e.g. increase active customer base this year by 25 per cent.

Constraints and Opportunities

Business operates in a real world and decisions are not taken in the abstract. Before making any decisions a manager must always assess the limitations of a situation. These exist both inside and outside the firm and affect every function. Some examples are given in the box.

Decision-making Constraints

Human
staff numbers
skills and experience
attitudes
trade unions
labour availability
national pay awards
education and training provision
employment laws

Marketing
market research data
new product research
product portfolio
sales team
distribution networks
competition
advertising codes/laws
aggregate demand
trade barriers

Production
installed machinery
capacity
technological base
warehousing
suppliers
environmental controls
planning laws

Finance
cash flow
liquidity
gearing
creditworthiness
availability of loans
interest rates

The decision maker is also confronted by internal and external opportunities. Inside the firm there may be staff with hidden skills, machinery with an interesting alternative use, or a potential source of new funding. Outside the firm a sudden gap in the market may emerge, or a significant new technology. The window of opportunity can open suddenly and profitability may depend on being able to respond before it closes.

Decision Models

In business, managers make decisions that involve large sums of money and other people's jobs. To achieve the optimum (best possible) outcome usually requires a systematic approach. For this purpose, a **decision model** is useful.

Typical elements are:

- **Become aware of problem**: detecting the existence of a problem before its details become clear.
- **Define objective**: clarifying the objectives or desired impact of the decision need that has arisen.
- **Identify constraints**: recognizing and analysing the key constraining factors both inside and outside the firm.
- **Collect information**: researching quantitative data and qualitative evidence; investigating possible causes and effects; identifying constraints.
- **Develop options**: generating ideas; selecting list of credible options.
- **Evaluate and decide**: assessing the plus and minus factors; projecting outcomes; testing and trialling against objective; deciding on optimum solution.
- **Implement**: planning necessary action; ensuring the decision is carried out; checking actual events; taking corrective measures.
- **Monitor consequences**: reviewing outcomes relative to objectives; learning from experience.

Monitoring consequences returns the manager to the problem awareness stage, so that all the stages together make up a continuous cyclical process.

▶ A **model** is a representation of reality that assists understanding of structure, operation and meaning.

▶ Notice the logical order for decision making.

Decision Making

Kennards Ltd

Richard Hopkins has recently been appointed managing director of Kennards Ltd, a traditional department store. Kennards has a loyal customer base and an excellent position in a university town. However, there are signs of underperformance. The objective for the first year is to increase return on capital to 20 per cent. An early target of Richard's attention is the in-store restaurant.

Problem awareness: the restaurant on the third floor is running at a slowly increasing loss; both menu and decor seem dreary and dated.

Define objective: make restaurant a key attraction for the store and profitable in its own right; otherwise find the best alternative use for the space.

Identify constraints: limited funds in budget for investment; older staff resistant to change; strong competition from other high street restaurants.

Collect information: investigate restaurant accounts; interview manageress and staff; devise questionnaire for a survey of all customers; check building regulations for possible alterations.

Develop options: collect numerous ideas from management and staff. Final options include: (1) straight refurbishment; (2) shifting company accounts from top floor and opening a new café/

▶ Every decision carries an opportunity cost.

restaurant with a roof garden; (3) closure and replacement with a new outdoor leisure department.

Evaluate and decide: obtain estimates for building, refurbishment and refitting work; draw up projected revenue and cost statements; test market for outdoor goods and new menus; make optimum choice: 'option 2'.

Implement: plan move of office space to basement; place fitting contracts; draw up timetable for all works; check progress; recruit and select new restaurant manager.

Monitor consequences: analyse any variance between budgeted and actual results for costs and revenues; assess impact on staff.

A more graphic picture of the decision process is shown in Figure 46.1 below:

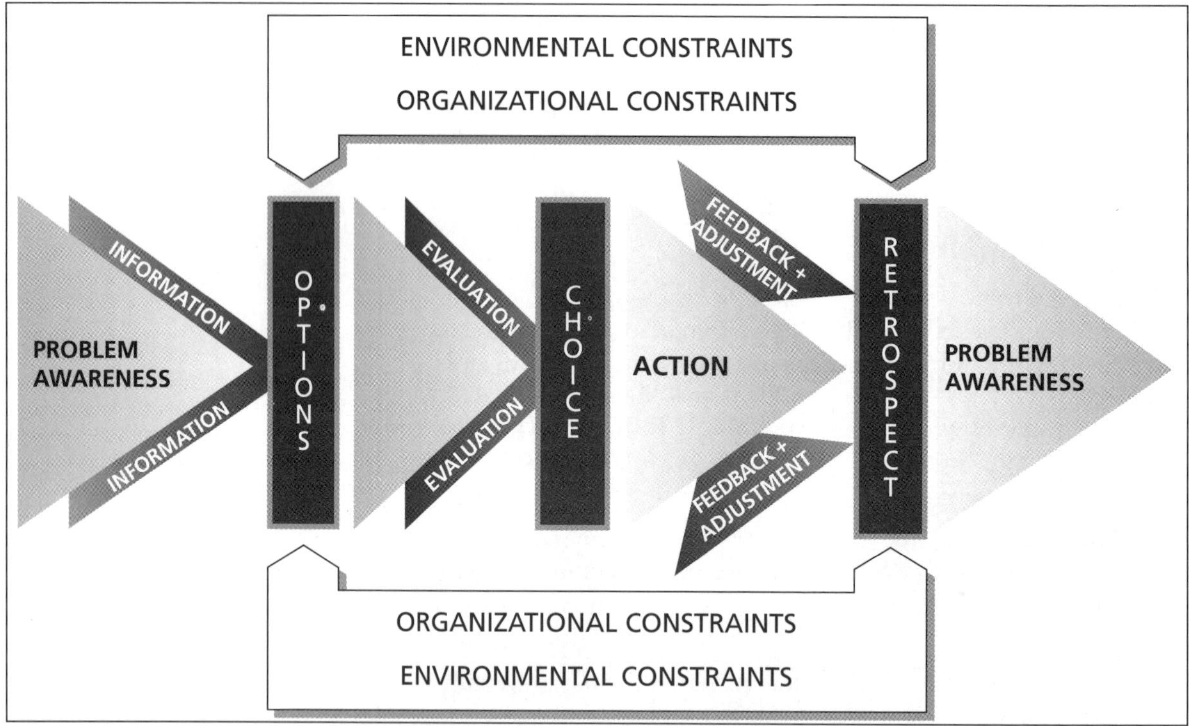

Figure 46.1
A decision-making model

This model offers an open-ended sequence, with a recurrent cycle. Notice that feedback begins to be received once the decision has been put into action, and this is likely to prompt adjustments to the original plan. ***Environmental constraints*** *refers to all limitations existing outside the organization.*

Use Figure 46.1 to illustrate the decision-making process at Kennards Ltd.

Reason Versus Intuition

No one fully understands the concept of **intuition**. Traditionally, it has been considered a stronger feature in women than in men. In any event, there are some weaknesses in the step-by-step rational approach, which tends:

- to overvalue quantities at the expense of qualities;
- to value predictability and rigid programmes of behaviour while discouraging imagination;
- to imprison managers in the **parts** of a decision, while intuition can absorb the **whole** situation and reach to its heart.

Of course, reason remains essential to managing any organization. For many problems there is unlikely to be an effective decision without thorough research, careful analysis of alternatives and vigilant control in practice.

Creativity

Creativity is the capacity to use an input of resources or ideas to produce an output of greater value. The process of **creative thinking** is of great significance, though it remains a partial mystery. The quality of any decision depends on the quality of the ideas originally conceived. The importance of creative thinking increases with the seniority of management.

Edward de Bono pioneered the idea of lateral thinking, which breaks from the patterns of normal vertical or logical thinking. The mind and imagination are free to make unlikely - even 'crazy' - connections, which can later be tested and developed using vertical thinking. According to de Bono, lateral thinking involves:

▶ 'The purpose of lateral thinking is the generation of new ideas and the escape from old ones.'
Edward de Bono, 1971

- escaping from clichés and fixed patterns;
- challenging assumptions;
- generating alternatives;
- jumping to new ideas and seeing what happens;
- finding new entry points from which to move forward.

Executive courses exist for its cultivation and many firms use brainstorming techniques to generate ideas. Some organizations have a creative style or culture of management, often allowing their staff greater personal freedom to explore - and to make mistakes.

▶ Abraham Zaleznik of Harvard Business School is highly critical of scientific management and believes that one of its effects is the suppression of imagination and creativity.

Uncertainty and Risk

Often risk and reward are inversely related. Launching an innovative product early increases the risk of failure yet may offer the chance of a dominant share in a vital market of the future.

Firms vary widely in their attitude to risk. If stability is the priority, then major risks will be avoided. But if fast growth and high returns are demanded, then risk taking becomes the art of management. The scale of acceptable risks is clearly related to the size of the enterprise. Some ambitious firms consciously develop a culture of risk taking among their management. This means that mistakes - within defined limits - are not only acceptable but regarded as evidence of managerial learning.

Where risks and outcomes can be quantified, **decision trees** are a useful device. They relate the outcome of an event to the probability that it will occur.

Suppose a friend owes you 50p. He offers to toss a coin: tails he owes you nothing, heads he pays you £1. Is this fair? For one toss of the coin you receive either nothing or £1. But over a series of tosses you would lose your money and receive £1 on an equal number of occasions. Thus the average value of one toss must be 50p. Put another way, you have a 50 per cent (written as 0.5) chance of receiving nothing and a 0.5 chance of receiving £1.

0.5 × 0p = 0p

0.5 × £1 = 50p

So your friend's proposal was fair!

The same principle can be applied to business.

A Decision Tree

Indie Records Ltd

An independent record company believes that it has a recording with great potential and an artist who could be a future star. Already it has received a cash offer of £300,000 for the rights. Alternatively, it could market the record in the UK, spending £200,000. There would then be an estimated 40 per cent chance of achieving higher sales projections, yielding £600,000 profit. But there would also be a 60 per cent chance of lower sales, yielding only £400,000. Finally, it could make a video and additionally release the record in America, for a total cost of £600,000. On the 20 per cent chance of a major hit, returns would then be £1,200,000, while there was a 70 per cent likelihood that a minor hit would generate £900,000. There would also be a 10 per cent risk of a flop in America, with total returns of only £500,000.

This information can be shown as a decision tree:

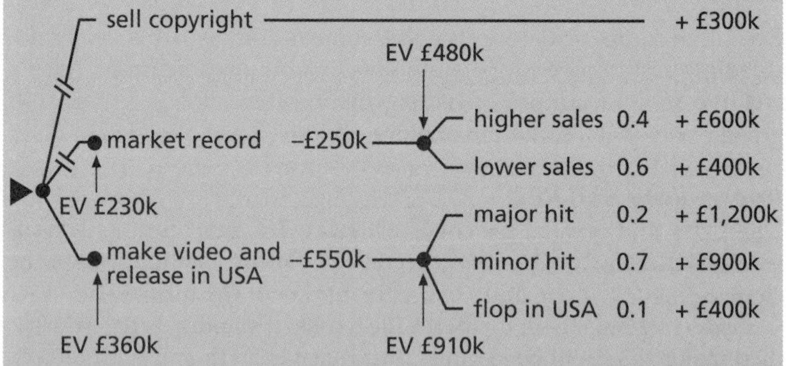

Figure 46.2
A decision tree

sell copyright + £300k
EV £480k
market record −£250k
higher sales 0.4 + £600k
lower sales 0.6 + £400k
EV £230k
major hit 0.2 + £1,200k
make video and release in USA −£550k
minor hit 0.7 + £900k
flop in USA 0.1 + £400k
EV £360k
EV £910k

The tree is drawn from left to right but interpreted from right to left. Start on the **right-hand side** and **work backwards**. The 'sell copyright' option is simple with its £300,000 yield. The 'market record' option has two possible outcomes and their combined expected value is shown projecting from the outcome noted. The 0.4 (40 per cent) probability of receiving £600,000 is worth 0.4 × £600,000 = £240,000. This figure is called an **expected value (EV)**. Similarly, the 0.6 probability of receiving £300,000 is also worth £240,000. Hence the total expected value is £480,000. We must then subtract the marketing costs of £200,000 to show a final expected value of £280,000 for the option. This is lower than the

▶ Calculations for the 'make video and release in America' option.

Expected values:

			£k		£k
major hit	0.2	×	1,200	=	240
minor hit	0.7	×	900	=	630
flop	0.1	×	400	=	40
expected value				=	910
less costs				=	550
final expected value				=	360

value of the 'sell copyright' option and thus can now be rejected. Notice the symbol used to indicate a branch of the tree that may be 'cut off'.

We now apply the same calculation process to the 'make video and release in America' option. Its final expected value turns out to be £360,000, implying rejection of the 'sell copyright' option and a decision to make the video and release in America.

Note that all the figures (except the copyright sale) would be estimates only. The expected values are not literally expected but are statements of average worth. The firm would actually choose the 'make video' option only if it could afford the risk of the worst outcome – a 10 per cent chance of receiving £400,000 and so losing £150,000 on the venture.

The decision tree would be only one element in the actual decision process. Other factors would vary from the implications of a £550,000 negative cash flow in making the video and financing the US release to the degree of uncertainty of the cash estimates themselves.

Make your notes on decision trees by drawing one for a company choosing between two options. Option 1 costs £420,000 with a 60 per cent possibility of sales of £500,000 and a 40 per cent possibility of sales of £700,000. Option 2 will cost £700,000 with a 10 per cent possibility of yielding £2,000,000, a 30 per cent chance of yielding £800,000 and a 60 per cent chance of yielding £700,000.

The Impact of Change

When making a short-term tactical decision, a manager can often assume that any unforeseen change of circumstances will be small. How many meals should a hotel restaurant prepare to serve next Saturday? Circumstances could change, but next Saturday will probably be similar to last Saturday. Now consider the directors of the hotel, deciding on a proposed building project to add fifty new bedrooms. It will be three years before any profit is expected. But how will the town's reputation change? Will demand for business conferences increase? Will the government authorize a link road to the motorway?

▶ Management that anticipates change is said to be **proactive**. Management that responds to change only when it has already occurred is called **reactive**.

Business is a kaleidoscope of risk and opportunity. The pattern changes continuously. To ignore or discount change is to invite disaster. In the 1970s, Swiss watch manufacturers decided to continue using mechanical technology. The result? Electronic watches from Japan destroyed nearly half of Switzerland's watch industry.

Often change is a continuous process, with its effects building steadily over time: for instance the growth of supermarkets and the decline of small grocers. But change can be **discontinuous** or take the form of a 'shock', when a whole business context changes quite abruptly.

Discontinuous Change or 'Shocks'

In 1974, the world price of oil quadrupled in a few months. Fuel economy was suddenly important. New oilfields became worth developing and the first serious post-war recession began.

Many large firms found all their projections and plans thrown into confusion. Led by Shell, a new approach called **scenario planning** developed. This involves planning for a whole range of 'what if ...?' situations, where in each case one or more of the basic assumptions are changed.

When the Gulf War broke out in 1991, Shell already had thorough plans to cope with any major crisis in the Middle East.

▶ In some markets, a company's ability to manage change successfully may be its greatest source of competitive advantage.

DECISION MAKING IN PRACTICE

▶ The gap between the theory and reality of decision making is often very wide.

There is always a gap between theories in textbooks and action in the real world. Decision models tend to assume that all managers are impartial and open-minded. In practice, managers have all kinds of personal reasons for favouring particular decisions. For instance, few marketing managers will favour cuts in the advertising budget. People become attached to particular causes or projects, which they may obstinately support long after any rational case has disappeared. Similarly, people find security in familiar patterns of behaviour and may oppose change in a defensive spirit.

Different people may perceive the same evidence differently. Often people's values and beliefs harden into prejudices that place a distorting filter between themselves and reality. Even experience can be a liability when it leads to automatic assumptions.

Personalities and internal politics are a crucial internal constraint in many organizations. 'Not upsetting Mr Jones' can easily become a major preoccupation. 'Pleasing Mrs Smith in personnel' may seem wise if an employee is hoping for early promotion. In other cases, whole departments may conduct private battles between one another and the abandonment of a new product may be seen in production as a victory over the marketing department.

There is often a great distance between the strategic decisions reached by a firm and the actual business of tactical management, which may be messy, compromised and inconclusive. Many middle and junior managers pay lip service to formal decisions while actually concerning themselves with day-to-day survival. Lack of time and pressure of work may mean that short cuts and second-best options are necessary. Managers may also adopt an approach that the US economist H.A. Simon calls 'satisficing'. This means making decisions to produce adequate or 'satisfactory' outcomes in terms of a few key criteria. For instance, a sales manager might wish to avoid any conflict with staff and yet achieve just enough sales to satisfy the board.

Krackle Krisps Ltd

Krackle Krisps Ltd was launched in 1989 to enter the highly competitive snacks market. The firm gradually introduced a range of six flavours in ordinary potato crisps and a further three flavours in a 'crinkle-cut' style. It also produced a snack for the adult market called 'Potato Pearls' and a novelty line for children called 'Tiger Tails'. Emphasis generally was on quality and freshness, with shorter distribution chains than the major manufacturers.

Strong sales in 1996 and optimistic sales forecasts for 1997 led the company to expand its production facilities. However, in practice it was not long before sales began to falter and only intense marketing efforts averted an actual decline. By the beginning of 1997 it was clear that significant over-capacity existed (about 25 per cent of a maximum of 2.5 million packets/year output). Simon Smith, the managing director, was anxious to consider a new product that might bridge the gap until some more general sales growth was resumed. When a special meeting took place in early March, two rival alternatives were proposed.

Sara Bassett, the marketing director, supported a new product called 'Quasars' based on a space theme. The target market would be children under sixteen, with sales in schools as well as in shops and supermarkets. Latest market research seemed most encouraging:

'Quasars': Sales forecast for first year

Original	Burger flavour	Total
400,000	200,000	600,000

The factory cost was projected at 10p per packet, with a selling price to wholesalers of 12p per packet. After distribution and mark-ups the product would retail at an average price of 20p per packet. Unfortunately, the production process would require machine modification costing £5,000.

On the other side of the table, the sales manager Graham Martin favoured another product called 'Bangles'. This would be a hoop-shaped snack in plain and pizza flavours. Its image would be young and fashionable, with marketing aimed at the 15–30 age group. The cost-price structure would be identical to that of 'Quasars' but, with a simpler machine process, the extra capital cost would be only £2,000. It was estimated that total sales in the first year would be 300,000 of the plain version and 150,000 for the pizza flavour.

1 Work through the decision-making process carefully, making notes under the headings below. Remember to make use of the numerical evidence.
   (a) Problem diagnosis
   (b) Objectives
   (c) Constraints
   (d) Information
   (e) Choice
   (f) Review
2 What further information would you consider obtaining before making your final decision?

Evaluation

- Objectives are the guidance system for decisions in matters of policy, strategy and tactics. Their effective communication to all staff is therefore essential.
- Most decisions do not exist on their own as discrete problems. They are vitally interconnected with many other decisions at different levels. Decisions are usually also interactive: tackling one problem may alter the optimum solution for another.

- In practice many decisions are **informal** and remain **implicit** (not openly announced). In small firms or closely knit management teams, decision making may be more a matter of mutual discussion and tacit understanding.
- The scientific approach to decision making is a powerful tool. However, many decisions have vital dimensions that are only accessible through intuition and creative thinking.
- Well-defined problems benefit most from tightly organized, rational decision processes. The most long-range and least clearly structured problems may benefit from speculative, unconventional and even 'crazy' thinking.
- The rigidity of some decision structures breeds a sub-culture of subversive or 'illegal' decision making. This occurs when some managers know that their proposals will not be accepted and so secretly pursue their own ideas regardless of official approval. Senior managers may even turn a blind eye in the hope of positive outcomes.
- When a group of people (e.g. a committee) addresses a decision, support may build too rapidly around a solution that appears to please the majority. A kind of 'groupthink' sets in and people uncritically support a decision that they would reject if thinking alone.
- In some firms decision making tends to be concentrated at the top of the management hierarchy. Such centralized firms face the problem of gaining staff identification with decisions passed down the organizational pyramid (see Chapter 45).
- Many firms are tending to push more decisions closer to their point of impact. This means increased **delegation** and greater personal responsibility for all managers.
- Decisions must often be made under pressure. Firms need increasingly rapid reactions in response to problems and opportunities.

Strategy and planning

Chapter objectives

After working through this chapter, you will:

- appreciate the meaning and significance of business strategy
- understand how PEST, SWOT and gap analysis contribute to strategy formation
- be able to apply some simple generic strategies
- know the critical factors in strategy implementation
- know the basic principles of operational and administrative planning
- know the meaning of the following key terms: objectives, strategy.

WHAT IS A STRATEGY?

A business organization brings together a range of valuable resources. Its purpose is usually expressed in the organization's **aims**, which are definite yet not specific. Profitability is always a key aim, but there may be others arising from the interests of stakeholders such as employees, customers or society in general.

Some firms choose to establish their aims in a **mission statement**, which should normally be a short and memorable declaration of essential intent: for example 'to be the leader in deep-sea drilling technology'.

These aims are important statements of direction, but they need hardening into specific **objectives**. For example, further profitability may suggest objectives such as sales expansion by a given percentage or entry into export markets. How are objectives to be fulfilled? This is a key question for senior management and the broad outline of an answer forms a **strategy**. This relates to a medium- or long-term horizon and is not merely a response to routine or day-to-day problems.

The need for a coherent strategy has been increased by the complexity of many organizations and the environment in which they operate. The quickening pace of technological and social change has also put a growing premium on good strategic planning.

> **Why we are in business**
> 'We are in business to delight our customers by offering them memorable products, good value for money and legendary service. Everyone in the Group should get real satisfaction from their work and contribute as much as they can to the success of their business. We want our shareholders to get a competitive return on their investment. We want our suppliers to profit from our success. We want the communities in which we work to be proud of our presence. As we achieve all this our future will be secure and profitable.'
> WH Smith Group plc, *Annual Report and Accounts*

Strategic Analysis

Every business has its own internal dynamics and operates in a dynamic external environment. The first step towards framing an

▶ A system for surveying the long-term business environment acts for the firm like 'antennae' in picking up messages that are still distant yet may be highly significant.

effective strategy is therefore an analysis of the firm in its environment. An approach often used here is PEST analysis.

PEST Analysis

This explores the firm's external environment under the following headings:

Political/legal
e.g. controlling waste disposal
Economic
e.g. rising real disposable incomes
Socio-cultural
e.g. shifts in lifestyle
Technological
e.g. development of faster microchips

When managers have identified the key external pressures they can try to assess their relative importance both now and in the future. The results of the analysis can then feed into the overall formulation of strategy.

All firms trade in a market of some kind. In almost all cases this is competitive – in other words, there are some firms offering similar or related products. These firms are usually keen to capture a competitor's market share. Thus, to a greater or lesser extent, a firm is under constant competitive pressure. Consequently, it must have a current strategy for its own defence and probably for some extension in existing or new markets. This is achieved through holding or gaining competitive advantage, the source of which needs careful analysis. Does the firm appeal to customers mainly on grounds of price? Or is product quality the distinctive factor? Or perhaps the strategy has been a balance between reasonable cost and satisfactory quality. Does the firm rely on a mass market or a small segment? Answering these questions throws light on possible strategies for the future.

▶ It is quite possible to manage a firm yet have illusions about its relative strengths and weaknesses.

SWOT Analysis

A particularly useful technique in the development of strategy is SWOT analysis (**S**trengths, **W**eaknesses, **O**pportunities, **T**hreats). This helps managers to identify key factors in the firm's strategic position.

Example of SWOT analysis for a manufacturer of printing equipment:

Strengths
e.g. worldwide sales team
Weaknesses
e.g. poor image
Opportunities
e.g. chance to enter Chinese market
Threats
e.g. expiry of patents

Strengths and weaknesses are factors **inside** the firm that may assist or obstruct the fulfilment of objectives. Opportunities and threats are factors **external** to the firm that may open up or close off possibilities in the effort to meet objectives.

Gap Analysis

A useful overview of what a new strategy needs to achieve is provided by **gap analysis**.

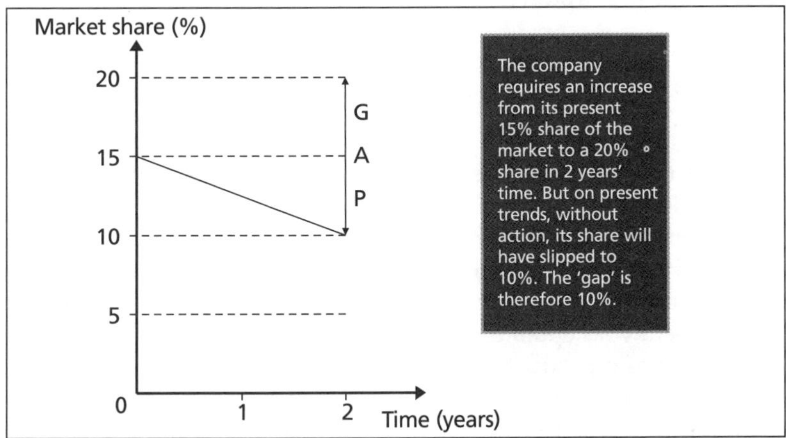
Market share (%)
20
15
10
5
0
1
2
Time (years)
G
A
P
The company requires an increase from its present 15% share of the market to a 20% share in 2 years' time. But on present trends, without action, its share will have slipped to 10%. The 'gap' is therefore 10%.

Figure 47.1 Gap analysis

This involves contrasting **objectives** for a date in the future with the likely position of the firm if strategy remains **unchanged**. The difference between the two positions is a 'gap' that the new strategy must fill.

CHOOSING A STRATEGY

The ultimate strategy of any firm is to add value within a competitive market. It is the means chosen to generate that added value that gives distinctive content to a strategy. This concept has been closely studied by Michael Porter at Harvard University. In *Competitive Strategy* (1980), he explains three 'generic strategies' or broad approaches to the achievement of competitive advantage - and consistent high profitability.

Porter's Generic Strategies

1 **Cost leadership**

In the marketplace this means price leadership. The firm achieves a scale and efficiency that give it a lower cost base than that of its competitors. Product quality is adequate without being special.

▶ In food retailing, Kwik-Save has pursued cost leadership.

2 **Differentiation**

The firm gives its products a distinctive character and quality that enable them to command a premium price in the market. These distinctive features may be based on quality alone or may focus on brand, style or uniqueness.

▶ Marks & Spencer has achieved differentiation.

3 **Focus**

In this context focus means meeting effectively the demands of customers in a narrow market segment. Because their wants are more precisely met than by mass market products, buyers are willing to pay a premium price.

▶ An Italian delicatessen pursues a focus strategy.

▶ What is the strategy of Sainsbury's? It appears to aim for both low prices **and** quality – its slogan is 'Where good food costs less'. Is this a contradiction in terms, or not?

Porter argues that a firm should be clear about which of these generic strategies it intends to pursue. Being 'stuck in the middle', he says, leads in the long term to underperformance.

'Making the ordinary extraordinary.' This slogan was used by Marks & Spencer in 1996 for promoting its foods. Prices for these products were high relative to those of competitors.

1 What exactly do you think the slogan means?
2 How might it increase sales and profitability?
3 What might be its strategic value?

Another theorist, Igor Ansoff (1965), identifies four growth vectors or directions for strategic business expansion. Current products in their current market may allow further **market penetration**. But equally, it may be wise to consolidate a period of growth or even to retreat or withdraw from a market once returns are expected to decline below acceptable levels. **Market development** means using the same basic product to enter new markets. These may be new segments of the same broad market or entirely new markets – for example in a different country or continent. By contrast, **product development** involves the necessary R&D to launch new products that may increase market share or gain market leadership. Finally, **diversification** means new products in new markets. This strategy may imply staying with the same industry, or it may require the firm to break out into a completely unrelated area of business enterprise.

▶ In 1996 Glaxo spent £342 million on research and development (R&D).

▶ In late 1996 Williams Holdings announced a major plan to focus on fire-fighting and security products and to sell its interests in gas fires and water heaters, kitchens, consumer electricals, fillers and coatings. The disposals were expected to be worth around £1 billion, and the whole strategy was designed to support investment in its chosen area of specialism and to boost the performance of its share price.

For any strategy to be realistic it must be likely to fulfil the firm's stated aims and satisfy the relevant range of stakeholders. Certainly, the final choice of strategy needs to exploit the firm's existing strengths. The achievement of competitive advantage requires excellence and firms generally build on those core competencies that maintain their 'edge' in the market. This was the idea underlying Peters and Waterman's advice (1982) to 'stick to the knitting'. Any feasible strategy must also be practical in terms of its implications for funding, human resources, technology and corporate culture.

IMPLEMENTATION

For a strategy to be effective, it needs the supportive mobilization of all resources throughout the organization. Senior management must work as a team towards the fulfilment of strategic goals. Sufficient funds must be allocated under the relevant budget headings. Any necessary R&D and investment programmes require careful scheduling. Particularly vital are the human resource implications. Plans for promotion, recruitment and training often run together with team building for tackling specific assignments within the new strategy. Some firms express their strategy in a 'vision' that is intended to capture the imagination of all employees. A mission statement can act as a spearhead in motivating staff towards a common goal. In any case, it is essential that the strategy becomes reflected in a shared commitment by staff at all levels.

There is often a real risk that the operational aspects of a strategy are implemented successfully, while the motivation of people falters. An organization may find itself drifting back towards the patterns of behaviour that were characteristic of the old strategy. Many individuals and elements within organizations are surprisingly conservative and resistant to change (see Chapter 48). It is especially disastrous if staff become cynical about management's intentions and treat their part in the new strategy as a pretence or even an irrelevance. It follows that the management of people within the vector of a new strategy is a top priority requiring the best skills in leadership and communication.

All strategies need to have embedded within them quite a high degree of flexibility. This is increasingly important as the speed of change in the business environment accelerates. As circumstances change - often unpredictably - strategies may need re-routing, reshaping and even remaking. Techniques such as PEST and SWOT analysis, market research and the expertise of managers all help to make the firm sensitive to developing or oncoming change. But the patterns of change can be kaleidoscopic in their complexity, while sudden 'shocks' are liable abruptly to modify - even revolutionize - a whole business environment. Thus a good strategy avoids rigidities and is sufficiently flexible to absorb or even to exploit unexpected change.

PLANNING

Plans are pathways of intention, defined by markers in terms of time and progress. For people and organizations, planning is the logical effort to impose order on events and to counteract the risks of confusion and unpredictability. Progress is possible without clear plans, but it is usually erratic and liable to unexpected and expensive setbacks.

Once a strategy has been agreed, it will need translation into **operational plans** for the various divisions, departments or teams. This process begins with senior management framing overall plans, which are then restated in increasing detail for each level downward through the organization. Planning normally involves programmes of events with targets set over the relevant timescale. There are also often ad hoc (purpose-specific) projects that are elements in the overall strategy and need their own detailed planning. In addition, the setting of budgets (see Chapter 31) is in itself a key form of planning and forms a critical support system for any strategy.

In pursuit of operational planning, firms also set **administrative plans**. These are designed to provide 'automatic' guidance for staff in dealing with events that are likely to recur. **Policies** are guidelines for managers who are making decisions in the context of a strategy. **Procedures** are much more detailed codes or rules that instruct staff in how to carry out certain tasks. They usually apply to staff at all levels.

▶ Policies are intended to limit the discretion of managers but, equally, there may be situations where a manager will override policy in the interests of overall strategy.

Business Plans

Smaller firms often express their strategy in an integrated **business**

plan. This typically includes a simple statement of objectives, with details of product range and personnel. A marketing plan is usually outlined in more detail, with market research data as relevant. There is then a series of detailed financial statements including a projected profit and loss account and cash-flow forecast. Plans for investment in fixed assets and the availability of working capital are also useful. Some small firms produce business plans only when required to do so by their bank as a condition for the granting of loans. However, a business plan is valuable in itself. The manager or business owner often benefits from thinking about the future beyond the immediate present and carrying out the necessary research. The plan can also be used as an effective control mechanism, with regular reviews and the use of variances as triggers for action.

Problems with Planning

Plans are not always successful. Sometimes they are based on faulty information or analysis. More often they founder because of poor communications or weak motivation among the people they are supposed to engage. There is also the risk that managers deviate from plans or fail to ensure that other people are fulfilling their agreed roles.

Perhaps the most serious problem with plans is their tendency to overdirect and induce managers to ignore changes that actually imply modifications to the plan or its replacement with a new approach. The process of planning can easily become mechanical and disregard the needs and feelings of the people affected. However, sensitive, well-constructed and flexible plans remain an essential tool of business management.

Regency Restaurants Ltd

Established in the 1970s, the firm operates a chain of family restaurants. These are mostly situated in the market and cathedral towns of Yorkshire and the Pennines. Regency is positioned mid-market in an increasingly competitive environment. Its appeal to customers has always been based on straightforward English food at reasonable prices. Decor is conventional, with 'Regency' styling for all the restaurants. Staffing is the greatest problem, with a high staff turnover ratio and substantial reliance on part-time and weekend work.

By the mid-1990s sales and return on capital were falling. Even the smaller towns with Regency restaurants were attracting the interest of the fast-food chains, while market research showed that customers found Regency's food acceptable but uninteresting.

Make a short strategic analysis of Regency's current position and offer a possible strategy for the next three years.

Evaluation

- No firm can achieve long-term profitability (or survival) without its particular source of competitive advantage. In the nature of competitive markets, this will always be under threat. Thus the defence, maintenance and extension of competitive advantage is the ultimate purpose of any strategy.

- Strategy involves every functional area of the business (marketing, operations, finance, human resources, etc.). It is therefore important that the directors or senior managers for each of these areas are fully involved in the strategy-setting process. Sometimes non-executive directors also have a useful role in offering a broad and unbiased perspective.
- Strategies and their allied mission statements are only as powerful as the commitment to them among people in the organization. It follows that ensuring identification with a strategy and motivation towards its realization are key priorities for managers.
- Strategy must be set on a timescale that is realistic and relevant for the firm and its environment. There is a danger of excessive 'short termism', where managers are overly influenced by an immediate crisis or by the expectations of one interest group, e.g. the City and its focus on share price. On the other hand, the further into the future a strategy is projected, the higher is the degree of uncertainty in its assumptions.
- Many areas of business activity are now subject to rapid and discontinuous change. This means that every strategy has a contingent quality and is subject to revision – perhaps radical revision.
- There is always a tension in planning between strong definition and adequate flexibility. The ideal trade-off varies according to the business environment and the level in the organization for which the plan is intended.

Corporate culture and change management

Chapter objectives

After working through this chapter, you will:

- understand the meaning of corporate culture
- be able to analyse a firm's culture
- recognize the pressures and need for change in business organizations
- know how change is resisted and achieved
- know the meaning of the following key terms: corporate culture, process of change, cultural types, management by exception.

▶ **Corporate culture**: a system of beliefs held by an organization or 'body'.

CORPORATE CULTURE?

Like people, firms have a personality:

'It was a genuinely friendly place.'
'The atmosphere was rather clinical.'
'Everyone was very keen.'
'They were all on first-name terms.'
'It was very much about making money.'
'A really stuffy and traditional firm.'

▶ The capacity to respond effectively to change is a key to business success.

These are the kinds of statement people make about business organizations. What do they mean? Clearly they are generalizations. Not everyone or everything was 'clinical', 'keen' or 'stuffy'. But the overall mood, style or ambience appeared to justify these descriptions. When a group of people work together it is inevitable that some distinctive patterns develop. The word 'culture' means beliefs about value and meaning and their expression in a way of life. Cultures exist in families, neighbourhoods, regions, countries – and firms. A **corporate culture** is a system of beliefs held by an organization or 'body' about its objectives, its products, its customers, its staff and itself – and how these are expressed through its decision making and operations. An understanding of corporate culture provides a deep insight into the behaviour of a firm and its likely response to the **process of change**.

▶ When firms adopt a new 'corporate identity', they are often trying to change their culture as well as the way in which they are seen by the outside world.

Some organizations have a culture that is highly responsive to change and seems eager to embrace its possibilities. Others feel their identity and security threatened by change and attempt to resist or slow down its impact.

Cultural Types

There are many criteria under which corporate culture can be classified. A useful model is provided by Roger Harrison (1972) and Charles Handy (1985). They distinguish four broad cultural types on a spectrum of discretion for the individual employee.

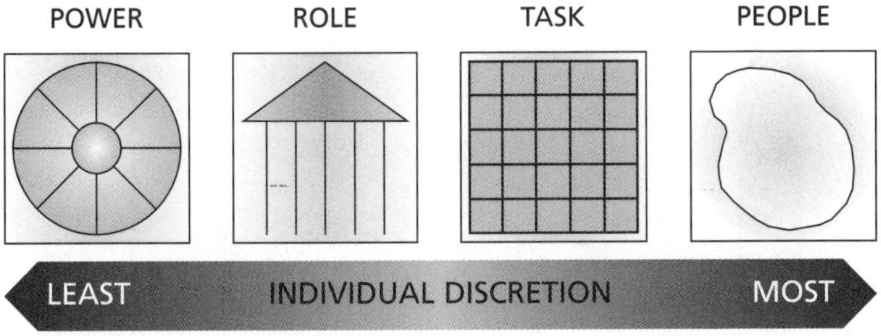

▶ Techniques of market segmentation (see Chapter 5) classify consumers according to their lifestyle. Firms can similarly be analysed by cultural type.

POWER ROLE TASK PEOPLE

LEAST INDIVIDUAL DISCRETION MOST

Figure 48.1
Types of corporate culture

Adapted from Roger Harrison, How to Describe Your Organization, *1972, and Charles Handy,* The Gods of Management, *1985*

- **Power cultures** are centralized and authoritarian. Senior managers keep a firm grip on power and employees must submit to organizational demands. The best service is given to the best customers.
- **Role cultures** are usually hierarchies where each person's job is tightly defined and highly specialized. The aim is to produce a uniformly high standard of service.
- **Task cultures** are less hierarchical, looser organizations where individuals and teams are relatively autonomous and are achievement driven.
- **Person cultures** allow complete discretion for the individual on a basis of equality and mutual cooperation.

In recent years there has been much discussion of an 'enterprise culture' (see Chapter 1). Correspondingly, firms can be classified according to the strength of their entrepreneurial characteristics.

▶ The entrepreneurial quality tends to be strong when a business is new or small, and weaker as it ages or grows. This is not necessarily true, however. Some large and long-established firms are strongly entrepreneurial, while a small family firm can have a low entrepreneurial propensity.

TYPE A	TYPE B
flexible	inflexible
market-led	product-led
change oriented	change-resistant
fast reflexes	slow reflexes
outward-focused	inward-focused
risk taking	risk avoiding

HIGH ENTREPRENEURIAL CHARACTERISTICS LOW

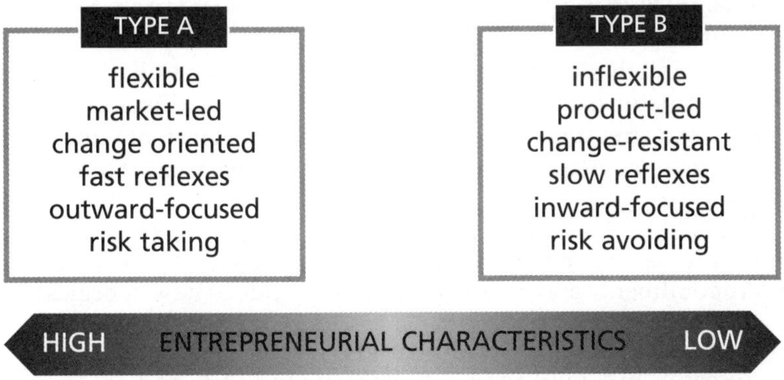

Figure 48.2
Type A and Type B: entrepreneurial characteristics

Another approach is to plot the ethos or culture of firms on a two-dimensional grid. The x-axis grades firms from being **atomistic** to **holistic**. An atomistic firm emphasizes the diversity of the individual and has only a weak identity with little sense of 'belonging'. A holistic firm is more than the sum of its parts, with a powerful ethos, a distinctive style and a strong sense of 'belonging'. The y-axis grades organizations from being **mechanistic** to **organic** models. Mechanistic firms are rigid and hierarchical, while organic firms are flexible and non-hierarchical.

▶ Firm A has a 'function culture', with well-defined roles and all its actions geared for practical results. The 'duty culture' of Firm B stresses the organization rather than the individual, with a strong sense of hierarchy. Firm C's 'rights culture' arises from the belief that each individual has a contract to fulfil, with a corresponding set of rights. A 'field culture' means that Firm D is cohesive yet non-hierarchical, with its staff interacting as though within a corporate 'magnetic field'.

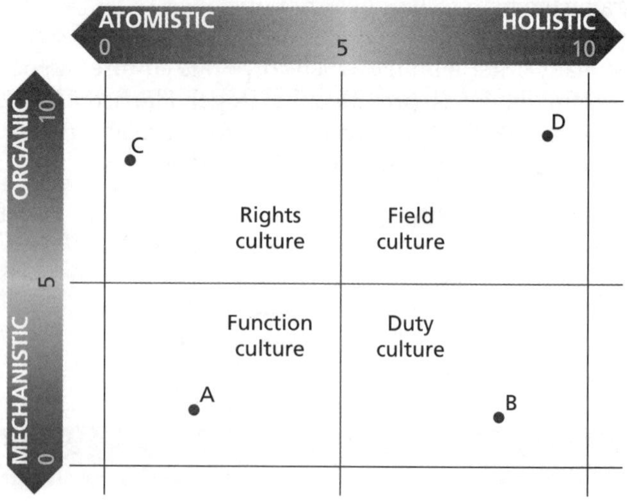

ATOMISTIC 0 5 HOLISTIC 10

ORGANIC 10 5 MECHANISTIC 0

C D

Rights culture | Field culture

Function culture | Duty culture

A B

Figure 48.3
Classifying corporate cultures

It is important to stress that no one type of corporate culture is either right or wrong. Different cultural types perform best in different business environments. However, all environments are subject to change.

Four ways of classifying corporate cultures have been given. Use one of them to classify the culture of any organization you know.

THE IMPORTANCE OF CHANGE

▶ The proactive firm searches the time horizon and deliberately initiates change, while the reactive firm tends to wait for evidence that change has become unavoidable.

Business conditions change with every day that passes. Some firms remain unaware of change or delay their response, with fatal results. As with the principle of natural selection, it is only the fittest that survive.

The ability to detect a need for change is a prime skill of management. Sometimes the need makes newspaper headlines (e.g. new safety laws after a major accident), but often it is virtually invisible. Forces for change may arise inside or outside the organization.

1 **Internal pressures**

- Objectives may change in content or emphasis.
- Appointments and resignations may introduce new energies or remove old barriers.
- Staff skills, backgrounds and needs change.
- Research and development brings new products and processes.
- Financial disciplines may demand economies or changes in direction.

2 **External pressures**

- Markets change with new customers and new demands.
- Competition may challenge products as well as markets.
- Society changes in its attitudes and values.
- New technology moves from laboratory to commercial applications.

- New management techniques are publicized.
- The government makes political changes (e.g. privatization) or introduces new laws (e.g. pollution regulations).
- Economic trends change direction (e.g. from recession to expansion).

Managers should aim to be aware of change before it makes any unplanned impact on the organization. In practice this is not always possible and, like doctors, they must become expert at using symptoms to make an early diagnosis.

Events that are unfolding according to plan do not require management attention. **Management by exception** means being constantly alert to those events that diverge from expectations and so may indicate unplanned change.

▶ **Symptoms of the need for change**: budget variances (see Chapter 31); changing sales and market share; employee relations problems; rising labour turnover; increased management conflict; critical feedback from customers; messages on the 'grapevine'.

Resistance to Change

Any period of stability creates a sense of familiarity and security. This causes a kind of solidifying process in attitudes, methods and patterns of behaviour. Loyalties develop towards systems and places as well as other people. Human beings are nest builders! Even reorganizing the desks in an office can cause staff a painful sense of dislocation. The phrase 'the end of an era' can become applied to very trivial matters. Typical reasons for resistance to change are:

- the possible threat of redundancy;
- expected loss of earnings or status in absolute terms or simply relative to others;
- deskilling, where a previously valued skill is no longer required;
- adverse effects on friendships, social patterns or domestic commitments;
- underlying suspicion towards management intentions;
- fear of the unknown, e.g. using new technology.

▶ When a long-established business closes down, it is often due to the failure of the owners to recognize and respond to change.

In resistance to change, motivation theory may swing sharply into reverse gear. The stronger the perceived threat to the security and other vital interests of employees, the stronger their likely resistance.

▶ The key to acceptance of change is the involvement of staff at all stages in its planning.

Achieving Change

Firms need systems for forward planning to avoid being overtaken by events. Statistical techniques, simulations and computer models can assist forecasting. Scenario planning (see Chapter 46) makes managers answer 'what if ...?' questions.

Key Factors in Achieving Change

- **Planning** by phases or in stages to a clear timetable that can be reviewed and revised as events and outcomes unfold.
- **Training** for staff, providing new skills and better prospects, combined with greater flexibility in accepting different work roles.
- **Awakening to benefits** for those employees who may have a

negative bias in their perception of change, e.g. new career opportunities.
- **Communications** that are open and thorough: the appearance of secretive manoeuvring should be avoided; negotiations with staff or their representatives should be honest and opened early; counselling can be offered to individuals most affected.
- **Participation** where possible of all staff in the change process: delegation enables staff to design their own parts of the change process – these are far more likely to be accepted than those imposed by management.
- **Compromise** where essential strategy is not endangered: symbolic compromise over details of working life (e.g. breaks) can help win agreement on the major issues.

The speed of change is partly driven by events and partly decided by management. Much depends on the build-up of change pressure. If events move very fast and the organization very slowly, then the likelihood of sudden and rapid change increases. If the structure of the organization is inflexible, then chaotic or revolutionary change may result.

▶ The line CC is the average rate of change acting on the two organizations. Firm A maintains a consistently high pace of change and is therefore unlikely to require sudden upheavals. Firm B is change-resistant and allows pressure to build until bursts of intense change are unavoidable.

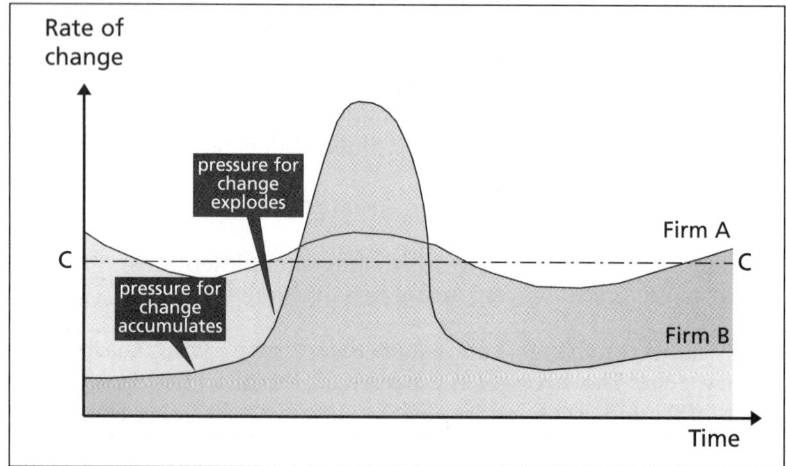

Figure 48.4
Organizational change

A Culture for Change

▶ Rosabeth Moss Kanter is an American theorist who has closely studied issues of change and flexibility. In *The Change Masters* (1983), she finds that innovative firms have an 'integrative' culture, looking at problems as a whole and challenging the ways of the past. Disciplined efficiency with spirited flexibility is urged in her next book, *When Giants Learn to Dance* (1989). Firms should combine 'the power of an elephant with the agility of a dancer'.

The capacity of any organization to recognize change pressures and to adapt effectively arises directly from its collective or corporate culture. Particularly important features of the organization are:

- the quality of its internal and external feedback systems;
- the flexibility of its structure.

This may help to explain why there is a trend in the 1990s away from tall, rigid and hierarchical structures (Type A) towards flat, flexible and open structures (Type B). In Type A firms, feedback is subject to delay, blockage and distortion as it climbs backwards up long chains of command. Type B organizations relay pressure for internal change rapidly through few layers of management. With responsibility diffused into virtually all work roles, the firm's perception of change is much increased. Such firms have an outward-focused culture that is vigorously interactive with, for example, customers and suppliers. The rigid hierarchies of Type A firms cannot adapt to change until they receive a command to do so. By contrast, Type B structures adapt continuously to change and staff begin to initiate their own training and to adjust their own roles.

Some major companies are now consciously developing a learning culture that thrives on change. This means a high level of motivation, initiative and experimentation among staff, where mistakes are treated as valuable opportunities to learn. A learning culture depends on people feeling secure. This means mutual support within teams and – within defined limits – real acceptance when mistakes are made. To cope with change is not enough: it needs to be embraced – and even celebrated.

▶ Peters (1994) argues that revolutionary change in the business environment is now the norm and that firms need the flexibility, courage and ingenuity to exploit the opportunities it offers.

Read the following case study and answer the questions below.

Pledgers

'A wonderful shop', said everyone in the town. Pledgers was a real ironmongers. It seemed to sell almost everything, from mousetraps to six-inch nails, from wheelbarrows to garden seats. Occupying a busy corner of the market square, the shop was cluttered and cramped. Staircases and narrow passages enabled customers to explore the rather dark interior. No one seemed to mind the slow service and some customers had been regulars since the 1950s.

Old Mr Pledger did not even bother to oppose the planning application from B&Q to build a large out-of-town store. Even his son, who ran the garden department, seemed uninterested. As for the other staff, they didn't want to upset Mr Pledger; they knew about his sudden rages. Besides, there was a question of loyalty. Pledgers was a landmark for the town. People would arrange to meet 'opposite Pledgers'.

The planning application was successful. By the following spring a large branch of B&Q saw its first customers arrive in the immense car park outside. There were no mousetraps and few staff. Meanwhile, life at Pledgers continued – and ended – without change. Old Mr Pledger was said to have retired. No one knew where his son had gone. The shop was empty. The posters on the whitewashed windows announced 'Final Sale'.

1. How would you describe the culture at Pledgers?
2. Why did such a well-established business fail?
3. What advice could you have given to enable the business to survive?

Evaluation

- Leadership style normally corresponds closely with corporate culture, except when leaders stake out a direction in which they intend the culture to shift.
- Senior appointments are a good guide to a firm's true cultural direction. It is usually only senior managers who are able to bring about real cultural change.

- Firms may acquire or develop splits in their corporate culture, causing serious conflict. These may be lateral – between divisions in the organization – or vertical – between the divisions and head office. Once cultural enclaves develop, they can be difficult to bring back into the mainstream culture.
- A firm's corporate culture determines the character of its employee relations. All organizations exert pressure on members to conform to their cultural norms. A spectrum exists between cultures of partnership and cultures of conflict.
- A major obstacle to the success of mergers is the difficulty of combining two different business cultures. In practice, some managers and many staff may leave a firm rather than submit to an alien culture.
- In planning for change, firms need always to allow for unexpected events. Contingency plans are a reserve support system to cope with change that would otherwise be overwhelming.
- Resistance to change can be valuable in forcing management to examine its assumptions and in highlighting likely problems for adjustment.
- Conservative elements in an organization can prevent excessively rapid change, while encouraging stability and continuity. Equally, they may be an obstacle in moving towards a new vision that is essential to the firm's success.

Business responsibility and business ethics

Chapter objectives

After working through this chapter, you will:

- appreciate the meaning of social responsibility in business
- know the legal basis for consumer protection
- be able to analyse the different motives for social responsibility
- understand the nature and influence of pressure groups
- understand the concept of finite natural resources
- recognize the threats that business activity can pose to the environment
- know the techniques used to measure social and environmental costs
- know the different motives firms have for social and environmental responsibility
- be able to evaluate the response of firms to ethical issues
- know the meaning of the following key terms: codes of practice, externalities, cost-benefit analysis.

THE IDEA OF SOCIAL RESPONSIBILITY

▶ What are the responsibilities of a business beyond making a profit?

Social responsibility is the concept that a business has obligations that extend beyond the lawful process of its profit-driven activity. Nearly two centuries of social reform have already brought many responsibilities within a firm's legal operation, but the outer boundary of responsibility is still blurred and subject to much argument. All firms have responsibility towards their shareholders, but they may also be argued to have social responsibility towards:

- employees
- suppliers
- consumers
- the local community
- the environment

These groups are often referred to as **stakeholders**. This means – at the minimum – that they have a stake in the outcome of the firm's decision making. A more radical interpretation suggests that all stakeholders have a right to influence the management and that the shareholders represent only one stakeholder among others. In practice, the extent to which firms accept responsibility

▶ 'Our task is to build on our traditions of quality and value to provide brands, products, financial results and management performance that meet the interests of our shareholders, consumers, employees, customers, suppliers and the communities in which we operate.'
Cadbury-Schweppes Annual Report

towards the various stakeholder groups varies widely. Some companies stress only their commitment to profitability and shareholder return. Others acknowledge the need for profitable trading but stress their commitment to a range of stakeholder interests. In general, it is the larger public companies with a high public profile (e.g. BP, Glaxo, Cadbury-Schweppes) that are most likely to embrace the stakeholder model.

For each of the business decisions below, identify the groups towards whom the firm might recognize social responsibility and briefly explain why.

1 A UK brewer plans press and poster advertising for a new brand of high-strength lager.
2 A bank mails its customers with brochures that offer personal loans to finance luxury purchases.
3 A large engineering company intends to relocate away from its existing base in a small town with high unemployment.
4 A national chain store which has previously stocked British handmade toys hopes to achieve small savings by switching its contract to a Far East supplier.
5 A timber merchant applies for planning permission to locate a sawmill and warehouse on the edge of a picturesque Sussex village.

Consumer Protection

▶ Responsibilities to employees were discussed in Chapter 37.

Historically, business was based on the principle 'caveat emptor', which means 'let the buyer beware'. Consumers were expected to use common sense in their purchases and it was not for the law to interfere. However, there have always been **common law rights** derived from custom and practice, which require reasonable conduct towards customers. For example, a firm cannot knowingly sell a product likely to cause injury or damage. Since the late nineteenth century, the law has gradually increased its regulation of the buyer/seller relationship.

Consumer Protection Laws

- **Sale of Goods Act, 1979** states that goods for sale must be (a) of merchantable quality, (b) fit for their purpose and (c) as described. In 1982 the law was extended to include services.
- **Trade Descriptions Act, 1968** protects consumers against false or misleading statements about goods and services.
- **Fair Trading Act, 1973** established the Office of Fair Trading (OFT) to monitor trading practices and to take or recommend legal action where necessary. The OFT is also responsible for controls of monopolies and mergers that might restrict competition against the public interest.
- **Consumer Credit Act, 1974** requires a statement of the annual percentage rate of interest (APR), in any credit agreement,

with time for the consumer to cancel a contract if he or she wishes.

- **Unfair Contract Terms Act, 1977** bans unfair disclaimers or exclusion clauses. Guarantees cannot disclaim responsibility and disclaimer notes cannot exclude the consequences of negligence.
- **Consumer Protection Act, 1987** makes it a criminal offence to sell unsafe goods, taking into account any associated marketing material, instructions or warnings. Sellers of defective goods are liable to civil action for any loss, damage or injury caused.

The Director General of Fair Trading (DGFT) encourages trade associations to operate **codes of practice** for their industry. These are not legally binding on members but could influence court judgements and are a flexible means to ensure up-to-date regulation.

▶ Well-known codes are maintained by the Motor Agents Association and the Association of British Travel Agents.

Consumer Protection Agencies

- **Trading Standards Departments** are run by local councils and have the power to enforce consumer protection laws. They also provide an important advisory service on everyday problems.
- **Environmental Health Departments** are also council-run and have power to protect public health, especially in relation to the sale of food.
- The **Office of Fair Trading** acts for the government in checking and enforcing all laws relating to fair trading.
- **National Consumer Council** is a government-funded organization that represents the consumer interest and is responsible for research, education services and related campaigning.
- The **Consumers' Association** has charitable status and carries out extensive research and testing on every type of product. Its findings are published in *Which?* magazine.
- **Regulatory bodies for privatized industries** have the task of monitoring the activities of the companies now supplying key public services, and representing the interests of their consumers, e.g. the Office of Telecommunications (OFTEL) or the Office of Gas Supply (OFGAS).
- **Advertising Standards Authority** (ASA) is a voluntary body that operates the British Code of Advertising Practice. This requires all advertisements to be 'legal, decent, honest and truthful', showing proper social responsibility and maintaining principles of fair competition. A similar code exists for sales promotion.
- **Independent Broadcasting Authority** (IBA) maintains a Code of Advertising Standards and Practice relating to television and radio.
- **British Standards Institute** (BSI) is a voluntary body encouraging health and safety in design, quality standards and environmental protection. Its kitemark logo indicates that a product reaches a BSI safety standard.

Select any three of the agencies above and find out the ways in which they affect the behaviour of business enterprise.

▶ Examples of pressure groups
Greenpeace and Friends of the Earth campaign for improved protection of the environment. The Health Education Council campaigns on health issues, and Action on Smoking and Health (ASH) campaigns for discouragement of smoking and for greater controls on cigarette marketing. Transport 2000 campaigns for better public transport; the Automobile Association (AA) campaigns on behalf of motorists.

Pressure Groups

A pressure group is an organization campaigning to achieve changes in attitudes and behaviour and often seeking changes in the law. Most pressure groups directly or indirectly wish to influence business decisions and often appeal to the concept of social responsibility.

Many organizations that are not specifically pressure groups are still important in campaigning for the interests of their members, e.g. trade unions, employers' associations and chambers of commerce. Inevitably, all groups appeal for public support and seek vital publicity. Pressure groups publish many kinds of supporting materials, campaign through advertising and mass media coverage, organize petitions and demonstrations, lobby MPs and represent their views to firms and the government. The business community may be influenced directly through changes in the law or indirectly through recognition that a significant part of public or local opinion has a point of view that cannot be ignored. This may affect the national policy of companies (e.g. not to sell products tested on animals) or a local decision (e.g. to provide litter bins outside a fast-food outlet).

Identify a pressure group that aims to make firms behave in a more socially and environmentally responsible way. Obtain the pressure group's literature and evaluate its likely effectiveness.

▶ To what extent is environmental impact included in business decision making?

BUSINESS AND THE ENVIRONMENT

Business activity involves the transformation of resources into the goods and services demanded by consumers. There are three physical phases in the process:

PRODUCTION → DISTRIBUTION → CONSUMPTION

Driven by the market forces of demand and supply, the physical cycle of production and consumption results in a continuous use of natural resources and a corresponding flow of waste entering the environment. This cycle raises many important questions:

- What are the environmental consequences of different business activities?
- What are their likely long-term implications?
- Can the environmental costs of production and consumption be measured?
- Do a company's accounts include all the costs of production?
- Should renewable and non-renewable resources be treated differently?
- Who should pay for environmental protection?

Until the 1970s such questions were rarely asked. Natural resources were merely raw materials and the free gift of nature. It was the task of business and technology to exploit these gifts as quickly and cheaply as possible. The progress of modern technology and mechanized production was filling the homes of the western world with an abundance of consumer goods. Nor did waste seem any problem.

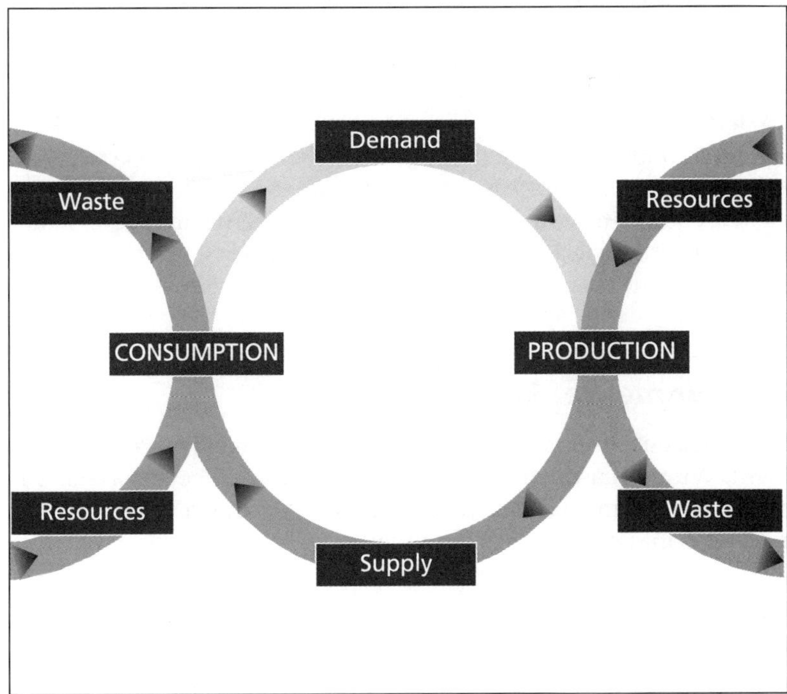

Figure 49.1
Waste from the production cycle

The atmosphere, the oceans and the areas of 'wasteland' seemed big enough to take everything. The first oil crisis (1973–4) began to change these perceptions. In *Small is Beautiful*, Schumacher (1973) argued that large-scale industrial economics were threatening the resources of ecosystems on which life depends. By the late 1980s there was mounting scientific evidence to indicate environmental problems. These included:

- the damage to lakes and forests from 'acid rain';
- the discovery of holes in the protective ozone layer caused by chlorofluorocarbon (CFC) gases;
- the likely 'greenhouse effect' arising from carbon dioxide emissions.

▶ 'We recognize that environmental care is among the most important corporate priorities. Our products are reviewed with our suppliers and customers on a total approach that looks at environmental impact and resource use from "cradle to grave".'

Pilkington plc

Growing public and governmental concern led to the Earth Summit at Rio de Janeiro in 1992, where 130 heads of state agreed on a range of pathways for environmental protection. And during the 1990s it became increasingly clear that all major companies would need to have regard for environmental responsibility in their strategic planning.

The Motor Car

To manufacture a car requires large amounts of metals, plastics and chemicals. It also needs a major input of energy. Once in use, the car converts – hugely inefficiently – non-renewable fossil fuel into mechanical power. In its short life it will burn about 20,000 litres of petrol, releasing into the atmosphere about 50 tonnes of the 'greenhouse' gas carbon dioxide and 5 kilos of the poisonous gas carbon monoxide. The roads along which it runs cover huge areas of once productive farmland, while scarring sensitive landscapes, sometimes beyond recognition. Each year in Britain alone, about 4,000 people are killed and 45,000 people are seriously injured by motor vehicles – many of them children or the elderly. The car's life ends prematurely when a repair is regarded as 'uneconomic' and the manufacturer's advertising persuades the driver to buy a newer model.

Of course, the car is a very useful and enjoyable possession, but does the showroom tell anyone its true cost?

▶ The USA has only 5 per cent of the world's population but produces 23 per cent of CO_2 emissions.

Environmental Impacts

Business activity cannot avoid making some impact on the environment. Within reasonable limits these impacts can be absorbed. But as the environmental demands of business grow, a wide range of problems may emerge. For example:

- the depletion of non-renewable resources such as minerals and oil;
- the consumption of renewable resources such as timber and fisheries faster than they are replaced;
- emissions from industrial processes that enter water systems and the atmosphere;
- the erosion of the topsoil and its contamination by chemical inputs;
- the entry of toxic waste into the environment through production processes and household consumption;
- the demands of transport systems on energy sources and land space while creating additional gas emissions.

The primary cause is the rapid increase in output and living standards across the richest parts of the world.

Many developing countries are now on the brink of large-scale industrialization. Consider the following data:

Country	*GNP ($bn)*	*Population (m)*	*GNP per capita ($)*
USA	6,744	261	25,880
China	631	1,191	530
India	292	914	320

Source: World Bank

If China and India were even in the future to reach the US living standards of today, then their output would need to expand by 49 times and 81 times respectively. This would impose on the environment the equivalent of 7.9 additional US total outputs of today – or 50.0 UK total outputs.

MEASURING SOCIAL AND ENVIRONMENTAL COSTS

A firm counts as the costs of its production those expenses that it is obliged to pay. But in many cases there are other, very real, costs that arise in society and in the environment.

Unpaid Costs

Buxton Quarries Ltd extracts limestone in the Peak District National Park and sells it to civil engineering firms for use in road building. The firm's profit and loss account shows those costs that are private and internal to the firm. But it does not reveal other costs that are public and external to the firm. These external costs might include:

- damage to the National Park landscape;
- reduced tourist trade in the locality;
- widening of country lanes for the firm's fleet of trucks;
- noise and accidents caused by these vehicles.

These social and environmental costs are called **externalities**. However, this term also includes any social or environmental **benefits** that arise from business activity. For example, a new reservoir will flood a rural valley yet create new opportunities for leisure pursuits such as water sports and fishing. Externalities raise a very interesting and important criticism of the market and its price mechanism. We have already met the simple supply curve which relates price to output (see Chapter 11).

▶ **Externalities** are costs external to the firm.

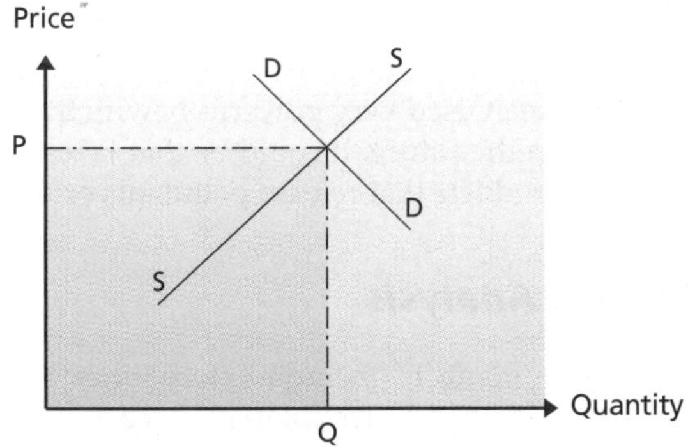

Figure 49.2
Simple market equilibrium

It is clear that the industry will produce Q units at price P.

Look closely again at the supply curve. If the industry's costs were to rise, there would be a fall in output at each price as profitability was squeezed. This must logically be represented by a shift in the supply curve to the left. In Figure 49.3 below, this movement in the supply curve reflects the addition of social and environmental costs to the usual internal costs of production. Although these externalities are not actually paid by the firm, the model allows us to explore their implications.

▶ Notice that input of social or environmental benefits would cause a shift in the supply curve to the right, with the implication of a lower price and a higher output.

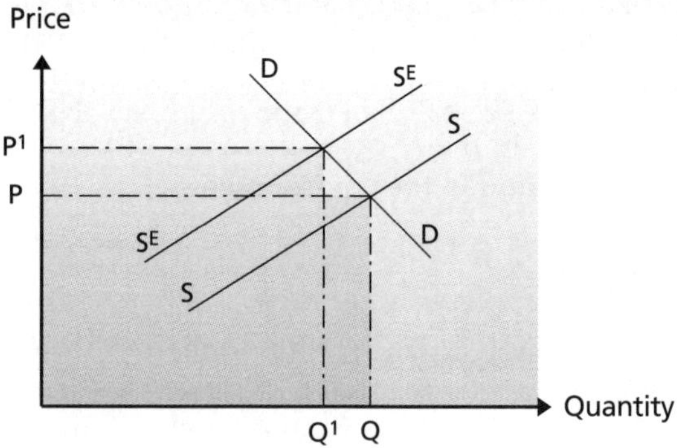

Figure 49.3
Equilibrium including external costs

▶ Externalities such as maintaining transport links in rural areas have been important justifications for the use of subsidies, e.g. to local bus services.

▶ Sir Crispin Tickell (scientist and former advisor to Margaret Thatcher) compared the environment with a boat. 'We can remove one, two or ten rivets without apparent damage. But at a certain point – it could be the eleventh or the thousandth rivet – we cause the timbers to fall apart.'

▶ Should the use of cars be reduced through taxation, with better facilities for cyclists and pedestrians, together with a policy of subsidies for buses and trains?

We can now see that if externalities were included in a firm's decision making, then:

- price would be higher, at price P^1
- output would be lower, at Q^1

Potentially, this principle of externalities has great significance. Most production by firms carries external costs that are rarely included in the price. How would the millions of private sector business decisions taken by producers and consumers every day differ if their analysis included social and environmental costs and benefits? A product could be highly profitable when its costs ignore its environmental impact. Inject environmental or social costs and it might well be dropped as unprofitable. Such a business world is interesting to imagine. Many present-day products would disappear or be radically redesigned. Others would become far more expensive and used only when really necessary. Yet others would be cheaper and presently non-existent products would come into being.

This picture is, of course, improbable! However, the price mechanism has already been used very powerfully with the lower duty on unleaded petrol. In the future, it could be that taxes are introduced on packaging or products that release pollutants or CO_2.

Cost–Benefit Analysis

Efforts have been made to include externalities in major public sector projects, using the technique of **cost–benefit analysis** (CBA). This was first applied in Britain during the 1960s to evaluate the Victoria Line Underground project and later in planning airport development for London. Each external (non-private) cost and benefit is assessed and given a financial value. For example, construction of a new rail-freight terminal might cause noise and nuisance to local residents (external cost) but help to reduce road congestion (external benefit). External costs are then added to a project's total internal costs, while external benefits are added to its expected internal revenues. Investment appraisal can then proceed as normal.

The valuation of externalities can be highly controversial. What is the value of a rare plant species threatened by a housing project? Or the value of a medieval church facing demolition to make way for a new airport? It can be argued that making such decisions is necessary to give external costs (and benefits) a more effective input to the decision-making process. Fuller use of CBA in the public sector was urged by the Pierce Report (1989). Similarly, there are moves to develop green accounting techniques that might lead to firms in both the public and private sectors publishing 'environmental audits' showing their net impact on the environment, expressed in financial terms.

▶ The Pierce Report recommended the calculation of sustainable income – the level of income we can enjoy without running down our overall capital stock – including natural resources.

THE ENVIRONMENT AND THE MARKET

Market forces (see Chapter 1) are effective in generating wealth and in allocating resources to the production of goods and services. The circular flow of income (see Chapter 38) expands a country's output and consumption as demand increases. All the industrial economies have experienced almost continuous growth since the Second World War, yet there is no sign of consumer demand being satisfied. Indeed, many priorities such as housing, health and education still represent major wants that are significantly unfulfilled.

Most political leaders argue that only economic growth will enable these needs to be met. Yet the larger part of any increase in national income is actually spent on luxuries such as cars, cameras and foreign holidays. Thus it would require a massive economic expansion to fulfil those more basic needs. Indeed, if consumer demand is insatiable, then the projection of economic growth is presumably infinitely upwards. What does this mean for a fragile environment and finite resources? Views on this subject are spread across a wide spectrum. Jeremy Seabrook (1990) suggests that in its demands on the environment, the market is a highly dangerous ratchet mechanism that knows no safety limit. An entirely opposite view comes from those who argue that threats to the environment are exaggerated and that the benefit of free market forces far outweigh any environmental costs. Between these positions lies the more widely held view that markets do respond to environmental concern and that the state can use the law and the pressures of taxation to provide environmental protection.

Arguably, there is some evidence to support this perspective. While formal cost–benefit analysis is confined to the public sector, private sector business decisions are increasingly influenced by environmental factors. Values and attitudes among consumers are shifting to reflect increased awareness of the environmental and moral dimensions to business. Across a range of issues - such as destruction of the world's rainforests or the practices of modern factory farming - consumer concern is growing. It is important to notice how, if market forces created these problems, the market is able to respond to the new pressures for change. While green products used to be found only in a few specialist shops, they can now be found on the shelves of every supermarket and chain store. This trend is even further developed in parts of Europe, especially in Germany. Some firms, of course, have taken the opportunity to exploit environmental awareness, treating it as little more than a sales promotion tactic. Others take the issues very seriously. Many public companies now include statements of environmental concern

▶ In Europe, Green Parties have some political influence (mainly in putting the environment on the agenda of other parties).

▶ The European Union has the authority in all member states to scrutinize major projects with serious environmental implications.

in their official objectives, and are adjusting their production methods and product mix accordingly. Pioneering companies such as The Body Shop International or Ecover (a producer of cleaning materials) have made the environment a first priority in their business values and in their marketing mix. Some firms are going further and are publishing an **environmental audit**. This examines all areas of operations with an analysis and evaluation of environmental impacts. Targets for improved performance are included, with assessment of progress over previous years.

Motives for Social and Environmental Responsibility

Many companies regard their public reputation not only as an asset to protect but also as a real source of added value. Brand names can build a 'personality' in public perception. This can affect every aspect of the firm's activity and is reflected in its corporate culture. Association with social and environmental responsibility may help to increase sales, support higher margins, reach new segments in the market and attract better staff.

In an even wider sense, when firms impose their own standards of responsible behaviour, there is less likelihood of government intervention through new laws or regulations. Finally, it should be remembered that social and environmental principles may represent the personal beliefs of directors and senior managers.

Dart Developments Ltd

The company is planning to site a holiday village on the cliffs of North Devon, close to the existing village of Withycombe. The development would feature a ten-acre site for caravans and mobile homes, plus twenty-five bungalows. A shop, bar and reception centre would be constructed next to the main car park. Plans for a takeaway restaurant, open-air swimming pool and children's playground are also included, together with a café on the beach. The necessary land would be purchased from a local farmer, while the South-West Coastal Path would have to be diverted inland. The lane connecting the A362 with the site would require improvement to cope with the summer traffic. Parking restrictions would be needed in the centre of Withycombe, with its narrow street of small shops. The twice-weekly bus service to and from Bideford would be increased to twice daily by the development company to cope with demand from visitors.

The whole scheme is something of a bombshell to the local community and at once there are strong feelings for and against the granting of planning permission.

1 Identify the likely external costs and benefits of the project.
2 Why would it not be satisfactory to leave all the decisions for market forces to resolve?

THE MEANING OF BUSINESS ETHICS

▶ Ethics are moral principles. Morals are judgements regarding what is right and wrong, good and bad.

Ethics are moral principles. Morals are judgements regarding right and wrong in human actions. Business decision making engages constantly with moral judgement, and ethics is therefore a central issue for management.

Ethical decision making in business has two dimensions. The first involves the ethics of the individual decision maker while the second involves the ethics of the organization as a corporate culture (see Chapter 48). Many ethical issues and priorities within firms are implicit, i.e. not directly stated but inferred by staff, who are familiar with corporate values and attitudes.

All firms are constrained by the framework of **law**, which clearly has an ethical basis: for instance cigarette advertising regulation. But in many ethical decisions, there is either a lack of legal definition or an expectation that the firm will set itself higher standards than those demanded by the law.

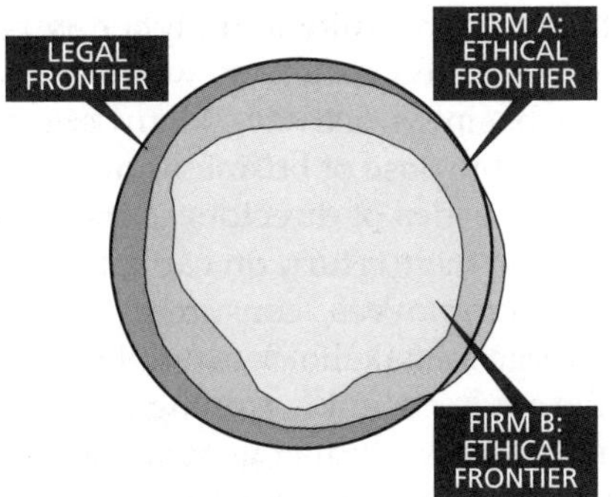

Figure 49.4
Legal and ethical limits

Firm A generally stays within the law in its ethical conduct and follows legal requirements, but in some cases will 'cut corners' to serve its own interests. Firm B works to standards well above the legal minimum and would regard itself as 'ahead' of the law on most ethical matters. In practical terms Firm A might create redundancies without warning and offer only the bare minimum in compensation. By contrast, Firm B might consult its staff over proposed redundancies and then offer generous financial terms, with individual consultation and support.

▶ Many modern firms have based their reputation on high ethical standards in the treatment of employees, customers, suppliers, the community and the environment. It is hard to imagine a serious scandal at a firm like Marks & Spencer, for instance. Companies known for their ethical standards are often among the most successful in commercial terms.

In practice, business activity raises numerous issues of ethical concern. A small sample might include:

- building projects for environmentally sensitive sites;
- payment of low wages to vulnerable, non-unionized workers;
- safety expenditure levels;
- factory closures in depressed areas;
- window dressing in accounts;
- promptness of payment to small firm creditors;
- use of executive expense accounts;
- gifts to clients or customers;
- depiction of women in advertising;
- exploitation of resources in developing countries.

In most of these situations there will be no simple answers.

There is a long historical tradition of firms setting themselves higher ethical standards than the law demands. In the 1820s Robert Owen was thought revolutionary at his New Lanark cotton mills when he offered good working conditions, decent housing and free education to his employees. This was at a time when employers faced virtually no legal constraints. Later in the nineteenth century, firms such as Pilkingtons and Rowntree were well known for their paternalistic but strongly ethical culture. Many modern firms have based their reputation on high ethical standards in the treatment of employees, customers, suppliers, the community and the environment. Significantly, companies known for their ethical standards are often among the most successful in commercial terms. This may be because high expectations in ethics are linked to high reputations in every activity. We meet again the concept of total quality as a culture.

▶ 'Business is, after all, just another form of human enterprise, so why should we expect less from it, in terms of social ethics, than we do from ourselves and our neighbours?'
Anita Roddick, in *Body and Soul*, the story of The Body Shop

Ethics in Business Today

Increasing educational opportunity and higher living standards are creating a more sophisticated society in which higher expectations are projected on to business activity. Many questions are asked about the fundamental purpose of business and the nature of corporate morality. The simple idea of directors acting for shareholders in attempting to maximize their return on capital may be criticized as ethically insufficient. Employees, consumers and the community are beginning to emerge as stakeholders, while the concept of **stewardship** towards the environment is gaining ground.

Major failures in business conduct generate worldwide publicity. The illegal tactics of the Guinness directors in the take-over of Distillers (1986) emphasized the risk of powerful managers acting without regard for the law. In 1991, the Bank of Credit and Commerce International (BCCI) collapsed, raising questions about the adequacy of legal controls over the operations of multinationals. When the *Exxon Valdez* released millions of gallons of crude oil off the coast of Alaska in 1989, the ethics of oil companies were criticized for practices that endangered the environment. Meanwhile, the *Herald of Free Enterprise* disaster (1988) highlighted the concept of corporate responsibility for breakdowns in safety systems.

Major companies in the USA and Europe are now increasingly concerned to make their ethical principles clearer and more rigorous. The reasons include:

- the supreme importance of protecting and building corporate reputation;
- the need to avoid costly law suits and damages;
- the reality that the failure of self-regulation leads to the enactment of tighter legal standards;
- growing recognition that responsibilities must be extended further beyond the financial interests of shareholders.

More firms are now issuing written ethical codes that make their moral principles explicit both to staff and the outside world. For example, BP's 'Policy on Business Conduct and Code of Business Ethics' stresses clearly to employees that they must observe both local law and the company code.

Business ethics is now a major subject for study at American universities and is being introduced to courses at British and European business schools. There is an increasing literature on the subject, arguing that ethics must be central to business culture and not a discretionary extra.

Michael Hoffman (a professor of philosophy and director of a centre for business ethics in Massachusetts) believes that the new interest in ethics reflects a breakdown of confidence in a purely rational and scientific view of the world:

> 'Science and materialism have flourished and ethics and values have been relegated to matters of emotion, attitude and feeling. Such an ideology permits no significant development of the non-material, non-measurable aspects of our lives, such as freedom, morality and divinity.'

How might ethical principles affect decision making in the business situations below?

1 A hi-fi manufacturer's advertising agency plans a poster featuring a new product alongside teenage girls in swimwear.
2 The export manager of an electronics firm is offered a contract to supply security equipment for the police force of a Third World dictatorship.
3 A toy manufacturer commissions a series of TV advertisements to cover the weeks before Christmas.
4 A building society offers a routine job to a sixteen-year-old who had intended to stay in the sixth form to take A levels.
5 A soft drinks company switches from returnable to non-returnable bottles to reduce cost.
6 A civil engineering company is aware that minor breaches of safety policy are occurring, yet also knows that costly man-hours are being saved as a result.

Evaluation

- The impact of business on the environment is a fundamental question concerning human beings and their relationship with nature.
- In their decisions, firms have a duty to shareholders in ensuring profitability. This means meeting demand in the market, i.e. the purchasing choices of ordinary people. However, it is possible for firms to influence and educate their shareholders, employees, suppliers and consumers in environmental values.
- Rising environmental standards for business in Europe and the USA can actually increase the environmental threats elsewhere. Firms may decide to relocate environmentally damaging activities to poorer countries with weaker legal constraints. Some multinational companies are careful in assessing the environmental impact of their business, but others will exploit local environments to the maximum degree permitted by law.
- Techniques for the measurement of social and environmental cost are still at an early stage of development. It is likely that cost–benefit analysis will be applied more widely in public sector decision making. For

the private sector, there may be increasing imposition of taxes to reflect environmental costs.

- The European Union Social Chapter (see Chapter 44) is an attempt to make business serve social goals as well as strictly business objectives. If all companies in all EU countries followed the proposed terms of the Social Chapter (for example, by paying a minimum wage), then none would be disadvantaged relative to another.
- An increase in some prices is implied as firms develop environmentally safer products with modified production techniques and materials. It is possible that this outcome will become increasingly acceptable to most people.
- Some researchers and writers are pessimistic about the capacity of a market economy to restrain its impact on the environment. Against this view, it may be argued that the democracy of the marketplace and the ballot box will jointly modify business activity to ensure environmental protection.
- While environmental protection demands constraints on the use of physical resources, future economic growth might occur through higher quality in products and an increased output of human services.
- It is worth remembering that serious environmental concern first appeared during the 1960s. Far from being a passing 'fashion', the issue has grown enormously in its influence on public and political awareness and on business behaviour.
- Ethical debate is often a good predictor of the social changes that later alter the patterns of economic demand.
- Some firms are initiating a change in response to ethical issues that is planned and proactive.
- To be effective, ethical standards need the decisive backing of top management.
- Ethical codes should be developed with the involvement and agreement of managers at all levels. Otherwise subordinate staff may fear the consequences of raising ethical objections to company decisions.

Further reading

Reading references from the text

An asterisk (*) indicates that the book is recommended for reading by students on A-level or Advanced GNVQ courses.

John Adair, *Understanding Motivation* (Talbot Adair Press, 1990).
Igor Ansoff, *Corporate Strategy* (Penguin, 1965).
*Charles Handy, *The Age of Unreason* (Century Business, 1989).
John Kay, *Foundations of Corporate Success* (Oxford, 1993).
*Tom Peters, *The Tom Peters Seminar* (Macmillan, 1994).
Tom Peters and Robert Waterman, *In Search of Excellence* (HarperCollins, 1982).
Jeremy Seabrook, *The Myth of the Market* (Green Books, 1990).

Also highly recommended for students

To gain an understanding of new thinking about business in the 1990s, try Handy (1989) and Peters (1994) above plus:

Peter Drucker, *The New Realities* (Butterworth Heinemann, 1989).

For a good support and supplement on general management:

Claudia Rawlins, *Introduction to Management* (HarperCollins, 1992).

For insights into marketing, read:

Walter Goldsmith and David Clutterbuck, *The Winning Streak* (Penguin, 1984).
Vance Packard, *The Hidden Persuaders* (Penguin, 1957).

Stories of people and their firms give a fascinating as well as integrated perspective on business management. Particularly readable are:

Anita Roddick, *Body and Soul* (Ebury Press, 1991).
David Thomas, *Alan Sugar – The Amstrad Story* (Pan, 1990).

Appendix 1: Money/real terms conversion table

Note on usage

To convert money to real values between any two years, first locate the money coefficient concerned. For example, to convert 1988 prices into 1994 terms, the coefficient is 1.348. So £5 in 1988 was equivalent to £5 × 1.348 = £6.74 in 1994. Simply divide by the coefficient to convert backwards in time.

1987	1.000									
1988	1.049	1.000								
1989	1.131	1.078	1.000							
1990	1.237	1.179	1.095	1.000						
1991	1.310	1.249	1.159	1.059	1.000					
1992	1.359	1.296	1.202	1.098	1.037	1.000				
1993	1.381	1.316	1.221	1.116	1.054	1.016	1.000			
1994	1.414	1.348	1.251	1.146	1.079	1.040	1.024	1.000		
1995	1.463	1.395	1.294	1.182	1.117	1.076	1.060	1.035	1.000	
1996	1.496	1.428	1.325	1.210	1.144	1.102	1.085	1.060	1.024	1.000
1997	–	–	–	–	–	–	–	–	–	–
	1987	**1988**	**1989**	**1990**	**1991**	**1992**	**1993**	**1994**	**1995**	**1996**

Appendix 2: Discount factors

End of year	Discount factors (%)					
	6	8	10	12	15	20
1	.943	.926	.909	.893	.870	.833
2	.900	.857	.826	.797	.756	.694
3	.840	.794	.751	.712	.658	.579
4	.792	.735	.683	.636	.572	.482
5	.747	.681	.621	.567	.497	.402
10	.558	.463	.386	.322	.247	.162

Index